FULLY INVOLVED

Members of Spokane #29 battle a fire at the Ridpath Hotel.

Fully Involved

A History of the
Washington State Council
of Fire Fighters

BY ELLIE BELEW

The Washington State Council of Fire Fighters
Olympia, Washington
2004

Washington State Council of Fire Fighters
1069 Adams Street Southeast
Olympia, Washington 98501

Affiliated with:
AFL-CIO
International Association of Fire Fighters
Washington State Labor Council

Fully Involved: A History of the Washington State Council of Fire Fighters

Design by Karen Johnson, Level 29 Design

Printed on acid-free paper

Publisher's Cataloging-In Publication
   Belew, Ellie B.

      Fully involved : a history of the Washington State Council of
      Fire Fighters / by Ellie Belew. -- Olympia, Wash. : Washington
      State Council of Fire Fighters, c2004.

         p. ; cm.

         ISBN: 0-9752720-3-9
         0-9752720-4-7 (pbk.)

         1. Washington State Council of Fire Fighters. 2. Fire
      fighters--Washington (State)--History. 3. Labor--Washington
      (State)--History. 4. Fire extinction--Washington (State)--
      History. I. Title.

      HD8039.F52 U634 2004
      363.37/8/06/09797--dc22   0404   2004102710

Printed in the United States of America
2 4 6 8 9 7 5 3 1

Major Donors

DiMartino and Associates, Inc.
Lighthouse Uniforms
WSCFF Benevolent Fund
WSCFF Burn Foundation

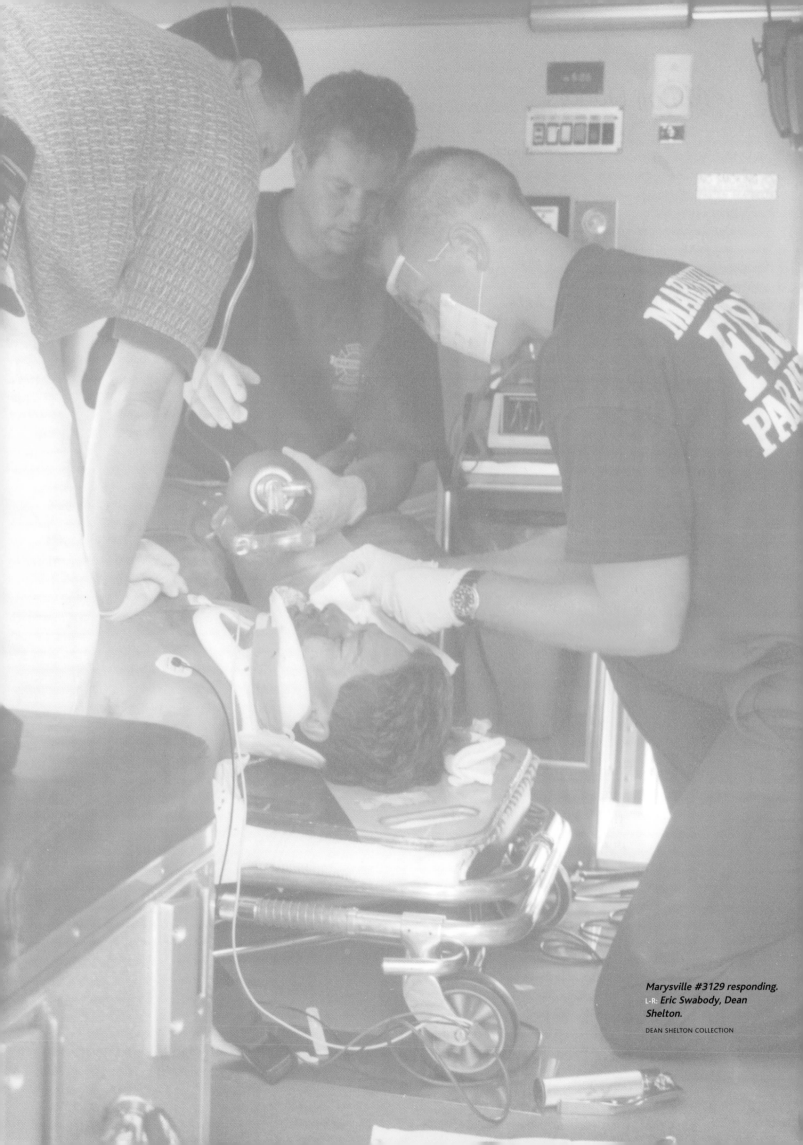

Marysville #3129 responding.
L-R: *Eric Swabody, Dean Shelton.*

DEAN SHELTON COLLECTION

Contents

Introduction

Memory is a terrible thing to lose. Today, an entire generation of young workers, most of them uneducated by either unions or universities, is entering the work world in almost complete ignorance of America's proud labor history. If they seem, all too often, passive and beaten down in the face of low-wages, lengthening hours and repressive conditions, this is because they know nothing of the struggles that brought us such victories as the eight-hour day, occupational and safety regulations, and the right to organize.

Working people's organizations and trade unions play an invaluable daily role in protecting their members from abuse and exploitation. But they also serve as organs of collective memory, preserving traditions of mutual cooperation and solidarity, and honoring the sacrifices and struggles of the working people who came before us. Keeping memory alive is every bit as important and empowering as the practical accomplishments of unions: when you know whose shoulders you stand on, you feel much less alone. When you understand that you are part of a long and courageous tradition, you gain the strength to carry that tradition on.

In the case of fire fighters, the public thinks of them as heroes, especially since the tragedy of 9/11, but seldom as workers. Yet, like steelworkers, miners and, more recently nurses and other service workers, fire fighters have their own history of fighting for tolerable hours and the right to bargain collectively. *Fully Involved* documents that history for the state of Washington, highlighting the larger-than-life personalities that built the Washington State Council of Fire Fighters, along with delicious details about their rivalries and strategic use of whiskey. It's not only fun to read, it's a gift to all fire fighters and to working people everywhere.

Read it, and remember!

Barbara Ehrenreich
Author of *Nickel and Dimed*

Editor's Note —— KEY TO LAYOUT

Fire fighters have a strong tradition of vivid storytelling. They are less inclined to archive records and documents in an orderly manner. If an exact date, law, or individual is cited, these details were documented. When a more general reference is given, it is because independent confirmation of such facts was not possible.

Title of Article appears in the margin of running text as a reference to another article that provides further detail about the topic highlighted. Individuals are not cross-referenced in this manner.

⬭ *Title of Article* **page number**

Wherever possible an individual's IAFF local name and number immediately follows reference to an individual. For example, E.C. Kuehner (Chehalis-Centralia #451) was the first president of the WSCFF.

WSCFF: Washington State Council of Fire Fighters, an organization devoted to the protection and support of professional fire fighters and paramedics in the state of Washington.

IAFF: International Association of Fire Fighters, the AFL-CIO, CLC affiliated labor union representing more than 250,000 professional fire fighters and emergency medical personnel in the United States and Canada.

Illustration credits appear with each illustration. NMCA is used as an abbreviation for the Northwest Museum of Arts and Culture in Spokane, Washington.

The Appendices provide summary and chronological information on major historical events in labor and the fire service, the leadership of the WSCFF, and its member locals.

Charging the Line:

A Summary History of the WSCFF

On November 29, 1938,
IAFF Vice President Max
Maximilian (#27) sent a
formal invitation to all IAFF
locals in Washington State to
consider forming a state
organization.

YAKIMA #469 COLLECTION

WSCFF 1939-1962

What exactly triggered twelve Washington State IAFF locals to create the WSCFF in 1939 remains unclear. Earlier attempts at organizing Washington's IAFF locals in concerted activity had failed, including a move in the late 1920s toward state legislation that would have required a two-platoon system.

Formation of any state IAFF association was problematic. As early as 1919, IAFF locals debated the role of state organizations, and how they might affect a local's political power. This was in part financially motivated, and in part to maintain large locals' political autonomy. Traditionally, smaller locals have had much to gain from a state association relative to what it costs them in per capita assessments. Large locals have been much more likely to be players in the AFL's city and state council system, and are often adverse to negotiating with smaller fire fighter locals within their states.

At some point in the mid-to-late 1930s Seattle Mayor Arthur Langlie called for a study of fire fighters' pension funding, and this study found the money was not there to pay for Seattle's pension program. Langley documented many of the financial shortfalls his administration faced. Pension funding does not appear to have been one of his top priorities; he seems to have put more energy into attempts to undercut existing labor agreements with Seattle employees' unions.

Certainly the 1935 amendments to RCW 41.16 (Firemen's Relief and Pension Act) placed greater fiscal demands upon Washington municipalities at a time when huge numbers of people were on relief and any government's ability to collect revenues was extremely low. Meanwhile, infighting dominated Washington State's labor movement. The CIO and the AFL-affiliated labor councils battled against each other for political control, and together against all manner of pay cuts, layoffs, and right-to-work legislation.

For whatever reasons, fire fighters from Bellingham #106, Bremerton #437, Centralia-Chehalis #451, Everett #46, Aberdeen-Hoquiam #315, Olympia #468, Seattle #27, Spokane #29, Tacoma #31, Vancouver-Camas #452, Wenatchee #453, and Yakima #469 gathered in Seattle on December 9, 1938. The meeting was called to order by IAFF District 7 Vice President Max Maximilian (Seattle #27). Seattle Chief Fitzgerald (not a delegate) welcomed the guests. Those present discussed the differences between a possible IAFF state organization, the already-existing Washington State Firemen's Association, and the Washington State Chief's Association.

Fire fighter Price (Wenatchee #453) made a motion, with Bennett (Yakima #469) seconding that "recommendations be made to state locals that a state organization

⬌ Spokane #29 **173**

⬌ Fractious Fraternity
27

⬌ At the End of the Day
137

⬌ Before the WSCFF **21**

be formed." After some discussion, the motion passed unanimously. Talk then turned to the need for civil service laws and problems with existing pension law. Minutes from the meeting indicate several hours of discussion followed on how to structure proportional representation in a state organization and what level of financial responsibility would fall to the new organization's member locals.

Unclear from the minutes is what exactly was being considered when representatives discussed some sort of affiliation with the Association of Washington Cities (AWC), which was meeting in Seattle at the time. Three individuals were authorized to attend the AWC gathering on behalf of the IAFF locals present.

The next meeting of Washington's IAFF local representatives took place on January 6, 1939, in Chehalis. The first order of business was a report from Maximilian (Seattle #27, IAFF District 7 vice president), who had attended the AWC meeting. Representatives from those IAFF locals present authorized a letter to the AWC "requesting them [the AWC] to do nothing detrimental toward the Police and Firemen's Civil Service Bill." Those present also directed that three delegates of the fire fighter group be accepted by the AWC as "delegates." Discussion then followed on "things to guard against if the fire fighters of the state of Washington affiliate with the AWC."

Representatives adopted the name "Washington State Council of Fire Fighters," elected officers, and authorized collection of a ten cent per capita assessment, to be held by each local for future funding of the organization, with the first month's per capita used to cover the costs of creating the WSCFF. Finally, a structure for delegate representation per local (based on hundred-member units) was adopted, and the newly elected officers were charged with drafting bylaws "for approval by the locals."

Eight days later, O.K. Coffin, president of Seattle #27 and acting secretary of the WSCFF, wrote locals asking for the first month's ten cent per capita:

> some of which has to be used for the purchase of stationery and stamps etc. I cannot afford to buy these things out of my own pocket and I can't use the local's [Seattle #27] stuff all the time gratis...

STATEWIDE SOLIDARITY: THE ORIGINAL MEMBERS OF THE WSCFF

Representatives attending the April 21, 1939 meeting of the WSCFF:

E.C. Kuehner	Chehalis-Centralia #451	President
H.L. Leach	Camas-Vancouver #452	Vice President
O.K. Coffin	Seattle #27	Secretary
F.E. Stearns	Bellingham #106	Treasurer
R.L. Warnock	Everett #46 (then #350)	Executive Board
A.D. McAdams	Seattle #27	Executive Board
C.E. Weeks	Spokane #29	Executive Board
Ernest Yett	Bremerton #437	Executive Board
E.A. Thompson	Tacoma #31	Executive Board and Host
Max Maximilian	Seattle #27	IAFF District 7 Vice President
Ernie Cassils	Bellingham #106	observer
F.W. Zumhoff	Seattle #27	observer

Founding locals of the WSCFF as of September 1, 1939:

Aberdeen-Hoquiam #315 (Aberdeen later became #2639)

Bellingham #106

Bremerton #437

Camas-Vancouver #452 (Camas later became #2444)

Chehalis-Centralia #451 (Chehalis later became #2510)

Everett #46 (then #350)

Olympia #468

Seattle #27

Spokane #29

Tacoma #31

Wenatchee #453

Yakima #469

The only IAFF local in existence at the time that did not affiliate was Walla Walla #404.

It is worth remembering how hard times were, and how many households had no source of income, in evaluating the degree of commitment represented by committing to a ten cent per capita assessment, and the expense of traveling to the fledgling WSCFF's meetings.

In April 1939 twelve IAFF locals sent representatives to a meeting hosted by Tacoma #31. Those present used the Oregon State Association of Fire Fighters' bylaws as a model to draft the WSCFF's and scheduled the first WSCFF Convention in Spokane the following July. Fifty-one dollars, one month's per capita assessment, was collected from those present, to cover the cost of correspondence and arrangements for the first convention. Three dollars of this fund was allocated to Secretary Coffin (Seattle #27) to send a copy of the "temporary" bylaws to each of the state's IAFF locals.

It must have been at that July 1939 Convention that a majority of Washington's IAFF locals requested that the IAFF charter the WSCFF (the IAFF protocol for establishing a state association), because a charter was issued on September 1, 1939. No minutes survive from this first convention, but based on affiliation dates, Walla Walla #404 was the only existing local that was not also a charter member of the WSCFF.

Records of WSCFF action are scattered and largely anecdotal for the next thirty years. In 1941 discussion focused on whether E.C. Kuehner (Chehalis-Centralia #451) could be president of the WSCFF and chief of his department. It was concluded that there was no reason he could not hold both offices since the situation wasn't covered in the WSCFF bylaws, didn't go against IAFF bylaws, and chiefs were dues-paying members of the IAFF.

In March 1944 the WSCFF's legislative team was reimbursed for expenses incurred while attending the state legislature's special session: $58.26, which included the cost of a room, a few meals, and a bottle of whisky. During the 1940s, any statewide gathering of WSCFF delegates was called a convention. At the May 1944 Convention there was contentious discussion as to whether Maximilian (Seattle #27) was doing his job as IAFF District 7 vice president. While debating the issue, representatives noted someone should contact IAFF locals in Montana and Idaho about this position. WSCFF delegates then cast their own votes for District 7 vice president at this same meeting.

Earl Brower (Everett #46) beat out Jack Waller (Spokane #29) by one vote after four rounds. Waller then agreed to cast the WSCFF's "unanimous" vote of support for Brower at the IAFF Convention. Seattle #27 concurred, but then made it clear it would not contribute to cover Brower's expenses in attending the convention. Other representatives considered this poor form. In the end Brower's expenses were covered by the WSCFF.

By 1947 Jack Waller (Spokane #29) was secretary of the WSCFF, Felix Arena (Seattle #27) its treasurer, and together Waller and Brower (Everett #46, IAFF District 7 vice president) were identified as the WSCFF's lobbying team. These three would keep their positions until 1956, when Brower retired and Waller was elected to replace him as IAFF District 7 vice president. Walt Lambert (Spokane #29) was then elected secretary of the WSCFF, replacing Waller. While WSCFF presidents came and went, Brower, Waller, Lambert, and Arena made up the core of the organization until 1964.

The original charter, issued to the WSCFF by the IAFF on September 1, 1939.
WSCFF COLLECTION

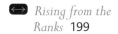 *Rising from the Ranks* **199**

From the 1940s until the early 1960s, the WSCFF was more of a clearing house for information between interested locals than a political player unto itself. Its lobbying efforts relied almost entirely on those few individuals who devoted themselves to attending legislative sessions and who met with other labor leaders. Consequently, advances in working conditions and wages occurred at the local level. For example, there is no record of any statewide response as World War II imposed major shifts in fire service staffing. During the war there was a shortage of qualified fire fighters. After World War II, fire fighters hired under the non-standard conditions of the war were in competition with returning, veteran fire fighters.

At the state level, the pension and benefits system for fire fighters was amended in 1947, 1955, 1957, and 1961, but much of the politicking that brought about these changes came from individual fire fighters who lobbied on behalf of their locals and used the WSCFF as a political platform, rather than the orchestrated actions of the WSCFF.

By 1950 there were approximately thirty locals in the WSCFF. In 1955 RCW 41.18 (Firemen's Relief and Pensions) established a new pension system, and modifications to the previous system (RCW 41.16) allowed professional fire fighters in fire districts, third class cities, and fourth class cities to be covered under both systems.

When the AFL and CIO merged in 1955, the IAFF shifted its affiliation from the AFL to the joint organization. It took two more years for the Washington State Federation of Labor (WSFL) and the Washington State Congress of Industrial Organizations (WSCIO) to do the same, to form the Washington State Labor Council (WSLC). That same year (1957), the WSCFF identified collective bargaining as its "primary legislative focus" and introduced its first bill, "Arbitration for Fire Fighters and Police," which was defeated in March.

In 1958 members of the WSCFF joined other labor groups in fending off the right-to-work Initiative 202, which was defeated almost two to one. The WSCFF changed its methods in 1960, and began use of a seven-member legislative team that toured the state, meeting with member locals to draft and revise legislative proposals before they were presented in Olympia. In November 1960, Washington State voters passed Initiative 207, which established the state civil service (codified in RCW 41.06).

The WSCFF's membership demonstrated its lobbying potential when it successfully supported HB 365, the Firemen's Pension Bill, in 1961. One aspect of this law, which further amended 41.18, was the creation of the Public Pension Commission, which began to document the immense under-funding of the state's pension systems. With this victory in hand, the WSCFF was poised for huge legislative action.

Logo from the 1958 WSCFF Convention. Held in Hoquiam, it was sponsored by Aberdeen-Hoquiam #315. (Aberdeen #2639 spun off to form a separate local in 1978.)

JERRY MCFEELY COLLECTION

John Alexander (#864) was president of the WSCFF from 1956-1958.

SPOKANE #29 COLLECTION

The 1963 Convention in Seattle, twenty-five years after the formation of the WSCFF, brought the organization into a new era. The first order of business was electing John Smith (Tacoma #31, WSCFF trustee) as president. Smith did not have the full backing of his own local, yet narrowly defeated Jack Baker (Bellingham #106, WSCFF vice president), who had Jack Waller's (Spokane #29, IAFF District 7 vice president) and Walt Lambert's (Spokane #29, WSCFF secretary) support. Resolutions passed included consideration of districting within the WSCFF, lobbying for a shorter workweek, and full support of the Washington State Labor Council's (WSLC) COPE (Committee on Political Education). A resolution entitled "Arbitration, Union Recognition, and Collective Bargaining for Fire Fighters" was also approved.

⬌ *Collectively Bargaining* **99**

John Richmond, newly elected secretary-treasurer of Seattle #27, Walt Lambert (Spokane #29, WSCFF secretary), George Roop (Spokane Valley Fire District 1 #876), and others took this resolution on collective bargaining to the WSLC and garnered its backing. The resolution died in the rules committee of the 1964 legislature, but with it the WSCFF had begun an ever-escalating campaign. Smith, Lambert, Waller, Richmond, John Willis (Tacoma #31) and other fire fighters swarmed Olympia. They would not take no for an answer until they won collective bargaining rights in 1967, with the passage of RCW 41.56 (the Public Employees' Collective Bargaining Act).

With the right to collective bargaining came the ability to have an IAFF local contractually recognized as the bargaining representative of the professional fire fighters in that jurisdiction. And although collective bargaining was still commonly referred to as "collective begging" (since it lacked the second punch of binding arbitration until 1973), winning passage of RCW 41.56 demonstrated the political clout WSCFF members had when they worked together.

As WSCFF president from 1963-1972, John Smith (#31) led the WSCFF to achieve collective bargaining and LEOFF. L-R: *unknown, Leo Weisfield "Seattle's friend," Smith, John Willis (#31), Axel Drugge (327), Walt Lambert (#29, IAFF District 7 vp).* SEATED: *Gov. Albert Rosellini, signing unidentified bill, circa 1970.*

AXEL DRUGGE COLLECTION

Passage of RCW 41.56 did not decrease the clash of personalities within the leadership of the WSCFF, however. Prior to Smith's election as president, it had been the WSCFF secretary, its treasurer, and the IAFF District 7 vice president who together pretty much ran the WSCFF. During Waller's and then Lambert's decades as WSCFF secretaries (with Seattle #27's Felix Arena as treasurer), the WSCFF president was more figurehead than leader or even key spokesperson for the organization. Smith changed this from the moment he was elected, and made few friends in the process. He had a vision of what was politically attainable, and although three of those who worked most closely with him (Waller, Spokane #29, WSCFF legislative representative and IAFF District 7 vice president, Lambert, Spokane #29, WSCFF recording secretary, and Willis, Tacoma #31), disliked Smith's approach, the WSCFF has never accomplished more than it did during his presidency.

In 1968, the secretary and treasurer positions were combined. Seattle #27 disaffiliated from the WSCFF the following year. At the fall 1968 IAFF Convention, a resolution requiring mandatory membership in state associations passed. IAFF dissention from large locals, including Seattle #27, was so divisive that enactment of the resolution was delayed. The IAFF then changed its representational system rather than requiring locals join state councils, and Seattle #27 stayed out of the WSCFF until 1978.

In 1969 LEOFF (RCW 41.26 Law Enforcement Officers' and Fire Fighters' Retirement System) was signed by Governor Dan Evans. The path this legislation took to get on the governor's desk and gain his signature was a masterful example of quick-witted and well-connected lobbying. It called upon the experience and relationships of every fire fighter who had been working the Olympia scene, and it remains a wonder that so many divergent interests pulled together to make it happen.

During this period, several longtime leaders in the WSCFF stepped aside. Jim Martinez (Boise, Idaho #672) succeeded Lambert (Spokane #29) as IAFF District 7 vice president in 1972, when Lambert followed Waller (Spokane #29) to join the IAFF research and lobbying staff. Howard Vietzke (Spokane #29) was elected secretary-treasurer in 1972, and Arena (Seattle #27) handed over to him all of the WSCFF's records in two cardboard boxes when he assumed office.

Smith, as spokesperson for the WSCFF, continued to push the envelope, publicly discussing the possibility of fire fighter walkouts if they didn't get binding arbitration. The WSCFF Convention of 1971 was Smith's last as council president; he served as the WSCFF's paid lobbyist in the 1973 legislative session and then retired, replaced by John Willis (Tacoma #31). In 1973 the WSCFF traded its members' questionable legal right to strike for binding arbitration with passage of HB 176, (the Mediation and Arbitration Collective Bargaining Rights Act, an amendment to RCW 41.56). The 1973 legislation also allowed for payroll check deduction of union dues, which greatly simplified the work of IAFF locals.

In 1974, the WSCFF began publication of the *Washington Professional Fire Fighter*. Later that year, at the IAFF convention in Baltimore, there was an ugly election for IAFF District 7 vice president. WSCFF President Hofmann (Everett #46) nominated incumbent Martinez (Boise #672). Martinez was challenged by WSCFF lobbyist John Willis (Tacoma #31). Weeks after this, Tacoma #31 followed Seattle #27 in disaffiliating from the WSCFF, in part because of this election.

Times got harder for the WSCFF and all IAFF locals as a backwash of legislative attacks and public criticism replaced what had been a fast-moving current of legislative victories. Some of this was due to the changing image of public employees in general. During the social strife and upheaval of the late 1960s and early 1970s, fire fighters literally put out the fires of race riots and seemed from the outside to offer a model of disciplined service. In fact, the fire service was facing the same social issues within its departments as the rest of society.

In early 1975, the Public Employment Relations Commission (PERC) was created by the legislature, and in 1976 PERC took over the administration of collective bargaining laws affecting many public employees, including those in the fire service. [The Washington State Department of Labor and Industries (L&I) had been administrator until this.]

By the mid-1970s, the fire service was beginning to formally incorporate emergency medical services (EMS), which changed the training, certification, duties,

PUBLIC SERVANTS ON STRIKE

I'm the public, and I'm not sure I can afford servants anymore.

1975 political cartoon summarizing sentiment toward public employees.
©1945 BY BILL MAULDIN. REPRINTED WITH PERMISSION.

and community expectations of fire fighters. Minutes from the January, 1975 WSCFF executive board meeting mention recommendations regarding EMS, but not their content.

Meanwhile, LEOFF became a focal point for public criticism. As each year passed after it took effect in 1970, more and more anecdotal stories of financial abuse by those it covered came to light. Combined with zooming inflation and actuarial predictions that missed their financial mark, it was only a matter of time before LEOFF became the target of legislative reform. Few in the fire service, and only a small minority within the WSCFF, could see the degree to which the tide of public opinion was turning.

At the End of the Day 137

The WSCFF tried to pull itself together. Districts were formed in 1976, with representatives to be elected by members of that district. Tacoma #31 reaffiliated in 1976. WSCFF lobbyist Willis (Tacoma #31) and others did their best in Olympia, but with Seattle #27 still out of the WSCFF, and many fire fighters somewhat complacent about the threat of legislative backlash, the axe fell. In June 1977, Washington State's public employees' pensions were reconfigured by the legislature. The Public Employees Retirement System (PERS), the Teachers' Retirement System (TRS), and LEOFF were each restructured to incorporate a two-tier benefits system. RCW 41.26 was amended, creating LEOFF 2, which was frequently referred to as "left out."

Fractious Fraternity 27

The late 1970s also saw changes in who joined the fire service. By 1977, both Seattle and Tacoma fire departments were in the thick of affirmative action programs, with varying success. In addition, EMS had become a critical part of Washington State's fire service, pushing departments and locals to find ways to integrate paramedics and other EMS personnel, while cross-training existing personnel.

At the End of the Day 137

Someone Like Me 83

EMS 69

Seattle #27 reaffiliated with the WSCFF in 1978, and that fall Washington State's fire fighters joined others in labor to support key political candidates as never before. Larry Vognild, a retired Everett #46 member, beat incumbent Senate Majority leader Augie Mardesich, thanks to such support. By the end of the year, the WSCFF purchased its condominium in Olympia, affirming its commitment to a political presence throughout the legislative session.

Campaigns and Candidates 126

Going into the 1980 IAFF Convention, IAFF District 7 Vice President Martinez had been challenged in his last three elections. As described earlier, Willis (Tacoma #31) had tried in 1974. In 1976, Vietzke (Spokane #29) ran, and in 1978 Dick Warbrouck (Seattle #27) also tried. Some remember that Vietzke lost because he didn't carry Seattle #27, and so Spokane #29 made sure Warbrouck didn't win in 1978. As one politico remembered, "by 1980 it was Tacoma's turn to try." Jim Hill beat Martinez, and Jimmy Cason (Tacoma #31) then replaced Hill as WSCFF District 6 representative.

On March 18, 1981, Washington labor held a rally to oppose the possible privatization of worker's compensation. Almost 8,000 workers from across the state,

In March 1981, thousands of Washington State's public employees rallied in Olympia to send a message to recently elected Governor John Spellman. The message was "Three-way, no-way," and meant that workers did not support possible privatization of the state's insurance plans.

TACOMA #31 COLLECTION

including numerous WSCFF members, gathered on the steps of the capitol to make their opposition to HB 31 clear to newly elected Governor John Spellman. Members of that same legislature attacked the existing collective bargaining rights of public employees. Teachers lost their right to collective bargaining on wages and fringe benefits when Spellman signed ESHB 166. Five other bills proposed changing binding arbitration to "last best offer" arbitration, but were defeated.

Going into the 1981 WSCFF Convention, WSCFF Secretary-Treasurer Vietzke (Spokane #29) announced he was stepping down. The election to replace him was contentious. Michael McGovern (Lakewood #1488, District 4 representative) nominated Tom Fieldstead (Yakima #469). Ron Morehouse (Bellingham #106) and Don Spangle (Spokane #29, District 1 representative) also ran, but Spangle was the only candidate with campaign hats. Fieldstead (Yakima #469) won. The vice-presidency was also up for election, after Hill (Tacoma #31) became IAFF District 7 vice president (1980). Ken Strong (Spokane #29) ran against Dan Downs (Richland #1052, District 2 representative) and Downs won.

Numerous resolutions were passed at the 1981 Convention, including several proposing legislative changes to LEOFF 2, with a LEOFF 2 Committee created to take action on these. There were also redistricting resolutions, although the content of these is lost. Resolution 38 directed the WSCFF to establish a political action fund which could collect voluntary contributions from individual members, another step in systematizing the WSCFF's political action.

That same fall, John Willis (Tacoma #31) stepped down as the WSCFF lobbyist to take a position with the Washington State Department of Labor and Industries (L&I). The executive board appointed Howard Vietzke (Spokane #29) to replace him, but also hired a professional lobbyist, Mike Ryherd, to train Vietzke. Vietzke and Ryherd then attended the legislature's emergency session in October, 1981. They helped defeat proposed PERC mediation user fees and the privatization of "employee services if a finding is made that such contracting will result in a cost savings" to state or local governments. At the time, many fire service jurisdictions were incorporating emergency medical services (EMS), and bids by private ambulance services made the option of contracting out for EMS popular to financially strapped governments.

In the midst of these changes, the WSCFF stepped up to technological changes. In October 1981, the executive board of the WSCFF held its first conference

Don Spangle (Spokane #29) went all out in his bid for WSCFF secretary-treasurer in 1981.

DENNIS PARLARI COLLECTION

EMS 69

call, which District 4 Representative Michael McGovern (Lakewood #1488) described in the winter *Washington Professional Fire Fighter*. "Although it seemed a bit confusing initially, everyone quickly adjusted… and the end result was successful."

As the 1982 Convention approached, Michael McGovern (Lakewood #1488) was committed to returning the WSCFF to its status as a real political player. At twenty-eight he had only been on the executive board for a year and a half, since replacing Dennis Parlari (Puyallup #726) as District 4 representative when Parlari was elected president. IAFF District 7 Vice President Jim Hill (Tacoma #31), McGovern's mentor, asked McGovern to consider running for president. When McGovern said he wasn't interested, Hill asked McGovern who it was he wanted to work for. McGovern thought Jimmy Cason (Tacoma #31, District 6 representative) might make a good president, but when he went to Tacoma and talked with Cason, McGovern found out Cason didn't want the presidency. McGovern decided he did. Then he heard Ken Strong (Spokane #29) was running.

WSCFF President Parlari (Puyallup #726) arranged a meeting between Strong and McGovern to see if they could resolve their differences so there would be only one candidate. Strong was not willing to commit to serving more than one term, but wanted Spokane #29 to be well-represented at the state level. When interviewed, Strong explained he felt he best served the union from within Spokane #29, and that serving at the WSCFF level involved more politicking than he was interested in over the long haul.

McGovern thought long-term commitment to the presidency was imperative, since he viewed the turnover in presidents immediately preceding 1982 as crippling the WSCFF's effectiveness. (There had been four presidents between 1972 and 1982, and John Smith's presidential legacy, 1963-1972, had either faded or been forgotten.) Merlin Halverson (Lynnwood #1968, District 3 representative), who had been on the executive board since 1977, then entered the fray.

The 1982 Convention in Yakima featured presidential campaign T-shirts, and dueling hospitality rooms. Only McGovern had his T-shirt modeled by a buxom female bartender, while Ted Rail (Spokane #29), who was in charge of Strong's hospitality room, neglected to purchase liquor before the Sunday night pre-convention gathering. Cason, managing McGovern's hospitality room, lent the Strong campaign what it needed. The next day, in the first round of voting by approximately 122 delegates, Halverson (nominated by Ron Morehouse, Bellingham #106) led by fifteen votes, McGovern (nominated by then President Parlari, Puyallup #726) came in second, and Strong (nominated by Ollie Morris, Pasco #1433) trailed McGovern by fewer than twenty votes. Strong's key supporters, the delegates from his own local (Spokane #29) as well as those from Spokane Valley, met with Halverson and McGovern individually to hear their pitches. Strong remembers that for this moment, Spokane #29 delegates had all the power. Votes were cast, and this time McGovern won by three.

Even after McGovern won the three-way election for WSCFF president in 1982, many Halverson supporters continued to wear their T-shirts with pride.

WASHINGTON PROFESSIONAL FIRE FIGHTER, SUMMER 1982.

One Vote Matters **83**

WASHINGTON STATE COUNCIL
OF FIRE FIGHTERS
VOLUNTARY POLITICAL ACTION FUND
for the nomination and election of certain individuals to federal
office in 1982.
VPAF is the WSCFF's political action fund. The WSCFF solicits
and accepts only voluntary contributions. A copy of our report
is filed with the Federal Election Commission and is available for
purchase from the Federal Election Commission, Washington,
D.C., and acknowledges receipt during 1982 of $_____
from _____

WSCFF VPAF
Dennis G. Parlari   Tom Fieldstead
President   Secretary-Treasurer
513 No. Front St., Suite G
Yakima, Washington 98901
*PLEASE RETAIN THIS PORTION FOR YOUR RECORDS

There are few notes on most of the rest of the convention's activities. Resolution 38 passed, authorizing creation of a "voluntary political action fund," and changing the WSCFF's future within Washington State and the IAFF. It would take more than a year to create this fund, but once it was in existence, it allowed the WSCFF to make political contributions as part of its ongoing political activities. One of McGovern's first actions as president was to eliminate Ryherd as the WSCFF's paid lobbyist, which meant Vietzke (Spokane #29) became the WSCFF's sole lobbyist. Later in 1982 the executive board appointed Greg Bergquist (Renton #864) as District 4 representative to fill the position McGovern had vacated.

During this same period, Seattle #27 approached the WSCFF in an attempt to have its per capita payments either waived or reduced, as it was feeling the financial pinch of various litigation it was party to. Discussions were already tense when WSCFF Secretary-Treasurer Fieldstead (Yakima #469) took it upon himself to offer Seattle #27 an ultimatum to pay up or get out. Seattle #27 eventually disaffiliated, and would remain out of the WSCFF until 1992.

A good part of the 1983 Convention concerned restructuring the WSCFF's finances to deal with Seattle #27's disaffiliation. As a result, the per capita assessment cleared the five dollar mark. A few months later, WSCFF District 6 Representative Jimmy Cason (Tacoma #31) reported in the *Washington State Professional Fire Fighter*:

> ...our per capita for the next twelve months will be $5.47 per member per month. This is an increase of $.51, due in part to the fact that Seattle is no longer affiliated... That per capita seems high and is one of the highest paid to a state organization in the country.

There was also considerable discussion about restructuring District 4, which had grown to include approximately twenty-eight locals and 742 fire fighters along the I-5 corridor. District 4 Representative Bergquist (Renton #864) pointed out this was "by far the largest district in the WSCFF" and that it deserved more than one position on the executive board. Resolution 83-25 directed a report and recommendations on redistricting be presented at the 1984 Convention. That summer's issue of the *Washington State Professional Fire Fighter* was the last published by Callan Publishing, Incorporated, a partnership that had produced a very slick magazine but failed to project an image of the WSCFF that met the council's approval.

In early 1984 the State Supreme Court issued a decision supporting Bellevue #1604 and overturning a City of Bellevue ordinance (from 1981) that banned certain nonpartisan political activities by city employees, a case that had begun in 1981 (*Bellevue Fire Fighters #1604 vs. the City of Bellevue*).

Delegates at the 1984 Convention voted for significant constitutional changes, in part a response to the executive board's appointment of Ron Morehouse (Bellingham #106) as secretary-treasurer in November, 1983, when Fieldstead (Yakima #468) became a deputy chief and resigned from the WSCFF. One amendment granted locals the power to fill a vacancy in the secretary-treasurer position, which district representatives had done in the past.

The WSCFF constitution was also amended to allow district membership rather than the executive board to nominate and elect district representatives, a huge shift in power from the board to the membership. WSCFF delegates changed the lobbyist position from one that was paid on a per diem, work-replacement basis, to a salaried position. Secretary-Treasurer Morehouse (Bellingham #106) summarized the rationale for this change, which had an estimated expense of forty cents per capita, in the fall 1984 *Washington Professional Fire Fighter*:

> ...this makes the position independent of the lobbyist's employment status, and removes the council from the responsibility of work replacement.

The work of the 1984 Convention continued. District 4 was split to create District 7 (a number formerly assigned to disaffiliated Seattle #27), in keeping with a May 1984 recommendation from the executive board. Resolution 84-4 was also passed, authorizing research and recommendations on a health and welfare trust for WSCFF members. (The WSCFF Health and Welfare Trust was established in 1986.)

From 1985 until 1989 the WSCFF executive board remained relatively stable, and the WSCFF focused on legislative action and member education. Lobbying targeted broadening collective bargaining and binding arbitration rights to include dispatchers, paramedics, and port workers, as well as whatever could be done to improve LEOFF 2. In 1987, the WSCFF successfully lobbied for passage of SB 5801 (RCW 51.32.185), which defines lung disease as a presumptive occupational disease for fire fighters. The WSCFF's educational efforts were directed toward increasing members' understanding of the LEOFF 2 system and the practicalities of contract negotiation.

In 1989 one election dominated the WSCFF's annual convention. Cason (Tacoma #31) ran for secretary-treasurer, challenging incumbent Morehouse (Bellingham #106). A general alliance of "non-Pierce County" locals backed Morehouse, lead by district representatives Halverson (Lynnwood #1984, District 3), Bergquist (Renton #864, District 4), and Dan Downs (Richland #1052, District 2). Morehouse recalls the election was also about a lack of communication between the executive board and McGovern, and that he felt at the time McGovern's initial democratic approach to the executive board had faded. McGovern (Lakewood #1488) and Cason (Tacoma #31) were close, so it was not surprising McGovern backed Cason's campaign, which further fed the charges of Pierce County domination within the WSCFF executive board. At the time, the WSCFF "office" (its business files) moved with the secretary-treasurer, which meant the office would shift from Bellingham to Tacoma if Cason beat Morehouse.

Cason, meanwhile, was a recognized leader in his own right both within the WSCFF and within Tacoma #31. Shortly before the election there were deals made within Tacoma #31. Out of these negotiations Cason emerged with Tacoma #31's full support, and Pat McElligott emerged knowing he would become District 6's

The 1987 WSCFF All Stars.
STANDING, L-R: *Jimmy Cason (#31), Al Nyman (#31), Ron Morehouse (#106, WSCFF s/t), Mike McGovern (#1488, WSCFF president), Bill Anderson (#876), Gary Brown (#29).* KNEELING, L-R: *Rex Lindquist, (#2545), Dan Downs, (#1052), Frank Spicklemire (#468), Jim Hill (#31, IAFF District 7 vp).*

TACOMA #31 COLLECTION

representative if Cason won. Spokane Valley #876 and Edmonds #1828 were targeted. In the end Cason won by two votes, generally attributed to carrying both of these locals.

After Cason won, there was a resolution from the floor, 89-31, which nominated Morehouse for secretary-treasurer emeritus. It passed. When Morehouse accepted the award, however, he made a crude gesture from the podium which reflected his frustration at the convention participants.

At the next year's convention, there were more executive board elections. Jim Rudd (Spokane #29, District 1 representative) defeated Downs (Richland #1052, District 2 representative) for the vice-presidency. Months earlier, at the spring 1990 Educational Seminar, Kelly Fox (Olympia #468) had declared for the District 5 position although at the time his mentor, Frank Spicklemire, also from Olympia #468, was not interested in stepping down. By convention time Fox faced off against and defeated Vancouver #452 President Joe Mackey, in a vote Fox characterized as emphasizing the north-south division within District 5.

⬅➡ *One Vote Matters* **33**

The 1990 Convention was also the first forum where delegates considered a source of funding that would greatly change the WSCFF. President McGovern announced a proposal from the Gehl Group, which would use telemarketing to promote WSCFF-sponsored concerts on the Westside of the state. McGovern remembers there was significant discussion about signing on with this program, some triggered by the difficulties the council remembered from Callan Publishing and its publication of the *Washington State Professional Fire Fighter*.

The next year's convention, in 1991, brought even bigger changes. Resolution 91-24 further expanded the executive board to ten districts. Dave West (Spokane #29) recalls heated discussion because only the Westside of the state was slated for new districts. Tremendous growth along the I-5 corridor triggered a parallel expansion of fire services, and the east-side locals didn't have the votes to challenge the proposed restructuring. The ten districts adopted in 1991 remain the basis for current districting; Seattle was added as District 11 when it reaffiliated the following year (1992).

The WSCFF executive board and guests gathered on the roof of the WSCFF's temporary offices in Tacoma before attending the first concert arranged by the Gehl Group.

L-R: *unknown, Cody Arledge (#2409), Kelly Fox (#468), someone from the Gehl Group, unknown, Jimmy Cason's back (#31), Dave West (#29), McMenamin.*

WSCFF COLLECTION

An equally basic change came after much discussion, when delegates voted 48 to 44 to move forward on fundraising by the Gehl group. Those who were involved with the WSCFF in 1991 remember that the WSCFF was guaranteed something like $20,000 for the first year's concerts. As it turned out, the concerts arranged by the Gehl Group generated tremendous income, far exceeding anyone's original expectations.

Most of those interviewed for this book identify the exponential increase in revenues from telemarketing as a major turning point for the WSCFF. Fire fighters who were involved with the WSCFF in decades past, when there was little funding, wonder if so much money diluted the passion of the WSCFF's leadership. Some also identify changes in fire fighters' wages, benefits, and working conditions as additional factors that have made the WSCFF and its membership, to them, less driven today than in years past. McGovern (Lakewood #1488, WSCFF president) remembers talking with Vietzke (Spokane #29, WSCFF legislative representative) as the WSCFF's income continued to grow. Vietzke told him that big money would bring with it big problems, and McGovern remembers thinking that he would welcome such difficulties, rather than being unable to fund programs the membership wanted.

In reality, the huge increase in available money did weave itself into bigger problems for McGovern. As mentioned earlier, Seattle #27 reaffiliated in 1992, creating District 11. At the WSCFF Convention that year, delegates passed a resolution which created the position of legislative assistant. This assured backup and an eventual transition when Legislative Director Vietzke (Spokane #29) stepped down. At this point it was also clear that there would come a time that McGovern would move on from the presidency of the WSCFF. Consideration of the new assistant lobbyist position and of McGovern's future became interwoven, since the two obvious possible positions he might move into were WSCFF lobbyist or IAFF District 7 vice president.

During the later years of McGovern's fourteen-year presidency, he and some of the executive board grew more distant. A larger income for the organization and the increasing number of financial decisions this dictated, combined with what some felt to be an increasingly distant or autocratic attitude from McGovern, made for increasing resentments. McGovern had helped to shape a very powerful executive board, but somewhere between 1992 and 1994, as he became clear in his own mind he would like to be the next WSCFF lobbyist, general support for such a plan faded within the WSCFF's executive board. And although the entire WSCFF had approved significant increases to the lobbyist's salary, this also counted against McGovern as it became more obvious he wanted appointment to that position.

During the early fall of 1992 three people were interviewed for the assistant lobbyist position, to begin during the upcoming legislative session: Fox (Olympia #468), Rick Gaines (Bellevue #1604), and Ken Snider (Spokane #29). Snider was appointed in October 1992, which Fox admits he took personally. During this time Secretary-Treasurer Cason (Tacoma #31) let several know, some on the executive board, but not McGovern, that he wanted to be lobbyist. With this, the subterranean fight for power within the executive board began to dominate all its meetings. Add to the situation that there was also some understanding that Fox was the fairly obvious eventual successor to McGovern as WSCFF president, and the stage was set for serious political maneuvering. The real rub was that McGovern was not interested in eventually replacing Hill as District 7 vice president, although Hill had expressed interest in serving until 2000, which would have given him a twenty-year term.

At the 1993 Convention Ricky Walsh (Richland #1052) barely defeated Downs (Richland #1052) as the District 2 Representative, and in 1994 Rick Chaney (Federal Way #2024) beat incumbent Gerry Gores (Burien #1461) for the District 9 position. During this convention delegates authorized the purchase of "a permanent office in Olympia," ending fifty-five years of organizational migration, wherein the WSCFF's office moved with the secretary-treasurer. Once again, although WSCFF delegates were the ones who approved purchase of permanent offices, this added "luxury" was attributed by some to McGovern personally.

Push came to shove within the executive board in 1995, when Vietzke (Spokane #29) formally announced he would step down as lobbyist at the end of the 1996 legislative session. When the WSCFF executive board met the day after the 1995 Convention, President McGovern announced he wanted to be lobbyist.

Secretary-Treasurer Cason immediately announced he did, too. McGovern and others remember a crushing silence while no one looked at anyone else. The board meeting then came to an abrupt end. Cason was appointed lobbyist at a special executive board meeting in September 1995, with Jim Rudd, as his assistant, replacing Ken Snider (Spokane #29).

When the Fall 1995 issue of the *Washington Professional Fire Fighter* came out, newly appointed Secretary-Treasurer Jack Andren's (Pierce County Professional Fire Fighters #2175) report outlined the domino-like series of retirements, appointments, resignations, and district elections that had swept the executive board and legislative team on the heels of Vietzke's retirement, including Andren's own appointment.

Cason (Tacoma #31) was Legislative Director Trainee, effective October 1, 1995. The executive board had then interviewed Andren (Pierce County Professional Fire Fighters #2175), Ted Rail (Spokane #29), and Lonnie Hampton (Tacoma #31), then appointed Andren secretary-treasurer, replacing Cason. Since Andren had been District 4 representative, an election for District 4 representative was held, and Mike Stead (Lakewood #1488) joined the executive board. When Vietzke retired, Snider (Spokane #29) decided not to continue as assistant lobbyist. The board then appointed Jim Rudd (Spokane #29) to this position, which meant election of a new District 1 representative. Spokane #29 picked Ted Rail. Rudd's shift also meant the vice presidency was vacant, and Walsh (Richland #1052, District 2 representative) was elected by the board near the end of 1995.

During the 1996 legislative session, Cason and Rudd trained under Vietzke and Snider. RCW 41.26.048 (Special Death Benefit—Death in the Course of Employment) $150,000 Death Benefit, (Line of Duty) was passed, in part because of the four Seattle fire fighter deaths the year before, during the Pang warehouse fire, granting $150,000 to families of fire fighters killed in the line of duty.

With less than six months to go to the 1996 Convention, the WSCFF executive board had been overhauled through appointments and district elections, and there was no common ground when it met. McGovern himself wasn't clear he wanted to serve another term; to others on the executive board this seemed apparent.

In his last report as District 5 representative, in the spring issue of the *Washington Professional Fire Fighter*, Fox pointed out all the principal officer positions and the odd-numbered district representatives would be up for election although only one position was contested at the time, with Hampton (Tacoma #31) challenging Andren (Pierce County Professional Fire Fighters #2175) for secretary-treasurer.

Behind the scenes, however, the distance between McGovern and the executive board had reached a point where there was opposition to McGovern's serving another two years. Fox was prepared to run for president, but was hoping to put it off until 1998 since he was facing a personal overload of family, work, and union responsibilities. A majority of the board rallied behind Fox, and he agreed to run.

Many who are currently active in the WSCFF remember the June 1996 WSCFF Convention in SeaTac. Fox declared his candidacy for president weeks before the convention, and in whirlwind fashion worked with the executive board to line up delegate votes. Greg Markley (Kent #1747) served as Fox's campaign director. McGovern knew Fox was running only when Fox told him three weeks before the convention, and knew then he did not have the executive board's support. Meanwhile Fox ran up so many minutes on his cell phone in such a short time that his phone company shut it down, thinking either his phone had been stolen or his account had been cloned. Nonetheless, McGovern went into the convention sure that the general membership would back him, based on the immense improvements to the WSCFF that had occurred during his presidency.

Fox won, 120-61. Then came the election for secretary-treasurer, which was perceived by most as a party ticket, with Fox and Hampton on one side and McGovern and Andren on the other. Hampton (Tacoma #31) won by about ten votes. Rail (Spokane #29, District 1 representative) challenged vice-president Walsh (Richland #1052, District 2 representative) and lost. Doug Willis, from Andren's local (Pierce County Professional Fire Fighters #2175) ran against Stead (Lakewood #1488) for District 4 representative, and won, in part because Stead, who was in McGovern's local, had not supported McGovern.

⬌ *One Vote Matters* **33**

As the smoke cleared after the 1996 Convention, many delegates went home stunned from the turn-around, since they had not been party to the ferment within the executive board. Fox was not particularly forgiving of those who had not supported him immediately after his election. Spokane #29 had backed McGovern, and it took some time to realign its loyalties, and for Fox to feel com-

⬌ *The LEOFF Health and Welfare Trust* **157**

fortable with its support. The WSCFF moved into its new office building in August 1996, as changes in the staffing of the WSCFF created additional turmoil within the organization.

That same August (1996) brought with it a contentious challenge for the IAFF District 7 vice presidency, held by Jim Hill (Tacoma #31) since 1980. The night before the IAFF convention was to convene, District 6 Representative McElligott, also a member of Tacoma #31, let his interest in running for the position be known. Hill had been McGovern's close friend and mentor for years, knew McElligott had backed Fox against McGovern, and was not interested in stepping down in 1996. After some late-night discussions McElligott did not formally declare his candidacy, although he did run in 1998.

The WSCFF moved into its current offices in Olympia in the summer of 1996. The building was dedicated to Jimmy Cason (#31) in 1997.

WSCFF COLLECTION

Then came tragedy. Jimmy Cason, newly appointed as director of governmental affairs, died suddenly, just before the 1997 legislative session. While still mourning, the WSCFF executive board held a special meeting on January 13, 1997, and appointed Cody Arledge (Tumwater #2409, District 5 representative) as lobbyist, with Rudd (Spokane #29) still on as assistant lobbyist. McElligott (Tacoma #31, District 6 representative) requested a formal role in the lobbying effort, and after a very close vote by the executive board, was approved as the third member of the WSCFF's legislative team. It is a testament to the commitment of the officers and executive board that they united so quickly to prepare for the 1997 legislative session.

That same January, the state attorney general's office closed its nine-month investigation and issued a consent decree on the Gehl Group's operational procedures. Although the WSCFF's telemarketing program had been included in this investigation, its operations were found without criticism. A few months later, in April 1997, the WSCFF office staff ratified its first contract, and has been represented by Office and Professional Employees International Union (OPEIU 23) ever since.

At the WSCFF Convention in Spokane in June 1997, two former officers of the WSCFF were honored. The position of WSCFF President Emeritus was created, and awarded to Michael McGovern, while the WSCFF's office building was named after Jimmy W. Cason. Chris Heminger (Auburn #1352, District 8 representative) defeated incumbent Secretary-Treasurer Lonnie Hampton (Tacoma #31), and two new district representatives were elected: Greg Markley (Kent #1747, District 8 representative), to replace Heminger and Brian Hurley (Tumwater #2409, District 5 representative) to replace Cody Arledge (Tumwater #2409), who had been appointed as Cason's replacement. Passage of Substitute Resolution 97-10, "Per Capita Budget Funding Policy," triggered what would be a two-year process of systematic organizational planning within the WSCFF.

The following May the *WSCFF Report of the Economic Summit* was released, and was included in the 1998 Convention notebook. Part of this study was a resolution (98-6), from the executive board, which directed the board to proceed with strategic planning that would make explicit the goals, objectives, and policies of the WSCFF. After the 1998 Convention, attention turned to the IAFF Convention in Orlando, Florida, and the contested election for IAFF District 7 vice president. Paul Harvey (Seattle #27) defeated Pat McElligott (Tacoma #31, District 6 representative) in a vote so close it was determined by the proxy votes of small locals.

← *One Vote Matters* **33**

During the 1999 legislative session the WSCFF successfully lobbied for legislation that allows for permanent EMS levies (RCW 84.52.069), as well as modifications to LEOFF 1 survivor benefits (RCW 41.26.160) and LEOFF 2 contribution refunds (amendments to RCW 41.26.470). In the meantime, the executive board did its homework and presented the *WSCFF Strategic Plan 2000* at the 1999 Convention. In it was the new mission statement of the WSCFF:

> ...to coordinate the statewide efforts of professional fire fighters by providing creative leadership and dedicated service, resulting in a unified, progressive membership that strives to improve social attitudes and promote legislation to benefit the fire and EMS communities and the citizens we serve, with a foundation anchored in the principals of honesty, integrity, and commitment.

← *On-the-Job Training*
95
← *I-790* **149**

The *Strategic Plan* also identified ten long-term strategic issues, and laid out an integrated action plan. Several recent accomplishments of the WSCFF stem from the plan's analysis: the apprenticeship program, passage of I-790, and the increased effectiveness of the WSCFF's legislative and educational seminars.

In December 1999, the World Trade Organization (WTO) met in Seattle. Approximately 30,000 individuals participated in a huge and peaceful AFL-CIO sponsored march to protest WTO policies undermining national health, safety, environmental, and labor laws. The WSCFF took no formal position and did not organize participation in WTO protest events, although many of its individual members participated. The Seattle Fire Department refused to use its hoses for crowd control, in a decision that was in keeping with lessons learned from the race riots of the late 1960s.

Seattle #27 **165**

During the next legislative session in 2000, the WSCFF worked to amend RCW 41.26.430, gaining a reduction in the LEOFF 2 retirement age, from 55 to 53. A few months later, at its spring educational seminar in Wenatchee, the first statewide new member orientation program was unveiled. It used the multimedia program, *Power Through Participation*, to walk new members through basic labor history, how a union works, and the specifics of the WSCFF. *Power Through Participation* won first place in the IAFF's Media Awards in 2001, thanks in large part to the work of Doug Baier (Bremerton #437) and Greg Markley (Kent #1747, District 8 representative).

In August 2000, Jim Rudd retired as the WSCFF's legislative liaison, and Keven Rojecki (City of SeaTac #2919) was appointed as his replacement. District 3 Representative Merlin Halverson (Lynnwood #1969) stepped down after twenty-two years on the executive board, and was replaced by Mike Wilson (Medic Seven #3524).

Labor rallied with environmental, peace, and justice groups in December 1999 to protest WTO policies that supercede individual governments' laws.

ELLIE BELEW COLLECTION

Then came the 2001 Convention. After much discussion, and some revision, resolutions were passed that would pave the way for passage of I-790. That fall, the tragedy of the September 11, 2001 attack on the World Trade Center and the deaths of 343 New York City fire fighters made those in the fire service sudden heroes. The WSCFF re-visited its political agenda, recognizing it had no desire to use the catastrophe as some kind of media opportunity, and also with a renewed knowledge of the risks their membership faced. During this same period Arledge stepped down as the WSCFF's Director of Legislative Affairs due to personal problems, and the WSCFF shifted to a lobbying team of President Fox (Olympia #468), Vice President Walsh (Richland #1052), and Lobbying Assistant Rojecki (City of SeaTac #2919).

I-790 **149**

During the 2002 legislative session the WSCFF successfully lobbied to expand coverage of presumptive occupational diseases for fire fighters, adding "heart problems occurring within seventy-two hours of exposure to smoke, fumes, or other toxins; cancer; and infectious diseases" (amending RCW 51.32.185). The WSCFF's proposed pension board reform legislation did not pass, however. At the 2002 Convention, WSCFF delegates authorized full support of initiative (I-790). Other convention action in 2002 included establishment of the WSCFF's Committee on Political Education (COPE).

Politics Costs Money **121**

In fall 2002 voters passed I-790, and the 2003 legislature then passed legislation codifying its changes to LEOFF's pension board. The WSCFF also lobbied successfully to gain passage of HB 1202, granting transfer of PERS service credits into LEOFF when a paramedic becomes a fire department employee. With the significant political success of I-790, the WSCFF is making plans for the future.

At the End of the Day **137**

Working streetside to build awareness and support for I-790, fall of 2002. L-R: *Guy Pennington (#726), Cory Bostick (#27, District 11 representative), Dennis Lawson (#726, District 4 representative).*

WSCFF COLLECTION

With over eighty percent of its locals representing fewer than 100 members, the WSCFF knows how important it is to protect the collective bargaining rights and the educated membership that allow professional fire fighters of Washington State to negotiate working conditions, benefits, and compensation in the future. Reduced government funding for public services while the demand for emergency services increases both in complexity and volume creates ever-growing challenges for the WSCFF. As per its mission statement, the WSCFF will continue to "improve social attitudes and promote legislation to benefit the fire and EMS communities and the citizens we serve, with a foundation anchored in the principals of honesty, integrity, and commitment."

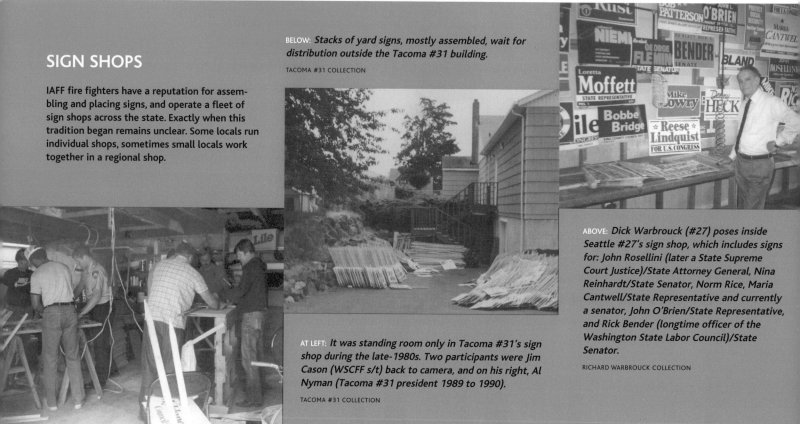

SIGN SHOPS

IAFF fire fighters have a reputation for assembling and placing signs, and operate a fleet of sign shops across the state. Exactly when this tradition began remains unclear. Some locals run individual shops, sometimes small locals work together in a regional shop.

BELOW: *Stacks of yard signs, mostly assembled, wait for distribution outside the Tacoma #31 building.*

TACOMA #31 COLLECTION

AT LEFT: *It was standing room only in Tacoma #31's sign shop during the late-1980s. Two participants were Jim Cason (WSCFF s/t) back to camera, and on his right, Al Nyman (Tacoma #31 president 1989 to 1990).*

TACOMA #31 COLLECTION

ABOVE: *Dick Warbrouck (#27) poses inside Seattle #27's sign shop, which includes signs for: John Rosellini (later a State Supreme Court Justice)/State Attorney General, Nina Reinhardt/State Senator, Norm Rice, Maria Cantwell/State Representative and currently a senator, John O'Brien/State Representative, and Rick Bender (longtime officer of the Washington State Labor Council)/State Senator.*

RICHARD WARBROUCK COLLECTION

Our Changing Profile

Delegates to the IAFF's first convention, in February 1918, included representatives from AFL locals in Seattle, Spokane, Tacoma, and Everett.

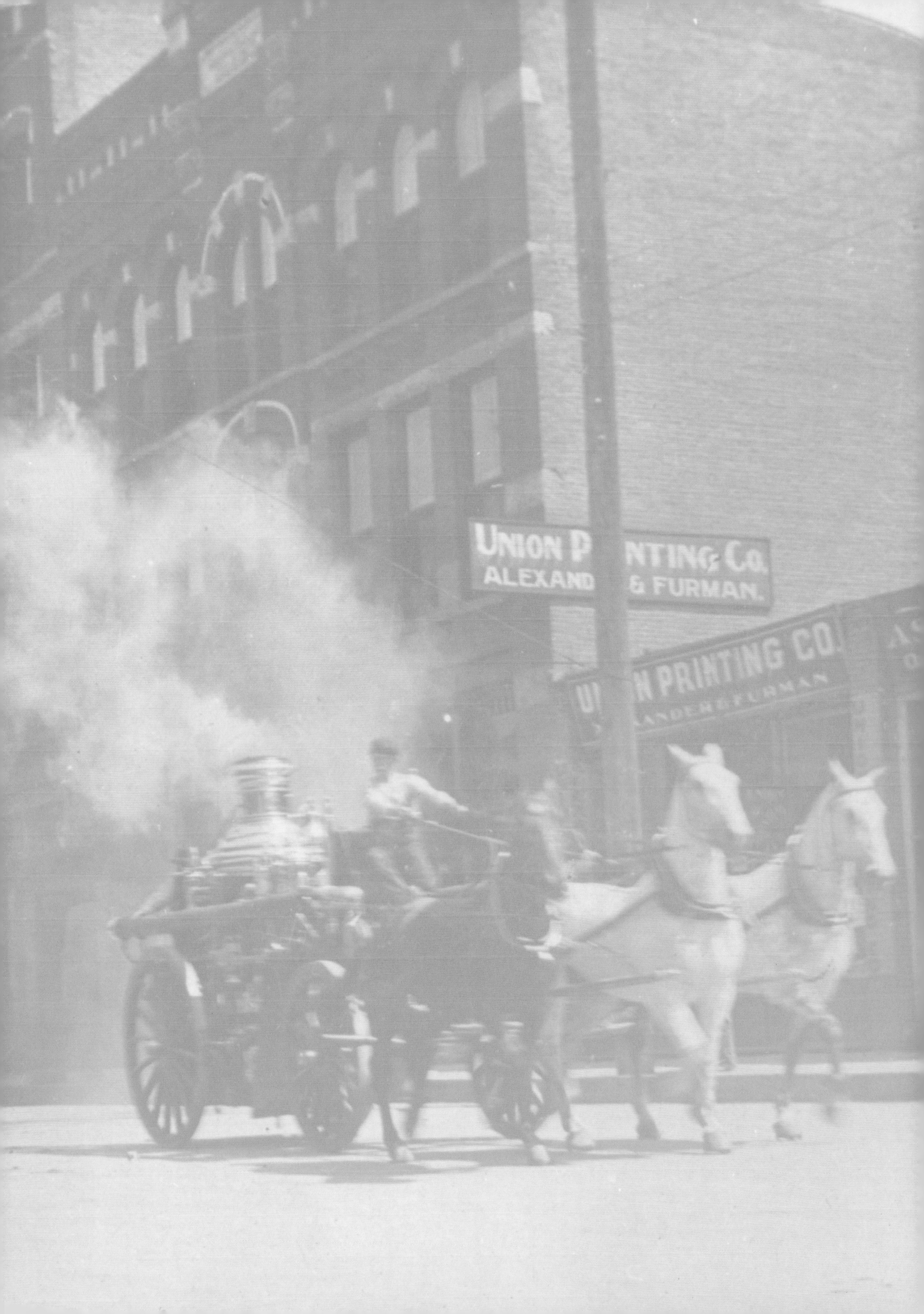
UNION PRINTING Co.
ALEXAND & FURMAN.
PRINTING CO.
FURMAN

Before the WSCFF:
Fire Fighters and the
Early Labor Movement

In 1901, the first AFL fire fighters' union in the US was organized in Washington, D.C. and called itself the "Union of Fire Fighters." At the time, the AFL allowed locals in recognized trades to affiliate directly if no international existed, and then issued the local a "Federal Labor Union" charter. "Federal" in this context referred to a local's affiliation at the national level, not to a local's federal employees. Two years later Pittsburgh organized, and is generally recognized as the first union of professional fire fighters. Its president, Frank Jones, was immediately fired but local members continued to pay his salary, and eventually won his reinstatement.

As cities across the US shifted from volunteer to professional fire departments, fire fighters were a rapidly growing group of workers, albeit at low wages with poor working conditions. As fire fighters continued to organize through World War I, they represented the heart of a turf war within the union movement. The AFL organized workers by craft, not where they worked, and sought to control a labor market by organizing all the workers within one trade. Within the AFL, its member unions, or internationals, were stretching the definitions of their trades as factories created new realms of jobs. Like factory workers, fire fighters were considered unskilled labor, although they were not much removed from the teamsters in their day-to-day use of horses, nor the telegraphers as they used early dispatch systems. In addition, many fire fighters had worked in other trades, and brought their experience as union members and their loyalties to particular unions with them.

In 1916 the AFL had seventeen fire fighter locals in the US, including Seattle City Fire Fighters Union (affiliated in 1913), and one in Canada, probably that of Vancouver, B.C. In 1917, there were sixty-six fire fighter locals directly affiliated with the AFL. Tacoma City Firemen's Union 15,601 (June 1917), Everett (February 1917), and Spokane City Firemen's Union 15,515 (April 1917) were among them.

At the November 1917 AFL Convention in Buffalo, New York, Thomas Spellacy, president of the Schenectady fire fighters' local, fought off member internationals' bids for fire fighters and proposed fire fighters be allowed to form their own locals. A motion was passed directing AFL president Samuel Gompers to form an international union within the AFL that would be granted complete jurisdiction over workers engaged in fire fighting.

Less than three months later, on February 26, 1918, under Gomper's direction, delegates from twenty-four of the AFL-affiliated fire fighter locals met at the AFL headquarters in Washington, D.C. and formed the IAFF. With a membership of 5,400,

OPPOSITE PAGE:
Steamer and horses returning from a Spokane fire.
NMAC COLLECTION, L86-70.10

The first annual convention of the IAFF, Feb. 27, 1918 in Washington, D.C.

SPOKANE #29 COLLECTION

its first constitution advised against strikes and made participation in legislative affairs a priority. When the IAFF held its first convention two days later, thirty-six delegates elected Thomas Spellacy president and adopted the constitution, formed a legislative committee and executive board, and established the newsletter, the *Fire Fighter*.

Each affiliated local was assigned a number. Pittsburgh was allowed to be IAFF #1. Seattle became #27, Spokane #29, Tacoma #31, and Everett #46. The IAFF's first convention delegates then lobbied their congressmen for a two-platoon system, something only thirty-four cities in the US had. (Seattle #27 and Tacoma #31 did, having gained the two-platoon system in 1913 and 1917, respectively.) By the end of 1918, the IAFF represented eighty-two fire fighter locals and had approximately 10,000 members out of an estimated 40,000 fire fighters in the US.

Three members of Spokane #29 who signed the original 1918 charter with the IAFF, posing with their local's charter, on Sept. 25, 1960.

L-R: *Jack Colgrove, Nels Burker, Jim Belamy (sic).*

NMAC COLLECTION, L93-25.22

The Seattle General Strike in February 1919 is an amazing indicator of the mixed feelings many in Washington State had about labor. It began in support of striking shipyard workers, then shut Seattle down for five days as 65,000-100,000 workers in a population of 300,000 walked out on (or were shut out from) their jobs. It is the only general strike in US history where local industry was paralyzed while the essentials were still distributed by strikers and strike supporters: milk for babies, emergency medical supplies for doctors, and strike kitchens which served 30,000 meals a day. "Nothing moved but the tide" is the classic description of the strike. Or, as Mayor Ole Hanson described it:

Streetcar gongs ceased their clamor; newsboys cast their unsold papers into the street; from the doors of mill and factory, store and workshop, streamed 65,000 workingmen. School children with fear in their hearts hurried homeward. The life stream of a great city stopped.

Much of the press and the public rallied behind Mayor Hanson's portrayal of the strike as an anarchist revolution in the making, while soldiers from Fort Lewis patrolled Seattle's streets. After five days the strike ended with more of a whimper than a bang. There hadn't been a specific goal when the strike had been called. Slowly groups of workers returned to their jobs until Seattle was back to work.

The IAFF held its second convention that August, in Portland, Oregon. By then it had 25,000 members, including those in newly affiliated Bellingham #106 and Yakima #217. (Yakima #217 was forced to disaffiliate, then reaffiliated as Yakima

⬅ *Yakima #217* 130

#469.) IAFF delegates rallied around resolutions calling for an eight-hour work day and universal health insurance. While the IAFF met, police in Boston went out on strike, a strike that backfired. Boston #19 fire fighters had threatened a strike the year before, and gotten their demands without having to go out on strike. When the police actually walked out the city was looted, the public was outraged, and Boston's police lost their union shortly thereafter. Boston #19 was forced to disaffiliate and did not reaffiliate until 1942, as #718.

Partially in response to this strike, Congress quickly passed a bill that prohibited Washington, D.C. fire fighters from affiliating with the IAFF. This federal action offered support to local jurisdictions as they abolished existing municipal employee locals and/or prohibited new ones. Other cities required IAFF locals to give up their charters in return for pay raises. IAFF membership dropped 5,000 in the next year and its headquarters was moved to Canada, where the labor movement was not under siege.

No fire fighter locals in the US were affiliated in the 1920s. As the pendulum swung against labor, the American plan became a slogan of anti-labor employers who decreed not belonging to a union was patriotic, and that a closed or union shop was subversive. "Company unions" were formed, where the company appointed worker representatives to negotiate working conditions, and "yellow dog contracts" came into being. Workers were required to sign yellow dog contracts at the time of employment, stating they would not join any union. From Canada, the IAFF helped its US locals lobby for civil service laws "to remove [the] fire service from politics."

By 1926, the IAFF was once again gaining membership, and for the first time professional education was included at its convention, with a presentation on dust explosion hazards. The general economy was showing signs of instability, however, with unemployment rising even as the infamous John Lewis led the United Mine Workers (UMW) in strike after strike. Black Tuesday hit the US Stock Market on October 29, 1929, ushering in the Great Depression.

The next year the IAFF formalized its position on strikes by changing its constitution from "deeming it [a strike] inadvisable" to an outright no-strike provision. Its membership continued to grow, and reached 23,000 by 1932. The Norris-La Guardia Act was passed, making it illegal for a federal court to prohibit general union activities, picketing, or actual strikes. It also removed an employer's ability to sue if an employee violated his or her yellow dog contract.

REPRESENTING THE REGION: IAFF DISTRICT 7 VICE PRESIDENTS BEFORE 1939

From the founding of the IAFF in 1918 until the WSCFF was chartered in 1939, the position of IAFF District 7 vice president was held by a member of Washington State's three biggest locals: Seattle #27, Tacoma #31, or Spokane #29. A listing of IAFF District 7 vice presidents from 1939 on is included in the Appendices, *A History of Leadership: The WSCFF Executive Board Since 1939.*

Year Elected	IAFF District 7 Vice President	IAFF Convention Location
1938	Max Maximilian (#27)	Atlanta, Georgia
1937	(no convention)	
1936	Max Maximilian (#27)	Asbury Park, New Jersey
1935	(no convention)	
1934	Max Maximilian (#27)	Cedar Point, Ohio
1933	(no convention)	
1932	E.W. Powell (#31)	San Diego, California
1931	(no convention)	
1930	E.W. Powell (#31)	Halifax, Nova Scotia
1929	(no convention)	
1928	E.W. Powell (#31)	Milwaukee, Wisconsin
1927	(no convention)	
1926	E.W. Powell (#31)	Philadelphia, Pennsylvania
1925	(no convention)	
1924	E.W. Powell (#31)	Kansas City, Missouri
1923	E.W. Powell (#31)	Montreal, Quebec
1922	J.A. Buck (#27)	Tulsa, Oklahoma
1921	J.A. Buck (#27)	Columbus, Ohio
1920	J.A. Buck (#27)	St . Louis, Missouri
1919	W.R. Brown (#29)	Portland, Oregon
1918	W.R. Brown (#29)	Washington, D.C.

On Strike 117

Throughout the Depression, fire fighters used their relationships within the community to help serve those in need. Unionized fire fighters struggled to keep their wages and working conditions, many times proposing their own scheduling, including voluntary days off, to avoid actual layoffs or reduced rates of pay.

Franklin Roosevelt became president in March 1933, when an estimated one in four American civilians was unemployed. In June of that year the National Industrial Recovery Act (NIRA) became law, establishing the National Recovery Administration (NRA). NIRA required identified industries to specify maximum hours, minimum wages, and codified privately-employed workers' right to organize; it also allowed businesses to fix prices and establish production quotas, waiving anti-trust law provisions. Once NIRA was in place John Lewis led the UMW in massive organizing campaigns, and then strikes. In 1934 there were 1,856 work stoppages in the US, the most since World War I. Organizing efforts and strikes in 1933 and 1934 gained huge advances for steel workers, garment workers, longshore workers, newspaper workers, and even movie stars.

During early 1935, the Washington State Federation of Labor (WSFL) lobbied in Olympia as it never had before. It focused on improvements to unemployment and pensions, and got much of what it wanted, including an amendment to the pension laws for fire fighters. Strikes were everywhere. Tacoma's mill workers went out in May 1935. While the National Guard walked the streets with fixed bayonets, these workers used federal mediation to gain union recognition.

That same May the Supreme Court ruled NIRA unconstitutional, on the grounds that its crop controls and price subsidies violated states' rights. In July Roosevelt signed the National Labor Relations Act (NLRA), also known as the Wagner Act. It allowed private-sector workers to select their union by majority vote, to strike, picket and boycott, created the National Labor Relations Board (NLRB), and obligated employers to bargain collectively. Fire fighters and other public employees gained nothing from the NLRA directly, but the political shift toward labor was a welcome change.

IAFF Christmas card from 1938, the year before the WSCFF was formed.

YAKIMA FIRE DEPT. COLLECTION

Seattle members of the recently formed American Newspaper Guild took on William Hearst's *Seattle Post Intelligencer*, and won representation in 1936. Later that year, John Lewis led the ten unions in the Committee for Industrial Organization (CIO) to form their own union after they were expelled from the AFL. (It changed its name to the Congress of Industrial Organizations in 1938.) The CIO was committed to both industrial unionism (organizing all the workers at a factory or workplace), and craft unions, and began by successfully taking on the auto industry.

Meanwhile, this national upheaval within labor meant the WSFL was no longer a solidified voice for Washington State labor, although its member unions grew 171% in five years (1935-1940), and some gains were made. In 1937 the Washington State legislature passed a minimum wage law for teachers and state employees, setting a national precedent. This was overshadowed by a showdown on AFL vs. CIO representation within the northwest timber industry. The timber workers, who had gone out on strike in 1935, looked to the CIO for better representation and organizing. In July 1937, the Federation of Woodworkers, led by its Pacific Northwest districts, voted to leave the AFL for the CIO, and became the International Woodworkers of America (IWA). The battle between AFL and CIO supporters continued. By 1940 physical fights broke out between Dave Beck's AFL Teamsters and IWA drivers while the NLRB tried to take a vote on representation.

It was in this atmosphere of labor upheaval that fire fighters, who were more than ready to work for better wages, benefits, and working conditions, considered a state-wide organization. Municipal funding was in a shambles, and in Washington State, this had gutted the fire fighters' pension system, established in 1909. Many of the state's IAFF locals were ready to try working together to influence legislation, and knew they needed to compare notes on their individual situations to do so. In 1939 the WSCFF was formed in hopes it could do both.

⟷ *At the End of the Day*
137

THE DAVIS FAMILY:
FOUR GENERATIONS OF FIRE FIGHTERS

Four generations of the Davis family have served on the Spokane Fire Department, with eight members of their extended family in the fire service. John Lindsey joined the Spokane Department two years after it was formed, in 1891, and retired as its chief in 1931. Two of his brothers-in-law then joined, Arthur Davis in 1907 and Russell Davis in about 1907. In 1946 Arthur Davis' son, Joseph Davis, became a Spokane fire fighter, serving until 1970. Two of Joseph Davis' sons also joined, Patrick in 1970, and Steven in 1972. Stan Stevenson, grandson of Arthur Davis, was a Seattle fire fighter from 1960 to 1990. Becky Davis, Steven Davis' daughter joined the Spokane department in 1997.

DAVIS FAMILY COLLECTION

Arthur Davis *Joseph Davis* *Steven Davis* *Becky Davis*

WSCFF President Gordon Hovik (#46) met with legislators on both sides of the aisle, including hardcore Republican Representative Jack Metcalf (seated).

AXEL DRUGGE COLLECTION

Karl Hofmann was president of the WSCFF from 1972 to 1976.

PHOTO BY JIM LEO

COMMITMENT TO LEADERSHIP: WSCFF PRESIDENTS

Information on the WSCFF's early presidents is almost non-existent. E.C. Kuehner (Chehalis-Centralia #451) was the first WSCFF president, and served from 1939 until sometime before 1946. Kuehner's dedication to his union work is still recounted. One legend tells of Kuehner hitchhiking from Centralia to Olympia to attend hearings. Another has him slipping out while on duty as a one-man crew, driving to Olympia and then back, thankful there was no fire call while he was gone.

Roy Warnock (Everett #46) was president from 1946 until 1951 or 1952. Bob Mesick (Bellingham #106) then followed, from 1951 or 1952 until 1954. Then came President Ray Greenleaf (Tacoma #31) from 1954 until 1956.

John Alexander (Renton #864) was WSCFF president from 1956 to 1961. The right-to-work movement attempted two initiatives during this time, I-198 in 1956, and I-202 in 1958. In both cases, they were defeated by coordinated efforts within Washington's labor movement. It was under Alexander that a WSCFF resolution first made it into draft legislation. The resolution would have required collective bargaining for fire fighters and police.

Gordon "Denny" Hovik (Everett #46) succeeded Alexander in 1961, and served as WSCFF president for two years. Hovik was forced to retire as president of the WSCFF in 1963, after he suffered his second heart attack while lobbying in Olympia. John W. Smith, Jr. (Tacoma #31) won that year's highly contested election, and served until 1972, when he became the organization's chief lobbyist. (Smith is profiled elsewhere in this chapter.)

In 1972, Karl Hofmann (Everett #46) became the WSCFF's president, and served four years. During the first year of his presidency, former president Smith served as the WSCFF's lobbyist, and RCW 41.56 was amended to authorize binding arbitration for all of Washington States' uniformed personnel. It was also during Hofmann's presidency that Tacoma disaffiliated from the WSCFF in 1974.

After serving as one of the WSCFF'S vice presidents for six years, Ken Groth (Yakima #469) was elected president in 1976. He served only one term but oversaw the restructuring of the WSCFF into represented districts, which laid the groundwork for the reaffiliation of Tacoma #31 (in 1976), and Seattle #27 (in 1978).

In 1977 Doug McNall (Everett #46) was elected president weeks after the infamous LEOFF 2 pension legislation passed. McNall served as the WSCFF's president for three years, until he was appointed chief of the Everett Fire Department in 1980.

Dennis "Denny" Parlari (Puyallup #726) was then elected, in 1980, after having served as WSCFF District 4 Representative for two years. Parlari, known for his well-mannered style of leadership, did not seek re-election because he had been promoted to assistant chief.

President Michael McGovern (Lakewood #1488) served from 1982 to 1996, followed by Kelly Fox (Olympia #468), from 1996 to present. Both are profiled elsewhere in this book.

Ken Groth (#469) provided critical leadership as the WSCFF Executive Board was restructured to consist of district representatives.

YAKIMA #469 COLLECTION

Collectively Bargaining 99

L-R Dennis Parlari (#726), Doug McNall (#46), and Howard Vietzke (#29), at a WSCFF convention in the late 1970s.

HOWARD VIETZKE COLLECTION

Fractious Fraternity: *Affiliation and Disaffiliation within the WSCFF*

As early as the 1919 Convention, IAFF locals debated the value of state associations. One delegate from Chicago #02, opposed to any such organizations, explained:

> Everything we have got, we have gotten by our own [the local's] efforts.... We are able to take care of our own condition, and do not have to call on anyone.

An IAFF local has always had to take separate action to affiliate with the WSCFF or any state association. For example, when the WSCFF was formed in 1939, Walla Walla #404 existed, but there is no record it took part in statewide discussions, nor is it listed as a charter affiliate. The IAFF took note of the growing numbers of affiliated state associations; from 1940 to 1950 their number grew from nineteen to thirty-three. G.J. Richardson, secretary-treasurer of the IAFF from 1920 to 1956, described the situation as of 1955 in *Symbol of Action*:

> A certain amount of friction developed between the smaller locals and the larger locals, largely on the question of the amount of per capita tax paid into the state association....In some states large locals paid on a limited number of members...

In addition, most large locals kept their own legislative representatives "to look after specific interests," as Richardson described the way large locals made sure their legislative positions were not dictated or compromised by a state association. What the larger locals traditionally valued were their connections to other AFL affiliates, and to the AFL's Central and State Labor Councils, which could be used to exert political pressure on elected officials. Many would not have affiliated with even the IAFF if they could have remained federal (at-large, direct) AFL affiliates.

Smaller locals, on the other hand, placed a high value on the collective clout of a state association, and usually did not have the resources to lobby and affect political change individually. They wanted the IAFF to require membership in state associations, which would force the large locals to pay hefty per capitas and negotiate their legislative lobbying priorities and positions. In 1945, the Texas state association, battling the Houston local, brought a resolution to the IAFF Convention that would have required the IAFF to revoke membership of a local that opposed legislation introduced and supported by its state association. The resolution did not pass, and several large locals dropped out of their respective state associations.

The WSCFF did not have locals disaffiliating at this point, but neither did it have any growth. Records from the IAFF and the WSCFF show no new fire fighter locals in the state from 1946 to 1955. In Seattle #27's January 1952 issue of the *Fire Fighter*, Walt Lambert (Spokane #29) described the benefits of WSCFF membership:

> By being affiliated with the Washington State Council of Fire Fighters, the International, and with other labor bodies, we are in fact striving for benefits and providing insurance against unfavorable actions and conditions instigated by those people who are detrimental to Labor and the working man. We must realize that selfish pro-management factions will always exist, and these groups wield a potent weapon, and take a realistic toll when the lack of union organization and affiliation is evident.... Outside of the benefits received by the large group of organized fire fighters, perhaps we have a tendency to forget the benefits and protection furnished individuals in the settlement of disputes before courts and city councils. The feelings of these fire fighters who have been defended successfully by affiliated organizations would be a true testimonial to the value of affiliation.... Only through affiliation have we been successful in passing pension laws and Civil Service legislation, electing friendly candidates, opposing integration (of fire and police services) securing skilled trade recognition, better working conditions, shorter hours, holiday pay, consideration for occupational diseases and disabilities, clothing allowance, annual vacations, etc....

By the 1955 IAFF Convention there were several resolutions requiring all locals to affiliate with their respective state or provincial association. None passed, and the entire question was referred to the IAFF Executive Committee. At each consecutive IAFF Convention, the issue was again raised by resolution, but none passed. John Richmond, secretary-treasurer of Seattle #27, made it clear that it was the IAFF, not state associations, that provided statistical information to each local. In the May 1965 issue of the *Fire Fighter* he wrote:

> All statistics which concern Fire Fighters are compiled by the International Association of Fire Fighters. With fire fighting being one of the most dangerous of occupations, all information regarding line of duty injuries such as heart disease, pulmonary disease, building collapse, explosions, burns, and suffocation, is compiled by the International and is at the disposal of all affiliated Locals.

In this same period, collective bargaining laws for public employees, and specific to fire fighters, were adopted in several states, including Washington (RCW 41.56 Public Employees' Collective Bargaining Act in 1967). This new right created a potential conflict between state associations and the IAFF, as to who would provide locals with support as they negotiated their individual contracts. IAFF District 7 Vice President Jack Waller (Spokane #29) was quick to line up IAFF resources for bargaining, and to keep the WSCFF focused on political lobbying. At the 1967 WSCFF Convention Seattle #27 Secretary-Treasurer John Richmond squared off against others in the WSCFF as its board was restructured.

When the convention was over the WSCFF had combined the secretary and treasurer positions, created seven vice presidential positions, and had eight district representatives (two from Seattle). These districts seem to have disappeared after this one convention.

The WSCFF must have been feeling the pressure of holding together its membership at the lobbying level, because at its 1968 Convention a resolution was brought to the floor by Seattle #27 and passed, barring an individual fire fighter or groups of fire fighters from introducing legislation without their local's and the WSCFF's approval. Penalties included WSCFF's automatic opposition of the legislation and expulsion of the offending member or members from their local union. Although Seattle #27 got its resolution, it still disaffiliated from the WSCFF within weeks of this convention.

Months later, when the fiftieth IAFF Convention opened in Toronto, a show-down was brewing within the IAFF over mandatory affiliation with state associations. After three rounds of voting Howie McClennan became IAFF president-elect. Almost immediately, Rochester (New York) put forth Resolution #6, requiring IAFF locals to affiliate with their state associations. Rochester knew its fiercest opponent was New York City #94. After significant and forceful discussion on the floor, the resolution passed, 454 to 411.

According to Richardson in *Symbol of Action*, New York City #94 President Maye then announced "his local would not live up to this resolution." Seattle #27's Richmond stood and announced that if New York City #94 left the IAFF, so would Seattle #27. According to Richardson "the whole afternoon was spent in parliamentary maneuvering, with no real progress being made towards any solution."

The next morning at 8 AM Maye took the floor representing New York City #94:

> On behalf of 40,000 dues paying members, we will not abide by resolution #6 under any circumstances. We are prepared to pay millions of dollars for the benefit of our membership, but will not pay one penny of state tribute.

Sixth District Vice President Gordon Anderson (Vancouver, B.C. #18) then made a motion that Resolution #6 not take effect for almost two years, until October 1, 1970. The motion was amended to include creation of a committee "to investigate the situation and bring back a resolution at next convention." The next resolution on the floor was made by Los Angeles #748, and was an attempt to change the voting structure to a "one-man, one-vote" system. Los Angeles #748 delegate Shonborn stated:

> ...the future of the International was placed in jeopardy because a minority sought to impose its will on the majority [with Resolution #6]. The minority is able to do this because of the unfair distribution of voting strength.

President-elect McClennan took the floor and asked that he be given a chance to solve the conflict during the next two years.

The convention took no further formal action on the matter, but the large locals were not willing to wait, and formed the Metro Group. Don Meyer was Seattle #27's ongoing representative and remembers the existing clique of the Chicago #02, New York City #94, the New York City officers' local, and Milwaukee locals formed the Metro group's core. Seattle #27, Washington D.C., Oklahoma City, Houston, New Orleans, and several other locals joined as well. The Metro Group met in Milwaukee shortly after the convention, agreed that the IAFF had a "responsibility" to change its constitution to the one-member one-vote system, and requested the IAFF hold a special convention on the matter. The IAFF refused. The Metro Group continued to meet around the US.

In January 1969 the IAFF executive board asked AFL President George Meany to intervene and secured a resolution from the Metro Group and a loose coalition of small locals in which they all pledged to "regard recommendations as binding upon them." According to Richardson, the Metro Group also agreed to "advise its supporters

Seattle #27, led by its S/T John Richmond, was a powerful political entity within the IAFF during the 1970s, and remained independent of the WSCFF (disaffiliated) from 1968-1978.

STANDING, L-R: *Don Meyer, Bill Gosnell, Cliff Hienselman, Roger Lovelace, Jim Hall, Frank Pelk, Dave Craig, Richard Warbrouck.* SEATED, L-R: *John Richmond, Bob Gough, Howie McClennan (IAFF president), Richard Sparks. (All members of #27 except McClennan, circa 1977).*

RICHARD WARBROUCK COLLECTION

While disaffiliated from the WSCFF, Seattle #27 purchased its first office building in the late 1970s, at 2407 1st Avenue. It used per capita assessments equivalent to WSCFF membership.

L-R: *Seattle #27's building committee: Gene Wilson, Bob Gough, Gary Medica, Bob Schuck, Bill Gosnell, Dick Warbrouck, A.E. "Bud" Leupold, John Kinsella.*

SEATTLE #27 COLLECTION

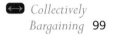 *Collectively Bargaining* **99**

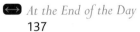 *At the End of the Day* **137**

who were withholding per-capita, all should make sure they were in good financial standing with IAFF." Meany, with the approval of the AFL executive board, appointed Communications Workers President Joseph Beire and Papermakers President Emeritus Paul Phillips to hear the dispute and offer recommendations.

These recommendations were adopted at the 1970 IAFF Convention as the first order of business, with few changes. Locals with one hundred members or less were granted one delegate, any local with more than 2,001 members received ten delegates, and those in between gained delegates incrementally. Proxy voting was introduced for the smallest locals, with no local allowed to vote proxies representing more than one hundred members. Per capita voting was allowed only when voting for officers or on roll-call votes, and required thirty percent of present and voting delegates' authorization. However, the IAFF never made local membership in the existing forty-two state associations mandatory.

Seattle #27 stayed out of the WSCFF until 1979, although in 1973 Richard Sparks made an attempt to have his local reaffiliate. In the meantime, there were plenty of fire fighters lobbying in Olympia, some on behalf of the WSCFF, and some on behalf of Seattle #27 and other individual locals. LEOFF 1 had passed in 1970, and WSCFF President John Smith led the WSCFF to win binding arbitration in 1973. By 1974 LEOFF 1 was being challenged by many as its fiscal impacts soared and anecdotes of its abuse made the rounds. At the 1974 IAFF convention, John Willis (Tacoma #31) lost to Jim Martinez (Boise #672) in an election for IAFF 7th District vice president that many felt should have been challenged. Instead, in September, Tacoma #31 disaffiliated from the WSCFF.

Dick Warbrouck, who would become Seattle #27's president in 1979, remembers his local used per capitas equivalent to what would have gone to the WSCFF to buy the local its building on 1st Avenue. Meyer (Seattle #27) remembers Seattle #27 and Tacoma #31 working together in Olympia, while John Willis (Tacoma #31) was the WSCFF's appointed lobbyist throughout the time Tacoma was disaffiliated.

Prior to the 1977 WSCFF Convention, President Ken Groth (Yakima #469), Secretary-Treasurer Howard Vietzke (Spokane #29), and Jim Hill, president of Tacoma #31, met in Tacoma and finalized negotiations on a redistricting plan. At the Walla-Walla Convention that year, WSCFF delegates adopted their plan, creating six districts, with Tacoma #31 as District 6, represented by Jim Hill, who was also elected vice president of the WSCFF.

The legislative fortunes of Washington's fire fighters were not improving, however. The 1977 legislative session passed LEOFF 2, commonly known as "Left Out" (amending RCW 41.26). Paul Harvey, who would become Seattle #27 president in 1984, remembers that LEOFF 2 made it clear to almost everyone the riff between Seattle #27 and the WSCFF had to be repaired. A period of intense negotiations to bring Seattle #27 back into the fold ensued, and a memory that many share is of

Seattle's representatives looking like the mafia as they appeared at negotiations in Bellingham, en mass, in dark suits, white shirts, and ties.

Finally, a deal emerged. Seattle #27 and Tacoma #31 would pay per capita on only their first 300 members, balancing their potential voting power, while keeping their expenses down, since they didn't require as many services as the smaller locals. In addition, Seattle #27 would hire its own lobbyist.

All of this kept Seattle in the WSCFF for about four years. At the 1982 Convention in Yakima, Seattle #27 asked for the WSCFF's dispensation on its 300 per capita. Harvey recalls "things were bad financially for Seattle, but maybe not that bad." In addition, Seattle #27 was having a hard time seeing what it was getting from the WSCFF for its per capita fees. Seattle's request was denied, it didn't pay its per capitas, although it did vote in the infamous 1982 presidential election.

⟷ *One Vote Matters* 33

Seattle #27 was out of the WSCFF by the end of the 1983 legislative session, following discordant discussions between WSCFF Secretary-Treasurer Tom Fieldstead (Yakima #469) and Seattle #27. WSCFF President McGovern (Lakewood #1488) remembers he was informed by Seattle #27's president, Conrad Clemston, that Seattle would again disaffiliate. Several members of Seattle #27 also remember that no one in the WSCFF seemed particularly interested in keeping their local in the WSCFF. In a 1983 issue of the WSCFF's *Professional Fire Fighter*, Jim Cason stated the council's per capita hike of $.51 was in part due to Seattle #27's disaffiliation.

When Paul Harvey was elected Seattle #27's president in 1984 he then attended the WSCFF's Presidents' meeting in Olympia and pledged to bring Seattle back into the WSCFF. It would take another eight years before his intention became reality.

Going into the WSCFF's 1991 Convention, Merlin Halverson (Lynnwood #1984, District 3 representative), Dan Downs (Richland #1052, District 2 representative), and Greg Bergquist (Renton #864, District 7 representative) successfully lobbied for redistricting of the WSCFF, through passage of Resolution 91-04:

> …that the WSCFF be redistricted by the executive board into ten (10) districts and be it further resolved that subsequent redistricting occur whenever any district exceeds four hundred (400) members.

This map shows WSCFF districting as of about 1977. The WSCFF created seven districts in 1976, including District 6, for Tacoma #31, which formally reaffiliated with the WSCFF in 1977. It also allowed for the creation of District 8, for Seattle #27, when it reaffiliated with the WSCFF the following year. In 1991 it sub-divided some of these original districts to create Districts 8, 9, and 10, and to once again allow for the reaffiliation of Seattle #27 in 1992.

WSCFF COLLECTION

As part of this change, WSCFF District 3 was split in two, creating the new District 10. Prior to this, District 3 had included most of Western Washington, except Seattle, which meant Halverson represented more than 1,000 individual fire fighters but had only one executive board vote. Part of this restructuring was in preparation for Seattle #27's reaffiliation in 1992.

In spring of 1992 Seattle was once again in the WSCFF, whose membership then rose to over 4,500. Harvey was still president of Seattle #27. He delivered a well-remembered speech, having to do with the tribal nature of the WSCFF, and used this analogy to make clear Seattle was ready to be an affiliated clan.

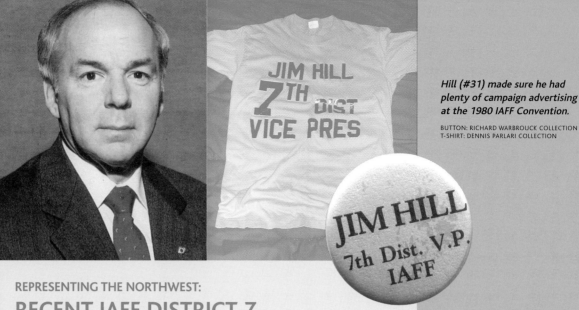

James Hill's (#31) terms as IAFF Dist. 7 vp spanned a period of huge modernization within the WSCFF. He also served as mentor to Michael McGovern (#1488), WSCFF's president from 1982-1996.

WSCFF COLLECTION

Hill (#31) made sure he had plenty of campaign advertising at the 1980 IAFF Convention.

BUTTON: RICHARD WARBROUCK COLLECTION
T-SHIRT: DENNIS PARLARI COLLECTION

REPRESENTING THE NORTHWEST:
RECENT IAFF DISTRICT 7 VICE PRESIDENTS

JAMES MARTINEZ (Boise #672) VP 1972-1980

James Martinez was elected when IAFF District 7 Vice President Walt Lambert (Spokane #29) shifted to a research position within the IAFF. Although the district covers Idaho, Alaska, Montana, and Washington, Martinez is the only non-Washingtonian to have held the position, and some say he was elected because of the in-fighting at the time between Seattle #27, Tacoma #31, and Spokane #29. While serving, he was known for his ability to work directly with smaller IAFF locals.

Martinez was challenged during every election he ran. In 1974, John Willis (Tacoma #31), longtime lobbyist for the WSCFF, ran. Two years later WSCFF Secretary-Treasurer Howard Vietzke (Spokane #29) ran. In 1978 Dick Warbrouck (Seattle #27) made an unsuccessful bid for the office. Martinez was again challenged in 1980, and lost to Jim Hill (Tacoma #31). The WSCFF awarded Martinez the IAFF's vice president emeritus in 1997 (Resolution 97-24).

JAMES HILL (Tacoma #31) VP 1980-1998

Hill contributed to the 1976 proposal to create districts within the WSCFF, which paved the way for both Tacoma #31's and Seattle #27's reaffiliations, in 1976 and 1978 respectively. Hill then became the first WSCFF District 6 representative, as well as vice president of the WSCFF. Two years later, he defeated Martinez to become IAFF District 7 vice president. While he was in this position more than seventy-five new IAFF locals organized in IAFF District 7.

PAUL HARVEY (Seattle #27) 1998-current

As president of Seattle #27 in 1992, Paul Harvey was extremely instrumental in negotiating Seattle #27's reaffiliation with the WSCFF. When Hill announced in 1997 he would retire in 1998, Paul Harvey declared his candidacy for the IAFF District 7 vice presidency, and spent the next year campaigning, as did Pat McElligott (Tacoma #31). Harvey won by a very slim margin and has held this office ever since. Harvey is renowned for his ability to address the larger issues and political import of individual, local, WSCFF, and IAFF action, and to do so with humor and thought-provoking analogy. He is the first IAFF District 7 vice president whose career within the fire service has emphasized EMS.

⬌ *One Vote Matters* 33

Paul Harvey in 1989, when he was president of Seattle #27.

SEATTLE #27 CENTENNIAL YEARBOOK 1989

Tacoma and Seattle played each other in benefit softball games, known as Fireball Classics.

L-R: *unidentified, Al Nyman (#31's president from 1989 to 1990), unidentified player, Claude Harris (Seattle chief 1985-1996), Paul Harvey.*

TACOMA #31 COLLECTION

One Vote Matters

"An election is not a footrace. There is no second place, so it doesn't matter in the end if you win by one vote or one hundred." **John W. Smith, Jr., WSCFF president, 1963-1971**

The following is a chronological list of WSCFF elections where a few votes made all the difference. A description of the political context for some of these elections is included within the first chapter of this book, "Charging the Line."

1944   IAFF DISTRICT 7 VICE PRESIDENT NOMINATION BY THE WSCFF, BROWER OVER WALLER BY ONE VOTE

Five years after the formation of the WSCFF, there were four candidates for IAFF District 7 vice president from within the WSCFF: Ed Thompson (Tacoma #31), George Renner (Seattle #27), Earl Brower (Everett #46), and Jack Waller (Spokane #29). Thompson was eliminated in the second round of voting, and Renner in the third. Brower then beat Waller by one vote. The next vote appointed Waller, who agreed to cast the WSCFF's "unanimous" vote of support for Brower. Seattle #27 concurred, but then made it clear it did not want to help pay Brower's expenses to attend the IAFF Convention. Other locals considered Seattle #27's response in poor form. In the end Brower's expenses were covered by the WSCFF.

1963   WSCFF PRESIDENT, SMITH OVER BAKER BY THREE VOTES

Smith's own local, Tacoma #31, did not back him. Neither did IAFF District 7 Vice President Waller (Spokane #29) nor Waller's protégé, Walt Lambert (Spokane #29). Smith had been a trustee, and beat Jack Baker (Bellingham #106) to replace Gordon Hovik, who'd had a heart attack while lobbying in Olympia.

1977   DISTRICT 2 REPRESENTATIVE, DOWNS OVER MORRIS BY THE FLIP OF A COIN

This was the first year there were districts within the WSCFF, so all positions were up for election. The first vote for District 2 representation was between three candidates: Dan Downs (Richland #1052), Gayland "Ollie" Morris (Pasco #1433),

WSCFF AWARDS

The WSCFF has recognized individuals who have helped in its pursuit of member education and legislative change. It did not, however, always keep records of its awards, so there is no way of knowing if Governor Wallgren was the WSCFF's only "honorary chief." (Wallgren received this after the 1947 passage of significant pension reforms.) In 1961 Leo Weisfield and John Cherberg were made honorary members of the WSCFF.

WSCFF President-Emeritus was created by resolution in 1997, and has been awarded only to Michael McGovern (#1488), in 1997. Jim Rudd (#29) and Don Spangle (#29) have received the position of distinguished service, created by resolution and awarded to Rudd in 1998. Spangle received this recognition in 1999, just a few months before his death.

Howard Vietzke (#29) was awarded the first WSCFF secretary-treasurer emeritus, in 1981. In 1989, Ron Morehouse (#106) also received this award.

Year	Walt Lambert Trade Union Leadership Award	Jack Waller Honorary Fire Fighter Award
1985		Sen. R. Ted Bottiger
1986		Sen. Larry Vognild
1987		Lt. Gov. John Cherberg
1988		Lee Stowell, admin LEOFF system
1989	Jack Gannon (IAFF pres)	Rep. Doug Sayan
1990	Ken Strong (#29, WSCFF pres)	Rep. Brian Ebersole
1991	James A. Hill (#31, IAFF District 7 vp)	Joseph Dear, director, L&I
1992		James Webster (attorney)
1993	Howard Vietzke (#29, WSCFF s/t and leg dir)	Sen. Marc Gaspard
1994	Al Brisbois	Rep. Mike Heavey
1995	Mike Watson (Wa. State L&I)	Richard A. King
1996	Alfred K. Whitehead (IAFF general pres)	Gov. Mike Lowry
1997	Jimmy Cason (#31, WSCFF S/T and lobbyist)	Rep. Steve Conway
1998	Greg Bergquist (#864, WSCFF Dist 7 rep)	Ron Sims, King County executive
1999	Merlin Halverson (#1984, WSCFF Dist 3 rep)	Sen. Patty Murray
2000	Jim Rudd (#29, leg liaison)	Co-Speaker Frank Chopp
2001	Michael McGovern (#1488, WSCFF pres)	Alex Skalbania (attorney)
2002	Vincent J. Bollon (IAFF general s/t)	Rep. Jerome Delvin
2003	Paul Harvey (IAFF 7th District vp)	Bill Hanson (executive director, WACOPS)

and Irvin Busby (Spokane Valley Fire District #876). Busby was eliminated in the first round of voting, although he had been one of the WSCFF's three vice presidents since 1972. Downs and Morris tied at the ballot box two or three more times; hence the coin toss. The WSCFF bylaws were amended by Resolution 1980-22 to incorporate coin-tossing protocol.

1982 WSCFF PRESIDENT,
MCGOVERN OVER HALVERSON BY THREE VOTES

In the first round of voting, Merlin Halverson (Lynnwood #1984) was only a few votes shy of a simple majority, fifteen votes ahead of Michael McGovern (Lakewood #1488), and twenty-seven votes ahead of Ken Strong (Spokane #29). Votes were cast again, and McGovern beat Halverson by three votes. Halverson remained on the executive board as District 3 representative until 2001.

1989 WSCFF SECRETARY-TREASURER,
CASON OVER MOREHOUSE BY TWO VOTES

Going into the 1989 Convention, most delegates knew that this was a very tight election. Jimmy Cason (Tacoma #31) was the WSCFF's vice president; Ron Morehouse (Bellingham #106) was the WSCFF's secretary-treasurer. After his victory, Cason liked to remind then-president McGovern that Cason had won by an even smaller margin than the vote that had made McGovern president.

1990 WSCFF DISTRICT 5 REPRESENTATIVE,
FOX OVER MACKEY BY ONE VOTE

Only fifteen votes total were cast in this election, those of the District 5 delegates as they chose a successor for Frank Spicklemire (Olympia #468). Kelly Fox (Olympia #468) defeated Joe Mackey (president of Vancouver #452) by one vote, and recalls delegates split pretty much according to the north-south geographic division within District 5.

1991 WSCFF SECRETARY-TREASURER,
CASON OVER CRAWFORD BY TWO VOTES

Jimmy Cason (Tacoma #31), incumbent, was challenged by Mick Crawford (Auburn #1352) and barely held on to his office.

1993 WSCFF DISTRICT 2 REPRESENTATIVE,
WALSH OVER DOWNS BY TWO VOTES

In 1993 Ricky Walsh had been president of Richland #1052 for three years when he ran for WSCFF District 2 representative. He ran against incumbent Dan Downs, also a member of Richland #1052. At the time, Downs had been District 2 representative since 1977, when the WSCFF created districts. After Walsh declared, his local voted to cast its votes for Downs, and against their own president. Downs' supporters then challenged Walsh's candidacy, asserting that his oath as a union member and officer was to support the mandates of his local.

Walsh sought clarification from IAFF District 7 Vice President Jim Hill (Tacoma #31), who consulted IAFF officials. The IAFF affirmed that any IAFF member in good standing "could dive in" and run for any position for which he or she was eligible. Walsh then defeated Downs by two votes.

1996 WSCFF VICE PRESIDENT,
WALSH OVER RAIL BY FIVE VOTES

Ricky Walsh had been appointed vice president late in 1995, after a series of changes on the WSCFF's executive board and lobbying team. He defeated Ted Rail (Spokane #29) who had been appointed District 1 representative as part of the same sweep of changes on the board. Walsh attributes his victory to a few delegates who left the convention after voting in the presidential election, and to several votes from Rail's own local, Spokane #29. Carrying one's own district has not always been critical to winning, however, as Smith's 1963 victory demonstrated.

1998 IAFF DISTRICT 7 VICE PRESIDENT,
HARVEY OVER MCELLIGOTT BY 358 VOTES

Out of 6,848 votes cast, Seattle #27's President Paul Harvey defeated Tacoma #31's President Pat McElligott by 358 votes, and people are still counting on their fingers trying to confirm which locals cast the deciding votes. Never before had the assignment of small, non-attending locals' proxy votes been so critical to an election. Boise, Idaho (#672) abstained, which removed 180 votes from the mix, and at least one local that had committed to McElligott changed its votes.

2002 WSCFF DISTRICT 11 REPRESENTATIVE,
BOSTICK OVER STEWART BY ONE VOTE

When Charles Hawkins, Jr., decided he no longer wanted to serve as both Seattle #27 president and WSCFF District 11 representative, two members of Seattle #27's executive board ran for the representative position. Cory B. Bostick had spoken to Hawkins almost a year before, expressing his interest in the position, and making it clear he did not want to run against Hawkins but did want to replace him. Kenny Stuart made a decision to run once Hawkins announced he was leaving the position. Seattle #27's executive board voted, and Bostick won the election by a vote.

Charlie Marsh represented Tacoma police officers and then police throughout the state beginning in the mid-1960s, working especially closely with Tacoma #31 and WSCFF President John Smith. During Michael McGovern's (#1488) term as WSCFF president, he and longtime WSCFF lobbyist Howard Vietzke (#29) reestablished connections with both Marsh and the larger state labor community.

WSCFF COLLECTION

Union Partners

A 1981 centennial AFL-CIO button. In reality the AFL and CIO merged in 1955. The AFL was formed in 1886, as an offshoot of the Federation of Organized Trades and Labor Unions of the United States and Canada, which was founded in 1881.

RICHARD WARBROUCK COLLECTION

Representatives of various IAFF locals and the WSCFF attended the 1977 WSLC Convention in Seattle, twenty years after the formation of the WSLC.

RICHARD WARBROUCK COLLECTION

The WSCFF has always worked with the larger labor community of Washington state, but it wasn't until the early 1960s that the WSCFF consistently did more than act as a clearinghouse and representative for the political agendas of its individual member locals. Seattle #27's December 1946 issue of the *Fire Fighter* covered the WSCFF's new membership in the Washington State Federation of Labor (WSFL, a state federation of the AFL), and mentioned the WSCFF's executive board had filled only four of the forty "entitled" or assigned positions within the 764-delegate federation, and that ninety-six WSFL delegates were women.

Jack Waller (Spokane #29) was one of the WSCFF's representatives, as was George Bundy (Seattle #27), who rallied significant WSFL support for the forty-eight-hour workweek Seattle #27 gained in 1948. Waller (Spokane #29) and Walt Lambert (Spokane #29) worked closely with the WSFL and labor's lobbying branch, the United Labor Lobby (ULL), throughout their careers in the WSCFF.

Two years after the AFL and the CIO merged, in July 1957, the Washington State Labor Council (WSLC) replaced both the WSFL and the Washington State Congress of Industrial Organizations, Washington State's CIO council. The WSLC immediately lobbied against the right-to-work initiatives of 1957 and 1958, then backed the WSCFF in its successful efforts to gain passage of the Firemen's Pension Bill of 1961 (amending RCW 41.18).

John Smith (Tacoma #31), WSCFF President from 1963 to 1972, felt his first duty was to represent fire fighters and did not consider coalition building with the larger labor movement a priority. The 1967 passage of collective bargaining for public employees (RCW 41.56) represented a huge shift in the way public employees cooperated within the labor movement. This was followed by the 1969 passage of RCW 41.26 (Law Enforcement Officers' and Fire Fighters' Retirement System/LEOFF), the 1975 creation of the Public Employment Relations Commission (PERC, RCW 41.58), and the 1981 "3-Way/No Way" rally in Olympia which helped block privatization of workers' compensation.

Mike McGovern (Lakewood #1488), the WSCFF's president from 1982 to 1996, broadened the WSCFF's connections with others in labor. During Kelly Fox's (Olympia #468) presidency, the WSCFF has continued to work closely with the WSLC and the Washington State Trial Lawyers Association. Most recently, the I-790 campaign reinforced WSCFF's partnership with the Washington Council of Police and Sheriffs (WACOPS) and the Council of Metropolitan Police and Sheriffs (COMPAS).

The WSCFF has also joined the WSLC's Labor Neighbor program, wherein union members doorbell other union members to support candidates. Perhaps most importantly, in an era of shifting support for the traditional union movement, the WSCFF has formally adopted the union education of its members as both a goal and an objective.

profile:
Jack Waller

Jack Waller is legendary within the WSCFF. He played a vital role within Spokane #29, worked to establish the WSCFF's reputation as a power to be reckoned with in Olympia, and went on to do the same for the IAFF in Washington, D.C.

Jack Waller's father died when he was nine. He wanted to go to medical school, but his stepfather, a "railroad man" according to Jack's oldest son, died while Jack was still in high school. Jack graduated as a National Merit Scholar and leader of the Rogers High School debate team, then worked on the railroad himself. After Prohibition ended in 1933, he got a job at the Bohemian Brewery, where he joined the brewers' union, then married Margaret in 1936. Two years later he followed an uncle and a brother-in-law into the Spokane Fire Department, completing his probationary period in June 1939. That September there were two major events in Waller's life: Darroll "Skip" Waller was born, and the WSCFF was chartered.

Waller made his first trip to Olympia to lobby during the 1941 legislative session. His wife Margaret told an earlier interviewer, "He went every year after that, too. As long as he was a fire fighter, he made those trips to Olympia." He and Margaret had two more children, he became secretary of Spokane #29, still working a second job at the brewery. In 1944 Waller was elected secretary of the WSCFF, a position he would hold for twelve years.

As secretary, Waller worked to make the WSCFF a part of the larger labor scene. In a letter to the Washington State Federation of Labor (WSFL) in December 1946, Waller offered the fire fighters' support in Olympia:

> In response to your letter of December 16, one of the two following men of the Washington State Council of Fire Fighters may be contacted in the event support in Olympia is desired: Earl Brower [then IAFF District 7 vice president], in care of the Fire Department, Everett, Washington. Jack Waller, in care of the Fire Department, Spokane, Washington.

Station 3, "the Threes," was his family's second home. Spokane was on the two-platoon system, twenty-four-on/twenty-four-off. Margaret Waller broke up her children's fights by saying, "I'm calling the station." If necessary, Darroll was told to "walk down to Threes to get his punishment," which most often was simply a question from his father, "Did you learn something?"

During the legislative sessions, Waller's local and the fire department offered enough backup for him to leave home at the beginning of the legislative session and be gone, even as he advanced to captain of a hook and ladder. Darroll remembers it was

Spokane Fire Chief James Blamey and Spokane #29 President E.E. Pruitt present a 12 gauge automatic shotgun to Captain Waller on February 21, 1947. Members of the department (both union and non-union) signed the accompanying certificate.

WALLER FAMILY COLLECTION

⟷ *Lobbying and Lambaste* 123

tough trying to do what he could to take care of whatever was needed around the house; at the time, his mother didn't drive.

By 1955 Jack and Margaret had two daughters (Helen and Lucy) as well as the two boys, and it took some doing to provide. Darroll was regularly sent to the Bohemian Brewery to pick up complementary flats of Squirt and beer. Harvey recalls everyone in his family wore water-damaged fluorescent socks for a long time after a warehouse fire. At some point Jack switched to union painting instead of working at the brewery, and took classes in arson investigation and labor management at Gonzaga University, as well as serving for some period as Spokane #29's president. By this time he had become friends with a man he would mentor for the rest of his life, Walt Lambert.

Lambert was secretary of Spokane #29, and began to join Waller in attending WSCFF and legislative events. The Wallers and the Lamberts attended the IAFF conferences as a foursome, which meant driving cross-country. Ruth Lambert can remember the trip to the 1956 IAFF Convention in Montreal in a 1950s blue Pontiac. "We made it to Grand Forks, that was sixteen hundred miles, pretty much non-stop." Once they got to Montreal, Waller won the election that made him IAFF District 7 Vice President. Lambert was then elected the WSCFF's Secretary.

Waller's years of activity in Olympia were paying off, as Howard Vietzke, who was a probie at Station 3, remembers. Vietzke was the assigned cook when Waller asked him if he had enough for a dinner guest. Vietzke said yes, and asked who was coming. Waller answered "the governor." "Sure" said Vietzke, and continued to cook. That evening a state-patrol escort pulled up to Station #3 and Governor Rosellini emerged to join the crew for dinner.

Family trips were planned around Waller's District 7 work with locals. Both sons can remember a summer's worth of travel in Idaho, going from local to local. In 1957 Waller was back in Olympia, working on the first arbitration bill for fire fighters and police. Waller organized the WSCFF's statewide lobbying effort, with a team that included Walt Barnes (WSCFF vice president, Tacoma #31), Earl Brower (WSCFF legislative representative, Everett #46), John Alexander (WSCFF president, Renton #864), and Felix Arena (WSCFF treasurer, Seattle #27). The bill died in the rules committee.

Darroll remembers his father had a line, and you followed it. He and his father were bird hunting near the Snake River when they saw some farmers steelhead fishing. It was before the dams had been built, but they both knew dams were coming. Darroll said he wanted to fish when he couldn't hunt anymore, and hoped the dams wouldn't ruin the fishing. His father asked him, "Which do you want— electricity and butter, or fish? You can't have them all. Dams mean jobs, and a better way of life."

Waller loved everything about fire fighting. Undated Spokane Fire Department crew with an antique steam engine.

ON APPARATUS, L-R: *C. Hobbs, L. Hallet, F. Cummins, J. Waller.*
ON GROUND, L-R: *M. Hobbs, D. Kelly, F. Hofman, M. Scotten.*

NMAC COLLECTION, L93-25.92

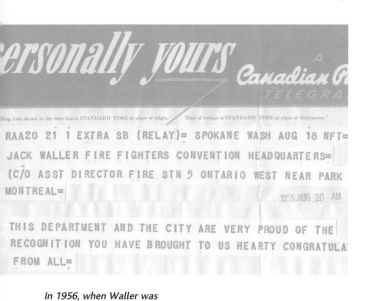

In 1956, when Waller was elected IAFF District 7 vp, Spokane Fire Chief Bill Dunham sent Waller a congratulatory telegram on behalf of the Spokane Fire Department.

SPOKANE #29 COLLECTION

Nineteen sixty-four was a turning point for Jack Waller. Jim Rudd remembers listening to his first union discussion that year, having just joined the Spokane Fire Department. Jim Bell, never known for his support of the union, was trying to get Waller out. After the union meeting many of the fire fighters went to one tavern, Rudd went to another. Another fire fighter joined Rudd and ranted about Waller. Rudd recalls, "I already knew Waller was a good guy, so I just wondered what was going on."

Sometime before the 1964 campaign season, Waller was approached by Warren Magnuson and Henry Jackson, to talk about Tom Foley, the new Democratic challenger for congress. Waller later told his sons he proceeded to make the biggest mistake of his life. He made it clear to the senators he "didn't think the kid [Foley] had it," although both Waller and Lambert worked on Foley's campaign once Foley declared.

Waller made another decision that year. He ran for IAFF secretary-treasurer, against Secretary-Treasurer Emeritus Al Albertoni, who had been in office for sixteen years. Waller had to resign as the IAFF's District 7 vice president to do so, and he encouraged Lambert to run for that position. At the 1964 San Diego IAFF Convention, Waller lost to Albertoni, the only time he lost any election and chose not to call for a recount, although his supporters wanted one. Albertoni had beaten him by three votes out of the twelve to fifteen hundred cast. Ruth Lambert recalls, "that was a very dark time for all of us," even though Lambert had won the District 7 vice presidency.

Waller came home to Spokane without any official position, but he was still a leader at the local and state level. Many municipal employees, including members of Spokane #29, were gathering signatures to change the city's charter, shifting it to a directly-elected mayor and council, with no city manager. On October 24th, 1965, the front page of the *Spokesman Review* ran a front page article naming Waller and other fire fighters and police as having "illegally" used union funds in their ballot campaign.

Those attacked filed suit for libel, and trusted Waller when he assured them they would win in the end, confident that if Jack Waller said it would work out, they could stop worrying. Waller was left to his own thoughts.

He retired in 1966, as captain, and ended his official lobbying for the WSCFF. Waller was then appointed Spokane County civil defense director. Vietzke remembers Waller pulling up to Station 3 in his civil defense car. They talked about the three or four candidates for the IAFF presidency, including Howie McClennan. Waller was so removed from the fire fighters' scene at this point that this was news to him. He suggested supporting McClennan. Interestingly, Waller once again challenged Albertoni for IAFF secretary-treasurer in 1967, losing 467-319. Harvey remembers his father working in the garden for hours during these years, taking care of his roses and producing huge crops of vegetables he then shared with the neighborhood, a trait he passed along to Darroll.

Ruth Lambert describes Waller as "having a Dutch temper," very slow to anger, fierce and hot when he did. Darroll remembers an event where his father lost his temper. At about this same time, Darroll worked painting houses under the direction of his father. One day he had fallen off a roof and was being extremely careful the next day, as he carried sheets of plywood up a ladder. His father yelled to him "just get on with it. You're not going to blow off."

"I might" said Darroll, a strapping young man in his late teens. When he came down the ladder his father told him, "Don't you ever embarrass me by going and taking the fireman's test when you act like that on a ladder." Darroll equally vehemently told him "I never will." Darroll became a union plumber, although his son, Jack Waller, is now a fire fighter (Tukwila #2088).

Margaret Waller didn't drive until after her son Darroll had his license. Darroll came home after what he remembers as an unfortunate encounter with a potato picker that "tore out all the window bars" of the new family car. His mother made him show his father. Jack Waller took note and said little. Margaret lost her temper and told her husband, "if you don't do anything when they wreck the car, then I'm going to learn to drive." And she did, although Jack Waller wouldn't teach her.

After the 1968 IAFF election of Howie McClennan at the Toronto Convention, a new position was created in the IAFF, Legislative Department Director. Jack Waller left Spokane's civil defense program in 1969 for Washington, D.C. to take on lobbying at the national level. Helen, a freshman in high school, and Lucy went back to D.C. with their parents, while Darroll and Harvey were old enough to stay behind.

Darroll asked his father about what he assumed was a bigger salary; Jack told him they were actually living on less because all the entertaining expenses of lobbying were his own. Waller stayed in Washington, D.C. until 1976, when he retired from the IAFF. One piece of federal legislation he lobbied for successfully was the Public Safety Officers Benefits Act (PL 94-430), which paid $50,000 to a fire fighter killed in the line of duty. The Lamberts joined the Wallers in the capital during the latter part of Waller's term, since Lambert was still District 7 vice president.

In 1980 Waller was appointed the Spokane manager for US census. Ruth Lambert remembers Tom Foley contacted Waller to run the program, and that "of course Walt was his assistant." When he finished this project, Waller retired. He died November 30, 1986.

The Jack Waller Honorary Fire Fighter Award was established by the WSCFF in 1985 in his honor.

On Thursday, April 24, 1969, Spokane #29 and the Spokane Fire Department sponsored a "going to Washington, D.C. party" for the Wallers.

SPOKANE #29 COLLECTION

WASHINGTON D.C.

JACK & MARGARET WALLER SEND OFF

THURSDAY   APRIL 24,   1969

SPOKANE ARMORY   8:00 - 12:00 PM

$2.00 per couple   B.Y.O.B.

profile:
Walt Lambert

Walt Lambert was the shorter, heftier member of the Waller and Lambert duo that has become legend within the WSCFF. He followed his good friend Jack Waller as fire fighter, secretary-treasurer of Spokane #29, secretary of the WSCFF, IAFF District 7 vice president, and then to Washington, D.C. to join the staff of the IAFF. Their careers and lives were so intimately entwined that Ruth Lambert recalls events in Waller's life and career as easily as those of her husband's.

Walt Lambert was the first baby born in New York City in 1920. He grew up in Brooklyn and came out west after serving in World War II in the Air Force medical corps, stationed at Fort Wright, near Spokane. Ruth Lambert remembers he applied as a fire fighter in the Spokane Department shortly after they were married:

> He wasn't tall enough to become a police officer, so he accepted a position as a fire fighter. He was just barely tall enough for that.

Lambert joined the Spokane Fire Department in 1946, starting at Station 5. His first duty was on the "meat wagon," an ambulance that was run out of the old City Hall. Lambert saw untold men "down" and eight babies born in the short time he was on this duty. Almost immediately he became friends with Spokane #29's secretary-treasurer, Jack Waller, who worked at Station 3. Within a year of being hired, Lambert passed his lieutenant's exam, and was the father of two sons. He was elected secretary-treasurer of his local when Waller gave up this position to run for secretary of the WSCFF. By 1955 Lambert was a seasoned assistant to Waller in Olympia, and helped gain passage of the Firemen's Relief and Pension Act (RCW 41.18). At the next WSCFF Convention, Lambert was elected secretary when Waller stepped down to run successfully for IAFF District 7 vice president that fall.

As WSCFF secretary, Lambert campaigned across the state, trying to get WSCFF locals to affiliate. He also lobbied hard for pension system changes, including those of 1957, which incorporated the first cost-of-living adjustments (ruled unconstitutional in 1959). That same session the WSCFF introduced its first bill on collective bargaining rights. In 1959 it took the collaborative efforts of labor to defeat a state right-to-work initiative, and Lambert again toured IAFF locals, whether they were in the WSCFF or not, to rally support.

Lambert's position within the WSCFF was restructured in 1962. Lambert became its recording secretary; Bus Cramer (Yakima #469) was elected financial

Walt Lambert poses in the office of Representative William J.C. "Bill" Day, the 3rd District Democrat. Day was also executive secretary of the Spokane Labor Council.

L-R: *Walt Lambert (#29) and Spokane's Representative Bill Day.*

RUTH LAMBERT COLLECTION

secretary; and Felix Arena (Seattle #27) remained treasurer. This may have been in response to federal passage of the Landrum-Griffin Labor-Management Reporting and Disclosure Act in 1959.

In 1963 John Smith (Tacoma #31) was elected president of the WSCFF in an extremely close election. Lambert had not supported Smith, and Smith recalls it took some time for him and Lambert to work out their differences. Perhaps it was because Lambert also had what his wife Ruth called an Irish temper. The following year, 1964, Lambert stepped down as secretary of the WSCFF. The Lamberts and the Wallers headed to the IAFF Convention in San Diego with high expectations. But Waller suffered defeat, losing his bid for IAFF secretary-treasurer to incumbent Albertoni.

Lambert was elected IAFF District 7 vice president, but his victory felt hollow in the face of Waller's defeat. When they returned home, both worked on Tom Foley's first campaign for Congress. In 1965 things got even darker for Waller when the

Spokesman Review, owned by the Cowles family, ran a front page article, falsely accusing Waller and other members of Spokane #29 of financial illegalities. Lambert was not

named but faced a different challenge. Relations between the WSCFF and Seattle #27 were contentious, and Lambert seems to have been in the thick of it. At the 1966 IAFF Convention, John Richmond (Seattle #27) challenged Lambert in his bid for re-election as IAFF District 7 vice president. It took two rounds of voting, and Lambert won by only three votes. Two years later, Spokane #29 hosted the 1968 WSCFF Convention, which included a celebration of the IAFF's fiftieth anniversary. At that fall's IAFF Convention, Howie McClennan replaced William Buck as IAFF president. Within a year McClennan created a new position, IAFF legislative department director, and hired Waller to fill it.

In 1971, Lambert retired after twenty-five years as a fire fighter, and moved to "the other Washington," to work as a researcher for the IAFF. Ruth Lambert remained in Spokane and dealt with selling their house. She recalls that during this time there was a strike at the IAFF offices, and while at least one IAFF officer crossed picket lines, Lambert did not. She also remembers Lambert hired the first African-American to work on the IAFF staff, as his secretary.

By 1980 Lambert was back in Spokane, retired from the IAFF, and assisting Waller, who had been appointed as the Spokane manager of that year's census by Congressman Foley. Lambert died in 1988. The Walt Lambert Union Leadership Award was established in 1989, in his honor.

The Lamberts and the Wallers maintained their friendship in Washington, D.C.

L-R: **Lambert (#29 and IAFF District 7 vp) , an unidentified Washington, D.C. dignatary, Ruth Lambert, Margaret Waller, and Jack Waller (#29, IAFF staffer).**

RUTH LAMBERT COLLECTION

profile: John Smith, Jr.

John W. Smith, Jr. (Tacoma #31) contributed as much to the WSCFF's legacy of political action as any other individual. Under his leadership, fire fighters in Washington State gained collective bargaining, binding arbitration, and the major pension improvements of LEOFF 1. Never bashful about his approach, Smith calls himself "a John Lewis union man," explaining he worked to represent fire fighters first, then worked within the larger union movement when it served fire fighters' interests.

Smith began in the fire service as a substitute while a student at the College of Puget Sound (now the University of Puget Sound), picking up enough shifts at one point to be the most highly paid member of the Tacoma fire department. He also sat in on labor discussions between the City of Tacoma and Tacoma #31. Tacoma #31 was one of very few IAFF locals in Washington that had a written labor agreement prior to passage of mandatory collective bargaining.

In 1952 Smith married. Nine days later he became a fulltime member of the Tacoma Department. He was elected president of Tacoma #31 within three years. He and Charlie Marsh, a representative of Tacoma police officers, negotiated identical terms for Tacoma's police and fire fighters, comparing notes after each department met with the city.

When Smith became president of Tacoma #31, he had his brother-in-law, Ernie Nelson, elected "as a committee of one" to find a union hall. Smith hated holding meetings in a fire hall "with the flag propped up in a Nesbit [soda] bottle." Smith knew the membership of the local wouldn't vote to build a union hall, so once Nelson found a building, Smith took a vote of the membership to determine how local members should be assessed to pay for it, not if they approved its purchase.

Smith was just as forceful as he increased his role representing Tacoma's fire fighters. He attended WSCFF conventions, and went to Olympia to lobby directly on behalf of Tacoma #31. He always recognized the importance of a state organization for fire fighters:

> Why did we need the WSCFF? You have to remember communication prior to Eisenhower's freeway system. Fire fighters needed a way to find out who was getting screwed the worst. And we needed a way to do something about it.

Smith was not convinced the WSCFF was doing what it could for its membership. By 1960, as one of the WSCFF's nine-member executive board, he tried to get representatives assigned to districts, and proposed a tenth be added to represent Tacoma. Discussion was vehement, with Spokane #29 and Everett #46 weighing in

Collectively Bargaining **99**

Signing the bill that would become RCW 41.18 in the Fireman's Pension Bill of 1961.

SEATED: *Governor Rosellini.*
STANDING, L-R: *Axel Drugge (#27, WSCFF trustee), Gordon Hovik (#46, WSCFF president), John Smith (#31, WSCFF trustee).*

WALLER FAMILY COLLECTION

against districting, while Seattle #27 did not oppose the proposal, which failed. Smith then ran for vice president in 1961 and lost.

Smith regrouped. When Gordon Hovik (Everett #46) was forced to step down as WSCFF president in 1963 after his second heart attack, Smith ran, although he had been told to wait his turn. Smith beat Jack Baker (Bellingham #106) by three votes, although Jack Waller (Spokane #29, IAFF District 7 vice president) and Walt Lambert (Spokane #29, WSCFF recording secretary) backed Baker. "A union is not a fraternity," Smith explains, "there's no taking turns."

Once elected, Smith moved on his ideas. He insisted upon directing the WSCFF's lobbying in Olympia, which did not sit particularly well with the Waller and Lambert team. Smith's legacy in Olympia included stringent rules for all of the WSCFF's lobbyists: they could not get drunk in public, there would be no dancing, and no lobbyist would "get a room with a woman, even if she was your wife, unless there was a child along. Just some child." He also kept track of every legislator's birthday, anniversary, and service record. The third part of Smith's strategy involved using the full membership of the WSCFF as volunteers. At the time, many locals had good volunteer systems in their own jurisdictions, but did not take part in statewide lobbying efforts.

As WSCFF president from 1963 until 1972, Smith worked both sides of the aisle, and secured strong bipartisan support for the WSCFF's legislative agenda. Smith was renowned for his take-no-prisoners approach. He required the WSCFF lobbyists to be above reproach because he used whatever information he had about legislators to convince them to support what was good for fire fighters. He told those who disagreed "a union is not a democracy, it's a dictatorship" once leadership is elected, and challenged them to run against him. No one did.

Smith stepped down as president in 1972, and then served as the WSCFF's lobbyist until 1974. It is only with time that some who worked beside Smith in the WSCFF have come to appreciate what his sometimes abrasive methods accomplished.

House Majority Leader Stewart Bledsoe banned WSCFF President John Smith (#31) from the house floor. Smith then copied Bledsoe in a letter to Ellensburg #1758, in which he told the local to continue to support their representative, Bledsoe, until Smith told them otherwise. Bledsoe immediatley responded by supporting Smith's lobbying for pension reform, and invited Smith back on the floor.

JOHN SMITH COLLECTION

profile:
Michael McGovern

Michael McGovern (Lakewood #1488) charged into adulthood, married, with a child and a mortgage within a year of graduating from high school. His first fulltime work was on Tacoma's tide flats, first in woodworking and later in heavy drilling and construction. A neighbor, Dick Herron, a Tacoma #31 fire fighter, kept pushing McGovern to consider a career change. McGovern eventually took Herron's advice and started classes at Bates in fall of 1974. He was hired by the Lakewood Fire Department on January 1, 1975.

McGovern's trademark intensity was then applied to his union involvement. He attended his first union meeting while still a probie, although at the time probies were not represented by Lakewood #1488. In less than a year he was elected its vice president. When Lakewood #1488 President Steve Marstrom stepped down in 1978, McGovern was elected to replace him.

In 1980, WSCFF District 4 Representative Dennis Parlari (Puyallup #726) stepped down to become its president, and McGovern was appointed to replace him. At the time the WSCFF lacked clear direction: Parlari was the fourth president of the WSCFF within five years, Tacoma #31 and Seattle #27 had recently reaffiliated, and district representative positions were experiencing significant turnover. That fall two IAFF elections signaled larger institutional change: John Gannon became IAFF president in a hotly contested election, and Jim Hill (Tacoma #31) defeated incumbent Jim Martinez (Boise #672) as IAFF District 7 vice president, bringing the office back to Washington State.

At the 1982 WSCFF Convention Parlari, promoted to assistant chief, stepped down as president. A three-way election ensued between McGovern, Merlin Halverson (Lynnwood #1984), and Ken Strong (Spokane #29). After two rounds of voting, McGovern emerged as president, winning by what became a mythic three vote margin. Jim Hill (Tacoma #31, IAFF District 7 vice president) made McGovern one of the IAFF's state representatives that same year.

McGovern took over the presidency under a tradition wherein the WSCFF's secretary-treasurer was the real power behind the organization, and therefore the WSCFF office moved with its secretary-treasurer. At the time, Tom Fieldstead (Yakima #469) was in his second year as secretary-treasurer. Seattle #27 proposed dispensation of its WSCFF dues, but discussions with Fieldstead were far from cordial. During the 1983 legislative session, McGovern remembers he was informed by then-president of Seattle #27, Conrad Clemston, that Seattle would again disaffiliate from the WSCFF.

From then on McGovern used his charisma and his ideas to lead the WSCFF into a new era. At the 1984 Convention the WSCFF's District 4 was split to address the exponential growth along the I-5 corridor on the Westside of the state,

Michael McGovern made lobbying in Olympia a focus of his fourteen-year presidency.

WSCFF COLLECTION

◧ *One Vote Matters* **33**

◧ *Fractious Fraternity*
27

⟷ *Giving Back to the Community* **49**

⟷ *Fractious Fraternity* **27**

creating District 7. A 1984 state supreme court case (*Bellevue Fire Fighters #1604 vs. the City of Bellevue*) reaffirmed fire fighters' rights to political action within their municipalities, and McGovern knew politics was where the WSCFF should be a player.

McGovern also worked to build a labor coalition within the state. Players included the Washington State Labor Council (WSLC), the Washington Federation of State Employees (WFSE), the Washington Educational Association (WEA), the retail clerks union, the trial lawyers, and the aerospace workers. Key legislation passed in 1985, amending LEOFF (RCW 41.26) to provide disability supplements for duty-related injuries.

In July, 1986, issues with the Northwest Burn Foundation led both McGovern and District 7 Vice President Jim Hill (Tacoma #31) to resign from its executive board. Less than a year later the WSCFF Burn Foundation was created. At about the same time the WSCFF's magazine, *Washington Professional Fire Fighter*, was restarted, at first as a semi-annual publication.

The WSCFF regrouped in the early 1990s, under McGovern. At the 1991 Convention, a resolution affirmed hiring the Joe Gehl Group to raise funds by telemarketing concerts. This would eventually generate sufficient funding to allow the purchase and renovation of the current WSCFF office building in 1995-1996, and many other modernizations within the organization. At that same convention, Resolution 91-24 expanded the executive board from seven to ten districts, paving the way for Seattle #27 to reaffiliate in 1992, as District 11.

Then came 1993, a huge year for legislative victories. Written exams for EMTs were replaced by a modular testing program (RCW 18.71.205). Collective bargaining and binding arbitration were granted to fire department dispatchers and paramedics who are employees of public hospitals (RCW 41.56.030). The third major legislative accomplishment that year was to reduce the LEOFF 2 retirement age from fifty-eight to fifty-five (RCW 41.26.430).

In 1995 McGovern worked to help achieve passage of SB 5322, (RCW 41.26.048) which established a $150,000 payment to a fire fighter's beneficiaries following death due to injuries sustained in the line of duty. This was passed months after the tragic Pang Warehouse fire in Seattle, which took the lives of four fire fighters. By 1996, there were 105 IAFF locals affiliated with the WSCFF, compared to the fifty-seven members when McGovern became president.

In 1996, Kelly Fox (Olympia #468, District 5 representative) launched his campaign for WSCFF president weeks before the convention, and won. McGovern then disengaged himself from most WSCFF duties, although he remained an IAFF state representative until 2000. He continued to serve as chief negotiator for Lakewood #1488 until his promotion to assistant chief in October 2000. Although he did not choose to stop being president of the WSCFF, he is now glad to have his life and career back, and agrees with what Howard Vietzke (Spokane #29) told him again and again, "the organization is bigger and more important than any individual."

profile:
Jimmy Cason

Chuck Jenkins (Tacoma #31) called Jimmy Wayne Cason a "fire fighter's fire fighter." More than that, Cason was a union fire fighter. He grew up in Weed, California, was all-state in football during high school, and won a scholarship to the University of Hawaii. Plans changed when Cason was drafted for the war in Vietnam. He and his high-school sweetheart, Jeanette, were married in October 1966, and ten days later Cason headed off to basic training. He completed his training at Fort Lewis, which gave him a taste for Washington State, where he and Jeanette settled when he came back from Vietnam in 1968.

Cason's first job out of the service was "busting tires" for B.F. Goodrich. Jeanette remembers he could have followed up on his scholarship offer, but "once he was out, he was ready to live, and have a family." At a barbecue, Jim Webster (Tacoma #31), a friend, mentioned his department was testing and suggested Cason take the test. Cason was hired by the Tacoma Fire Department on January 16, 1971, six months after the birth of his first child, Jeff. (Daughter Jodie was born in 1972.) Cason started as tillerman on a ladder company out of Station 1. He also became the personal driver for Tacoma Chief Lou Chambers, who had been a battalion chief with Tacoma the year Cason was born. Like most who crossed paths with Cason, Chambers became a personal friend.

Within three or four years of joining Tacoma #31, Cason was on his local's executive board. Chuck Jenkins, president of the local at the time, remembered:

> Jim was always working for us [the local].... we spent lots of time together—we ate and played, and thanks to the tight traveling budget we were on, we even slept together. And with Jim, it was all fun.

Jim Cason (#31) at a fishing derby, circa 1980.

JEANETTE CASON COLLECTION

By 1980, Cason had served as Tacoma #31's secretary-treasurer, and was its vice president when he went to the IAFF Convention in Toronto, Ontario. Jeanette remembered he accompanied Jim Hill (WSCFF District 6 representative, Tacoma #31) with a suitcase full of proxy votes and at some point, liquor bottles. Cason was there to help deliver the votes for Hill. When Hill won, Cason was appointed WSCFF District 6 representative, to replace Hill.

Once he was on the WSCFF executive board, Cason upped his political involvement both within the WSCFF and in electoral campaigns. His district report in the Spring 1981 *Washington Professional Fire Fighter* noted 335 Tacoma #31 members had volunteered in the campaigns of sixteen endorsed candidates, and contributed to fifteen victories. The following year Michael McGovern (Lakewood #1488) was elected WSCFF president. In recognition of Cason's leadership at the time, McGovern consulted with Cason before declaring for the office.

⟷ *Tacoma #31* 185

Jim Cason (#31) and pooch Smoky in 1996.

JEANETTE CASON COLLECTION

At the next WSCFF Convention in 1983, Cason was elected vice president of the WSCFF, defeating Dan Downs (District 2 representative, Richland #1052). "There was nothing subtle or delicate about Jimmy," Tacoma Mayor Brian Ebersole later eulogized. This was demonstrated at the 1986 WSCFF Convention in Spokane, when the Tacoma #31 delegation emerged from a caucus with various black eyes and bruises from a brawl that had ensued when Cason felt there had been enough talk.

Cason continued to broaden his union involvement, networking with others in the Washington State Labor Council (WSLC), the International Longshoremen's and Warehousemen's Union (ILWU), and elected representatives. The *Tacoma Morning News Tribune* named Tacoma #31 one of the ten "most influential persons or organizations in Pierce County" in 1989. That year Cason ran for secretary-treasurer of the WSCFF, challenging incumbent Ron Morehouse (Bellingham #106). In a hotly contested race, Morehouse campaigned against what he and others saw as "the Pierce County" consolidation of power within the WSCFF. Cason won, and continued to serve as WSCFF secretary-treasurer until 1995.

No one speaks of Jim Cason without remembering his legendary partying abilities. Pat McElligott (Tacoma #31) remembers that Cason "knew every place on the hill [Olympia] where you could get a drink or a cigarette." Jeanette remembers politicians like Representative Norm Dicks (6th District) coming to Cason's birthday party, and that Governor Booth Gardner was as much friend as political ally.

People gathered on most free-way overpasses as fire fight-ing rigs made their way down eerily empty pavement of I-5.

CASON'S PALLBEARERS, L (BACK TO FRONT): *Pat McElligott (#31), Jack Babbitt, Chuck Jenkins (#31).*

R (BACK TO FRONT): *unknown, Bruce Baurichter (#31), George Orr (#876).*

TACOMA #31 COLLECTION

McGovern and Cason worked closely as officers of the WSCFF. They sought out and successfully lobbied for increased fundraising through telemarketing, and both worked with Howard Vietzke (WSCFF legislative director, Spokane #29) to build the WSCFF's presence in Olympia. Cason and McGovern formally parted ways over who was to replace Vietzke when Vietzke announced his retirement in 1995, to take effect in 1996. The WSCFF executive board then appointed Cason as Vietzke's replacement, with Jim Rudd as his assistant. Cason stepped down as secretary-treasurer, and with Rudd, trained under Vietzke during the 1996 legislative session.

Days before the 1997 legislative session was to begin, Cason died of a heart attack. All who knew him were stunned. Estimates of those attending his funeral service are close to 10,000, and the names of those present read like a who's-who in the fire service, the legislature, and Tacoma politics. I-5 was closed as a convoy of fire engines carried Cason from the service in Tacoma to Shelton, where he was buried.

Tacoma Fire Department Chief Dick Moore spoke at the memorial service "Jimmy would have loved to be here, like Tom Sawyer, looking around at everybody, listening to what we are saying."

Moore went on to say "Jimmy could have done anything he wanted. But he chose to drive a fire engine." Cason also chose to work tirelessly for his union brothers and sisters in the fire service. He lobbied long and hard for safety standard revisions, including ordinances regulating sprinkler systems. More than any one contract or legislative change, Cason changed the people he worked and played with, inspiring them to work together to benefit those in the fire service. The WSCFF office building in Olympia was named the Jimmy W. Cason Building in 1997.

Giving Back to the Community

Climbing the Seattle Bank of America Tower's 788 vertical feet in 1,311 steps was the 2003 Firefighter Challenge. In its twelfth year, prizes are given for fastest finishers who race in full combat gear: boots, pants, and coats (with liners intact), helmet (no hood), gloves, and breathing apparatus, which is used for the entire race.

LEUKEMIA AND LYMPHOMA SOCIETY COLLECTION

Union fire fighters in Washington State have a tradition of volunteering which predates the formation of the WSCFF. During the Depression, many locals gathered donations of food, clothing, children's toys, and firewood, and then set up distribution systems to get these donations to those who needed them most. The WSCFF has continued the tradition, coordinating fundraising events for the Muscular Dystrophy Association (MDA), the Leukemia and Lymphoma Society, and the WSCFF Burn Foundation. In addition, member locals have continued to donate time and arrange their own fundraisers, both for organized non-profits and in support of individual members and members' families.

Service and Solidarity **61**

Members of Spokane #29 took over operation of a private gas station for two days and donated all profits to "Spokane's needy families."

SPOKANE FIRE STATION MUSEUM COLLECTION

Members of many locals, including Tacoma #31 (pictured here), have helped run Special Olympics activities.

TACOMA #31 COLLECTION

DONATIONS TO PERUVIAN VOLUNTEER FIRE FIGHTERS

A 2001 trade delegation from Washington State to South America, which included WSCFF representatives, has become an ongoing commitment to provide fire fighting equipment to the all-volunteer fire service of Peru. The WSCFF delegation returned in 2003 with donated fire service gear and a vehicle.

Tom Damborg (#1052) and Ricky Walsh (#1052, WSCFF vp) join volunteers at Station 165, in the poorest part of Lima. The six sets of turnouts donated by the WSCFF doubled the number of turnouts shared by the station's forty-four volunteers.

RICKY WALSH COLLECTION

MUSCULAR DYSTROPHY ASSOCIATION

The IAFF began its formal affiliation with the Muscular Dystrophy Association in 1953. The WSCFF membership has stepped up its participation through the Fill the Boot program, wherein those in the fire service use fire boots to collect donations. Funds are used to subsidize summer camp for children with various muscle diseases, as well as funding MDA research.

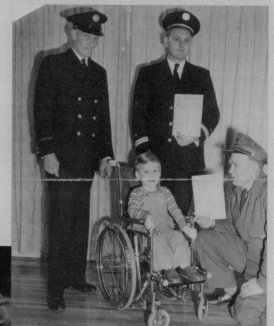

The MDA was one of the first national charitable organizations the IAFF and its member locals supported. This little boy posed with members of the Tacoma Fire Department (and a third, unidentified individual) to announce a door-to-door collection for MDA.

TACOMA #31 COLLECTION

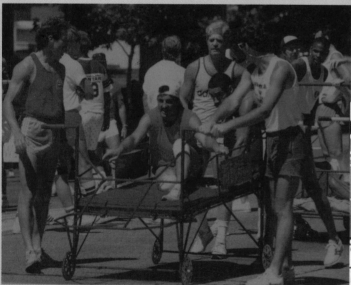

Members of Tacoma #31, including Pat McElligott (#31 president, WSCFF District 6 representative) get ready to race their bed as a fundraiser for MDA.

TACOMA #31 COLLECTION

In 2002, WSCFF members raised $373,000 in their Fill the Boot program, run in conjuction with the IAFF.

WSCFF COLLECTION

Those in the fire service have felt a special need to help fund treatment and research for burn victims. Over time the nature of their fundraising activities has changed, but not their commitment. This newspaper recycling drop box was operated by Tacoma #31 when it donated directly to medical treatment facilities.

TACOMA #31 COLLECTION

WSCFF BURN FOUNDATION

Beginning in the early 1980s, the WSCFF and member locals were active supporters of the Northwest Burn Foundation. There was a falling out in July 1986, when Kathleen Rasmussen, Director of the Northwest Burn Foundation, wrote a letter to the *Seattle Post-Intelligencer* denouncing the "Fireball Classic," a benefit softball game between Tacoma #31 and Bellevue #1604 fire fighters, scheduled for a month later, in the Tacoma Dome. There had been internal discussions on the types of fundraising activities that were appropriate, and how tickets should be marketed, but no indication such a letter would be circulated. Within weeks, Michael McGovern (WSCFF president, Lakewood #1488) and Jim Hill (IAFF District 7 vice president, Tacoma #31) resigned from the foundation's board.

The WSCFF Burn Foundation was formed in less than a year, with Rod Heivilin (Shoreline #1760) as president. One of its first fundraising events was a "Football Night," an event premiered by Tacoma #31. This became a model for similar events sponsored by numerous locals and held at Keg restaurants around the state. By 1991 differences between the WSCFF Burn Foundation and the Northwest Burn Foundation had been minimized, although they continue as separate organizations.

In 1994, the WSCFF Burn Foundation came up with an idea that has proven itself as a major source of funding: the fire fighter calendar. What started as a poster quickly became a full-size glossy edition, with judged competitions for each year's models. In 2002, the WSCFF Burn Foundation underwent a slight restructuring, replacing the office of president with executive director, a position still held by Heivilin.

L-R: *Shannon Buenting, Marina Shea, and David Cantwell model for the February 2003 page.*

WSCFF BURN FOUNDATION FIRE FIGHTERS CALENDAR COLLECTION, 2003 ©ROD HEIVILIN AND MICHAEL RIEDEL

L-R: *Kevin Miller and Charles Peiffer model for the August 2003 page.*

WSCFF BURN FOUNDATION FIRE FIGHTERS CALENDAR COLLECTION, 2003 ©ROD HEIVILIN AND MICHAEL RIEDEL

LADIES AUXILIARIES

Ladies auxiliaries were established by the IAFF on September 7, 1930, and were sponsored by the local, not the department. Little had changed in the IAFF's vision as late as January 1981, when the *International Fire Fighter* ran an article explaining the auxiliaries could:

serve important public relations and support functions, including assisting in public service programs, furthering cooperation with local charities, aiding in fund drives, helping out at social events, and providing support and assistance for local political activities under the direction of the local union.

Someone Like Me 83

The same issue of *International Fire Fighter* included coverage of court cases challenging women's participation in fire department training programs.

Sign Shops 18

The wives of union fire fighters in Washington actively contributed to the success of fire fighter legislation, improvements in working conditions and wages, and the infamous campaign signs since the first paid departments were formed, and their volunteer work has had much to do with improving fire fighters' images within their communities.

Mickey Vietzke recalls that the Ladies Auxiliary of Spokane met "for a noon luncheon. Most of us couldn't attend because we were stay-at-home Moms, working girls, or both." In response, the Fire Belles were created in 1957, taking the name of a women's bowling team made up of the wives of Spokane fire fighters. The Fire Belles donated to the Salvation Army, provided aid at all major fires, collected for Muscular Dystrophy, made Christmas baskets for the needy, created and sold cookbooks (including many fire house specialties), and had masquerade dances.

The WSCFF continued to offer separate convention programs, called "Women's Programs," or the "Women's Agenda" as late as 1985. In that year's post-convention report from Bellevue #1604, sponsored activities included a poolside fashion show and a lunch with "Kirkland's woman Mayor," childcare provided. It is unclear when the WSCFF dropped this programming at its convention, and also when locals stopped sponsoring ladies auxiliaries.

BELOW: *Members and mascot of the Yakima Fire Fighters Auxiliary.* L-R: *Jean Gefre, Shirley Beiger, Judy Thomas, Beth Dopps, Firebuff (the dog), Joyce (last name unknown), Jerri (last name unknown), Barbara (last name unknown), Judy Nugent, unidentified.*

YAKIMA #469 COLLECTION

AT LEFT: *Wives of Spokane #29 members attended the WSCFF Convention in Bellingham.* L-R: *Doris Strong, Peggy Bambino, Virginia Mills, unidentified, Mickey Vietzke, Liz Munk, Ruth Lambert. Each had sewn her own dress, and they called themselves the Lilac Ladies, after Spokane, the City of Lilacs.*

HOWARD VIETZKE COLLECTION

ABOVE: *In 1913 the families of Spokane fire fighters campaigned hard in support of a ballot measure to enact the two-platoon system. Opposed by many influential voices, including that of the* Spokesman Review, *it passed and on January 2, 1914 Captain W.W. Eichelberger left work at 6 PM saying, "Goodbye boys; I guess I'll spend the evening with the wife and kids."*

SPOKANE FIRE STATION MUSEUM COLLECTION

ABOVE: *Seattle #27 formally created its ladies auxiliary in 1967. Richard Warbrouck presides at the officers installation of the Fire Fighters Ladies Auxiliary of Seattle.* L-R: *Gerri Anderson (president), Deidre Sherman (vp), Karen VanTrojen (secy), Jo Ann Hutchison (tr), Sharon Medica, and Els-Britt Pankievich (sergeant-at-arms). This auxiliary presented programs at a residential center for those with MD, as well as sewing towels and volunteering at the center's pool.*

RICHARD WARBROUCK COLLECTION

Growing Up with the WSCFF

Families of those who have played key roles in the WSCFF have lived their lives around this organization. In decades past, the extreme work schedules of fire fighters, and residency requirements kept their families close by, and because of this, their families were a tight social group.

In addition, there have occasionally been more dramatic threats to the families of those active in the WSCFF. Harvey Waller, son of Jack Waller (Spokane #29, WSCFF lobbyist, IAFF District 7 vice president), can remember their house as the focus for anonymous phone calls and threats during one citywide initiative:

> We had rocks through the window. I can remember the phone would ring, and I'd answer it. And it would be some grown man yelling obscenities. And I was just a kid, I'd give the phone to my mother. I didn't know what they were all yelling about…. Some people said the calls came from the newspaper but no one could ever prove anything.

Since the mid-1980s, fewer family members join WSCFF members in union activities. Statistically, fire fighters have a high divorce rate. In addition, as the political power and involvement of the WSCFF has increased, the personal demands upon its

Children of Tacoma #31 members visit their fathers at the station. Prior to the two-platoon system, fire fighters were given few days off. Many children of fire fighters recall spending most of their free time at their fathers' stations. In addition, some stations were community centers, such as in Spokane where one fire station held regular Friday or Saturday night dances.

RALPH DECKER COLLECTION

leadership have also increased. Anecdotes abound documenting the non-stop engagement of WSCFF members with their work. Many WSCFF family members have pride in their partners' union work, but feel the sacrifice. Ricky Walsh's (Richland #1052, WSCFF vice president) three teenage children offered balancing perspectives. Jason Walsh is used to his father "living" on his cell phone. Jennifer thinks her father's intensity in his work is one reason she can talk to him as a teenager, while Ryan Walsh, the oldest of three Walsh offspring, thinks his own independence was fostered by traveling around the state and even the country with his father.

Dennis Lawson (#726, District 4 representative) and his family spend a little time together on the island of Maui. L-R: *Kyle, Megan, Brenda, Dennis.*

DENNIS LAWSON COLLECTION

Karl Hofmann (#46, WSCFF president) with his family. L-R: *Karleen, Kenneth, Bertine, Kristine (Hofmann).*

HOWARD VIETZKE COLLECTION

Four-year-old Dallas Shelton stood for hours with his father, Dean Shelton (WSCFF trustee, #3219) campaigning for I-790 on election day, 2002.

MARYSVILLE #3219 COLLECTION

The
Workplace

L-R: *Don Monroe and Jack Lambert, both members of Yakima #469. Moments after this picture was taken, the wall collapsed, breaking Lambert's back and permanently injuring him.*

LINE OF DUTY DEATHS

The following Washington State fire fighters died serving. One fire fighter clarified that what he does is not heroic, because it is the job of each individual in the fire service to respond to catastrophe and disaster. The risks and responsibilities of each situation are evaluated according to best available information. In serving, these individuals minimize their emotional reaction to an event, and instead systematically reduce peril and provide aid. Courage is required: the ability to face danger with self-possession, confidence, and resolution.

Name	Location	Date
Herman Larson	Seattle, Local 27	March 9,1891
W.O. Phillips	Tacoma, Local 31	April 6,1892
George T. Chapman	Spokane, Local 29	May 25, 1894
Charles E. Brabon	Seattle, Local 27	March 6, 1899
John F. Lynch	Spokane, Local 29	October 8, 1902
Herman A. Mero	Spokane, Local 29	March 6, 1905
George Hill	Tacoma, Local 31	February 24,1908
Jack Govert	Tacoma, Local 31	1908
Daniel Noonan	Tacoma, Local 31	January 30,1909
Henry J. Maynard	Spokane, Local 29	July 25, 1909
Jacob N.Longfellow	Seattle, Local 27	December 15,1910
Jesse Hill	Tacoma, Local 31	February 15,1911
Robert J. Wolff	Walla Walla, Local 404	January 27, 1912
G. F. McLure	Tacoma, Local 31	April 7, 1920
Albert Schwarzer	Tacoma, Local 31	October 6, 1912
Patrick Cooper	Seattle, Local 27	August 2, 1914
E. G. Deardorf	Spokane, Local 29	September 21, 1914
Fred G. Gilham	Seattle. Local 27	January 20, 1917
Ole G. Rust	Seattle, Local 27	July 24, 1917
Warren S. Willis	Spokane, Local 29	January 11, 1920
Charles F. Lacasse	Seattle, Local 27	April 7, 1920
Tom Cunningham	Centralia, Local 451	June 25, 1920
Horace E. Roberts	Seattle, Local 27	June 23, 1923
Dennis T. Boyle	Everett, Local 350	October 29, 1923
William A. Taro	Everett, Local 350	November 10, 1923
William A. Hutchinson	Spokane, Local 29	May 3, 1924
George Crane	Tacoma, Local 31	May 3, 1924
William E. Shuberg	Seattle, Local 27	September 22, 1924
Cecil McKenzie	Seattle, Local 27	August 7, 1925
Darwin R. Lund	Seattle, Local 27	June 30, 1927
Charles E. Wheeler	Seattle, Local 27	May 3, 1928
Charles Bunnell	Spokane, Local 29	October 6, 1930
Conrad Heymel	Tacoma, Local 31	February 9, 1934
Albert S. Wolpert	Seattle, Local 27	October 1, 1937
Ted R. Cousland	Seattle, Local 27	June 2, 1938
Thomas E. Sparrow	Spokane, Local 29	July 15, 1939
Clarence Johnson	Tacoma, Local 31	November 18, 1940
Jess L. Booher	Spokane, Local 29	February 25, 1942
Luther D. Bonner	Seattle, Local 27	February 20, 1943
Walter F. Gustafson	Spokane, Local 29	December 27, 1944
Andrew G. Beattie	Seattle, Local 27	December 11, 1945
Fred O. Larsen	Seattle, Local 27	March 22, 1947
Clyde Jenkins	Tacoma, Local 31	October 17, 1948
Jack W. McGee	Seattle, Local 27	May 7, 1949
Glen S. Murphy	Seattle, Local 27	November 11, 1949
John D. Jansen	Tacoma, Local 31	August 21, 1951
Willis A. Cunnington	Walla Walla, Local 404	June 2, 1952
Oscar F. Knierim	Tacoma, Local 31	September 12, 1953
W. Orval Childers	Walla Walla, Local 404	June 10, 1955
Leonard W. Doyle	Spokane, Local 29	June 2, 1956
James Willey	Seattle, Local 27	January 10, 1957
Raymond Strozinsky	Walla Walla, Local 404	June 7, 1961
Arthur Strong	Tacoma, Local 31	June 14, 1963
John F. Herron	Seattle, Local 27	July 23, 1964
Leroy A. Mackey	Spokane, Local 29	January 14, 1966
Harold W. Webb	Seattle, Local 27	October 14, 1966
Henry C. Gronnerud	Seattle, Local 27	November 29, 1968
Carroll G. Wagaman	Tacoma, Local 31	December 4, 1972
Woodrow W. Groom, Jr.	Walla Walla, Local 404	January 1, 1974
Gabriel Tichi	Walla Walla, Local 404	January 1, 1974
Dale F. Jones	Tacoma, Local 31	February 25, 1974
Gerald Miller	Seattle, Local 27	May 10, 1976
Robert G. Hanna	Spokane, Local 29	March 3, 1980
Paul J. Heidenreich	Spokane, Local 29	September 12, 1982
Lisa J. Long	Seattle, Local 27	July 7, 1983
Mary R. Matthews	Seattle, Local 27	January 14, 1984
Gary Parks	Everett, Local 31	February 16, 1987
Robert D. Earhart	Seattle, Local 27	July12, 1987
Irving D. Day	Tacoma, Local 31	February 1, 1988
Matthew W. Johnson	Seattle, Local 27	September 9, 1989
Donald Perry	Seattle, Local 27	June 5, 1991
Walter D. Kilgore	Seattle, Local 27	January 5, 1995
Gregory A. Shoemaker	Seattle, Local 27	January 5, 1995
Randall R. Terlicker	Seattle. Local 27	January 5, 1995
James T. Brown	Seattle, Local 27	January 5, 1995
William R. Angel	Edmonds, Local 1828	April 3, 1995
Gary V. Medica	Seattle, Local 27	December 19, 1996
Curt Rogers	Vancouver, Local 452	January 1997
Russet S. (Rusty) Hauber	Yakima, Local 469	March 15, 1997
Lawrence Eager	Renton, Local 864	June 29, 1997
Steve Haworth	Renton, Local 864	March 11, 2002
Robert Morehouse	Snohomish Co. 1, Local 1997	September 9, 2002
Richard James Tiffany	Clark County Fire District 12, Local 4229	November 17, 2003
Timothy Ross	Everett, Local 46	December 5, 2003

Platoons, Kelly Days and Transit Passes

In 1917, Tacoma #31, then AFL #15601, waged a successful campaign for a two-platoon system.

RALPH DECKER COLLECTION

The first professional fire fighters in Washington State worked continuous duty, which allowed them as much as one day in seven to be away from the station. However, most departments required notice if a fire fighter were to leave town for any reason. In 1912 the citizens of Seattle approved a two-platoon system, eighty-four-hour workweek for members of the newly formed City Fire Fighters Union. This went into effect in April 1913, making Seattle the third city in the United States to have a two-platoon system. Tacoma put the two-platoon system to a public vote in 1913, and lost.

Spokane adopted a "day-on/day-off shift plan" in February 1928, which included two eight-hour shifts of volunteer inspections and drills. Yakima #469 conducted extensive correspondence with other IAFF locals around the state, trying to coordinate wage and hour issues even before the WSCFF.

By 1939 most departments had two platoons, and fire fighters focused on reducing the number of hours in a workweek and improving their rate of pay. Kelly Days, an extra day off that rotated within shifts, came into play during this period. (It gets its name from Chicago's Mayor Kelly.) Seattle #27 rallied in 1946 and staged a massive and successful campaign to gain the forty-eight-hour workweek. During that same year Bremerton fire fighters' ballot measure passed a sixty-three and one-half-hour workweek, while failing to pass a pay raise.

Two unidentified members of Tacoma #31 play music together in a station (note classic station chair).

RALPH DECKER COLLECTION

STARTING STEAM ENGINE FIRES

According to *100 Years of Firefighting in the City of Destiny Tacoma, Washington,* fire fighters started their steam engine fires with a chemical mix. A lever on the firebox of a steam engine allowed sulphuric acid to drop into a cup containing sugar of potassium, which generated a fire hot enough to light coal around the cup on fire. A head of steam could be generated within about five minutes this way.

Tacoma's downtown stations had devices within the stations that connected to the steam engine boilers, circulating hot water into the engines' boilers.

A steam engine could hold enough coal for fifteen minutes worth of operation. If the response to the fire wasn't over within fifteen minutes, a separate cart of coal would be hauled from the nearest station.

Steamer and horses returning from a Spokane fire.

NMAC COLLECTION, L86-70.10

Local	March 1947 Monthly Wages	March 1947 Workweek (hrs.)	1952 Workweek (hrs.)
Tacoma #31	$240	62.5	56
Everett #46	$249.50	60	56
Spokane #29	$215	62.5	63
Vancouver #452	$245	60	N/A
Camas (part of Vancouver #452)	$250	40	N/A
Port Angeles #656	$245	62.5	N/A
Seattle #27	$245	48	47
Centralia #451	N/A	N/A	56
Aberdeen (then part of Aberdeen-Hoquiam #315)	$245	70	56
Yakima #469	N/A	N/A	56

It was not uncommon for those opposed to salary increases for fire fighters to run ads which listed all members of a department by name, rank, and weekly rate of pay. In this ad (circa 1930s-1940s), voters are reminded "the firemen are asking you to dig down and increase their wages to $170 when not one man in the fire department receives less than $134.50 a month." The ad then went on to threaten station closures and increased fire insurance premiums if the pay raise was passed.

TACOMA #31 COLLECTION

Statistics for 1947 were personally compiled by Felix Arena (#27, WSCFF treasurer), with salaries specific to "1st Grade Fireman," and sent, in a handwritten letter, to R.B. Poley (#469's s/t). Workweek hours for 1952 were included in Spokane #29's June 23, 1952 newsletter as part of a campaign to get a three-platoon system, with a 56-hour workweek. Spokane #29 got its 56-hour workweek in December 1957.

Even when weekly assigned hours were reduced, "call-backs" brought fire fighters back to work without pay. Jim Rudd (Spokane #29) remembers being called back so regularly that experienced fire fighters "didn't answer the phone if we saw smoke." Rudd also told the story of a Spokane #29 member, Swede Hanson, who was called back to fill sandbags during a flood. Hanson was assigned next to a man who worked for the city's water department. Rudd described:

> The water department employee was making time-and-half, which was probably all of three to four dollars an hour, but the Swede was making nothing, since it was a callback. So the Swede walked, and never came back. Ever. Seven to eight men total quit, including Hanson, Steve Foster, Mason, and Tuttle.

NO MORE HORSES: YAKIMA'S MOTORIZATION

In 1909 North Yakima put its brand new Dart fire engine on display at the 1909 Alaska-Yukon-Pacific Exposition in Seattle. Looking more like a buckboard wagon with a radiator for the driver's footrest, this engine was the first motor-driven fire apparatus west of the Mississippi. Many visitors to the exposition presumed NYFD was an abbreviation for New York Fire Department, a more logical location for such modernity. North Yakima's fire fighters were indignant and quickly sent along a plaque with the full name of their department, which was added to the display.

YAKIMA FIRE DEPARTMENT COLLECTION

↔ North Yakima Fire Department continued to motorize its equipment, through the efforts of three fire fighters (Captain Carl Brown, Gus Perkins, and Roscoe Clair) who built motorized undercarriages and then transferred onto them the bodies of the horse drawn equipment. On April 12, 1912 North Yakima became the only all-mechanized fire department west of the Mississippi, when it sold all its horses.

YAKIMA FIRE DEPARTMENT COLLECTION

HOSE CART RACES

A six-man hose cart team from Tacoma #15601, sometime between June 1917 and 1919. Fire department hose carts races were held across the Pacific Northwest, beginning in the mid-1880s and continuing until departments became fully motorized. In one twelve-man race, on July 4, 1885 in Spokane Falls, the home town Hose Company 2 won. It pulled its 1,345 pound cart six hundred feet to a hydrant, made the connection, laid 300 feet of hose, and "produced water" in 58 seconds.

RALPH DECKER COLLECTION

A 1972 transit pass for a Seattle #27 member. Free transit passes, usually while in uniform, were a part of many fire fighter contracts, beginning in the early 1900s. Some contracts still include this, although almost no one uses it. There was also a tradition in several cities that allowed fire fighters to attend movies for free.

RICHARD WARBROUCK COLLECTION

John McAuliffe (#31 trustee) shows off his recipe for asparagus. Not all stations still cook and eat together.

TACOMA #31 COLLECTION

Department by department, both the hours within a workweek and the rate of pay improved for union fire fighters. As fire fighters gained the autonomy that came from being able to have a life apart from the station, the relationship between department and fire fighter has become more typical of other professions.

Residency requirements, wherein a fire fighter had to live in the district or municipality of service, have disappeared. The longstanding tradition of cooking and eating together is no longer universal. Unwritten standards of behavior and grooming have become written policies that in theory address a more diverse workforce. The tradition of working a second job, which began when fire fighters' pay couldn't support a family, has now become, for some, the means for a parallel career.

Although fire fighters remain an incredibly tight group, far fewer families of fire fighters seem to socialize intensely with those of other fire fighters. When asked about this, Rudd (Spokane #29) remembered that when Spokane shifted to four platoons, he no longer saw everyone at his station. (With the earlier three-platoon system he knew those who worked the shift before him, and those on the shift after him.)

 *Growing Up with the WSCFF* **53**

Gary Medica (#27) models the haircut for which he was suspended. He was ordered to get a haircut on July 4, 1971. That night, at home, he trimmed his hair. A few hours later, on his next shift, he was then suspended for insubordination when he refused a battalion chief's order to have another fire fighter cut his hair while on duty. Medica was active in Seattle #27 throughout his career, which ended when he was killed in the line of duty on December 19, 1996. In August 1981 state law was modified so that "anyone who has to wear a breathing apparatus may not have facial hair" according to the explanation given the following summer by Larry Church (#2491, WSCFF District 5 representative). Mustaches of certain dimensions were eventually formally allowed.

RICHARD WARBROUCK COLLECTION

"Wildcat eating in the chairs"— these unidentified members of Bremerton #437 were challenging a rule that no eating was allowed in their loungers.

BREMERTON #437 COLLECTION

Unidentified members of Tacoma #31 pose for reasons that are now obscure. The lounge chair has become a fixture of many stations, with at least one fire fighter referring to them as "rapid-response deployers."

TACOMA #31 COLLECTION

Camaraderie remains a hallmark of the fire service, but it has become more of an option than an inescapable feature of the work.

While the scheduling and pay of fire fighters has improved, their scope of duties has broadened. Building inspection was added, in some degree, within some departments, as early as the 1890s, usually in response to catastrophic municipal fires. During and after World War II, civil defense operations were channeled, at least in part, to fire departments.

By the 1950s "fire protection" was another aspect of the fire service, which included an educational component. Perhaps the biggest professional change within the fire service has been the incorporation of EMS services, beginning in the late 1960s. As of the 1980s HAZMAT was also added. With the federal government's response to the bombing of the World Trade Towers in 2001, the fire service has been further drawn into becoming an integrated "first responder" service.

Fire inspection duties were integrated into the fire service in Washington State after the big municipal fires of the late 1880s. As fire fighters have observed how certain types of construction burn and do not burn, they have focused more attention on lobbying for specific building code provisions.

SPOKANE FIRE STATION MUSEUM COLLECTION

An unidentified member of Tacoma #31 lecturing on match safety. Beginning in the late 1940s, fire fighters started going into the schools with educational programs, as well as doing more general public education and outreach.

TACOMA #31 COLLECTION

Service and
Solidarity: *Depression-Era Tacoma*

After the stock market crashed in October of 1929, Tacoma #31 stepped in to provide an increasingly coordinated program of services, fundraisers, and legwork to other agencies as everyone tried to identify who was neediest as times got harder and harder.

In 1930 Tacoma's fire fighters played football against the police at Tacoma's Stadium Bowl, ending in a tie of 13-13. The game attracted an audience of 10,000, with the proceeds going to charity.

By 1931 the city of Tacoma's general fund was more than $425,000 in debt, with $771,827 in uncollected taxes as the ranks of unemployed kept growing. Somehow the money for ten additional fire fighters was found, which brought the department to 198. Fire fighters were assigned to different districts that included all of Tacoma. When relief agencies heard about a needy family, fire fighters would visit and then report back to the agencies. The local established two wood yards, one at Engine Company #7 in south Tacoma, and the other at Engine Company #11 (38th and McKinley Avenue). Unemployed heads of needy families applied, and were allowed to cut three racks of wood, and to take two. The third rack was delivered to widows with children by garbage-department workers, on their own time.

Fire fighters at Engine Company #6 (headquarters) also ran a program known as Grub Box. This included a food bank and prepared lunches for unemployed men who were then working tearing down a bridge at Yakima and Center street. Wood from the bridge was salvaged and taken to the wood yards for distribution as firewood. Fire fighters also set up a collection system to gather toys, repaired and repainted them, and distributed them to the children of Tacoma. This program continued at Station #5 into the early 1960s.

In 1932 things only got worse. On May 1 all City of Tacoma employees received a ten percent cut in pay. Tacoma #31 took the city to court, and made the case that their rate of pay had been determined by popular vote. When Judge Freed Renmann awarded Tacoma #31 members and police $200,000 in back pay, the city appealed to the state supreme court, which would not hear the case until 1935. Meanwhile, the city put the matter onto another ballot, asking voters to rescind the 1930 voter-approved pay raise for both police and fire fighters. The council won voter authorization six to one. Records seem to indicate a pay cut of twelve percent. Tacoma did put all its payroll on a warrant basis as of November 1, 1932.

Fire Chief Emory Whitaker and the chief of police each received fifty-dollar-a-month raises in 1933. As the city council reviewed its budget for 1934, it voted against a proposed emergency expenditure of $15,000 that would have allowed the police and fire departments to remain at then-current levels. The lack of funding forced two

During the Tacoma Hotel Fire (October 17, 1935) a member of Tacoma #31 assists a woman who has descended a bed sheet.

WASHINGTON STATE HISTORICAL SOCIETY, TACOMA TAC/FIR 38

Tacoma #31 fire fighters evacuate residents of the Tacoma Hotel during the fire of October 17, 1935.

WASHINGTON STATE HISTORICAL SOCIETY, TACOMA TAC/FIR 36

engine companies and one hose wagon out of service, and twenty-one fire fighters and twelve police were laid off.

The Tacoma Hotel, which covered a square block and had been designed by Stanford White, burned to a brick hulk on October 17, 1935. Four minutes after the first alarm, Assistant Chief Sylvester Buck struck a third alarm, skipping the second. Virtually every fire fighter, on or off-duty, fought fire that day, as well as many police. The $288,000 loss remained the largest in Tacoma until 1947.

While Tacoma fire fighters were battling this blaze, the state supreme court issued its decision, and upheld Superior Court Judge Renmann's back pay award. Tacoma #31 officials quickly formed a committee that went to every fire station and got every fire fighter to sign over his portion of the award to the union committee. Police tried to get their members to do the same but failed. Fire fighter W.P. Leo then filed a class-action suit against the City of Tacoma, Mayor George Smitely, and City Controller Thomas Swayze. On March 11, 1935, the Tacoma City Council authorized the sale of $225,000 in bonds so the city could issue the back pay, and it was paid out at the beginning of June.

Nineteen thirty-eight brought shift changes to the fire department, although it remained grossly understaffed. A twelve-day cycle was instituted, with ten-hour day and fourteen-hour night shifts. Each fire fighter worked five day shifts and five night shifts, back-to-back, then had forty-eight hours off. The WSCFF was formed in the next February, and it is easy to see why Tacoma #31 hosted the WSCFF's first official meeting on April 21, 1939.

RIGHT: *The Tacoma Hotel was the pride of the City of Tacoma in 1935. In this picture the S.S. President Jefferson is tied up in the City Waterway. Note also old Station 6 across the street to the left of the hotel.*

CLYDE TALBOT (RALPH DECKER) COLLECTION

FAR RIGHT: *What remained of the Tacoma Hotel after the October 17, 1935 fire.*

CLYDE TALBOT (RALPH DECKER) COLLECTION

Pounding the Pavement: *Seattle Gets the Forty-Eight-Hour Workweek*

According to Axel Drugge, who came on in 1942, Seattle fire fighters made some kind of an initiative attempt at a forty-eight-hour workweek in the early 1940s, and were thoroughly defeated. When Drugge was elected secretary and treasurer of Local #27 in 1945, a shorter workweek became his mandate. He talked with local members and convinced them to go for what they really wanted, a three-platoon system with a forty-eight-hour workweek, rather than putting their efforts toward a lesser set of shift improvements. The city council was less than sympathetic; some accounts indicate the council unofficially put forward a lesser offer.

Some sort of workplace improvements were overdue. Fire fighters throughout the US had compromised on pay, worked beyond contractual hours and shifts, and made do with wartime equipment shortages during World War II; veterans were returning home and needed jobs. Seattle #27's initiative proposed a solution to all but the equipment needs: dropping the two-platoon system and seventy-hour workweek would make existing fire department jobs more livable and create new jobs for the returning vets.

Members hit the streets to gather signatures on a proposal that would author-ize a forty-eight-hour workweek; no specific language on shift changes was included. John Shifman collected 25,000 signatures and wore out a pair of shoes doing so. The union joked it would buy him a new pair, but the budget was tight and it never did. Meanwhile Drugge gathered endorsements within the labor community. He brought a supporting resolution to the WSCFF's 1945 Convention in Spokane, where it passed by a single vote. Seattle #27 was used to such narrow margins of support within the WSCFF. It was by far the largest local in the WSCFF and, in Seattle's view, other locals tended to vote somewhat blindly against Seattle because of its formidable bulk. Drugge also attended the Central Labor Council's 1945 Convention and brought home its endorsement.

Seattle fire fighters campaigned during the fall of 1946. The city council coun-tered by putting its own proposal on the same ballot, one that would require putting an approved expenditure over a given amount on hold until the next budget cycle. Drugge remembers the expenditure amount as $25,000, and describes the council at the time as "cold hearted and venomous."

George Bundy, who would later become editor of the *Fire Fighter*, came on as the initiative's campaign manager in late September, and lost twenty pounds in two months, according to Drugge. Bundy lined up support from many of Seattle's bigger

◀▶ *Seattle #27* **165**

◀▶ *Platoons, Kelly Days and Transit Passes* **57**

businesses, and arranged to have major department stores display supporting photos and campaign posters. And while membership in Seattle #27 was at about fifty percent of all fire fighters, the rank and file rallied. Every fire fighter, union member or not, was assessed twenty dollars. Jim McCoy, campaign treasurer, collected the assessments and was careful to make sure the city administration never found out who gave what. Every residential block of Seattle was pamphleted three times as each fire station covered its own service area.

But member support wavered. As secretary of Seattle #27, Drugge received an unsigned letter from "the Committee to Investigate the 48-Hour Week Committee." Drugge took the envelope and letter to a good friend who taught forensics at the University of Washington. A Seattle #27 member's fingerprints were identified. This fire fighter was against the forty-eight-hour workweek because he thought a deal had been made behind the scenes, wherein Seattle #27 would also accept an eight-hour day (that is, three eight-hour shifts per day). Drugge caught wind of a petition circulated among Seattle #27 members to retract support for the proposal. Drugge immediately contacted every station-house steward with a clear message.

Drugge would file charges that signatories violated the local's bylaws. Almost immediately Drugge received a visit from a battalion chief who wanted to know "why you're threatening members with the bylaws." Drugge explained "we took an oath when we joined and the petition doesn't comply with it. Our union is voluntary, nobody was forced to join." The battalion chief stormed out, while Drugge encouraged him to stop by anytime he wanted to talk.

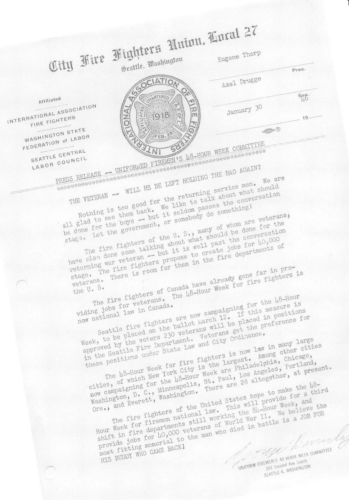

George Bundy (#27) was key to his local's campaign for the forty-eight-hour workweek. In this January 30, 1946, press release Bundy makes the campaign a matter of fairness to vets coming home from WW II and points out, " the 48-hour week for fire fighters is now national law in Canada."

AXEL DRUGGE COLLECTION

The campaign contracted for about twenty billboards. At first they had only a few words, "Support Proposition #1. Help make jobs for veterans." A third of each billboard remained blank until a few weeks before the vote. Then a color picture of a GI in battle dress, slogging down some South Pacific beach with his rifle slung over his shoulder was added, along with the campaign slogan "He did his job then, he needs a job now." It had taken Drugge's stubborn finesse to get this slogan approved. When he brought the ad copy in the billboard company wouldn't display Drugge's first attempt, "Proposition #1 will make jobs for veterans." The billboard representative said it wasn't truthful since the proposition would only provide a few jobs, not jobs for every vet. Drugge changed the wording to "help make jobs" and it was approved.

The entire campaign had a budget of $9,500, all of which went to expenses, not time. The night before the vote, Bundy and Drugge reviewed their finances and found $500 left in the kitty. Although Drugge later wished he'd given the money to Bundy in recognition of all of Bundy's volunteer work, they instead hired fifty service men from a downtown veteran's service center at ten dollars a man. Each veteran was to hand out literature at those precinct voting stations considered borderline. And so they did, in uniform, for as long as the polls were open, on a day Drugge remembers as extremely cold and wet. At least one of these pamphleteers joined the Seattle Fire Department when the initiative was finally enacted, and he became a captain.

The forty-eight-hour workweek initiative passed by a large margin. The City of Seattle then took the position that its new City Charter had precedence, and that there was no legal way to fund the change to a forty-eight-hour workweek until the following fiscal year. Chief Fitzgerald, who had never publicly opposed the workweek changes, went on record that this lack of funding combined with changes in shifts would force the closure of sixteen engine and two ladder companies.

Seattle #27 took the matter to court, which found the charter took precedence over the initiative until January 1, 1947, when funding should be made available. Ordinance #77487 established the forty-eight-hour workweek. Then another obstacle arose. The resolution did not specifically stipulate what the work schedule would be. Seattle #27 had written the resolution thinking it would have no problem negotiating scheduling with the city council later, but when the time came the council was in no mood to work with the fire fighters. A plan was then recommended by the Municipal League and adopted by the Seattle City Council: three eight-hour shifts (midnight-8 AM, 8 AM to 4 PM, and 4 PM to midnight) with each fire fighter working six days a week, and rotating between various shifts every few weeks. No fire fighter was to sleep on any of these shifts. The new schedule added 235 fire fighters, but Engine #24 and Truck #5 were shutdown, and the fireboat *Duwamish* was demoted to a backup unit that required a land-based crew from another company when put into service.

Seattle #27 had hoped for a schedule similar to Los Angeles', and continued to lobby for it in the summer of 1947: eight-hour day shifts and sixteen-hour night shifts, to fit a forty-eight-hour workweek (Los Angeles fire fighters had a forty-hour workweek). The local also cited the new city charter which granted the council authority to adjust fire fighters' work hours. Finally, the council said it would accept the recommendation of those in the fire department. Councilman Bob Harlin, a strong labor supporter, said the eight-hour day was the only acceptable possibility in the "eyes of labor." Drugge took this as warning that he would be shot down if he tried for labor backing outside of Seattle #27 and instead polled all department membership, offering three choices: the "L.A. plan," the existing eight-hour day, and a ten-hour day with fourteen-hour night shifts. Working fire fighters chose the ten-hour day shift/fourteen-hour night shift proposal.

The city council wanted to wait until after the 1948 elections to make such changes, though they said they didn't oppose them. On January 1, 1949, a ten-hour day with fourteen-hour night shifts went into effect, after another of Drugge's WSFL endorsements weighed in.

After much turmoil the city hired 235 new firemen and passed what they called a twenty-dollar-per-month raise. This was an actual raise of ten dollars per month, because it included a wartime raise of ten dollars. (Another version gives the total increase as thirty dollars, with fifteen in place as a wartime increase.) Seattle #27 knew it had gotten as much as it was going to on these issues, and wrote an open letter to Chief Fitzgerald, Mayor Devin, and the Seattle City Council thanking them for approving "the Seattle Plan" work schedule.

WW II and the Cold War

In January 1942, IAFF Secretary-Treasurer George Richardson sent a letter to all locals which outlined selective service procedures for fire fighters "since the entry of the United States into the war." The letter documented why a fire fighter should qualify for deferment, but made it clear it was up to each individual to apply, and that decisions to defer rested primarily with local draft boards.

Enough Washington State fire fighters went into the military, whether they enlisted or were drafted, to force major cities to devise special staffing procedures to replace them. At the same time there was a distinct wave of federal anti-unionism which portrayed itself in the guise of patriotism, not unlike post-September 11, 2001, federal labor policies. The National Defense Mediation Board was created in March 1941. Less than a year later, the National War Labor Board (WLB) replaced it, by executive order of President Roosevelt. The WLB's function was to resolve labor disputes so they did not affect the production and distribution of "war materials." In fact, all manners of goods and service came under its purview. Unions' abilities to strike were almost entirely curtailed, but a "maintenance of membership" clause meant working at a unionized workplace required union membership.

LAYING HOSE: YAKIMA'S INNOVATIONS

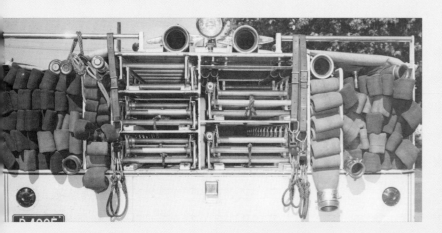

One of Yakima's trucks, set up for "Yakima hose" (four-inch diameter). Members of the Yakima Fire Department built this truck.

YAKIMA FIRE DEPARTMENT COLLECTION

When Yakima Chief W.K. "Pete" Moore was making calls to suppliers to locate more civil defense sirens in 1952, he didn't know he was on his way to a technological innovation. One supplier he called, in Colorado, was out of sirens but had some cheap four-inch hose. Moore bought it. At about the same time Yakima #469 negotiated a change from a two-platoon to a three-platoon system which reduced crew size from five to three.

Bill Kuehn, the appointed training officer at the time, was looking for greater efficiencies because of the reduced crew size but also because he was a fanatic for efficiencies. Many fire fighters in Yakima remember Kuehn spending his evenings figuring water coefficients so that the crews could spend the next day practicing hose drills which generally proved his calculations correct. It is not clear the incorporation of four-inch hose into standard fire response was Kuehn's idea, but the department adopted a new way of laying hose to a fire. This method ran four-inch hose from a hydrant to the water-pumping truck, and from the pumper truck to large master water streams, also called water monitors or stangs. This also meant the truck and all its equipment could be parked closer to the fire. At about the same time Yakima also began to use pre-connected hose on its trucks, which came to be known in some circles as the "Yakima load."

Early on, there were doubters as to the new system's efficacy. At Yakima command school, a Yakima squad, with its new equipment and technique, faced off against a Seattle squad to see who could deliver something like one thousand gallons of water to a fire. Seattle fire fighters used the more traditional method, laying two-and-one-half-inch hose from the fire to the hydrant, with the pumper truck necessarily close to the hydrant.

Yakima won hands down. By 1964 Chief Moore was touring the US explaining Yakima's techniques, what some called a forward lay, to other departments. Moore also instituted the first statewide command school to address the need he saw for some kind of standardization of training for fire service officers. This was held in Yakima from the mid-1950s until about 1985, when its location began to move around the state.

A lunchtime meeting held at Spokane's Station 15 met under a banner that tied fire prevention to citizen efforts during wartime.

Each fire department came up with its own way to deal with the shortage of qualified fire fighters during the war. A few passing references to Seattle's wartime "auxiliaries" can be found, which seem to have been some kind of crew of volunteers, who sometimes operated donated equipment. No documentation was found regarding how auxiliary members were integrated or rejected from the department when World War II ended and returning veterans wanted their fire fighter jobs back. Don W. Meyer, (Seattle #27, WSCFF secretary-treasurer 1965-1968) joined the Seattle department just before he went into the Navy. When he came back, he reapplied, re-took the written and oral exams, and his name was "reinstated on the eligibility list." He was hired the next day, on February 12, 1946, but he also had a father-in-law in the department at the time, which he considers equally important in getting his job. Other vets in Seattle had a harder time, as documented by Seattle #27's campaign slogan, rallying for a forty-eight-hour workweek: "The Veteran—Will He Be Left Holding the Bag Again?"

Tacoma took a different approach. Instead of volunteers, "duration men" were hired, who were exempt from existing hiring standards. Tacoma #31 eventually decided to allow the duration men in as members when the war ended, but no information was found regarding how local members returning from military service were dealt with.

Several departments were reshaped by World War II. Bremerton used what it called "replacement" fire fighters, as the population it served exploded from twenty-five thousand people in 1937, to eighty thousand in 1943. Most of the newcomers were shipyard workers, who lived in makeshift housing. Other cities were equally hard hit by the explosion of factories and shipyards, and fire service demands escalated with increasing populations and expanding industrial sites.

The Tri-Cities and Hanford were reconfigured, and in part created, by the sudden appearance of the Manhattan Project, which is now known as the US Department of Energy's Hanford Site. Fire fighters at Hanford were originally members of the

Pounding the Pavement 63

In 1942, the Spokane's Station 17 service area included Felts Airport.
L-R: *Brask, C. Dean, D. Zaph, three members of Spokane #29, facing the camera.*

SPOKANE FIRE STATION MUSEUM COLLECTION

Two unidentified members of Tacoma #31 stand by a rescue vehicle equipped to deal with Civil Defense emergencies (circa 1950s).

RALPH DECKER COLLECTION

Building Service Employees International Union (BSEIU), along with the janitors, since they were considered unskilled laborers. Meantime the Richland area became the largest voting precinct in the US, and fire protection was provided in a unique combination of military, federal, and municipal departments.

In addition to staffing reductions and workweek increases, those in the fire service during World War II had to deal with ancient and worn-out equipment. Most departments replaced almost nothing between 1940 and 1946. Given the Depression-era shortages that led into this period, the situation was bleak. Such equipment as was in use, also had to be modified. Tacoma painted Engine 6 black, with "all bright work dulled with black paint, eliminating reflections the enemy might see."

Wartime also added to the responsibilities and duties of the fire service. Tacoma fire department officers were required to stand "preparedness watches" during the night, and fire fighters were asked to stay within Tacoma at all times. Similar wartime practices became incorporated into fire department responsibilities, and even increased, as part of a program of Civil Defense. In many ways, the duties assigned to the fire service during World War II were a precursor to its development as first responder.

Members of the IAFF who returned from military service during WWII received this certificate. At the time, the IAFF could do little to actually improve the working conditions or wages of those who received this certificate.

BREMERTON #437 COLLECTION

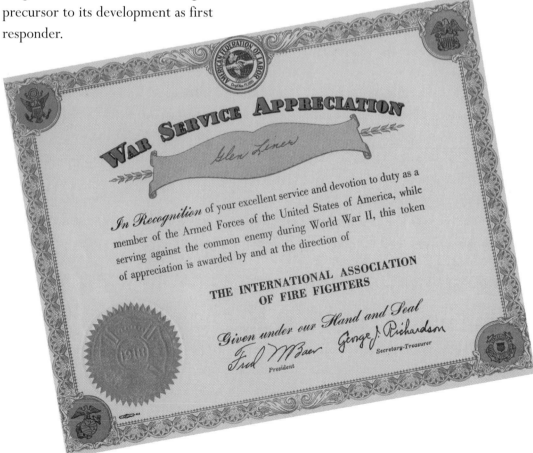

EMS:
The Fire Service Responds

An Overview

If you talk to older fire fighters about emergency medical services in decades past, you will hear about aid cars, and the nickname "meat wagon" fits services offered prior to about 1970. The precursor to fire-service based Emergency Medical Services (EMS) was an aid car, or more likely, a few fire fighters with some first aid training who stayed with a patient until an ambulance, many times run by a mortuary, arrived to transport the patient to the nearest hospital. In 1916 the Everett Fire Department had an aid squad of three fire fighters, who were certified by the Bureau of Mines for mine rescue, which meant they knew some first aid and how to use the pulmotor resuscitator and the smoke helmet. Five years later, this equipment was referred to as a "lungmotor" after the motorized bellows it operated. Pressure regulation was by touch. When members of Everett #46 revived a "stillborn" child, he was named Lungmotor in honor of their efforts, according to *The Fire Boys* (a history of the Everett Fire Department). Chester Peterson (Everett #46), a resuscitator operator, remembered response time was critical:

Spokane Fire Department Aid Car in 1949.

L-R: *Bailey Reynolds, Wes Cedars, Rudy Mead, Jim Bell, Walt Lambert, Omar Buffioux.*

SPOKANE FIRE STATION MUSEUM COLLECTION

> The sheriff picked us up, and we drove at 100 miles-per-hour to North Seattle. When we arrived I wasn't in very good shape to work on the victims. At 100 miles-per-hour the car was actually outrunning the siren, and it seemed like traffic would not move out of the way.

The Bremerton Fire Department discontinued its early ambulance service because of difficulties with vehicle maintenance and staffing. Three Bremerton businessmen created competing ambulance services; and as was the case everywhere until at least the mid-1960s, ambulance service simply meant victim transport to a hospital.

In the 1950s certain procedures were developed that changed the nature of emergency medicine. In 1956, Doctors Elan and Safar developed the technique of mouth-to-mouth resuscitation, and three years later researchers at John's Hopkins Hospital developed the first portable defibrillator and CPR. By 1964, a Dr. Banks of the American Academy of Orthopedic Surgeons started a three-day training for EMTs, although it is unclear what an EMT was in 1964.

The 1966 publication of a report by the National Academy of Sciences–National Research Council was perhaps the most pivotal event in the development of EMS. It is commonly referred to as the "White Paper," or (according to the IAFF) "Death in a Ditch." *Accidental Death and Disability—The Neglected Disease of Modern Society* detailed the inadequacies of existing treatment of medical and traumatic incidents in light of the US military's new medic regime during the Vietnam War, wherein traumatic care was administered in the field by a cadre of specially trained medical personnel, with transport to surgery a priority. This had remarkable medical results, and in comparison, domestic care was found lacking:

> Expert consultants returning from both Korea and Vietnam have publicly asserted that, if seriously wounded, their chances for survival would be better in the zone of combat than on the average city street.

Partially in response to the White Paper's analysis of existing ambulance services, the National Traffic and Motor Safety Act and the Highway Safety Act were both passed (1966), establishing national standards for ambulance design, construction, and the inspection of used emergency services vehicles.

While the White Paper analyzed all traumatic and emergency medical services, medical advances were particularly focused on cardiac issues. Dr. Frank Pantridge of the Royal Victoria Hospital in Belfast, Northern Ireland, began a pre-hospital coronary care response and transport system, also in 1966. He called it the "Flying Squad," used physician-staffed ambulances, and was able to document significant improvement in patient survivability for out-of-hospital cardiac events.

A little over a year later, in Miami, Dr. Eugene Nagel began using radios to allow hospital physicians to direct trained fire fighters in administering care.

The same Dr. Safar who helped develop mouth-to-mouth resuscitation in the 1950s started Freedom House Ambulance Service in Pittsburgh in 1967. The IAFF's *EMS Guidebook* describes his program:

> Funded by grant money, Dr. Safar took 44 unemployed 18-60 year old men and gave them 3,000 hours of advanced medical training. After completing training these men responded with physicians and assisted with on-scene medical treatment and transport.

In 1968 AT&T began to identify 9-1-1 as a universal emergency phone number. That same year, St. Vincent's Hospital of New York City established the first pre-hospital cardiac care unit (mobile coronary care unit), which was staffed by physicians and used bio-telemetry. Dr. Michael Criley used Los Angeles Fire Department fire fighters and their rigs to start a mobile life support program in 1969. Columbus, Ohio established a "Heartmobile" that was staffed with a physician and fire fighters. Dr. Nagel began the nation's first paramedic training program in Miami, for fire fighters, at the University of Miami Medical School. Called Physician Extenders, these para-professionals used a fifty-four-pound telemetry/defibrillator unit to send heart rhythms to Miami's Jackson Memorial Hospital.

Seattle's Harborview Hospital's emergency services director Dr. Michael Copass, a Vietnam vet, had been part of the initial discussions that triggered a number of these first programs. In 1968, Dr. Leonard Cobb, Chief of Cardiology at

TOP TO BOTTOM: **Dr. Michael K. Copass and Dr. Leonard A. Cobb have been the driving force behind the quality of EMS services in the Seattle area.**

HARBORVIEW HOSPITAL SEATTLE COLLECTION

Harborview Medical Center, met with Seattle Fire Chief Gordon F. Vickery to discuss using fire personnel and first-aid cars to provide "out-of-hospital" care to cardiac patients. A research project was established, funded through June 1972, by the US Department of Health, Education, and Welfare (HEW). (The IAFF cites a slightly different chronology during this period.)

Nineteen fire fighters who had worked on the Seattle department's aid cars went through 150 hours of training, and then staffed Medic One, a customized motorhome with a supervising physician onboard, that could administer Advanced Life Support (ALS). Medic One went into service on March 7, 1970. In January 1971, the physician no longer rode on Medic One, but was instead called by the on-site paramedics. That same month a fire at Seattle's Highland Park Church of the Nazarene brought home another benefit of Medic One. Fire fighter Dean McReynolds received serious burns and Medic One administered intravenous lines as it rushed him to Harborview Hospital's burn center.

EMS VEHICLES

SEATTLE:
The first "mobile hospital" was an Oldsmobile Tornado front-drive chassis with a motor home body mounted to it, and was radio-dispatched as Medic One. The first Medic One was a Winnebago affectionately known as "Mobie Pig" by the fire fighter/paramedics assigned to it.

SEATTLE FIRE DEPARTMENT MEDIC ONE COLLECTION

BREMERTON:
In 1972, Gary Larson planned, organized and placed into service our first dedicated rescue unit, a 1967 Chevrolet van converted from use as a training vehicle. This van was equipped with a color-coordinated, auxiliary roof-mounted aluminum boat. The first rescue unit was also the first to display the unique "Bremerton stripe," originally intended as flames. Frank Coppinger provided his expertise to custom paint this first rescue unit. Fire departments all across the country followed Bremerton's example and started painting stripes on their apparatus. Shaub-Ellison, a local tire store, donated wide chrome wheels for the rescue vehicle, but then Mayor Jarsted felt this appeared extravagant and made the fire fighters paint them white. L-R: Renny Mason and Gary Larson display equipment on Bremerton's first R-1 unit, known as "Doggie 1." (Circa 1976.)

BREMERTON #437 COLLECTION

TACOMA:
Nineteen fifty-three was the year Tacoma initiated Rescue Company 1, nicknamed "the Breadwagon." This unit supplied advanced first aid, and responded to eighteen aid calls in its first year. L-R: Lamar Bartell and Jack Wilbert, both part of its original crew.

RALPH DECKER COLLECTION

SPOKANE:
Spokane added a new first aid and rescue unit to its fleet on September 9, 1963. Its interior was built by the fire department shop to hold two stretchers. L-R: Lt. Clifford F. Kingsmore, Roy Strong, Chief W.A. Dunham.

SPOKANE FIRE STATION MUSEUM COLLECTION

During the 1971 legislative session RCW 18.71.200 (Emergency Medical Service Personnel—Definitions) was passed, which made Washington State one of the first to legally address where paramedics would fit in the realm of medical personnel. A second class of Harborview paramedics graduated, and by June, Aid Car #10 became a back-up medic unit, acting primarily as a first-aid car, but with the equipment and personnel to respond if Medic One was out of service.

It might seem that Seattle's medic program had proved itself, but that was not the case. Its HEW funding would run out on June 30, 1972, yet the City of Seattle refused to authorize funding to continue the program. Seattle fire fighters began a public solicitation campaign to cover expenses until the next fiscal year and raised enough money to fund the program for several years. Funding was also used to initiate the Medic II program, which trains citizens in CPR, and later that year an aid car, Aid Car #17, was upgraded to medic status, in the city's north end.

Seattle's EMS was one of the first, but many departments in Washington State were soon catching up, as the legislature passed RCW 18.71.200 (Emergency Medical Service Personnel Definitions). The television show *Emergency!* debuted in 1972, and captivated many with the concept of EMS. More than a few paramedics interviewed for this book admit that this show influenced their decision to pursue a career in EMS. Before *Emergency!*, there were only twelve paramedic staffed units in the entire US. After four years of viewing Johnny and Roy, about one-half of the nation's population was within a ten-minute response radius of a paramedic unit.

In 1973, the Washington State Department of Transportation unveiled the Star of Life to identify and symbolize the essential components of an emergency medical response system. This was part of a move toward national EMS coverage.

BREMERTON #437 COLLECTION

Nationally, 1972 heralded the Department of Transportation (DOT) and the Department of Defense's (DoD) joint development of a program using helicopters for medical evacuation. A year later Denver's St. Anthony's Hospital started the nation's first civilian aero-medical transport service. In Seattle the Medic Two program was established to provide CPR training to the general public as Harborview Medical Center began the nation's most intensive paramedic training program, which required 5,000 hours of training.

In that same year, 1973, two laws were passed that formed the backbone of the move to national EMS system coverage. Congress passed the EMS Systems Act (PL 93-154), which laid out the process and authorized funding for 300 new regional EMS systems. Once this passed, it became clear that many states lacked enabling legislation. Washington passed RCW 18.73 (Emergency Medical Care and Transportation Services) to address this, although it did not address the need for a "good Samaritan law" until two years later, when it passed RCW 4.24.300 (Persons Rendering Emergency Care or Rransportation—Immunity from Liability). This was to remove liability from non-professionals providing medical treatment such as CPR, many EMS systems' first tier of response.

Once the federal EMS Systems Act had passed, it was up to each state to decide how EMS systems should function. There was little uniformity as to which jurisdiction and/or existing service would become the EMS provider and administrator as Washington communities rushed to receive EMS services. Many private ambulance services wanted the transport aspect of EMS, but not necessarily the paramedic staffing requirements. Hospitals, doctors, and nurses had professional concerns about the new breed of medical technicians, and about pre-hospital care. In addition, an EMS system meant some entity would have authority over it, and would need to have a funding source.

Fire departments and fire fighters had mixed feelings about stepping into medical services and meeting staffing and certification

Industrial First Aid badge, circa 1960.

RICHARD WARBROUCK COLLECTION

requirements. Within a variety of EMS systems, many fire fighters were cross-trained as EMTs and paramedics and used fire department vehicles to respond to medical emergencies. The IAFF Executive Board adopted nine recommendations in January 1975. As reported in the April 1975 *International Fire Fighter*:

> The board agreed that every community is entitled to this type [of] emergency medical service [paramedic] and that it should be within the 'jurisdiction' of the fire department.... that service as medics shall not reduce the present table of representation, 'but any expansion would be in addition thereto.'
>
> Although the term 'paramedic' has been generally accepted... they [should] be identified as 'Firemedics,' as has already been done in Philadelphia.... that medic training be available to all and that it be on a voluntary basis.

Meanwhile, Seattle's Medic One program received national recognition in a 1976 profile on the television show "60 Minutes" that described Seattle as "the best place in the country to have a heart attack."

In 1977 Washington State's paramedic certification requirements were upped with passage of RCW 18.71.205 (Emergency medical service personnel—Certification). By 1981 seventy-three percent of all US fire departments provided some level of EMS service. The federal 1981 Omnibus Budget Reconciliation Act (OBRA) consolidated seven Department of Health and Human Services (DHHS) programs, including those under the EMS Act into a block grant program. This shifted responsibility for EMS programs to the states, who could decide how much of these large block grant funds should be directed to EMS.

As the mix of EMS and fire services spread through many jurisdictions, so did issues of applicable labor law. In 1985, EMS personnel who were not cross-trained as fire fighters won clarification of their overtime rights under the Fair Labor Standards Act (FLSA) with the US Supreme Court decision *Garcia v. San Antonio*. Fire fighters are partially exempt from overtime requirements, as are EMTs who are also fire fighters. This decision made it more efficient and cheaper to use cross-trained fire fighters in the growing number of EMS positions.

Collectively
Bargaining 99

An action against one of the WSCFF's executive board members helped bring issues of certification to the forefront. In 1985, District 5 Representative Larry Church (Clark County Fire District 5) was suspended, charged with having cheated on his EMS written examination because he had a copy of an earlier exam at a fire station. In reality, the state Department of Health (DoH) had been using the same EMT re-certification test materials almost since certification had been legislated, and copies circulated relatively freely, with the DoH issuing practice questions that were part of the test. Church lost his arbitration decision and eventually, his job.

Church's removal, which many felt stemmed more from his union activity than the testing issue, led the WSCFF into the issue of cities making ongoing EMT certification a condition of fire fighter employment. The WSCFF took formal action to recognize EMS was part of its future at its 1986 Convention, when it established the EMS Committee, by Resolution 86-26. Those on the committee, which included Merlin Halverson (Lynnwood #1984, longtime WSCFF District 3 representative), were directed to "identify how the state EMS hierarchy works, and who controls it, and to begin the process of working the WSCFF into a position of influence in that system." The committee noted professional fire fighters would continue to provide EMS to the public, and that EMS "enhances the professional image of fire fighters and dramatically improves public support for the fire service." It recommended locals take part in developing:

> a system of quality fire service EMTs and paramedics without the arbitrary and meaningless testing system that now exists, and to provide adequate safety procedures for EMS personnel via state standards.

At the 1987 WSCFF Convention, the EMS committee presented six resolutions which identified key legislative issues. The "number one priority" was EMT recertification, with communicable disease screening and mandatory inclusion of gloves and masks in safety gear requirements also named. Voicing the concern of many in the fire service, the committee also recommended EMT certification not be a condition of continued employment, at least until certification testing procedures were improved.

In 1988 HB 1543 was signed, creating OTEP, an alternative system of recertification for EMTs. OTEP took effect in 1990.

STANDING, L-R: *John Sinclair (#1488), Ron Morehouse (WSCFF s/t #106), Michael McGovern (WSCFF pres #1488), Jimmy Cason (WSCFF vp #31), Howard Vietzke (lobbyist #29), Rep. Maria Cantwell, Rex Lindquist (7th Dist rep #2545).*
SEATED: *Gov. Booth Gardner.*
WSCFF COLLECTION

In the 1992 legislative session, the WSCFF demonstrated its political power. State Representative George Orr (Spokane Valley Fire District 1 #876) introduced HB 1543, while Howard Vietzke (Spokane #29), WSCFF's legislative representative, led the lobbying effort. Revisions to RCW 43.70 (Department of Health Sections) and RCW 18.71 (Physicians) allowed creation of the Ongoing Training and Evaluation Program (OTEP WAC 246-976), although OTEP didn't take full effect until 1990. OTEP offers an alternative to the single practical exam that had been required for EMT recertification. EMTs could meet recertification requirements under OTEP by receiving evaluation at the time training in each skill area was completed.

Later that year, at the 1988 IAFF Convention, Al Whitehead was elected president. A few months later he attended the IAFF's EMS Convention in Miami, announced that EMS would no longer be "the bastard child" of the fire service, and that the IAFF would embrace it. At the time many fire departments were increasing their role in EMS, while others allowed private companies or what was called the third service, a publicly run EMS that was not affiliated with police or fire services, to meet their communities' needs.

Those departments that did include paramedics had new policies to address as their paramedics gained seniority. Three issues are interwoven: promotional opportunities for paramedics within the fire service, rates of pay to address the additional training and ongoing certification requirements of paramedics, and priorities of response as a cross-trained fire fighter/paramedic. Ted Rail (Spokane #29), who has been a paramedic himself since 1980, and has served on a variety of EMS-related committees, outlined typical policy choices departments have made. In establishing department practices, factors used include the cost to a department of maintaining well-trained and experienced paramedics, the tradition of the fire service as fire fighters, and the community's perception of fire and EMS when it approves funding.

One fairly common choice is to pay paramedics a differential of somewhere between ten and fifteen percent, and to assume all costs of recertification and ongoing education. In some scenarios, departments have decided paramedics cannot be part of the line of progression to officer ranks because their primary duty is to respond to medical situations, which might conflict with fire command or other fire service leadership responsibilities.

In Seattle, policy further dictates that paramedics do not actually go inside to fight fire, but respond to fires and perform duties outside a structure. In other departments, paramedics receive no differential, can test for promotion, and be promoted. Spokane and Tacoma have rules wherein they have both paramedic lieutenant and fire lieutenant positions, and an individual can test for each and become both, and be paid accordingly.

While departments were adapting to integrating EMS staffing, promotions, and the delivery of services, AIDS brought the issue of exposure to communicable diseases to the forefront for those who provided medical treatment. At the federal level, the Ryan White Law (PL 101-381) was adopted in August 1990. Implemented in 1991 by the Centers for Disease Control, it requires notification be given to emergency response personnel who have documented exposure to infectious diseases while attending, treating, assisting, or transporting a victim, and provides some funding to do so. (It was reauthorized in 1996 and 2000.)

The reality of such notification, in Washington State and elsewhere, tends to illustrate what WSCFF District 3 Representative Mike Wilson (Medic 7 #3524) calls a "schizophrenic situation. Paramedics practice advanced medicine, like doctors and nurse practitioners, but they are certified, not licensed." When the decision is made to notify health care providers who are exposed, paramedics have had to fight for the same knowledge routinely given to emergency room care providers.

Eleven years after IAFF President Whitehead spoke about recognizing EMS within the fire service, the IAFF issued a position paper in 1999, the *Emergency Medical Services—A Guide Book For Fire-Based Systems* which concludes, "Fire departments are strongly encouraged to add injury prevention activities to established fire prevention programs." What is less clear is what the role of paramedics within the IAFF will be as their numbers increase.

Bruce Nelson (#437) administers mouth-to-mouth resuscitation to a fire victim. The little girl survived.

BREMERTON #437 COLLECTION

Aid calls now represent a huge majority of calls within many fire departments. Whatever policy and practices a fire department adopts in regard to its paramedics, the traditional concept of the fire service as those who fight fire, vs. the broader and newer role of integrated fire protection, EMS, and hazardous response has not been resolved. Meanwhile, more and more urban and suburban departments are coordinating service plans, if not merging or becoming partners in regional EMS systems. The WSCFF put significant effort into creating portability of pension benefits for paramedics. During the 2003 legislative session it gained passage of HB 1202, granting transfer of PERS service credits into LEOFF when a paramedic becomes a fire department employee.

⟷ *Unknown Risks* 82

⟷ *At the End of the Day* 137

Several different locals and their EMS systems are profiled elsewhere in this article. Each has faced the issues of privatization; jurisdictional, political, and financial control of EMS; the geography and population densities of EMS service areas; and the integration of volunteers and CPR-trained civilians to maximize the level of service available. EMS delivery is a huge part of the fire service as fire departments incorporate an ever-growing range of response services.

BREMERTON:
Municipal Resistance

Personnel within the Bremerton Fire Department were the driving force to bring EMS to Bremerton, and actually faced opposition from Bremerton's administration during early attempts to expand the scope of its EMS system. The program began in 1972 when six fire fighters completed their training at Olympic College and were certified as EMTs. Dr. Yekel, a local physician, was their EMT program advisor. There was considerable initial opposition to the idea of a fire department rescue or medic unit, particularly from Mayor Jarsted. The major objection cited was the fear of placing the fire department in competition with a local ambulance company owned by Mitchie King. When Bremerton's fire fighters managed to set up the department's first mobile unit, there were further objections.

A year later, in 1973, all fire fighters not certified as EMTs or paramedics were trained in "Fire Service First Aid and Rescue." Advanced Life Support (ALS) was added in 1976, when three Bremerton fire fighters completed necessary training. Lack of support, especially inadequate funding, forced the department to borrow some equipment from a local nurse-anesthetist. The provision of remaining equipment and medications was negotiated by Ken Beach, a Seattle fire fighter/paramedic working part-time with the Bainbridge Island Fire Department. Ken's brother, Don Beach, was the Fire Chief on Bainbridge Island at the time and authorized the transfer, while Bremerton's Chief, Max Meigs, drove to Bainbridge Island on his own time to pick up what was needed. Dr. Davis, first medical program director for Kitsap County, issued four pages of standing orders to allow paramedics to initiate certain treatments and ALS became a functional part of Bremerton's EMS.

The Bremerton Fire Department added paramedic service at the same time CEN-COM, a coordinated county-wide central dispatch and communications system, began. Once CEN-COM was in place, the Bremerton Fire Department discontinued decades of call receipt and self-dispatch service from Station 1. Within a year, in 1977, Bremerton's aid calls outnumbered fire calls, 1658 to 910.

By 1980 all Bremerton fire fighters were certified to at least the EMT level. The city was still providing $25,000 to a private ambulance service, Leyde Ambulance, to respond with the fire department and to transport patients. During this year the council did approve putting the first six-year medical bond levy to the voters. The fire department backed passage of the levy once the council promised to increase staffing by six people. The levy passed, but the city later reneged on its promise. Staffing was never increased to accommodate the additional response demands. In 1981, Bremerton began to pay its paramedics overtime for all mandatory continuing education (not to exceed fifty hours per year), while aid calls increased to almost two thirds of all calls.

In 1983, paramedics finally received formal representation in staff meetings, and Larry Rankin was hired to fill the newly created medical officer position. In 1985 air transport of patients who required Seattle trauma facilities shifted from MAST (Military Assistance in Safety and Traffic) to a new helicopter service, AirLift NW, which had been started by Harborview's Dr. Copass. This ended the practice of letting Bremerton's paramedics find their own way home once they had flown to Seattle with their patients.

By 1987, chronic staffing problems dominated Bremerton's EMS service. Two long-time paramedics resigned, continuing to work as fire fighters. This left only six active paramedics to run two fulltime ALS units over three shifts. In a year aid calls tripled the number of fire calls. The following year, the City of Bremerton took control of the Rescue 1 funds from the fire department. In 1989 three contracts with fire districts outside the city were terminated. Rescue units began ALS transports to the hospital in 1992, replacing a system where a Bremerton paramedic rode onboard a private BLS unit when transport was required. In 1993 Kitsap County standardized designation of all mobile EMS units and Bremerton's Rescue Units became Medic Units. Aid calls quadrupled fire calls in 1996, twenty years after Bremerton initiated its EMS system.

THURSTON COUNTY:
Coordinated Services

Established in 1974, Thurston County's Medic One is the first public, fire-based, county-wide, tiered EMS response system in the United States. It provides emergency medical and trauma care and transport to over 210,200 residents within the county's 758 square miles. Medic One pays eighty percent of salary and benefits as well as all training and equipment costs. The fire departments, as employers, pick up the other twenty percent, train, and utilize their EMS staff as fire fighters. All jurisdictional entities are participants in the system (offering at least BLS), rather than one entity being the sole provider. The policy-making body is the Thurston County Board of County Commissioners (BoCC). Advisory to the BoCC and the Medic One office is the Thurston County EMS Council.

Part of the motivation to set up Medic One came from insufficient private ambulance services in Thurston County in 1973, with additional county laws to take effect in 1975 that required all ambulance staff to have EMT certification. Lacey's chief, Floyd Pugh, saw the writing on the wall:

Charter members of Tumwater #2409, affiliated in 1974.

L-R: *Rick Sapp (now chief), Roger Woodside, Jim Simmons, Rick Taylor, Chief E.F. "Bud" Ridgeway, Bob Sapp (currently in bargaining unit), Brice Alvord, Robert Kraemer.*

TUMWATER #2409 COLLECTION

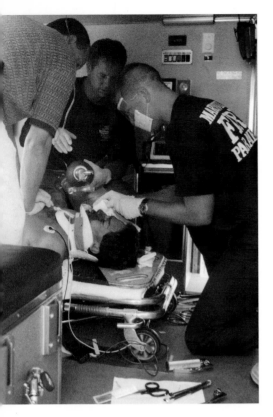

Marysville Medic One #3129 responding.

L-R: *Eric Swobody, Dean Shelton.*

DEAN SHELTON COLLECTION

It's clear neither the fire district nor the private ambulance companies can provide the kind of service we need without a direct subsidy.

Five fire departments were part of the original Medic One. Medic One began operation with funding from an annual excess levy, and a $50,000 federal grant made available when the EMS Systems Act passed in 1973.

Medic One converted to a three-level response system of Criteria Based Dispatch (CBD) on July 1, 1998. The first level of EMS care is the informed citizen, the second is Basic Life Support (BLS), and the third level is paramedic Advanced Life Support (ALS).

Today, Medic One uses seventeen fire departments/districts as providers of BLS, with personnel certified as First Responder or EMT levels. Many of these are volunteers, and all their training, certification, and supplies are paid for by Medic One. There are approximately forty-seven fire fighter-paramedics in Thurston County, who are employed by Olympia, Tumwater, Lacey Fire District 3, and Rochester Fire District 1 and integrated as county-wide providers of ALS. Their salaries are paid eighty to one hundred percent by Medic One. In about 2000, a permanent EMS levy passed, replacing decades of annual excess levies. (This type of levy was championed in the legislature by the WSCFF as a stable, long-term funding source that others, like University Place and Tacoma, have utilized as well.)

In addition to standard paramedic units, Medic One provides support at the ALS level with SPRINT 14 (Single Paramedic Rapid-Intervention Non-Transport), a single paramedic with gear in an SUV. A full medic unit must respond as well when transport is needed. SPRINT 14 is part of the West Thurston #3825 Rochester bargaining unit, and is a temporary working solution to the problem of providing rapid ALS response.

KING COUNTY PARAMEDICS #2595:
Fighting for Representation

In October 1976, almost six years after the Seattle Fire Department and Harborview Medical Center formally initiated their EMS program, the Seattle Fire Department conducted its first paramedic training for those who were not in its department. King County was interested in replicating Seattle's improving EMS system, and had formed three provider groups. Each sent employees to be trained: Shoreline Provider Group, Highline Provider Group, and Valley Provider Group. One of those who attended was Tom Gudmestad (now a medical services officer) who had been an EMT with the Burien Fire Department since 1972. He remembers that the training lasted almost a year, and that it emphasized the Seattle-Harborview way of doing things. Members of this training group were civilian employees of provider groups, and those in charge of the Seattle Fire Department's program were leery of certifying paramedics who were not already professional fire fighters.

Gudmestad's class graduated and went into service in September 1977. The Shoreline Provider Group rapidly cross-trained its paramedics and incorporated them into its fire department. Members of the Valley Provider Group shifted their day-to-day operational control and administration to Valley Hospital. The Highline Provider Group continued to use its executive board as its administrative body. This board is made up of member-entity representatives, and there were difficulties in selecting an operations administrator from any one entity who was not already a fulltime employee.

As all three provider groups began to provide ALS, adequate staffing became an issue. By the time training was complete, Highline had eight fulltime paramedics, and could therefore staff around the clock. Valley had only six, which meant it required extensive overtime shifts to provide uninterrupted coverage (three of its candidates did not complete the training). In addition, there was no mutual aid agreement, further stretching the service either provider group could provide. Gudmestad cited another demand on service. Adjacent areas, including a large portion of southern King County, had no ALS. This meant Highline calls included meeting aid cars that had driven a patient to the edge of Highline's service area.

Paramedics for these provider groups also knew they were paid significantly less than those working for the Seattle and Bellevue fire departments, since they received only a fifty-dollar raise from their training pay (of one thousand dollars per month) when they went to work. As they tried to address these staffing and pay issues, they realized they had no representation. Those in the Highline group invited those in the Valley group to talk about going union. Gudmestad, an IAFF member on "withdrawn" status from the King County Fire District 2 Department (Burien), argued long and hard that IAFF affiliation was the way to go. Others, who had worked for Shepard

MERSON RESUSCITATORS
o protect YOU and safeguard your COMMUNITY

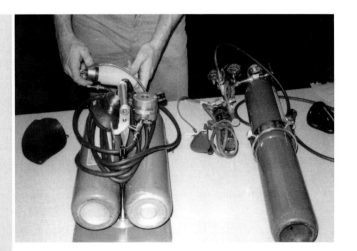

The 1953 IAFF Convention brochure featured this ad for a state-of-the-art resuscitator.

IAFF COLLECTION

A "demand" or "E&J" resuscitator and oxygen tank, used by the Camas Fire Department.

DON FULTHORP / CAMAS #2444 COLLECTION

Ambulance, wanted to go back to the union that had represented them, the Teamsters. By the end of the meeting, Gudmestad had convinced his coworkers to go IAFF.

The next hurdle was the IAFF itself. At this time there were no IAFF members who were not fire fighters. The IAFF Executive Board had adopted resolutions in 1975 that:

> this type emergency medical service [paramedic]... should be within the 'jurisdiction' of the fire department.

What the IAFF hadn't addressed was what to do with paramedics who were not fire fighters. Jim Martinez (Boise #672), then IAFF District 7 vice president, went to bat for the paramedics, and helped affiliate one of the first paramedic locals. The IAFF cites September 2, 1977, as King County Paramedics #2595's affiliation date. (Since they went into service on September 1, the affiliation date may have been slightly back-dated, to honor the commitments and intentions of its members.)

Having a local didn't make things much easier. When the provider groups refused to recognize the local, King County Paramedics #2595 was forced to go to the Public Employment Relations Commission (PERC). Once PERC ruled the local represented the paramedics, negotiations began, and eventually finished, granting parity pay with others in the region, such as paramedics working for the Seattle and Bellevue Fire Departments, and for the Evergreen Provider Group.

At this point the provider groups and King County used a strategy that is fairly common within public and private employer management circles, claiming that although the provider groups would be happy to meet their contractual pay requirements, King County was the one with the money, and it wouldn't pay. The providers made it clear they had no funding to cover the additional expense. When King County Paramedics #2595 went to King County, charging that it was the employer, the county said the provider groups were the employers. The local sued King County, claiming it was the de facto employer. Just before the court date, King County agreed to provide funding to meet the paramedics' negotiated contract. King County's relationship with METRO at the time helped motivate the county to avoid a court decision that would have set a precedent.

Both Highline and Valley Provider Groups were shifted to King County in 1980, and became King County Medic One. Eventually, another provider group within the county, serving Auburn and Federal Way, also became part of King County Medic One.

During the time they were negotiating with the county, King County Paramedics #2595 applied for membership in the WSCFF. Gudmestad remembers a meeting with the WSCFF's president, Doug McNall (Everett #46), and another WSCFF representative. They met in a bar and the WSCFF contingent had a fair bit to drink and little to say other than "there's nothing we can do for you." By April 1983, the WSCFF changed its tune. King County Paramedics #2595 became part of the WSCFF.

About five years later, King County Paramedics #2595 were the focus of a contentious lobbying effort by the WSCFF. Eventually, the 1988 legislature amended RCW 41.56 to grant binding arbitration to paramedics who were public employees, unless they worked for public hospital districts. Al Ross, King County's labor representative at the time, had insisted that the only way the county would concede was "over my dead body." When members of King County Paramedics #2595 won, Gudmestad recalls his local sent a funeral bouquet to Ross.

Unidentified members of Seattle #27, Seattle Engine Co. 17, in 1958.

RICHARD WARBROUCK COLLECTION

BEYOND BUNKERS: IMPROVEMENTS IN TURNOUTS AND UNIFORMS

Fire fighter gear has evolved tremendously, and many of the safety improvements have been quite recent. As late as the 1980s many fire fighters paid for their uniforms. Some departments provided uniform allowances, some didn't. Currently, most departments provide turnouts, and an allowance for work and dress uniforms.

In 1969 a statewide, state-administered, and one hundred percent state-funded pension system (LEOFF, Law Enforcement Officers and Fire Fighters Retirement System, RCW 41.26) was passed. From this the Department of Labor and Industries (L&I) moved toward explicitly requiring more standardized equipment and work practices, since LEOFF made it in the state's financial interest to reduce work-related injuries and deaths. As callous as this might sound, there is a constant financial pressure on fire departments to minimize spending when it comes to providing for the equipment and staffing that allow for best safety practices. As the fire service has taken on EMS, HAZMAT, and as building construction uses a higher percentage of artificial materials, there are more and more risks to fire fighters and paramedics, and the cost of equipment and staffing that reduce these risks are constantly on the rise.

⟷ *Helmets* 184
⟷ *Breathing Apparatus* 115
⟷ *EMS* 69
⟷ *Unknown Risks* 82

On June 14, 1974, an arsonist started what would come to be known as Seattle's Polson Fire. The Polson Building was a six-story masonry and heavy timber building on the southwest corner of Western Avenue and Columbia Street. Eleven fire fighters were hospitalized, with five more suffering injuries. Note this unidentified Seattle fire fighter's full turnouts: street shoes, work pants, a raincoat, a leather helmet, and work gloves.

SEATTLE FIRE DEPARTMENT YEARBOOK 1978

Unidentified Hanford I-24 fire fighters practice in full turnouts, which as of the mid-1980s included "dayboots" (rubber hip-height boots), plastic helmets with visors, and self-contained breathing apparatus (SCBA). Truck in background has a small foamer.

HANFORD FIRE DEPARTMENT COLLECTION

Puyallup #726 members on a practice maneuver. L-R: Carl Barker, Adam Jackson, Dale Anderson, (unnamed), Dennis Lawson (WSCFF District 4 representative). The Vancouver Fire Department includes the cost of some issued gear on its website: helmet $129, self-contained breathing apparatus (SCBA) $1,700, Kevlar turnout coat $632, Kevlar turnout pants $465, rubber boots $84, radio $2,500.

DENNIS LAWSON COLLECTION, PHOTO BY BILL JACKSON

Unknown Risks: HAZMAT

There is very little documentation that fire fighters received any systematized training on how to respond to situations involving hazardous materials prior to the late 1970s. In the mid-1950s there were occasional articles in Seattle #27's *Fire Fighter* suggesting fire fighters would have no problem dealing with radioactive materials. No other mention of hazardous materials appeared for over a decade.

Richard Warbrouck (Seattle #27) has a clipping from the mid-1970s. In it, Warbrouck and four other fire fighters are reported to have "become ill… after they breathed phosgene gas" while responding to an electrical fire at a Seattle restaurant. Warbrouck remembers seeing plastic benches on fire, then having trouble breathing (no one was wearing breathing apparatus), then sitting on the curb until he felt somewhat better.

In the early 1980s, Yakima #469 fire fighters received their first HAZMAT training at the command school, in classes taught by Don Monroe (Yakima #469). At the time, Monroe had to scrounge materials from a presentation he had seen in Oregon. Ric Bowman, also of Yakima #469 remembered that when his department had its first "turn in" of hazardous materials they had to call the bomb squad from Walla Walla. More than a few reservists from the Yakima Firing Center, who were residents of Yakima, turned in various explosives they had taken home at some point.

In 1986 the federal Hazard Communication Standard, also called the "right-to-know" law took effect, requiring employers to make their workers aware of hazardous material in the workplace. Further legislation followed, along with upgraded equipment and practices.

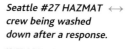
↔ *Two unidentified members of Tacoma #31 stand drenched in oil after an incident.*

TACOMA #31 COLLECTION

Seattle #27 HAZMAT ↔ crew being washed down after a response.

SEATTLE FIRE DEPARTMENT CENTENNIAL YEARBOOK 1989

Someone Like Me:
Affirmative Action

Introduction

The history of diversity within the professional fire service of Washington State parallels changes (or lack thereof) in many professions and trades in the US. In the early 1900s fire fighting was an unskilled, poorly paying job for white men, many times Irish Catholics. Changes in civil service laws, unionization, and an increasing recognition of the value of reliable and trained personnel in municipal fire protection brought improvements to working conditions and benefits, but did nothing to broaden these demographics.

Professional fire fighters eat together, sleep together, trust their lives and careers to each other, and end up spending a third of their lives together. The unique work shifts and intense teamwork fire fighting requires, combined with the inherent risks of the job, foster intense camaraderie. In addition, fire fighters take pride in meeting the standards to which they are held physically, and less obviously, intellectually and emotionally.

Taken between 1911-1914 at a reunion, members of the original (1886-1889) Spokane Falls Fire Department pose in front of the Spokane Chronicle offices. (Note African-American member sitting, first on left.)

NMAC COLLECTION, L93-34.42

Increasing diversity within the fire service has meant different kinds of people have had to demonstrate, or prove, that they could meet the demands of the job. It has also meant that station by station, department by department, union local by union local, these same people have had to find a way to become accepted within the very tight society of fire fighters. Membership in this tightly bound group is based ultimately on "doing the job," and this has added to the still-existing tension over how to determine who should be hired for the job.

By the late 1960s Washington State fire fighters had become expert at using their solidarity to achieve gains in wages and working conditions. Like many of the building trades, the fire service had become a career in which, as Bill Gosnell (Seattle #27) put it, "you could make good money with a high school degree and a driver's license" since in large part, it provided its own training. Both the benefits and require-

Robert Davis (#27) joined members of Miami #587 in picketing the 1988 IAFF Convention, which was held in Miami. Miami #587 dropped members who joined the International Association of Black Professional Fire Fighters (IABPFF), claiming it was a competing union. The IABPFF is a professional association, not a union.

ROBERT DAVIS COLLECTION

ments of being a professional fire fighter and EMS provider have increased exponentially since the 1960s, but the diversity of fire fighters has not.

Almost everyone has an opinion on why this is, and on what, if anything, should be done about it. Two articles in this book describe the evolution of affirmative action within the Seattle and Tacoma fire departments, and the roles Seattle #27 and Tacoma #31 have played. These articles focus upon the experiences of African-Americans and women. Other individuals, including Latinos, Native Americans, Asians and Pacific Islanders, lesbians, and gays have their own stories, which are not addressed in the limited scope of this book.

SEATTLE

⬅ *Seattle #27* 165

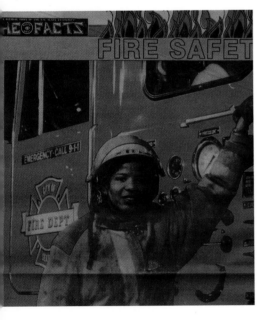

Michelle Williams, the first African-American woman on the Seattle Fire Department (circa 1985). This layout comes from the front page of The Facts, a Seattle newspaper.

ROBERT DAVIS COLLECTION

In January 1959 Claude Harris was hired and became the first black fire fighter in Seattle (and perhaps the state), with no other African Americans hired by Seattle until mid-1967. The Seattle Fire Department began to address the issue of affirmative action in 1968 with a minority recruitment program, and by June it had recruited twelve black applicants.

A year later, there were fourteen black fire fighters in Seattle, the highest percentage of minority recruitment in any of the city's departments. Even with these gains, the 1970 Seattle Human Rights Commission's study found only 3.2% of the fire department's personnel were minorities, although minorities were 13.5% of the city's "available work force." Soon after these figures were released, some sort of case was brought against the city alleging discrimination in hiring and promotion; the specifics of this case (including a citation and outcome) are obscure.

In 1971 the city and the fire department's affirmative action programs approved the use of selective certification in entry level and promotional hiring, as directed by Civil Service Rule 7.03j. Selective certification allows for the highest ranking candidates of a particular minority who are already eligible for a position to be certified, if they are not already certifiable under regular civil service provisions. This puts minority candidates into the final pool of candidates, but does not give them a job.

Seattle Mayor Wes Uhlman issued an executive order in August 1972 that established a specific affirmative action program for all of the city's departments. This order had an explicit goal of increasing the numbers of city employees who were "minorities, women, and persons over forty years of age" until such individuals held jobs within each department in proportion to their numbers within the available work force of the city. The fire department adopted a revised affirmative action program that September, a month before the city council mandated the creation of affirmative action programs in all departments. The city then approved its own affirmative action program in May 1973.

The city's formal adoption of a program meant the fire department had to revise its affirmative action program, which it did, although the Seattle Human Rights Commission did not approve it until 1976. In 1975 the fire department (with 8.6% minorities) was lagging behind other city departments (with 15.2%) in the move toward diversity. It was the dearth of minorities in the fire department's officer positions that triggered use of selective certification, however. When the Seattle Fire Department's revised affirmative action program was approved by the city in 1976, the department had no minorities in its thirty "official and administral (sic) positions" and only eight in its one hundred fifty-five captain and lieutenant positions.

Two promotions which used selective certification were legally challenged in 1976. One was Harris' promotion to battalion chief, and the other was Donald Taylor's promotion to lieutenant. Non-minority applicants charged they had been unfairly passed over. Harris recalls looking at his battalion chief's jacket days before his promotion took effect, and that its gold braid "was like a beautiful sunset." As it turned out, an injunction prevented him from assuming his rank until the case went to court. The two cases were combined, and came to be known within the fire department as the Church case, although its actual name is *Maehren v. Seattle (1979)*.

When the circuit court upheld the promotions, Seattle #27 backed an immediate appeal. The local chose not to be the actual appellant based on legal advice that the union's standing in the case might become an issue. Dick Warbrouck and Bill Gosnell, who both served as Seattle #27 presidents, acknowledge their local funded almost thirteen years of court battles, eventually losing in the US Supreme Court in 1985. Gosnell recalls the local wanted to take selective certification "all the way to the Supreme Court" to eliminate ongoing disputes between the city and the fire department.

The use of union funds in these appeals has been a source of rancor for some black members of Seattle #27, one of whom said, "it's like we paid for the bullets and the gun." During the sixteen years of legal challenges funded by their union, those fire fighters belonging to the Seattle Black Fire Fighters Association (SBFFA) assessed

BONNIE BEERS

In 1975 Bonnie Beers was a junior at the University of Washington when her brother mentioned there were openings with the Seattle Fire Department, so Beers put in her own application. Almost two years later, Beers was the first woman fire fighter in Seattle. During these two years (1975-1977), Beers learned what she needed to know about everything from hose couplings to building construction, while the Seattle Fire Department had reconfigured its recruitment and pre-recruitment programs.

Beers recalled one situation that illustrates, for her, the challenges faced by women as they went out into the stations. A lieutenant ordered two women to raise a fifty-five foot ladder, with tormentor poles, which weighed about 350 pounds. He was fairly sure they couldn't do it, and according to Beers it would have been more usual for four fire fighters to raise the ladder. The two women hoisted it as ordered.

Beers, now a battalion chief (Battalion 5), chooses to work at busy stations whenever possible, because she has learned it is easier to fit in when there is a lot of work to be done.

1998 Members of the SBFFA (Seattle Black Fire Fighters Association).

STANDING, L-R: *Reggie Ball, Marvin Larry, Kenneth Mitchell, Nathaniel Ford, Irwin Chappelle, Lenny Roberts (not a fire fighter), Curtis Gayden, Charles Gill, Michael Poole, Chief Angelo Duggins, Greg Bennett, Darnell Factory, Gregory Dean, Lonnie Reed, Horace Benjamin, Robert Nelson, Gilbert Campbell, Howard Ward, Donald Taylor, Lenro Morgan, Robert Niles, Robert Davis, Freddy Hayes, Roberto Jourdan, Grady Poole, Albert Smalls.*

SEATED, L-R: *Harold Webb, William Murphy, Gerald Jones, Claude Harris, Howard Lavert, Friendly Mitchell.*

ROBERT DAVIS COLLECTION

themselves enough to pay for Harris' legal representation, which supported the City of Seattle's defense of the original decision.

As the Maehren case worked its way through the courts, the first women entered the fire department's recruit school, although none made it through the first class. Eight women applied to the 1976 class; six made it into the program, including Twyla Bryant and Bonnie Beers (Seattle #27) who both remember all the women who made it through the program were terminated after drill school. One, Lori Lakshas, took the matter to court, then settled.

The trainee program was dissolved in 1977 and was immediately replaced with a pre-recruitment class. This consisted of twenty-five to thirty-five weeks of supervised preparation, with pre-recruits paid $4.87 per hour. (Eileen Lewis, now chief of the Tacoma Fire Department, worked her way through Seattle's pre-recruitment program, entered the standard recruitment class, became a probie, then went to work at the Bangor Submarine Base.) In October 1977, Barbara "Bonnie" Beers became the first woman to enter the uniformed ranks of the Seattle Fire Department.

Seattle #27 featured its legal team on the front page of its magazine in May 1979 as the Maehren-Church case was before the State Supreme Court.

L-R: *James Kennedy and Joel Rindal, both of Carroll, Rindal, Kennedy, and Schuck.*

SEATTLE #27 *FIRE FIGHTER,* MAY 1979

The Maehren case, in challenging use of selective certification and by stretching from 1977 to 1985, encouraged divisiveness between those who came into the department through affirmative action programs and those who came in "the regular way." During the same period, the city and the fire department and Seattle #27 also disagreed on the specifics of the ever-changing physical test components. Even now those in the Seattle Fire Department have strong and divergent opinions on whether the alterations in testing protocol and use of selective certification constituted a lowering of standards, or a way to add qualified minority applicants to the final hiring and/or promotional pool.

By 1984 there were forty-five women working as fire fighters and paramedics. The following year Mayor Royer appointed Harris as Seattle's first minority chief. (Harris served until the end of 1996.) From the mid-1980s on, emphasis on the pre-recruitment program seems to have dwindled, as did its funding. The number of minority fire fighters never increased after the pre-recruitment program's first few years.

To this day there is much emotion and little agreement as to what would constitute a fair process to increase the numbers of minority and women fire fighters, and as to whether such increases are important. The fire department no longer has pre-recruitment programs, nor any other formal program to encourage diversity.

L-R: *Mayor Charles Royer, Chief Claude Harris, Seattle #27 President Bill Gosnell attending the graduation ceremony of Seattle's 1985 pre-recruitment class.*

ROBERT DAVIS COLLECTION

Members of the SBFFA volunteer to offer some training in preparation for the department's exams. As of 2002, diversity within the Seattle Department is declining as many of the original minority hires retire, and there are few new hires from under-represented minorities. The percentage of women continues to increase, slowly. Both of these trends are duplicated in the Tacoma Fire Department, and so any gains in fire service diversity will come from future efforts.

TACOMA

In 1970, agents of the US Commission on Civil Rights investigated hiring practices in Tacoma's fire service and Chief J.W. Reiser was invited to attend. The Commission found the department significantly deficient in the number of minorities on its payroll. These and other hearings around the country identified a dearth of minorities within the fire service. In response, the IAFF initiated an historic recruiting program, funded by the US Department of Labor. The IAFF then selected Tacoma as one of twelve cities in the US to participate in its pilot program, with a goal of seeking out and recruiting minorities into the fire service. Tacoma #31's John Willis remembers the fire chief wouldn't go with him to receive the first grant of $127,000. When Willis appeared at the presentation ceremony alone he was informed he needed someone from administration. Willis quickly made arrangements for city police to rush the city manager to the presentation.

Many of the active members of Tacoma #31 were also Free Masons. This lodge was sponsored by the fire department.

FRONT ROW, L-R: *Orrin Anderson, Walt Barnes, Harold Harris, civilian, Earl More.* 2ND ROW, L-R: *George B. Anderson, John Brever, Charles Rancipher, Art Youk, Vernon Eyres, William Schegel.* 3RD ROW, L-R: *Rev. W.J. Brook, Clyde Talbot, Roy Willar (sic), William Koch, Royce Waldrep, C.F. "Spud" Erickson.* 4TH ROW, L-R: *William Snavely, Batt. Chief Harold Fisk, William T. Sherwin, Glenn Lawson.*

RALPH DECKER COLLECTION

The Minority Recruitment Program was jointly developed by Tacoma #31 and the fire department, and began in April 1971, after a series of public hearings. A committee of fire fighters and others began by reviewing past trainee programs to identify the source of the existing bias in hiring. On-duty personnel and volunteers from the Tacoma Fire Department then distributed recruitment posters in grocery stores, barber shops, recreation rooms, post offices, businesses, and public buildings, targeting Tacoma's Hilltop, McKinley Hill, Portland Avenue, and Salishan neighborhoods. They also made contact with many organizations, associations, and individuals within Tacoma's minority leadership to identify people who might make good recruits.

According to the *Affirmative Action Report* the Tacoma Fire Department later issued, qualifications to apply to the program were:

1) a high rating in a screening test administered by Fort Steilacoom Community College, which included spatial relationships, reading comprehension, vocabulary, mathematics, tool recognition, mechanical ability and specific job-related knowledge

2) completion of the required agility test within the allotted time

3) proof of status of citizenship

4) medical examination requirements

The first two black recruits were accepted into the program June 28, 1971. By December 27 of that year, the eighth and last recruit was accepted into what was called

L-R: **WSCFF Secretary-Treasurer Lonnie Hampton and WSCFF Director of Legislative Relations Jim Cason, both members of Tacoma #31, celebrate in 1996.**

In 1971, Lonnie Hampton (Tacoma #31) was one of the first black fire fighters to join the Tacoma Department.

TACOMA #31 COLLECTION

the Cadet Corps, and Lonnie Hampton, who was later to become the WSCFF's secretary-treasurer was one. Cadets took English and mathematics classes at Fort Steilacoom Community College, with tuition and books paid for by the program. Department entrance exams were postponed several times as the program was expanded to incorporate new cadets.

At the end of the first session, the committee issued an evaluation of the program. In the report, many members of Tacoma #31 made it clear they thought recruitment should be focused on those still in high school, because they felt educational background was the most important factor in determining which recruits successfully completed the program. In 1972, the committee proposed fire fighting be part of the job fair in Tacoma's junior and senior high schools.

Willis oversaw the first and second programs with a frugal eye, and took the funds still remaining with him back to IAFF headquarters in Washington, D.C. To this day he is extremely frustrated with the waste he saw in other cities' programs. While keeping the cost of the actual program down, Willis also worked hard to try to find employment for "his recruits" that would allow them to make a living and still be available when their names came up for hiring.

One of the most interesting and productive aspects of Tacoma's various recruitment programs has been that they prepared their cadets to score high on the standard tests issued to all who applied to the Tacoma Fire Department. This meant that there was no selective certification procedure. Both the fire department and Tacoma #31 knew they had to develop an affirmative action program that would deliver a more diverse workforce, but Tacoma #31 also felt strongly that selective certification was equivalent to lowering standards. This issue is hotly debated within the fire service to this day.

Tacoma #31 and the Tacoma Fire Department were awarded an additional IAFF recruitment grant in May 1973. The recruiting director of the second program was Damon Herd, and the goal of this round of recruiting was to increase the number of minorities on the department's hiring list to at least thirty. Two hundred individuals applied to the program, one hundred fifty-two were accepted, and sixty-seven made the recruitment list. Of these, thirty-five were minorities. From 1972 to 1976 the Tacoma Fire Department, in large part because of its recruitment programs, increased the number of minority fire fighters from six to twenty-nine. Herd was hired as field coordinator and promoted to senior field coordinator for the IAFF's encompassing recruitment program.

When the Tacoma Fire Department and Tacoma #31 received their third Labor Recruitment Program Grant from the IAFF in April 1976, retention of minority fire fighters was a bigger problem than their recruitment. Out of twenty-four minority applicants who had been hired off the last list, eleven had been terminated. The new fire chief, Chief Mitchell, blamed these eleven terminations on the personal failings of the applicants. He consulted with Bates Technical College and decided "it is difficult to teach someone mechanical aptitude" although later programs would do exactly this. The committee overseeing the program seems to have gone along with Mitchell's opinions, because pre-screening was used to eliminate candidates with poor mechanical aptitude before they entered the program.

The substance of the third program, directed by Lonnie Hampton, was almost identical to the first two programs. Four weeks were spent on community outreach, followed by a recruitment night put on by the IAFF staff. For the next six to eight weeks 489 recruits were tutored on general subject matter in preparation for the written exam. The 218 who passed were again helped to prepare for the physical agility test. The 170 who passed this were identified by the program report as: 111 minorities, 51 non-minorities, and 8 females (some women were also minorities). These individuals were tutored for the oral exam. Including graduates from this class, the number of minority individuals in all aspects of the Tacoma Fire Department increased to fourteen percent.

In 1977 Chief Mitchell, Tacoma's Civil Service Board, and Tacoma #31 (represented by its president, Ralph Guelfi) held frequent meetings to discuss affirmative action and the possible implementation of selective certification. Chief Mitchell committed his department to future recruitment efforts, but did not feel Tacoma was behind other departments in its efforts. Tacoma #31 was willing to continue its participation in affirmative action programs, but wanted assurances:

> …past methods of hiring would not be changed, and that selective certification will not be used.

The union then agreed to use a modified version of "the rule of three" to increase the number of minorities promoted within the department. Under Tacoma Civil Service law, the rule of three required its administration to hire from the top three eligible candidates. Tacoma had modified this to allow hiring of a minority candidate from the top three eligible minority candidates. This did not address the Civil Service Board's concern about women recruits. There were no women in the department and the board stated females were hindered by the department's preferential point system for veterans, since the military had a percentile limit for women.

At this time, Tacoma's fire department was the only department in the city that did not incorporate selective certification, and Tacoma #31 wanted to keep it that way. In 1980 Tacoma #31 started its own recruitment program, but there is no documentation as to whether anyone was recruited under it.

In 1981 Eileen Lewis was hired as Tacoma's first female fire fighter, using selective certification. Her hiring was challenged by a male applicant who claimed he was unfairly passed over. The Tacoma Civil Service Board held a hearing, and Tacoma #31's president, Chuck Jenkins, submitted a letter on behalf of Tacoma #31 that "as far as the union is concerned Hodges [Lewis] did not deserve the job." Jenkins then told Lewis at the same hearing "it was nothing personal." The Civil Service upheld Lewis' hiring, and she went on to become Chief of the Tacoma Fire Department in February 2000.

Judie Fortier of Tacoma's Human Relations Department and Lonnie Hampton were working closely together at this point on a fire fighter pre-recruitment program. As soon as Lewis completed her probation, she added her volunteer time to their efforts. At this point the pre-recruitment program emphasized training to prepare women to meet the physical demands of the department's exams. Fortier remembers that outreach was for minorities and women:

> There were different testing issues for women and for minority men, but everybody needed preparation for the exams and we didn't differentiate.

In 1982 the Tacoma YMCA offered pre-training to women, at the Y's expense. Lewis was there, literally showing recruits the ropes. In 1984 six women passed Tacoma's fire department exams, and five of them had participated in this program. The next year the city and the Tacoma YMCA co-sponsored a six-month pre-recruitment program which included individualized and group coaching for the physical exam, classes on terminology and equipment and preparation for the written exam.

In August 1986 Joyce Heggen became the first woman in Tacoma's department to achieve a rank higher than fire fighter, when she became its first female paramedic. During the late 1980s Tacoma #31's involvement with affirmative action focused on review of the changing exam requirements, especially the physical or agility test. Al Nyman, president of Tacoma #31 from 1989 to 1990, submitted comments to the Civil Service Board denouncing the changes of the time:

> Competitive appraisal of applicants seems racially and sexually limited to white males, while "protected classes" are offered a free ride to city employment.

Eventually the unions' position softened, and it joined in volunteering at the pre-recruitment classes. These are no longer in existence, and, as in Seattle, the percentage of minorities within the fire department is dropping as those hired during the 1970s retire. Also in parallel to Seattle, the number of women recruits is slowly increasing. As more than one fire fighter had observed, the tremendous efforts and gains toward diversity in the fire service are disappearing, which means any future attempts to broaden the make up of fire fighters will have little to build upon.

profile:
Claude Harris

Seattle Fire Chief Claude Harris, circa 1987.

ROBERT DAVIS COLLECTION

Claude Harris never considered he might be the first black fire fighter in Seattle when he applied. It was late in 1958 and he was working at Boeing, about six months out of the army and looking for a job that didn't involve erratic layoffs. A friend pointed out a recruiting billboard to him: the City of Seattle was seeking both fire fighters and police. Harris went to the city's employment office about an hour before closing on the last day he could apply. Although he had his paycheck from Boeing in his pocket, he did not have the two dollars cash he needed for the two separate applications, so he picked the fire service over police and put his dollar down. At the time there were five blacks on the police force, and Harris assumed there must be others in the fire department.

He passed the written exam, the physical agility test, the oral interview, and then worked his way through three rounds of physicals that identified medical conditions later found to be untrue. Harris joined the department on January 5, 1959. His first real interaction with Seattle #27 was less than a month later, when the local picked up the medical tab for the birth of his second child, an expense that wasn't covered by the army, Boeing, or the fire department.

⬌ *Seattle #27* **165**

Harris spent his first seven years "detailing" (substituting) all over Seattle. He was promoted to lieutenant in 1966, to captain in 1971, and first applied to be fire chief that same year. In the fall of 1976, Harris was promoted to battalion chief. Because selective certification had placed his name on the list of final candidates, this promotion was legally challenged by other applicants (and financed by Seattle #27), on the grounds they had been unfairly passed over, in a series of cases that came to be known as the Church case *(Maehren v. Seattle, 1979)*. Mayor Uhlman directed that Harris be made an acting battalion chief in personnel while the court injunction was in place.

⬌ *Someone Like Me* **83**

Harris stayed in personnel after his promotion was upheld, and once again applied for appointment as fire chief. In 1980 he was appointed deputy chief. Five years later he applied for the chief's position once again. On July 16, 1985, Mayor Royer appointed Harris chief of the Seattle Fire Department, making him the first African-American fire chief in Washington State. As Harris remembers, "by the third time I applied, I was well-prepared."

As fire chief, Harris assigned minority and women fire fighters throughout the city to make sure the citizens of Seattle had ample opportunity to see and meet the diverse members of the department. This cut both ways, since some who had not welcomed affirmative action wanted to avoid "segregated" companies, and some minority fire fighters would have preferred to serve in their own communities.

Harris also brought computers into every fire station. He upgraded or replaced safety equipment and technologies, in part to respond to legal challenges and union demands. These included new bunking gear and a rehydration system to address problems with the new gear, customized face pieces (for a better fit), and use of positive pressure ventilation.

Although some of these were in place in 1989, one fire fighter died during a fire at the Blackstock Lumber Company. During the mandatory Department of Labor and Industries (L&I) investigation, the Seattle Fire Department was found negligent. Harris then instituted a number of additional improvements to address problems identified by L&I, some of which had their own problems. Fire fighters then filed anonymous complaints to L&I about their working conditions. Real solutions to full, timely, and functional communication between and accountability for all personnel at the scene of a fire do not come easily. During the early 1990s Harris tried to find such solutions and to put them into operation. Some criticized Harris for not fully incorporating a new generation of leadership, as the chief's duties further shifted from on-site fire fighting leadership to administrative direction of a city department.

In 1995 four Seattle fire fighters died in the Pang warehouse fire. Communication and personnel accountability were once again found lacking. Harris makes it clear that as fire chief at the time he was ultimately responsible for his department, "the buck stops here." Harris retired in 1996. In considering his career, he reflected, "Nobody wants to be a pioneer [of integration]. The goal is to allow a person to show up and do the job."

⬌ *Seattle #27* **165**

CAMP BLAZE

In 2000, under the umbrella of the Women in the Fire Service Inc. (WFS), Camp Blaze started as a nonprofit, one-week residential fire camp for young women between the ages of sixteen and nineteen. Professional female fire fighters from across the country donate their time as instructors, leaders, directors, and medics. Camp Blaze believes that:

through visionary female collaboration and community involvement... we can increase and insure the presence of confident and strong women leaders.

With this in mind, twenty-four young women are selected from a national pool of applicants. Their expenses (other than transportation) are covered by the camp. Upon arrival, campers are issued full turnouts, then train as firefighters: they operate a chainsaw and the Jaws of Life, rappel five stories, practice search and rescue, fight fire, and learn interview skills. Medics are on duty at all times.

Members of WSCFF locals (including Amy Bannister of Seattle #27 and Jolene Davis of Tacoma #31) have had a large part in establishing, administering, and staffing Camp Blaze. The WSCFF became a contributor to Camp Blaze in 2003.

Two young women observe a flammable liquids fire and prepare to fight fire during the 2003 session of Camp Blaze.

CAMP BLAZE COLLECTION

profile: Eileen Lewis

Eileen Lewis in 1986, when she was named by the Tacoma YWCA as Woman of the Year.

EILEEN LEWIS COLLECTION

Chief of the Tacoma Fire Department, Eileen Lewis stands all of five foot three, speaks plainly, and loves her work. She describes herself as "very type A," and originally sought out the fire service because although she liked the challenge of physical work, she found most other jobs boring within a year of when she started them.

Lewis first tested with the Tacoma Fire Department, and made it as far as the physical agility test, but wasn't fast enough, due to a fractured ankle. She joined the Seattle Fire Department's pre-recruitment training program not much later, in May 1977, as part of the second class that included women. Lewis made it through the pre-recruitment program, then entered the standard recruitment class, and became a probie.

Lewis left the Seattle Department in July 1978, and was immediately hired by the Bangor Submarine Base, in what was then a privately contracted fire service. She was the second woman in that department, and the first to become a fire fighter. While working at Bangor, she tested with the Tacoma Department. Not much later, one of her coworkers, Pat McElligott (WSCFF District 6 representative), would also test with and join the Tacoma Department.

After her negative experiences with the Seattle department, Lewis had reservations about joining the Tacoma Department. During pre-hire interviews, Fire Chief Tony Mitchell convinced her:

> they [those in the Tacoma Fire Department] were serious about hiring a woman. I told them that I could be successful if they were serious, but I wasn't interested if they wanted to use a female hire to demonstrate unsuccess *(sic)*.

On March 15, 1981, Lewis was hired by the Tacoma Fire Department as a recruit. A male applicant who claimed he was unfairly passed over in the hiring process filed an appeal under Tacoma's Civil Service rules. Selective certification had been used in Lewis' hiring, and Tacoma #31 was vehement in supporting the appeal against Lewis. Chuck Jenkins, Tacoma #31's president, told the *Tacoma Tribune* that "as far as the union was concerned, Hodges [Eileen Hodges Lewis] did not deserve the job."

The Civil Service Board vote was split, so the appeal was denied. Lewis' hiring date was changed to March 16 because of the hearing, and she went on to rank first in her recruit class when its thirty-three days of training were completed.

Lewis completed her probationary period in spring 1982. Within a few months she was volunteering to help recruit and train women for the next fire department tests, and offering personal support for candidates. Lewis also made her way through criticism from some wives of fire fighters, as the first female to bunk in what had been all-male quarters. In 1983 she was quoted in the *Tacoma Tribune*:

> After two years, I think I have the acceptance.... and it's allowed me to relax more. There are no special exceptions made for me.... There are so many women out there who are really qualified for the job, but I think the mental abuse they take drives them out.

In 1986 the Tacoma YWCA named her its Woman of the Year, in honor of her demonstrated professionalism and her ongoing and extensive volunteer work to place more women within Tacoma's Fire Department. Lewis was promoted to lieutenant in 1988. Five years later she made captain. Then came a series of administrative appointments: assistant chief of administrative services (September 1993), deputy chief of administrative services (April 1996), and special assistant to the mayor (April to June 1997).

But Lewis wanted to get "back into the field." In February 1999 she transferred to become a battalion chief, anxious to "see what issues our fire fighters are facing on a day-to-day basis." On February 26, 2000, Eileen Lewis was appointed chief of the Tacoma Fire Department. At the time there were thirty-five women in the department, and one all-woman engine company.

Since she became chief, Lewis has worked with Tacoma #31 to foster a strong recruitment program, and made sure there has been staffing to make the program work. Her goal has been to make the department "an environment for possibility," where those with talent and commitment can rise in the department, bringing diversity to all levels of the fire service. Knowing that such a goal can only be met if the best person gets the job, Lewis has worked to foster a department that hires "the best people" to begin with. She knows the work itself deserves the best:

> Once you have a taste of being a fire fighter, it makes everything else worthwhile. You have the reliance upon others, and the closeness, plus your job is to help people. Women in the service have brought their compassion to the job, and that's been good for everybody.

JEANETTE WOLDSETH

When Jeanette Woldseth (Bellevue #1604) was hired by the Bellevue Fire Department on January 3, 1977, she became the first fulltime woman fire fighter in Washington State. (Bonnie Beers, Seattle #27 was hired in September, 1977). Woldseth went on to become a captain, and has been active in Bellevue #1604 for years, including serving as a delegate to the WSCFF until her retirement in July 2002. Woldseth has always shunned any special recognition of being a "first," because, as she said during her media blitz of 1977, "I'm just doing the job I want to."

On-the-Job Training: *Apprenticeship Programs*

Apprenticeship programs have not, until recently, been a big part of fire service training in Washington State. Fire fighters traditionally received their initial training during a six-month to one-year probationary period, and then through on-the-job drills and work experience. This has meant a minimum of transferability between fire departments.

Apprenticeships were standardized in 1937, with passage of the National Apprenticeship Act, which allowed the federal government to legislate such programs. Three years later Washington State then passed RCW 49.04 (Apprenticeship Act) and assumed jurisdiction, creating the Washington State Apprenticeship Training Council (WSATC), and making Labor and Industry (L&I) the administrative body for such programs. Other trades almost immediately established statewide programs. It wasn't until about 1970 that individual fire departments set up their own programs within Washington State, which allowed fire fighters to take advantage of the GI bill.

In the late 1980s several WSCFF executive board members, Michael McGovern (WSCFF president, Lakewood #1488), Jack Andren (District 4 representative, Pierce County #2175), and Frank Spicklemire (District 5 representative, Olympia #468) studied California's apprenticeship program, along with other delegates from the Washington State Fire Protection Policy Board (WSFPPB). These included management representatives (Washington State Fire Marshals Organization, WSFMO) and representatives from fire service apprenticeship councils. All of them liked what they saw in California well enough to include it in the WSFPPB's Master Plan, although little more came of it.

The WSCFF *Strategic Plan 2000*, released in 1999, targeted improved apprenticeship opportunities. In early 2001 the existing sixteen fire department programs worked together to form an umbrella program that would standardize training and gain better representation on the Joint Apprenticeship Training Council (JATC). On July 18, 2002, the Washington State Firefighter Apprenticeship Training Standard was approved by WSAC.

WSCFF District 9 Representative Rick Chaney (Federal Way #2024) has worked tenaciously to help make a coordinated, statewide, certified apprenticeship program a reality for fire fighters. He currently serves as chair of the WSFF JATC, which can now grant apprenticeship certification in International Fire Service Accreditation Congress (IFSAC), Fire Fighter I, Fire Fighter II, and that of an Associate of Science Degree in one process. The next goal will be to involve more fire departments in this program, while expanding the certifications and degrees which are incorporated into it.

Circa 1930.

NMAC COLLECTION, L87-1.42727-30

Station 6 in 1958, a year before it was replaced.

NMAC COLLECTION, L93-25.116

Spokane's Station 6 was built in 1900, and opened that 4th of July. Spokane fire fighters built this station (and quite a number of others), all of which were two-story, with gambrel roofs, cupolas, exposed beams and rafters, and ornate multi-paned windows. Station 6 was probably one of the last in Spokane to use horses, which were totally phased out in 1917. Station 6 was replaced in 1959.

STATIONS

As working conditions for fire fighters have improved, so have the amenities of the stations they work in. At the beginning of the twentieth century, fire fighters were only allowed to leave their stations for a few shifts a month, and lived in buildings that could best be described as bunkhouses combined with storage sheds.

Partly because of the quasi-military aspect of the fire service, partly because orderly equipment makes for fast response times, and partly out of pride, fire fighters take good care of their stations. Older stations from a few locals demonstrate the beauty and functionality that were hallmarks of stations around Washington State.

1 Fire fighters pose in one of Spokane's stations, playing cards. Note the horse-drawn steam engine in the background. Early fire stations usually had a sleeping area upstairs with a downstairs that was used for all equipment storage, living, and cooking areas.

NMAC COLLECTION, L91-158.18

2 Originally built as Yakima's fire station and city hall, this building is now part of Yakima's Opera House.

YAKIMA FIRE DEPARTMENT COLLECTION

3 Spokane's Washington Hose Company 3, at Station 3, circa 1889. This station was located on the "courthouse block" north of the river.

NMAC COLLECTION, L86-359

4 Spokane's Engine Company 3 poses with two rigs using horse harnesses with a steam engine in the background. L-R MacClain, Taylor (seated), Boyle (standing closer), unidentified (standing in rear), Lynch (seated), Asst. Chief Joyce (standing), Thieman (seated).

NMAC COLLECTION, L86-357

5 Tacoma Fire Department's old headquarters and Station 6 in 1974, two days before it was torn down. Vines had been planted in 1919, and Clyde Talbot (#31), who took this picture, helped plant them.

CLYDE TALBOT COLLECTION

6 Spokane Station 7's kitchen, in 1957. This picture was one of a series taken to document the need for improvements in fire station living conditions.

NMAC COLLECTION, L93-25.112

The Law of the Contract

J. W. HOOVER
DIRECTOR

CLAUDE H. MORAN
LABOR COMMISSIONER
EASTERN DISTRICT

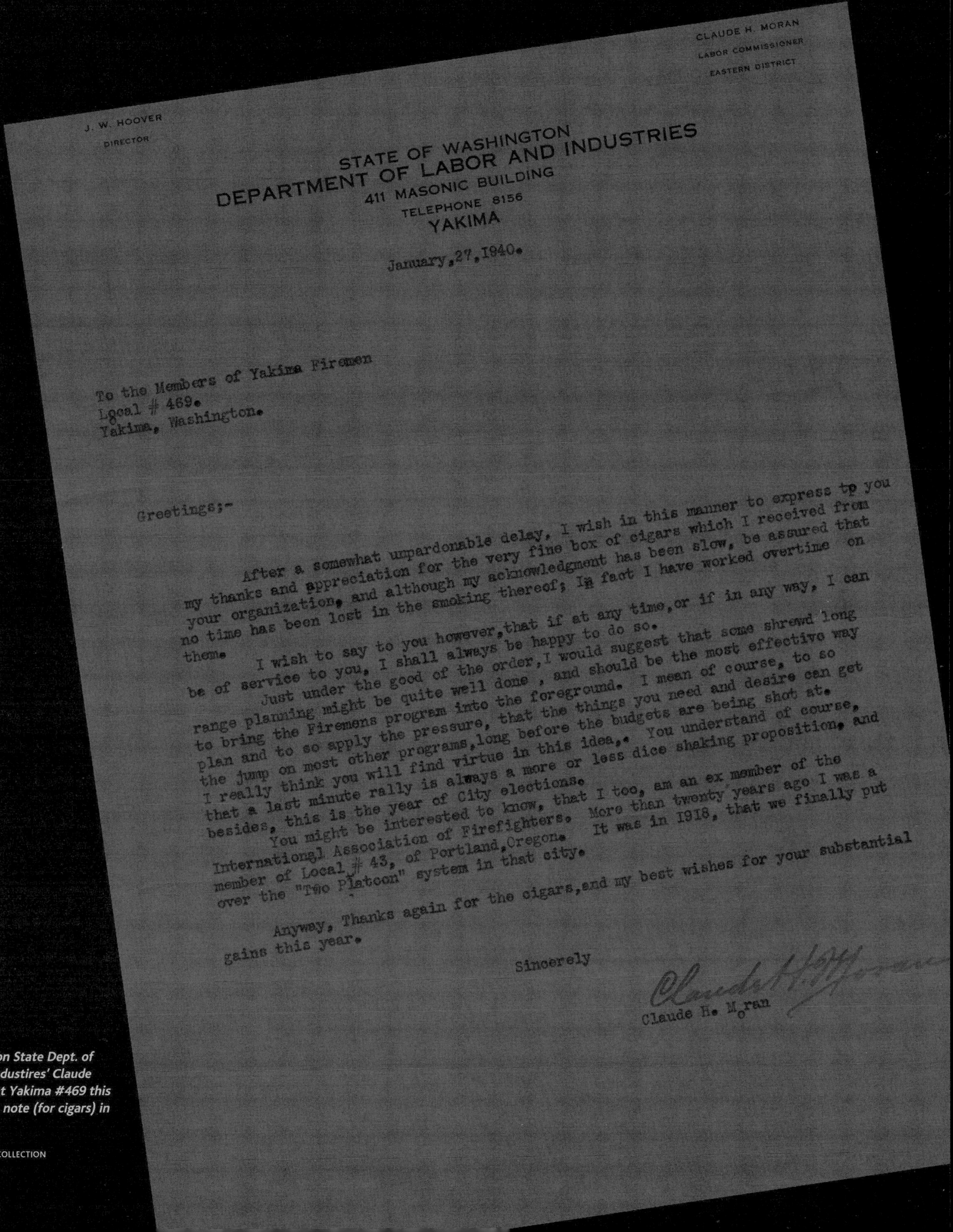

STATE OF WASHINGTON
DEPARTMENT OF LABOR AND INDUSTRIES
411 MASONIC BUILDING
TELEPHONE 8156
YAKIMA

January,27,1940.

To the Members of Yakima Firemen
Local # 469.
Yakima, Washington.

Greetings;-

After a somewhat unpardonable delay, I wish in this manner to express to you my thanks and appreciation for the very fine box of cigars which I received from your organization, and although my acknowledgment has been slow, be assured that no time has been lost in the smoking thereof; In fact I have worked overtime on them.

I wish to say to you however, that if at any time, or if in any way, I can be of service to you, I shall always be happy to do so.

Just under the good of the order, I would suggest that some shrewd long range planning might be quite well done , and should be the most effective way to bring the Firemens program into the foreground. I mean of course, to so plan and to so apply the pressure, that the things you need and desire can get the jump on most other programs, long before the budgets are being shot at. I really think you will find virtue in this idea,. You understand of course, that a last minute rally is always a more or less dice shaking proposition, and besides, this is the year of City elections.

You might be interested to know, that I too, am an ex member of the International Association of Firefighters. More than twenty years ago I was a member of Local # 43, of Portland, Oregon. It was in 1918, that we finally put over the "Two Platoon" system in that city.

Anyway, Thanks again for the cigars, and my best wishes for your substantial gains this year.

Sincerely

Claude H. Moran

Washington State Dept. of Labor & Industires' Claude Moran sent Yakima #469 this thank-you note (for cigars) in 1940.

YAKIMA #469 COLLECTION

LEGACY OF LEGISLATION

The WSCFF has been a major force in passage of legislation at the state level that improves the terms, working conditions, pensions, and benefits of those in the fire service. From Governor Langlie on, WSCFF representatives have had opportunities to pose with each governor, except Dixie Lee Ray (1977-1981).

A STANDING, L-R: *unknown, probably Earl Brower (#46, WSCFF director of governmental relations 1941-1963, IAFF Dist 7 vp 1944-1956), Jack Waller (#29, WSCFF secretary 1944-1955, WSCFF legislative representative 1941-1963, IAFF Dist 7 vp 1956-1962), possibly Bill McCormick, unknown.* SEATED: *Monrad Charles Wallgren (Governor, 1945-1949).*

WALLER FAMILY COLLECTION

B *Probably the 1961 signing of the Firemen's Pension bill (amending RCW 41.18 Firemen's Relief and Pension Act of 1955).* STANDING, L-R: *Walt Lambert (#29, WSCFF secy), Zane Mitchell (#315, WSCFF exec board), John Alexander (#864, WSCFF president), Bus Kramer (#469, WSCFF exec board), Jack Waller (#29, IAFF Dist 7 vp and WSCFF "legislative representative"), Harold Nilsen (#27), Axel Drugge (#27, WSCFF exec board), Gordon Hovik (#46), John Smith, Jr. (#31, WSCFF exec board), unknown, unknown.* SEATED: *Governor Albert Rosellini.*

AXEL DRUGGE COLLECTION

C *Representatives of the WSCFF witness the 1983 passage of HB 434 (RCW 53.18.015 Application of Public Employees' Collective Bargaining Act), which granted port district employees coverage under RCW 41.56.* STANDING, L-R: *Michelle Jaincanich, Michael McGovern (#1488, WSCFF president), Mike Ryherd (WSCFF lobbyist), Howard Vietzke (#29, WSCFF legislative representative), Jim Cason (#31, WSCFF vp), State Representative Dick King, Ron Ullrich.* SEATED: *Governor John Spellman.*

WSCFF COLLECTION

D *WSCFF representatives posed during the 1985 signing of SH 1010/HB 435 (RCW 41.04.515 Disability Leave Supplement for Law Enforcement Officers and*

Fire Fighters) which granted up to six months of disability leave supplement. STANDING, L-R: *Howard Vietzke (#29, WSCFF legislative rep), State Representative Mike Patrick, Michael McGovern (#1488, WSCFF president), aid to State Rep. Sayan, State Representative Doug Sayan, Jim Cason (#31, WSCFF vp), Ron Morehouse (#106, WSCFF s/t), Charlie Marsh (WSCPO executive director).* SEATED: *Governor Booth Gardner.*

WSCFF COLLECTION

E *In 1993, WSCFF gained passage of HB 1541 (amending RCW 18.71.205) EMT recertification provides option of eiminating written exam in favor of a modular testing program.* STANDING, L-R: *Ken Snider (#29), Ted Rail (#29), Michael McGovern (#1488, WSCFF president), Cody Arledge (#2409), State Representative George Orr (4th District, #876), Howard Vietzke (#29, WSCFF legislative director), Jim Cason (#31, WSCFF s/t).* SEATED: *Governor Mike Lowry.*

WSCFF COLLECTION

F *WSCFF and others in the fire service gained the 1999 passage of HB 1154 (RCW 84.52.069 Emergency medical care and service levies) which authorized permanent levies, rather than only those with time limits.* STANDING, L-R: *Senator Jeri Costa, State Representative Mike Cooper (District 21, #1760), Chris Heminger (#1352, WSCFF s/t), unknown, Brian Hurley (#2409, WSCFF District 5 representative, WSCFF's representative on Dept. of Health committees: EMS and Trauma Steering Committee, State EMS Education Committee, Bioterrorism Committee), Duane Malo (White Center fire chief, lobbyist for fire chiefs), unknown, unknown (fire commissioners).* SEATED: *Governor Gary Locke.*

WSCFF COLLECTION

Collectively Bargaining

Based on a Handshake 1930-1959

This article has been one of the most difficult to research. While every attempt has been made to verify citations, dates, and details, there are surely some omissions and errors that remain.

In the 1930s, the federal government enacted laws that granted some workers the right to organize, and to have unions that were not created by the company or employer. The National Industrial Recovery Act (NIRA) was passed in 1933, part of Roosevelt's New Deal. NIRA established the National Recovery Administration (NRA), included terms for establishing maximum hours and minimum wages by industry, and granted some workers the right to organize and collectively bargain. But by May 1935, business interests convinced the US Supreme Court to rule NIRA was unconstitutional, on the grounds its crop controls and price subsidies violated states' rights. The NRA was eliminated with this ruling.

Two months later the Wagner Act (also known as the National Labor Relations Act, or NLRA) became law and incorporated some of what had been in NIRA. It granted many rights to many workers but applied only to workers whose industry engaged in interstate commerce, which meant it did not cover public employees. For the industries covered, the Wagner Act did establish the National Labor Relations Board (NLRB), allowed for secret elections to determine bargaining agents, and out-lawed a management-directed system of representation, the "company union."

The WSCFF's first constitution, in 1939, lists seven objectives, one of which is "to encourage and protect civil service laws in all cities in the State of Washington who have paid men in their fire departments." At the time, civil service seemed the best system to provide for an explicit and fair system of workplace negotiation for public employees.

It would take binding arbitration, gained thirty-five years later (in 1973) before WSCFF locals could escape asking for each wage increase and every improvement in working conditions through a vote of the people. Tacoma #31 was ahead of its time in gaining negotiated written agreements with its employer, the Tacoma City Council. John Smith (Tacoma #31) remembers fire fighters and police in Tacoma had separate agreements but worked together on their negotiations. After every meeting with the city, police and fire fighters traded notes, making sure they "got the same pay, the same everything." During these negotiations, Smith bonded with a major negotiator and representative of the Tacoma police, Charlie Marsh, who was also president of the

Members of Yakima #469 signed a petition opposing adoption of the "Hartley-Taft Labor Bill." Passed in 1947, this law prohibits secondary boycotts and closed shops, while allowing states to enact right-to-work laws. It also established procedures for settling "national emergency strikes."

YAKIMA #469 COLLECTION

⬌ *Platoons, Kelly Days and Transit Passes* 57

⬌ *Union Partners* 36

Washington State Police Officers Association (which later became the Washington State Council of Police Officers, WSCPO and still later, WACOPS). In the end, like other IAFF locals without written agreements, what Tacoma #31 couldn't get through discussion it got by pounding the pavement. According to Clair Hansen, a member of Tacoma #31:

> I remember in 1941 and 1942 walking through neighborhoods and going house to house, telling people that fire fighters were trying to get a pay raise and that they should vote for it. We really tried to get across that fire fighters needed a raise and an improvement in working conditions. Getting the support of the citizens of this city was the only way we could get a raise back then.... It didn't seem like the city ever wanted to give us fire fighters a raise. We always had to work for what we got.

Federal law did not get friendlier toward unions during the early and mid-1940s. The Taft-Hartley Act of 1947 (also known as the Labor-Management Relations Act) amended the Wagner Act to make secondary boycotts and closed shops illegal (union membership could not be required prior to employment). In addition, it allowed states to adopt right-to-work laws which prohibit union shops or any other arrangement that requires employees to belong to a union. The Taft-Hartley Act also established a way of settling "national emergency strikes," language that has since been used by the federal government to intervene in the Professional Air Traffic Controllers Organization (PATCO) strike of 1981 and the International Longshoremen's and Warehousemen's Union (ILWU) contract negotiations of 2002.

In 1949 Washington State did pass what Marvin Schurke refers to as "the first fully-administered public sector collective bargaining law in the nation." (Schurke is the current executive director of the Public Employment Relations Commission, PERC.) Workers at the Black Ball Ferry Line went on strike (as allowed under the NLRA). The state then bought out the company, and became the ferry workers' employer. RCW 47.64 was then passed, creating the Marine Employees Commission, and allowing these ferry workers to retain their collective bargaining rights (with terms approximating interest arbitration).

In March 1952 Everett voters passed an initiative amending the city's charter "to provide for the submission of disputes arising between the firemen and the city as to working conditions, wages, and pensions to a board of arbitrators." But when Everett #46 (then Everett #350) tried to collectively bargain its salaries, the city commissioners refused to follow the arbitration procedure outlined in its new ordinance, and instead went for a court decision which found the charter amendment unconstitutional. Everett #46 appealed the decision to the state supreme court, *Everett Fire Fighters local No. 350 v. C. Arvid Johnson* (1955), and lost.

There is little record the WSCFF pursued a significant course of action on collective bargaining until the mid-fifties. Sam Kinville, who was beginning his career with the AFSCME (American Federation of State County and Municipal

Everett #46   161

Employees, a federation, not a union), remembers fire fighters as more concerned with their pensions than with collective bargaining rights. But the civil service system proved itself to be generally ineffective and at times unfortunate for those employees who worked under it.

Since most civil service boards are controlled or staffed by mayoral and city council appointments, municipal employees found their workplace negotiations could jeopardize their very employment. Public employees around the state and the country began to rally around their desire for collective bargaining rights, rights many who worked in the private sector had come to expect.

In 1957, the WSCFF made collective bargaining rights its major legislative focus and brought forward language that became HB 369, Arbitration for Firemen and Policemen. Seattle #27's *Fire Fighter* came out with numerous supporting articles, and quoted a speech made at AFSCME's 1956 Convention, by Secretary-Treasurer of the newly merged AFL-CIO, William Schnitzer:

FRONT, L-R: **Rep. Slade Gorton, Avery Garrett, Bill McCormick.** REAR: **Walt Lambert (#29), Axel Drugge (#27), Jack Waller (#29). This may have been part of the WSCFF's efforts in 1957 when it introduced its first bill, Arbitration for Firemen and Policemen.**

AXEL DRUGGE COLLECTION

> It does not make much sense for a government to insist on collective bargaining rights for workers in private industry and then to refuse to apply the same rules to itself.

The WSCFF did its best in Olympia with Jack Waller (Spokane #29) as legislative representative, backed by Vice President Walt Barnes (Tacoma #31), Director of Government Relations Earl Brower (Everett #46), President John Alexander (Renton #864), and Treasurer Felix Arena (Seattle #27). Arbitration for Firemen and Policemen was opposed by the Association of Washington Cities (AWC), individual cities, and individual counties. Alex Drugge (Seattle #27) summarized the bill's defeat in the March 1957 *Fire Fighter*:

> Organized labor was shocked that this session did not approve of their basic legislative programs.... we are grateful for whatever the [Seattle] city council does to improve our salaries and working conditions, nobody denies this. However, we also desire something more, the right to bargain collectively, and the right to sign written agreements. In common terms, we want to sit as equals and deliberate our problems, and if there is a dispute, the right to arbitrate the same.

Collective Begging to Binding Arbitration 1960-1973

By the early 1960s civil-service wages were below those of organized labor in the private sector. Across the United States public workers began to disrupt public services with actions, including slowdowns and strikes. The issue of collective bargaining rights was in the forefront for most public workers, especially after President Kennedy's Federal Executive Order 10988 (1962) granted federal workers the right to organize. During this period public employees in general, and fire fighters in particular, debated using strikes as a tool to improve their working conditions. Within Washington State's labor community this was a divisive issue. Private-sector unions had no interest

⬅ *On Strike* 117

in giving up their ability to strike, and did not want to support public employees in doing so, even those who provided "essential services." Bill Gosnell (Seattle #27) remembers the Teamsters' concern with a milk truck drivers' strike in New York City which was framed in terms of the "essential service" of providing milk for school children.

Fire fighters debated within their locals, within the WSCFF, and within the IAFF about the no-strike policy of the IAFF. Many felt the inability to strike and the lack of collective bargaining rights made any sort of negotiations for better working conditions and wages impossible. Others agreed with John Willis (Tacoma #31), long-time lobbyist for his local and the WSCFF:

> I told them striking was a stupid idea. What's going to happen when you're out on strike and there's a fire and some little kid burns up?

There were also concerns that cities might rethink their long-standing commitment to funding publicly operated, professional fire protection services. Municipal professional fire protection had been established in response to devastating fires and inept private fire protection, and strikes might trigger a return to privatization. At the WSCFF's 1963 Convention in Seattle, twenty-five years after its founding, delegates were ready to change the WSCFF's approach, and did so. Gordon Hovik (Everett #46), WSCFF's president since 1961, had suffered his second heart attack during the previous legislative session, and could no longer serve. John Smith (Tacoma #31), who had been a trustee, was narrowly elected president, without the full support of his own local. Bob Munk (Spokane #29), who helped deliver to Smith three critical votes from Spokane #29, explained why he backed Smith:

> The other guy [Jack Baker (Bellingham #106)] never showed up to even talk to us in Spokane. I ended up on an elevator with him at the convention, and he wouldn't say a word even then. John Smith had a plan, and he wanted our votes.

Seattle #27, host for the convention, introduced a resolution that passed, Arbitration, Union Recognition, and Collective Bargaining for Fire Fighters. Governor Albert Rosellini and Seattle Mayor Gordon Clinton were present at the convention to offer their support. The WSCFF, represented by Smith (Tacoma #31), Axel Drugge (Seattle #27), and John Richmond, secretary-treasurer of Seattle #27, then went to the Washington State Labor Council (WSLC) Convention with Resolution 43, Mandatory Collective Bargaining for Fire Fighters:

> WHEREAS: Fire fighters are prohibited from striking because of the civic responsibility and seriousness of providing protection from fire for life and property, and therefore be it
>
> RESOLVED: That the Washington State Labor Council go on record in support of establishing mandatory collective bargaining for fire fighters, with the option to arbitrate and the decision to be binding...

The WSCFF's resolution was adopted as part of that year's WSLC legislative action package. This bill was then passed by the 1964 Senate before dying in the House Rules Committee.

After the legislative session was over, Richmond (Seattle #27), a consummate Olympia lobbyist, was convinced public support was with the fire fighters, and wrote in his local's magazine, the *Fire Fighter*:

...it can be assumed that the majority of people haven't changed their attitude toward sound labor legislation, and with the proper presentation and support by all public employees, it seems quite logical to believe that the people would again support a sound plea from labor to allow public employees, who are prohibited from striking, the right to collective bargaining and the settlement of disputes by means of arbitration.

There is no real documentation on what discussion or action was taken at the 1964 WSCFF Convention in Yakima. In 1965, the WSCFF again supported legislation for public employee collective bargaining. Lambert (Spokane #29, IAFF District 7 vice president) was tired of legislative defeat, and rallied support for the concept Seattle #27 had developed, preparing for an initiative if the legislature wouldn't budge. Going into the session he wrote in the *Fire Fighter*:

> If the 1965 legislature fails to enact this legislation, then the issue is to be submitted to the people via the initiative petition route in the 1966 fall general election.

The 1965 legislature did pass RCW 28A.72 Negotiations by Certified Personnel, which allowed teachers ("certificated personnel") to "meet, confer and negotiate," but this did not provide for actual negotiations. The 1965 bill backed by fire fighters' HB 360, which would have granted collective bargaining, grievance arbitration, and interest arbitration for the most public employees, including fire fighters, made it to the governor's desk. But Governor Dan Evans vetoed the entire bill on the grounds it intruded upon the existing civil service system, which covered state employees.

Meanwhile the federal Fair Labor Standards Act (FLSA) was amended (in 1961 and again in 1966), broadening its definition of employers who were required to meet mandatory minimum-wage and overtime pay requirements. Although documentation is hazy, it appears some part of these changes caused Washington State's Department of Labor and Industries (L&I) to either promulgate rules, or to formalize its future practices in regard to the FLSA. (There may have been some amendment to existing state law as well, but no citation could be found.) Employers would be required to have contracts with workers who worked over forty hours a week. The fire fighters watched these changes carefully, and lobbied to make sure they did not become one of its few exceptions.

Notice was sent to all organizations, both unions and employers, who would need to have these newly required contracts in place. Notice was also given that Harold Petrie, then director of L&I, would conduct a seminar in Olympia to provide information on the new requirements. A lot of fire fighter locals came to Petrie's seminar, few employers attended. Petrie explained the law's requirements: any employer with more than four employees had to comply with minimum wage and hourly law, and when any employee worked more than forty hours a week, there would need to be a written contract. Petrie reminded all present that no existing benefits could be "taken off the table," or rescinded, as this contract was drafted.

Many employers were prepared to ignore these requirements. George Roop's (Spokane Valley Fire District 1 #876) employer, Spokane Valley Fire District 1, was one. After Roop and some of his coworkers returned from Petrie's seminar, they explained to the district that compliance was not optional, and that there were penalties, including fines Roop remembers as being about fifteen hundred dollars, for noncompliance. Spokane Valley Fire District 1 #876 invited the fire district's commissioners

Karl V. Herrmann (4th District) in the 1963 pictorial directory of the state legislature. Herrmann helped Spokane Valley Fire District 1 #876 negotiate their first written contract years before collective bargaining was enacted.

GEORGE ROOP COLLECTION

⟺ *Everett #46* **161**

to a meeting to draft the required contract. Then Roop heard the Commissioners would have a lawyer there to represent them. Roop got in touch with someone he knew from his lobbying work, Senator Karl Herrmann, who had been on the committee that drafted the bill. When the Commissioners announced their attorney would be speaking for them, Roop, after introducing Senator Herrmann to the Commissioners, explained that Herrmann would be speaking for the fire fighters. "That made for a shorter meeting," Roop recalls with some humor. With that first contract Local #876 left behind its twenty-four-hour-on, twenty-four-hour-off schedule. "We went to twenty-four-on, forty-eight-off, and got Kelly days and all of that."

There is no documentation of what discussions took place after the 1965 legislative session; there is also no documentation that an initiative on collective bargaining was actually considered. In 1966 one local managed to move ahead without mandatory collective bargaining law. Everett #46, under its president Joseph McDonald, became the first local in Washington to have a binding contract. (Everett's local hadn't had its original #46 reissued yet, and so was called Everett #350.) This contract established Everett #46 as the sole and exclusive bargaining agent for Everett's fire fighters, a first in Washington State.

Perhaps this helped the WSCFF gear up. President Smith announced the WSCFF was establishing a strike fund, and in the weeks before the 1967 legislative session began, told the press:

> If we [the WSCFF] are not successful in getting the law we want, the cities of the state will be faced with walkouts by their fire fighters. This isn't a threat. It's a reality. We're through playing games.

Smith let it be known Washington State fire fighters were willing to trade collective-bargaining rights for a law making such strikes illegal. What he didn't need to mention directly was that other fire fighters had gone out on strike in the last year (1966) in cities including Atlanta, St. Louis, and Kansas City, Missouri. As the 1967 legislature convened, the WSCFF's executive board, individual fire fighters, and lobbyists for specific locals arrived, including George Roop (Spokane Valley Fire District 1 #876), John Willis (Tacoma #31), representatives from Bellingham #106, and a team from Seattle that included John Richmond, Richard Sparks, Dick Warbrouck, and Bill Gosnell. These men and their locals did not necessarily like each other, they did not pursue the same lobbying methods, nor were their efforts always well-coordinated, but together they moved collective bargaining legislation ahead.

Public employees and unions across the state joined the WSCFF in Olympia. Sam Kinville, then lobbyist for the WSLC, described labor's position in the *Fire Fighter*:

> ...the labor movement and the public employee unions are no longer satisfied to collectively beg. They expect, and, in fact, will demand nothing less than honest-to-God collective bargaining.

There are credible stories of what it took to pass this bill: previous years of courting legislators, months of favors being called forth, private conversations that were as much threat as promise, weeks spent sleeping in cars close to the Capitol. President Smith (Tacoma #31) continued his aggressive, take-no-prisoners approach to setting the WSCFF's agenda. As the legislature deliberated, Smith went to Cincinnati at the request of the IAFF, to give testimony on the IAFF's no-strike policy,

⟺ *Lobbying and*
Lambaste **123**

⟺ *On Strike* **117**

which he opposed. Weeks later RCW 41.56 (the Public Employees' Collective Bargaining Act) passed, to take effect July 1, 1967. The efforts of the WSCFF and its members were critical in making it happen.

Collective bargaining was also granted to port employees with passage of SB 34 (RCW 53.18, Port Districts—Employment Relations—Collective Bargaining and Arbitration), although security and supervisory personnel were explicitly required to be covered under separate labor agreements from other port employees.

With passage of RCW 41.56 and RCW 53.18, Washington State became one of the first in the nation to grant collective bargaining rights to public employees. IAFF District 7 Vice President Lambert (Spokane #29) came to the June 1967 Convention with Resolution 67-18, to prepare fire fighters for the negotiations that were already beginning:

> That the Collective Bargaining Committee set up a form [process] whereby all member Locals of the WSCFF may follow a given procedure before signing Contracts with their respective municipalities.

From the beginning of collective bargaining the IAFF has provided training on collective bargaining at events organized by the WSCFF. Another staple of contract negotiation was also supported by Lambert's resolution: active fire fighters negotiated their own contracts, and compared contractual terms with other locals. Those locals with better wages and working conditions, such as Seattle #27 and Tacoma #31, provided support to smaller locals as fire service jurisdictions entered into their first contractual negotiations.

But as fast as such negotiations were initiated, the issue of who could be in a bargaining unit was challenged. Prior to passage of RCW 41.56, there had been little or no consideration by IAFF locals as to which positions within a department would be covered since local membership had always included all those employed in the fire service, up to and including chiefs.

A few months after RCW 41.56 took effect Seattle #27 faced the first bargaining unit challenge. Bill Gosnell (Seattle #27) remembers this legal challenge was in keeping with Seattle's role as a testing ground for contract negotiations. On May 14, 1968, Harold J. Petrie, director of Washington State's L&I, ruled Seattle's bargaining unit:

> …shall consist of all uniformed personnel below the grade of Battalion Chief, and that Seattle Fire Fighters Union Local No. 27 represents a majority of employees within the above-designated unit and should be recognized as the exclusive bargaining representative of such unit.

The issue of whether officers could be included within the same local as those of lesser rank within the same department would remain a focus of negotiation challenges for years to come.

Petrie's decision was a hot topic later that same summer when fire fighters gathered in Spokane for the WSCFF's thirtieth convention. WSCFF Secretary Robert Munk (Spokane #29) was quoted on the matter in a Spokane newspaper:

> It is our understanding that Harold Petrie, state director of labor and industries, has ruled that only chiefs and battalion chiefs are not to be recognized as union negotiators, but that decision has been challenged and a court action has been threatened.

Before talk on the convention floor turned to the details of collective bargaining, discussion focused on WSCFF representation in Olympia. The WSCFF was a significant legislative player, and its member locals had mixed feelings about deferring to the WSCFF when it came time to lobby. Seattle #27 came in with a resolution:

> Any individual or group of individuals who are members of the International Association of Fire Fighters [IAFF] who shall introduce legislation to the legislature of the State of Washington affecting fire fighters of the state, without first going through and receiving the approval of their local union and the Washington State Council of Fire Fighters, shall be suspended from their local union.

⟷ *Fractious Fraternity* **27**

Exactly who the loose cannons were that this resolution sought to address remains unclear. It is also not clear whether it was a number of issues or particular lobbying positions and/or styles that were causing significant dissention. What was clear is that shortly after the 1968 Convention Seattle #27, the WSCFF's single largest local, left the WSCFF and was out for ten years, until 1978. It was also clear to Seattle #27 at the time that locals within the WSCFF were not interested in doing much to keep Seattle a member.

The Spokane Convention also commemorated the IAFF's Jubilee, or fiftieth, anniversary. William D. Buck, retiring IAFF president, was present, and delivered a speech on potential strikes that the *Spokane Daily Chronicle* covered:

> Buck... reported that several proposals concerning the no-strike provision have been submitted [to the IAFF]. He told the convention that locals are pushing for a change in the international union constitution's 'no strike' clause because some public officials have taken advantage of that policy.

⟷ *On Strike* **117**

In fact, the IAFF did vote to remove all language concerning a local's decision to go out on strike.

Across the state locals used the Collective Bargaining Act to negotiate their contracts. In 1969, RCW 41.56 was targeted for amendment. The WSCFF maintained its presence and influence in Olympia through IAFF District 7 Vice President Lambert (Spokane #29), John Willis (lobbyist for Tacoma #31), George Roop (Spokane Valley Fire District 1 #876) and WSCFF President Smith. Many other locals and individuals were part of the effort, but not all their names are in the records. Working with Seattle #27's lobbying team, fire fighters achieved another huge legislative victory. In 1969 Law Enforcement Officers' and Fire Fighters' Retirement System (RCW 41.26 LEOFF) was passed, effective October 10, 1970.

⟷ *At the End of the Day* **137**

By the end of that same session, a committee had been established (by RCW 41.56.400) to study optional binding arbitration as it existed within 41.56. The Public Employees Collective Bargaining Committee was chaired by Representative Dick King, and issued its report in 1971.

A "commission to prevent unfair labor practices and issue remedial orders and cease-and-desist orders" was also created (under 41.56.160). The two amendments together were in response to what RCW 41.56 didn't address: the need for binding arbitration. The IAFF held a hearing on its constitutional strike provisions, and invited

George Roop (#876) was one of many in the WSCFF who worked with other public employee associations and unions to gain collective bargaining.

GEORGE ROOP COLLECTION

Even after RCW 41.56 took effect, in 1967, each local had to negotiate its first contract, and did not have binding arbitration to force timely good-faith bargaining. Officers of Spokane #29 watch Spokane Mayor David Rogers sign their first collectively bargained contract in about 1972.

L-R: **Ken Strong (#29 president), Howard Vietzke (#29 s/t), Gary Brown (#29 vp).**

WSCFF President Smith to testify. Smith continued to maintain that if all other avenues of negotiation failed, a walkout might be something a local would use.

Without binding arbitration or the right to strike, when collective bargaining reached impasse the employee had no leverage. This meant that winning collective bargaining rights left fire fighters in a sort of limbo since there was still no hammer to force both sides to actually finalize a contract. Many locals bargained, but few contracts were signed. What would happen if fire fighters went out on strike was not clear; municipal and other public jurisdictions were unlikely to lock out fire fighters. Consequently, few contracts were resolved.

Howard Vietzke (Spokane #29) remembers that during this period his local had to fight hard for fifteen and twenty-dollar-a-month raises, going door-to-door in the last few days before each referendum, in what many quickly came to call collective begging:

⬌ *Platoons, Kelly Days and Transit Passes* **57**

> The city [Spokane] said 'sure, we'll go for your raises. But that means we'll have to raise taxes and cut services.' So we would have to go out door-to-door in the last few days to convince people to support us.

Throughout the United States other public employees were striking, and in many cases it worked. Jim Webster, a Seattle labor lawyer who has represented the WSCFF and IAFF locals, remembers "teachers were striking, and got raises when they did." Bill Horst, president of Yakima #469 at the time, described his local's first contract, negotiated in 1969:

> What we got mostly was the right to meet... there wasn't much content to that first contract. Somewhere there's a picture—we got all dressed up to sign it. I wanted to make as big a deal of it as I could, but there really wasn't much to it.

In 1970 the most interesting advances in contracts came when Everett #46 (then #350) signed, and gained binding arbitration, a first in the state. (Everett #46 had also been the first fire fighters' local to sign a binding contract as its members' sole and exclusive bargaining agent, in 1966.) An article in the IAFF's May 1970 *International Fire Fighter* summarized:

⬌ *Everett #46* **161**

> An across the board ten percent pay increase, a binding arbitration clause and the right to withhold services were the highlights of a collective bargaining contract recently negotiated by Local 350 [Everett #46] and the City of Everett, Wash....
> Other benefits won by the local include the following:
> • The union is sole bargaining agent for all positions up to and including battalion chief.
> • A 42-hour work week that includes a 10- and 14-hour schedule.

- Paid vacations of fourteen working shifts and ten paid holidays per year. Double-time pay for all work performed on a holiday.
- Dues check off.
- A clause stating, that if the employer fails to honor any and all items in the contract, the fire fighters covered by the contract have the right to strike to redress their grievances without fear of prosecution.

Jay Weewie, president of Everett #46, credited the newly adopted form of government (mayor-city council) and a "crack negotiating team…. These boys are pros."

In 1971 the Public Employees Collective Bargaining Committee issued its report, recommending the legislature enact one of three sets of laws:

SEATED, L-R: **Bob Anderson (mayor), Jay Weewie (Everett #46 president).**

STANDING, L-R: **Ray Smith (Everett fire chief), Larry Vognild (#46's chief negotiator), John Smith (WSCFF president), Dick Rowley (#46), Larry Jasper (#46 secretary), Karl Hofmann (WSCFF vice president), Jim Branstrom (Everett #46).**

INTERNATIONAL FIRE FIGHTER, MAY 1970

1) …a comprehensive State Labor Relations Act encompassing both the private and public sectors… [with] procedures… administered by a single administrative agency.…
2) …a comprehensive Public Employees Labor Relations Act…
3) …in any event, the legislature should enact the following amendments to… RCW 41.56.

The committee then identified key issues within RCW 41.56 that needed changes: definitions relating to supervisory and management positions, authority to determine appropriate bargaining units, allowance of union security clauses in negotiated contracts that would supercede civil service rules or regulations.

By 1972 the WSCFF was dealing more with internal matters than a cohesive and aggressive legislative plan for action. That year's legislature moved a measure similar to what came out of the WSCFF's Convention on binding arbitration through both houses during its special session. It later died, "largely due to lack of labor support" according to a newspaper account of the day. In April WSCFF President Smith (Tacoma #31) was appointed to the Public Employees' Collective Bargaining Committee by Governor Dan Evans.

At the June 1972 Convention at Ocean Shores there was a changing of the guard within the WSCFF. Smith resigned as president for medical reasons, but not before he led the final charge toward binding arbitration. Governor Evans attended the convention as its featured luncheon speaker. He made it clear he wanted to reach some kind of administrative agreement with the fire fighters. A newspaper article covering the convention summarized Evans' remarks and the WSCFF's response:

> [Evans] called for a "framework for resolution" of contract disputes between fire fighters and their city governments without costly work stoppages or strikes. The fire fighters continued today to mold their own answer to that problem, a resolution calling for an amendment to the state's collective bargaining law for public employees providing "binding arbitration" in such disputes when impasses occur.
> John Smith, WSCFF president, said fire fighters have traditionally refused to strike because of the public interest, but at the same time they feel they should have leverage in dealing with cities.

Karl Hofmann (Everett #46) ran unopposed to replace Smith as WSCFF president. Howard Vietzke (Spokane #29) was elected secretary-treasurer, replacing Bob

Munk (Spokane #29) who retired from office. That fall Walt Lambert retired as the IAFF District 7 vice president and for the first time since the founding of the WSCFF, IAFF District 7 was represented by someone from outside Washington. Jim Martinez, who credited Washington as a model for his efforts in Boise, assumed IAFF representation for Alaska, Idaho, Montana, and Washington. In November 1972, Smith signed a contract with the WSCFF to serve as the WSCFF's "Legislative and Political Director" for a salary of five hundred dollars a month. The terms of his contract do more than emphasize the attempt to formally coordinate the WSCFF's representation in Olympia. They make it clear that Smith would direct what happened in Olympia:

> Any [WSCFF executive] board member wishing to take part in legislative or political work (endorsement of candidates, etc.) will secure the advice of the employee [Smith] and the consent of the president of the board of the Washington State Council of Fire Fighters. Should consent be given, he shall subsequently report to the same employee [Smith].
>
> No board member shall go to Olympia during a legislative session to promote or defeat fire-related legislation without the advice of the employee [Smith] and the consent of the president.

John Willis continued to lobby for Tacoma #31, Smith's own local, during this time, and was not alone in opposing Smith's use of the "strike card." Smith recalls that the 1973 arbitration amendment came to the floor as a governor's request bill, and that he had been working with Governor Evans to make sure it did. Certainly Smith's public statements on the possibility of walkouts made it possible to successfully trade the right to strike for binding arbitration.

Fire fighters worked every angle in Olympia to get binding arbitration, and the force of their cumulative styles and connections swept Olympia. Some came representing individual locals (including Seattle #27, still disaffiliated). Whenever the call went out, carloads of IAFF members came to Olympia. Fire fighters, renowned for delivering both campaign yard signs and votes, now proved themselves to be forceful and effective lobbyists. They won passage of two bills that enormously improved RCW 41.56. One amendment (RCW 41.56.110) required public employers to allow a monthly payroll deduction for a member's union dues. The other enacted binding arbitration.

With the 1973 passage of HB 176 (Mediation and Arbitration Collective Bargaining Rights Act), fire fighters (and other uniformed personnel) traded an explicit prohibition on strikes (RWC 41.56.430) for binding arbitration. This amendment to RCW 41.56 defined uniformed personnel, allowed a union security provision in collective bargaining agreements, and most importantly required mediation, fact-finding, and binding arbitration (including a method for selecting arbitrators) as a means of dispute resolution for such uniformed personnel. Municipal and fire district fire fighters and police were the only public employees covered by these additions, and other public employees have scrambled for years to catch up. The May 1973 *Fire Fighter* was jubilant:

> It was amazing to observe how fearful Mayors and other government officials were of this particular bill. It is hard to convey to you the effort made over the years to kill this type of legislation…

In the fall of 1974 incumbent IAFF District 7 Vice President Martinez beat Willis (Tacoma #31) in a very close election. Tacoma disaffiliated from the WSCFF shortly after Willis lost his election, and remained out until 1976, although Willis continued to work for the WSCFF as its lobbyist until 1982.

Learning to Negotiate 1974-2003

By late 1974, the politics of public employee collective bargaining had shifted. Teachers in the Washington Educational Association (WEA is an association, not a union) had originally preferred to remain separate from other organized public employees, and had considered themselves professionals rather than "labor." By early 1975, the WEA was ready for stronger language on their bargaining rights. State college and university professors and state troopers had bills on the floor in earlier legislative sessions that would have granted them collective bargaining rights, but these were vetoed by Governor John Spellman.

In the meantime, uniformed personnel had learned from experience that L&I lacked knowledgeable expertise as the administrator of their collective bargaining rights under RCW 41.56. Also, in 1973, 41.56 had been amended to "provide unfair labor practice protections and interest arbitration" to uniformed personnel. RCW 53.18 (which covers port employees) was not amended, although there was some overlap in who was affected.

PERC (Public Employment Relations Commission) was created in 1975 to provide "more uniform and impartial... efficient and expert" administration of state collective bargaining laws.

PERC COLLECTION

These various groups of organized public employees lobbied together during the 1975 legislative session. Some sources mention legislation relating specifically to formation of an education commission was passed by the legislature, but then vetoed by Governor Evans, during the regular session. In the legislatures' second "extraordinary" session RCW 41.58 (Public Employment Labor Relations) was passed and then signed by Governor Evans. This created the Public Employment Relations Commission (PERC) and assigned to it the administration of most public employees' collective bargaining rights.

RCW 41.59 (the Education Employment Relations Act), which dealt with certificated school district employees, came under PERC as did RCW 28B.52, covering the academic faculty of community and technical college districts. Both of these had been administered by the superintendent of public instruction. Collective bargaining of uniformed personnel (RCW 41.56) and port employees (RCW 53.18) switched from L&I to PERC, as did some portion of the private sector (RCW 49.08). All of these changes went into effect January 1, 1976. PERC's mandate is:

> ...to provide, in the area of public employment, for the more uniform and impartial (a) adjustment and settlement of complaints, grievances, and disputes arising out of employer-employee relations and, (b) selection and certification of bargaining representatives by transferring jurisdiction of such matters to the public employment relations commission from other boards and commissions.

Once PERC was established, its decisions became the definitive interpretation and application of collective bargaining and binding arbitration law. Incorporated below are some key PERC decisions that affect WSCFF members. Some were appealed to the courts, and are so noted.

City of Spokane v. Spokane Police Guild (1976) upheld the constitutionality of the RCW 41.56 amendment which made binding (interest) arbitration compulsory. Issues addressed included wage increase "demands."

City of Everett v. Fire Fighters Local #350 (1976) ~ This case found that the RCW 41.56 amendment making binding (interest) arbitration compulsory does not violate "home rule" powers of cities.

⬌ *Everett #46* **161**

Municipality of Metropolitan Seattle (METRO) v. Department of Labor and Industries (1977) found that public employee supervisors have bargaining rights under 41.56, and may be included in separate bargaining units.

In 1979 RCW 41.56 was amended. PERC summarizes the effects of these changes. They:

> eliminate redundant fact-finding procedure and streamline... moving contract negotiations' disputes concerning uniformed personnel to interest arbitration, streamlining... procedures for moving contract disputes (uniformed personnel) to interest arbitration.

IAFF Local 1052 v. PERC (1981) was a case where Richland #1052 tried to overturn a PERC decision that removed its battalion chiefs from the bargaining unit. It was a particularly convoluted case because it began while RCW 41.56 was administered by L&I, and then shifted to PERC's purview.

⬌ *Rising From the Ranks* **199**

In 1983 there were more legislative changes made to the laws affecting PERC. Marvin L. Schurke, executive director of PERC since its founding, wrote a summary of the 1983 legislative session in the spring 1983 issue of the WSCFF *Washington Professional Fire Fighter*. These changes came from PERC's agency-requested bill (HB 136, Chapter 58, laws of 1983) and focused mainly on adding a six-month statute of limitations for filing unfair labor practices (ULPs) with PERC. This made PERC's timing parallel to that in the National Labor Relations Act (NLRA). At the time, PERC was facing a huge backlog of cases, due to budget cuts.

In addition, port employees' bargaining rights were amended by HB 434. This modified RCW 53.18 to clarify port employees were covered under RCW 41.56 regarding binding arbitration. It seems it was originally structured to apply only to Port of Seattle employees, who did not work at its airport, although details are sketchy. Senator Vognild, a retired member of Everett #46, reported to the WSCFF that this change came from a WSCFF proposal, but had been significantly amended.

⬌ *Campaigns and Candidates* **126**

In 1985, EMS personnel who were not cross-trained as fire fighters won clarification of their overtime rights under the Fair Labor Standards Act (FLSA) with the US Supreme Court decision *Garcia v. San Antonio*. Fire fighters are partially exempt from overtime requirements, as are EMTs who are also fire fighters. This decision made it more efficient and cheaper to use cross-trained fire fighters in the growing number of EMS positions.

⬌ *EMS* **69**

Port of Bellingham (circa 1986-1987) was a huge battle for the WSCFF, although documentation remains somewhat convoluted and patchy. This case involved the

interrelated definitions of who was covered under LEOFF, as part of the determination on who was defined as a uniformed employee for purposes of collective bargaining. Port districts really fought this, according to Howard Vietzke (Spokane #29), WSCFF's lobbyist at the time. Vietzke remembers the ports were not against having their employees covered by LEOFF (RCW 41.26), but they did staunchly oppose collective bargaining rights (RCW 41.56). The legal catch came from two other bits of legislation, RCW 14.08.010, which defined port employees of airports, while RCW 53 is less clear. By 1990 Bellingham Airport #3266 was formed, and its members were covered by RCW 41.56.

PERC preliminary ruling in Bellevue #1604 (1987) found that it is a ULP to insist that language which excludes payment of legal fees be included in a contract. In combination with *IAFF Local #46 v. City of Everett* a plan for negotiation on this matter is laid out. That is, if management and a local are getting along well through a year or two of negotiations living with their contract, then a local could agree to take such language out of its contract.

⬅ *EMS* 69

The 1988 legislature amended RCW 41.56, granting binding arbitration to paramedics who were public employees, **unless** they worked for public hospital districts. (Those working for "public employers" were later included, in a 1993 amendment to RCW 41.56).

City of Bellevue v. IAFF #1604 and PERC (1988) considered whether it is a ULP when a city violates "good faith bargaining" in interest arbitration. The City of Bellevue wanted information Bellevue #1604 had requested in arbitration excluded from binding arbitration. PERC found in favor of Bellevue #1604, determined that PERC had proper jurisdiction, and ordered the city to return to bargaining with the local, and to provide it certain information, as requested.

IAFF Local #1052 v. PERC and the City of Richland (1989) determined employers must bargain about staffing proposals that affect safety and workload.

City of Yakima v. IAFF Local #469, PERC and the Yakima Police Patrolmen's Association; City of Yakima v. IAFF Local #469; City of Yakima v. PERC (December 1989–November 1991) ~ Jim Webster, a Seattle-based labor lawyer, represented Yakima #469, and remembers the WSCFF sponsored and/or joined in on this case. An article in the December 1989 *Washington Professional Fire Fighter* summarized the case at the time:

Whether [the] City [of Yakima] was required to collectively bargain with [its] police officers and fire fighters on matters the city had delegated to its civil service commission...

The City of Yakima filed suit against Yakima #469 for filing a ULP because the city refused to negotiate several changes to Yakima's civil service law that had impacts to the local. The city claimed PERC has no jurisdiction to hear ULPs regarding civil service rules because these are exempt from RCW 41.56. Fourth District Congressman Sid Morrison wrote in, offering his opinion that RCW 41.56 limited negotiation on issues commonly provided by a civil service board (as per RCW 41.06 State Civil Service Law). (The limitations cited actually refer to the State Personnel Board, which has far greater authority than any city's civil service board.) The Supreme Court agreed with Yakima #469 that collective bargaining agreements take precedence over municipal civil service law.

IAFF #1445 v. City of Kelso and PERC (1990) ~ Originally Kelso #1445 charged the City of Kelso had made retaliatory layoffs during its annexation into a fire district. PERC found in the local's favor. Both Kelso #1445 and the city then cross-appealed. The court found the city's refusal to submit to interest arbitration on effects of annexation was not a ULP: "refusal to participate in interest arbitration is not an unfair labor practice [ULP]."

⬌ *Merging Fire Departments* **114**

In 1993, HB 1081 modified RCW 41.56 to provide binding arbitration for law enforcement and fire dispatchers, public hospital district paramedics, and "airport fire fighters employed by the Port of Seattle."

Jim Webster noted that there was a general reduction in the number of collective bargaining cases after 1992, "because the system of comparables actually works." From 1982 through 1992 he represented three to five arbitration cases per year, whereas after 1992 these dropped to less than one a year.

In 1993, passage of HB 1081 (amending RCW 41.56.30) granted collective bargaining rights to law enforcement and fire department dispatchers, and public hospital paramedics.

STANDING, L-R: **Michael McGovern (#1488, WSCFF pres), Jimmy Cason (#31, WSCFF s/t), Howard Vietzke (#29, WSCFF legislative director), Rep. Mike Heavy (chair House Commerce and Labor Committee), Mike Patrick (WSCPO executive director).** SEATED: **Governor Mike Lowry.**

WSCFF COLLECTION

Centralia #451 v. City of Centralia (1995) ~ The union alleged that the City of Centralia had violated RCW 41.56.140(4), by unilaterally changing its crew size and equipment staffing without giving notice or providing an opportunity for collective bargaining. Centralia #451 raised its concerns with employee safety; the city argued it had the right to establish staffing levels. PERC found that some aspects of staffing did fall within the scope of "personnel matters" that are mandatory subjects of bargaining, but that the city, in "failing or refusing to bargain in response to the union's undifferentiated demand for bargaining on its staffing decision," did not violate RCW 41.56.

Pasco Police Officers' Association v. City of Pasco (1997) ~ The WSCFF filed an amicus curiae brief on this case, in which PERC found a management rights proposal was a mandatory subject of arbitration. This meant the proposal had to be submitted to interest arbitration at impasse. Judge Talmadge's minority opinion was that this case made it clear the "scope of management clauses" was overdue for clarification by PERC.

Seattle Local #27 v. City of Seattle (1998) ~ In this case it was found that a city cannot create a supplementary retirement benefit to LEOFF 2, and that such benefits are not "mandatory" issues in bargaining. The decision prohibited Seattle #27 from making similar proposals in future negotiations.

IAFF Local #46 v. City of Everett (2002) ~ Two individuals were suspended for alleged misconduct. Arbitration ruled there was no just cause, and required back payment of wages. Everett #46 had spent between $25,000-$28,000 to carry its members' case through grievance arbitration, and the contract didn't cover court costs. Everett #46 argued that since the cost of its legal defense would have been covered under collective bargaining, and since arbitration was to be encouraged, not avoided (on the basis of this financial exposure), their costs should be covered. The Association of Washington Cities (AWC) filed an amicus brief in support of the city's position.

  The State Supreme Court, by one vote, agreed with Everett #46 that if "the contract doesn't explicitly waive lawyer fees, and wages are collected" through grievance arbitration (not interest arbitration), then the collection of attorney fees is allowed.

MERGING FIRE DEPARTMENTS: KELSO #1445 AND COWLITZ FIRE DISTRICT 2

Early in 1985, the Kelso's municipal fire department was in poor shape. Kelso #1445 had an active contract with the city, but "longevity and pay rates were so high they [the city] didn't have the money to pay," remembers Dan Baxter (Cowlitz #3828), who was in the department at the time. In addition the EMTs within the department were going to recertify, but as part of a regional crackdown on EMS testing for recertification, they were all decertified. General practices within the department were also terrible, with one officer on sick leave while working another job, and virtually no inspection program in place because of staffing issues.

 EMS 69

The city of Kelso then approached Cowlitz Fire District 2, a mostly volunteer department, about contracting out its fire service, including future hiring. Kelso #1445 got a court injunction to block such contracting, at which point the fire district decided to take the matter to the voters. The voters supported annexing Kelso into Cowlitz Fire District 2. This created openings for professional fire fighters within the fire district but also eliminated all jobs within the Kelso fire department. Kelso #1445 members then negotiated with the fire district on the details of testing for the new hires.

In the meantime, the WSCFF learned from the debacle unfolding, and worked to gain the 1986 passage of HB 1388 (RCW 35.10.370 Job Security for Fire Fighters Annexed To/From Fire Districts and Cities). This provided fire fighters with some job security when cities and/or fire districts merge.

By sometime in 1987, some members of Kelso #1445 had transferred into Cowlitz Fire District 2, and then made the shift from volunteers back to professional fire fighters. Others were hired into the Longview Fire Department, and became members of Longview #828. Kelso #1445 charged the city of Kelso had made retaliatory layoffs during its annexation into a fire district, and took the case before the state's Public Employment Relations Commission (*IAFF #1445 v. City of Kelso and PERC*, 1990).

Cowlitz Fire District 2 first affiliated as a Teamsters local, in about 1992. Some six years later they disaffiliated from the Teamsters, amid talk of merging with the Longview Department. According to one source, Jim Hill, IAFF District 7 vice president at the time, "picked them up the next day." On February 15, 1998, Cowlitz #3828 affiliated with the IAFF, and joined the WSCFF about a month later.

The WSCFF lobbied for passage of HB 1388 in 1986 after union fire fighters lost their jobs as a result of Cowlitz County Fire District 2 annexing the City of Kelso. L-R: *Jimmy Cason (#31, WSCFF vp), Howard Vietzke (#29, WSCFF legislative representative), Ron Morehouse (WSCFF s/t), Rep. Art Wang, Michael McGovern (#1488, WSCFF president), Jim Hill (#31, IAFF District 7 vp).* SEATED: *Governor Booth Gardner.*

WSCFF COLLECTION

SELF-CONTAINED BREATHING APPARATUS (SCBA)

SCBA designs have evolved. World War II created a surplus of military-issued equipment, which many departments bought. It wasn't until worker safety standards began requiring use of SCBA that such equipment became a standard and usual part of responding to a fire. Many fire fighters who worked prior to the 1960s tell accounts of SCBA gear being considered too expensive to train with, and that the tradition was that "real" fire fighters didn't use SCBA. In addition, many departments screened potential fire fighters by putting them in a "smoke box" without SCBA, to see how long they could maintain without oxygen, and without being able to see where they were. Two early types of SCBA are illustrated here and on page 116: the cannister style and the oxygen style.

CANNISTER STYLE SCBA

Spokane's Fire Department, like many, issued every fire fighter a manual on all aspects of fire fighter protocol. In Spokane this manual was called "the brown book" and described one SCBA as follows: "All types of poisonous gases are removed or eliminated... as air passing through the canister... by combination with the caustic... by absorption pregnated charcoal... [and] by oxidation through catalytic effect of hopcalcite."

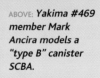

ABOVE: *Yakima #469 member Mark Ancira models a "type B" canister SCBA.*

YAKIMA FIRE DEPARTMENT COLLECTION

ABOVE: *Members of Tacoma's Engine Co. 6 line up in front of their truck. Two are wearing "Chem-Ox" apparatus.* L-R: *Bud Baron, unknown, unknown, Stan Gorsky. Navy surplus, these SCBA required the operator to give a pull on the bottom lever and then start breathing through it, since it took some time for the passing gas to initiate the chemical reaction. Inexperienced fire fighters occasionally passed out because they went in to a situation before they were receiving oxygen.*

RALPH DECKER COLLECTION

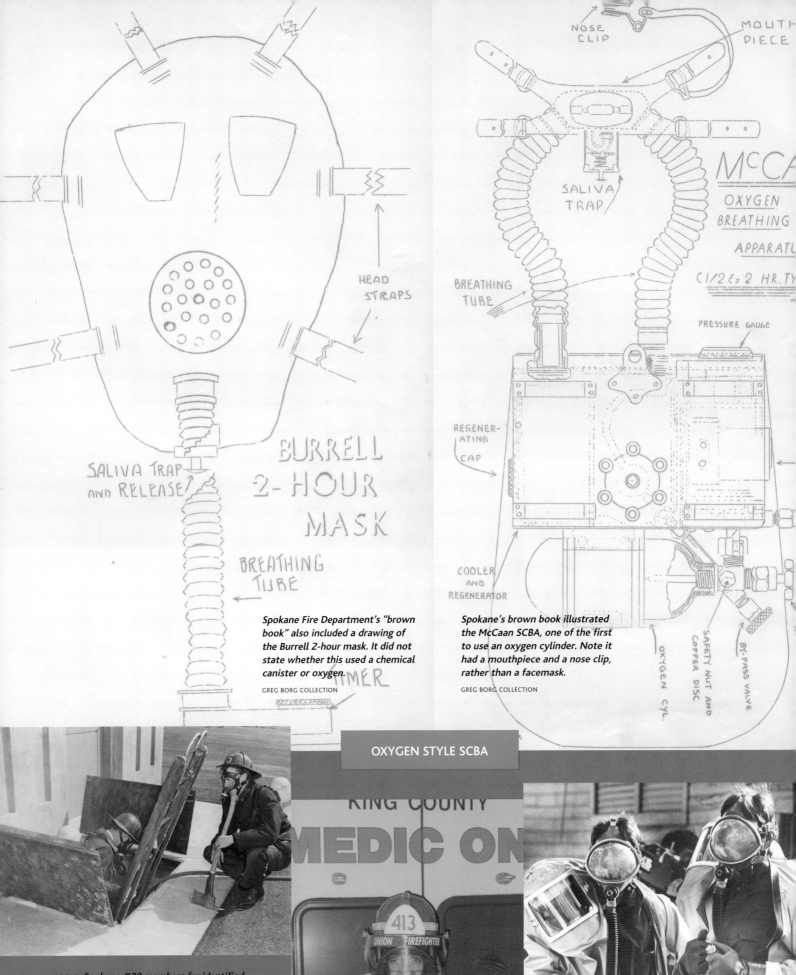

HEAD
STRAPS

SALIVA TRAP
AND RELEASE

BURRELL
2-HOUR
MASK

BREATHING
TUBE

TIMER

NOSE
CLIP

MOUTH
PIECE

SALIVA
TRAP

BREATHING
TUBE

REGENER-
ATING
CAP

COOLER
AND
REGENERATOR

McCA

OXYGEN
BREATHING

APPARATU

C 1/2 & 2 HR. TY

PRESSURE GAUGE

OXYGEN CYL.

SAFETY NUT AND
COPPER DISC

BY-PASS VALVE

Spokane Fire Department's "brown book" also included a drawing of the Burrell 2-hour mask. It did not state whether this used a chemical canister or oxygen.

GREG BORG COLLECTION

Spokane's brown book illustrated the McCaan SCBA, one of the first to use an oxygen cylinder. Note it had a mouthpiece and a nose clip, rather than a facemask.

GREG BORG COLLECTION

OXYGEN STYLE SCBA

ABOVE *Spokane #29 members (unidentified, circa 1951) wear some of the first SCBA that used air tanks.*

SPOKANE FIRE STATION MUSEUM COLLECTION

AT RIGHT *An unknown union fire fighter models current SCBA.*

WSCFF COLLECTION

ABOVE *Unidentified Seattle #27 fire fighters in breathing apparatus circa 1989.*

SEATTLE FIRE DEPARTMENT, CENTENNIAL YEARBOOK 1989

On Strike:
Fire Fighters Walk the Line

The possibility of fire fighters striking has a moral rub: withholding systematic fire protection threatens the safety of a community. The ethical lapse of a community which fails to provide wages, working conditions, and benefits in keeping with the risks of the fire service and in relation to those within private industry is rarely considered.

When the IAFF held its charter convention in February 1918, Section 2, Article 11 of the adopted constitution read:

> It shall be deemed inadvisable to strike, or take active part in strikes as our position is peculiar to most organized workers, as we are formed to protect the lives and property of communities in case of fire or other serious hazards.

This replaced an earlier resolution that proposed an IAFF local would need to consult with the president of the IAFF before calling a strike. Mr. Wedekind, a member of what would become Seattle #27, made the case that since the IAFF had no strike benefits, locals should make their own decisions. At least nine IAFF locals struck, walked out, and/or resigned en masse that year. Four resulted in union gains, sometimes as a result of decisions issued by the US War Labor Board: Newport (Kentucky) #45, Cleveland #93, Pittsburgh #1, and Montreal #125. Four other IAFF locals were not so lucky. All members of Oak Park (Illinois) #95, Jacksonville, Colorado Springs #5, and Cincinnati #48 were fired, sometimes simply for being union members.

The Seattle General Strike of February 1919 demonstrated general support for union workers. That August the IAFF held its convention in Portland, Oregon, overlapping the Boston police strike. When Boston was then looted, legislative, if not public, sentiment turned against the police. Congress prohibited Washington D.C. fire fighters from affiliating with the IAFF, and many local jurisdictions followed suit. In November 1919 Yakima #217 members threatened a walkout, and were summarily replaced with nonunion workers.

Before the WSCFF **21**

Yakima #217 **130**

The IAFF constitution was amended at the 1920 Convention, and "forbid locals to issue an 'ultimatum' to city officials or take 'decisive action' until the IAFF executive committee responded to any request to take strike action," according to Jack Stieber's *Public Employee Unionism, Structure, Growth, Policy*. In 1930 IAFF Convention delegates unanimously amended the constitution to explicitly prohibit strikes.

In 1932 the Norris-LaGuardia Act passed, making it illegal for a federal court to prohibit general union activities, picketing, or strikes; it also prohibited employers from suing employees for violating yellow dog contracts. The next year saw passage of the National Industrial Recovery Act (NIRA) as part of Roosevelt's New Deal legislation. This triggered numerous strikes nationally (1,856 work stoppages in 1934),

In 1968, the union [Auburn #1352] voted to go on strike because the City of Auburn would not bargain in good faith, they just went through the motions. They offered a five dollar a month raise and we said B.S.... they would not give a written agreement, because of mass PR about the fire department possibly going on strike....

The City had threatened to replace the paid fire fighters with volunteers if they actually struck. Well, many of those volunteers were also union members. So we went to the Machinists, the Teamsters, and everyone else and they told their members to honor any picket line around the fire station or else. So the City's threat was neutralized since there would be almost no volunteers available....

The City of Auburn finally decided to take their chances in arbitration. They lost! We got the 'first' written contract with the pay raise we wanted.

⬅➡ *Collectively Bargaining* **99**

⬅➡ *One Vote Matters* **33**

including the Great Maritime Strike of 1934, which affected many West Coast ports. Work stoppages in turn led to the Wagner Act (or the National Labor Relations Act, NLRA) of 1935, which applied only to workers in industries engaged in interstate commerce, not to public employees.

Tacoma lumberyard workers went on strike in 1935. The national guard was brought in and patrolled the city with bayonets, although eventually a federally mediated decision supported the striking workers. A year later the IAFF demonstrated it meant business with its no-strike language when Vancouver, B.C. #18 voted to strike. Although the local never went out, the IAFF revoked its charter. During this same year the United Auto Workers (UAW) used sit-down strikes to gain union recognition, as did Seattle members of the Newspaper Guild who struck William Hearst's *Seattle Post Intelligencer*.

In 1939 the WSCFF was formed. Its first constitution included a no-strike provision parallel to the IAFF's:

> We shall not strike or take active part in any sympathetic strikes as our position is peculiar to most organized workers, as we are formed to protect the lives and property of communities in case of fire or other serious hazards.

Executive Order 9017 (1942) established the National War Labor Board as a replacement for the National Defense Mediation Board, and banned strikes and lock-outs, with provisions for the "peaceful adjustment" of labor disputes. This was further bolstered by the Taft-Hartley Act of 1947, which provided for federal intervention in "national emergency strikes," allowed state passage of right-to-work laws, and prohibited secondary boycotts and closed shops.

In 1950, the WSCFF reaffirmed its constitutional prohibition on strikes. At the 1952 IAFF Convention in Seattle, representatives of Illinois' state association brought forward a resolution that would allow a local to strike after "all other means of reaching agreement have been exhausted," but required the permission of the IAFF district vice president and the IAFF executive board. According to George J. Richardson's *Symbol of Action*, an unnamed Seattle delegate supported the resolution, stating:

> ... the fire fighter is gradually losing ground. We must use every possible resource to bring back some of the things we are losing.

By the end of the IAFF Convention, Resolution 59 had been adopted, stating that "rather than affirm the right to strike" it sought implementation of impasse procedures, including compulsory arbitration. That September the AFL Convention passed a similar resolution.

By 1955, the WSCFF was lobbying the state legislature for binding arbitration, and it continued this effort for the next ten years, while the WSCFF and the IAFF's constitutional prohibitions on strikes remained. In 1959, the *Spokane Chronicle* quoted Spokane #29 member Howard Vietzke:

> When we fire fighters of Washington hear of strikes in other states by public employee groups, we are thankful that the health and safety of the citizens of Washington are not put in jeopardy because of labor management disputes.

The Landrum-Griffin Act passed in 1959, further restricting strikes, picketing, and boycotts. In 1963 John Smith (Tacoma #31) was narrowly elected president of the

WSCFF. Smith made no secret of his tactics. He wanted collective bargaining and binding arbitration, and he wasn't categorically opposed to potential work stoppages.

The IAFF reaffirmed its no-strike position at its 1964 Convention, in a vote Stieber describes as "almost unanimous." But in 1966 at least three IAFF locals went out on strike: Atlanta #134, Kansas City (Missouri) #42, and St. Louis. At the 1966 IAFF Convention a special (non-IAFF member) commission was appointed to review the IAFF's strike prohibition. WSCFF President Smith testified before the commission in Cincinnati, in 1967. During this same period Smith led the WSCFF to gain legislative passage of collective bargaining (RCW 41.56 Public Employees' Collective Bargaining Act), and used threats of work stoppage to do so.

⟷ *Collectively Bargaining* **99**

At the 1968 IAFF Convention, delegates, in what Richardson calls "a complete defeat of Executive Board's recommendation… deleted in its entirety" the no-strike provision with passage of Resolution 67-18. That same year Auburn #1352 voted to strike, although they did not actually go out. The IAFF executive board created another study commission during 1969, although little documentation of its 1970 report is available.

⟷ *Auburn #1352 Calls for a Vote* **118**

IAFF Secretary-Treasurer Albert Albertoni (Oakland #55) reported at the 1970 IAFF Convention that in the two years since the IAFF had removed its strike prohibition:

> The militancy of our membership, and the adoption of Resolution 67-18 have resulted in approximately 100 strike situations [between 1968 and 1970]. By "strike situations" I mean anything from the threat of work stoppage up to and including slow-downs, mass sickness, and actual work stoppages. etc.

This "militancy" put financial strains upon the IAFF, leading Albertoni to propose a ten percent increase in the per capita fees to fund a Defense and Emergency Fund. (It is not clear whether this increase passed.) Eleven IAFF locals went out on strike in 1970. When Sacramento #522 walked, Governor Ronald Reagan ordered replacement fire fighters and equipment from the California State Division of Forestry. The December 1970 issue of the IAFF *International Fire Fighter* reported a superior court judge had ruled "California public employees have no right to strike, nor do they have collective bargaining rights." IAFF President McClennan was quoted, "Our hopes are that the ruling will not stand up in the higher courts." The final disposition of this case is not clear.

The WSCFF and its members increased their political pressure despite this ruling. Although many within the state's fire service opposed using "the strike card" to bargain for binding arbitration, Smith made sure the card stayed on the table while he was president and then as WSCFF lobbyist. In 1973 RCW 41.56 was amended (Mediation and Arbitration Collective Bargaining Rights Act) to mandate mediation, fact-finding, and arbitration in contract disputes, and explicitly prohibited strikes.

⟷ *Collectively Bargaining* **99**

IAFF locals in other states were not so fortunate. In 1973 over 10,000 IAFF members went out on strike, including New York City #94. The October 1975 issue of the IAFF *International Fire Fighter* included an article, "Strikes Involving 2,399 Members Outline Need for Federal Labor Relations Statute." At that time Pine Bluff (Arkansas) #358, San Francisco #798, Berkeley #1227, Findlay (Ohio) #381, Tucson #479, and Kansas City (Missouri) #42 were all out on strike. In response, the IAFF sought federal legislation for public employees that offered the "same kind of protection as the Wagner Act provides for unions in industry." This hasn't happened, to date, at the federal level.

BADGES AND BUTTONS

The badges that are part of a fire fighter's dress uniform are as ornate as jewelry, and usually signify rank, company, and department. The silver or gold uniform buttons are usually standard to a department.

Tradition decrees lieutenants badges have one bugle, with one bar on the collar to match. Captains' badges usually have two bugles, those of a battalion chief have three, assistant chief four, and the department chief's badge bears five.

BELOW: *Spokane Station 11's ledger (1921-1927) contained this handwritten, unsigned "Proposed State Uniform Bill" which would have required "any Company City Corporation Hospital or Individual in this state of Washington" which required badges or uniforms to pay for them. Ma departments provided certain limited clothing and/or uniform allowances into the late 1980s.*
GREG BORG COLLECTION

TOP TO BOTTOM, AT LEFT:

Cadet badge, Tacoma. Issued to those in the department's recruitment school in the late 1970s.
RALPH DECKER COLLECTION

Fireman's badge, Richland Department.
GREG BORG COLLECTION

Engine lieutenant badge, Tacoma, with one bugle.
RALPH DECKER COLLECTION

Captain's badge, Spokane. The City of Spokane had "Junior Captains" until the 1940s, when lieutenants were added. At the time, lieutenants were on trucks, while captains commanded stations. Lieutenant's badges have two bugles, side by side, Captain's badges have two crossed bugles.
GREG BORG COLLECTION

Truck captain's badge, Tacoma, with two uncrossed hatchets.
RALPH DECKER COLLECTION

Engine captain's badge, Tacoma, with two uncrossed bugles.
RALPH DECKER COLLECTION

Chief's badge, Spokane, gold with five bugles.
SPOKANE FIRE STATION MUSEUM COLLECTION

A hand clasping bolts of electricity represents the Fire Alarm Division of the Tacoma Department.
RALPH DECKER COLLECTION

The oldest known Seattle badge in existence, circa 1930s, was handcrafted by Joseph Mayer Company in sterling silver with bugles and a wreath of gold. Crest reads "Senior Fire A.V. Arm Operator."
SPOKANE FIRE STATION MUSEUM COLLECTION

Issued by the City of Spokar it reads "Fire Department, Spokane Special Police." It may have been issued durin World War II, when fire departments incorporated non-career and, in some cas volunteer fire fighters, or it may have been issued to ide tify early fire prevention or investigation personnel.
SPOKANE FIRE STATION MUSEUM COLLECTION

A sterling button, Tacoma.
RALPH DECKER COLLECTION

Politics Costs Money

GEORGE ROOP COLLECTION

The Labor-Management Reporting and Disclosure Act of 1959, also known as the Landrum-Griffin Act, amended the Taft-Hartley Act, placing controls on internal union practices, and included a "bill of rights" for union members, which requires unions to file annual reports, while further restricting strikes, picketing, and boycotts.

Lobbying is the art of political persuasion made manifest. In Washington State lobbying activities by individuals and organizations are defined and legislated under RCW 42.17 (Disclosure—Campaign Finances—Lobbying—Records). The WSCFF has focused on changing legislation to improve working conditions, pensions, and benefits since its inception in 1939. Individual members' and IAFF locals' lobbying activities have always played a critical role in this. The rules of political action and campaign contributions have changed considerably during the past seven decades, and so have the appointed positions and funding methods within the WSCFF.

COPEs, Committees on Political Education, are essentially one way an organization can meet to decide upon political endorsements. COPEs were formed shortly after the AFL and the CIO merged in 1955, and combined the CIO's Political Action Committees with the AFL's Labor's League for Political Education.

Individual members of IAFF locals have contributed directly to state and regional labor council COPE committees.

RICHARD WARBROUCK COLLECTION

The WSCFF and its locals have participated in the Washington State Labor Council's COPE, and individual locals have participated in their county and regional AFL Labor Council COPEs. At its 2002 Convention, WSCFF delegates passed a resolution to consider creating a COPE. A year later, the WSCFF COPE was created with passage of Resolution 03-13. The COPE will allow the WSCFF to prepare a slate of statewide and congressional endorsements to be presented at each year's convention, for delegate consideration.

Political Action Committees (PACs) originated in the 1940s, but gained significance beginning in the mid-1970s. They raise and distribute voluntary campaign contributions to candidates. PACs are legislated within Washington State by the Public Disclosure Commission (PDC), and at the national level by the Federal Elections Commission (FEC).

The IAFF gives 1974 as the year FIREPAC was created. At the time, there were about six hundred federal PACs, with donations to congressional campaigns totaling approximately twelve million dollars. Michael McGovern (Lakewood #1488, WSCFF President 1982-1996) doesn't remember having heard of FIREPAC until about 1987, at which time he and others began contributing. By 1996, there were more than 4,000 federal PACs, and their congressional contributions totaled more than $193 million. Members of the WSCFF have increased their contributions over the years, as is indicated by their ranking within FIREPAC.

In late 1982 the WSCFF established the WSCFF Voluntary Political Action Fund (V-PAF) to make contributions to candidates for federal office. Its goal was one dollar per month per member. During this period WSCFF district representatives were responsible for reporting on PAC funding.

Ten years later, in 1992, the passage of Initiative 134 placed additional restrictions on state campaign contributions. Although contributions by labor organizations were a target of this initiative, the changes that came from I-134 did not affect the WSCFF's ability to work effectively in Olympia, as it represented its members' interests.

Early in 2003, a Tacoma Appeals Court ruled the Washington State PDC cannot allow different locals of the same union to contribute to one candidate's campaign, even if the parent union makes no contributions to this candidate. As this book goes to press, the State Attorney General's Office has filed an appeal. Until it is decided, the rules prior to the Tacoma Appeals Court decision remain in effect.

FIREPAC CONTRIBUTIONS 2002

WSCFF member locals that gave over 1000% of their Century Club Targets, as defined by the IAFF:

LOCAL	NAME	AMOUNT RAISED	% TARGET
#3674	Clark County	$ 3,078.00	9,327.27
#3524	Medic Seven Paramedic Association	3,141.00	6,543.75
#2868	Washougal	775.44	3,692.57
#1052	Richland	4,154.39	2,612.82
#726	Puyallup	3,474.32	1,631.14
#2878	Eastside Fire & Rescue	5,331.58	1,336.24
#1862	Montesano	200.00	1,333.33
#1488	Lakewood Professional Fire Fighters	4,021.49	1,288.94
#437	Bremerton	1,900.00	1,266.67
#3711	Spokane County Fire District 8	425.00	1,089.74
#2105	University Place	954.00	1,025.81

FIREPAC was created by the IAFF in 1974, as a Political Action Committee (PAC), and was one of only about six hundred at that time. As a PAC it raises and distributes campaign contributions to political candidates. The above WSCFF locals raised over 1000% of the targets established by the IAFF. (Targets are determined by membership size and previous participation in FIREPAC.)

The WSCFF ranked third in total FIREPAC contributions, and fifth in percentage of Century Club Targets, as defined by the IAFF:

NAME OF STATE ASSOCIATION	# MEMBERS	AMOUNT	% TARGET
TOP BY DOLLARS CONTRIBUTED			
Associated Fire Fighters of Illinois	11,788	$ 89,008.59	251.6927
California Professional Fire Fighters	28,281	76,325.94	89.96139
Washington State Council of Fire Fighters	**6,770**	**73,441.60**	**361.6032**
Professional Fire Fighters of Oklahoma	3,954	64,983.00	547.825
TOP BY PERCENT OF FIREPAC TARGET			
Professional Fire Fighters Assn. of New Jersey	3,128	62,395.88	664.9177
Arkansas Professional Fire Fighters	1,304	24,767.17	633.1076
Professional Fire Fighters of Oklahoma	3,954	64,983.00	547.825
Professional Fire Fighters of Wisconsin	3,682	57,323.16	518.9495
Washington State Council of Fire Fighters	**6,770**	**73,441.60**	**361.6032**
Professional Fire Fighters Assn. of New Jersey	3,128	62,395.88	664.9177

Lobbying and Lambaste

Dan Downs, WSCFF District 2 representative, went to Washington D.C. as part of the IAFF's legislative lobbying at the federal level.

WASHINGTON PROFESSIONAL FIRE FIGHTER, MAY 1988

"[Publicly employed fire fighters] are 'political animals,' in reality, creatures of the legislative system. Their pension rights, civil service protection, and their right to bargain for hours, wages, and conditions are all given and controlled through the State Legislature. Even the very existence of their jobs in a fire department and the existence of the fire department itself is provided for by legislation at some level such as county, city, district, etc...."

Dan Downs (Richland #1052)
Washington Professional Fire Fighter, **summer 1982**

WINING AND DINING

In 1956, shortly after he was hired, Howard Vietzke (Spokane #29) remembers working his turn as cook at Station 3. Jack Waller, who would be elected IAFF District 7 vice president later that fall, told Vietzke to "set an extra plate, for a guest." Vietzke asked who the guest might be. Waller told him, "the governor." Vietzke thought Waller was telling him to quit asking so many questions, and got on with his cooking. About lunchtime a State Patrol escort pulled up to Station 3 and Governor Albert Rosellini emerged from his car. Everyone working at the station, and the governor, ate lunch together.

Interestingly, George Roop (Spokane Fire District 1 #876) has similar memories of Rosellini coming by his station, and was surprised to hear Rosellini was stopping in the city of Spokane as well. Clearly Governor Rosellini also knew how to lobby.

NECESSARY EQUIPMENT

A special kind of briefcase was used by WSCFF lobbyists in legislatures past. Exactly how many fifths of liquor could be placed inside has become legend, but more than a few WSCFF representatives new to Olympia were introduced to legislators and

WSCFF activists take a break, circa 1955.

L-R: **Earl Brower (IAFF Dist 7 vp, Felix Arena (WSCFF treasurer, #27), honorary IAFF Professional Fire Fighter in leopard skin, Jack Waller (WSCFF secretary, #29), Ray Greenleaf (#31).**

other lobbyists by the WSCFF's more elder statesmen while presenting the briefcase. There were also plenty of errands for newcomers involving the transfer of cases of Bohemian beer to certain car trunks. Whether this brand of beer had anything to do with Jack Waller's (Spokane #29) years of employment at the Bohemian Brewery is unknown.

PUBLIC STATEMENTS

↔ *Collectively Bargaining* 99

In 1966, the WSCFF's President Smith prepared for the 1967 session in Olympia, laying the groundwork for the WSCFF's victory, passage of binding arbitration rights. He began by going to every newspaper that would listen. Within each of his proclamations he let it be known the WSCFF was establishing a strike fund. What he made sure he never mentioned was how little was actually in the fund:

> We didn't have anything resembling a real strike fund. And I never threatened with a strike. I talked about walkouts, because I wanted to make it clear we were ready.

↔ *On Strike* 117

His posturing served fire fighters well, although these public comments alienated many within the WSCFF and the professional fire service who believed striking was neither legal nor ethical.

MORE WINING AND DINING

One legislator who shall remain unnamed "wouldn't vote for fire fighters, no matter what." In his gentlemanly but unremitting way, George Roop (Spokane Fire District 1 #876) continued to approach this legislator on each piece of proposed legislation. Roop can no longer remember whether one particular evening's socializing took place at an Olympia bar or at a private location. He does remember there was a fair bit of drinking, and that this legislator was extremely drunk.

Roop got the legislator out of the party, and delivered him home "so he wouldn't get picked up by the police." Ever after, this legislator told Roop, "Just tell me the damn bill numbers. I don't want to hear about them. But I will vote for them."

STILL MORE WINING AND DINING

A relatively recent participant in the Olympia scene waxed philosophical, the morning after a long late night of sipping some very special tequila he had provided to a potentially sympathetic supporter. "You know, things haven't changed that much. It's all about people, you gotta make the connections."

STAY IN TOUCH WITH YOUR LEGISLATOR

John Harnett, then vice president of Bremerton #437, did his part to make sure fire fighters got the legislation for binding arbitration passed. During the vote, one key legislator who had promised his support was nowhere to be found. Harnett and other fire fighters went looking, and tracked the unfortunate official to a bathroom stall, where he was standing crouched upon the toilet, hiding. Harnett and others escorted him to the floor so he could cast his critical vote. Harnett loved to tell this story.

POLITICIANS DO THEIR OWN PROMOTION

Part of learning to work in Olympia was to know whom you were dealing with. Senator Karl Herrmann (4th District representative) was a consistent supporter of fire fighters who later became Washington State Insurance Commissioner. This position also made him State Fire Marshall, and as such he issued signs which were required to be posted in public buildings. On each sign, the lettering KARL HERRMANN dominated a much smaller message, NO SMOKING.

STAY IN TOUCH WITH YOUR LEGISLATOR, CONT.

Legislators bluff. Kelly Fox (WSCFF president, Olympia #468) remembers an incident from the early 1990s, during one of his first WSCFF Legislative Conferences. Mike Spring (Walla Walla #404 president) approached Fox and furiously related a conversation he'd had with his legislator, Representative Dick Neher. As Spring discussed issues with Neher, he'd made mention of WSCFF's lobbyist, Howard Vietzke (Spokane #29). Neher then informed Spring, "I never heard of Vietzke." Spring was livid. What had Vietzke been doing in Olympia? Fox pointed out:

> … it would be Nearly (pun intended!) impossible for Representative Neher not to know Vietzke because Neher was on the JCPP [Joint Committee on Pension Policy] and Howard testified at or attended those meetings. Spring was not convinced—why would "his" legislator lie to him? Fearing the worst, I went to Howard and attempted to alert him to the situation.

> Vietzke exploded, and made it clear that from then on Neher would never forget Vietzke.

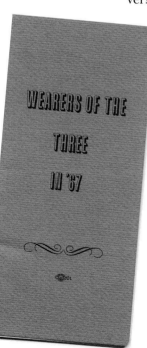

Registered lobbyists in Olympia are known as the "Wearers of the Three" and were listed in this 1967 directory (note union bug).

GEORGE ROOP COLLECTION

Claude Moran, Wa. State Dept. of L&I's Labor Commissioner (Eastern region) sent a thank you note to Yakima #469 in January 1940, for the "very fine box of cigars" he received. He wrote: I would suggest that some long-range planning might be quite well done... to bring the Firemens' program into the foreground."

YAKIMA #469 COLLECTION

CAMPAIGNS AND CANDIDATES

See also *Lobbying and Lambaste* 123, *Politics Costs Money* 121, *I-790* 149, *At the End of the Day* 137, *Seattle #27* 165

The WSCFF has fostered long-term relationships with elected officials since its formation in 1939. In addition to lobbying in Olympia, the WSCFF endorses and helps campaign for candidates and initiatives. It also works to defeat campaigns and candidates.

In 1978, the WSCFF rallied with other state labor interests, backing Larry Vognild (Everett #46). Augie Mardesich was Senate majority leader in Washington State and helped make sure LEOFF 2 passed in 1977, as well as winning parallel changes to PERS. Labor within Washington State, and fire fighters in particular, wanted Mardesich out. Larry Vognild, a recently retired member of Everett #46, took on Mardesich. With incredible support from WSCFF members, other public employee unions, and the Washington State Labor Council (WSLC), Mardesich was defeated.

Locals have been just as active at the municipal level. Seattle #27 attempted a recall of Mayor Uhlman in 1975. Sixty-three thousand signatures were gathered, but the recall failed. In 1981, the City of Bellevue passed an ordinance which banned city employees from "actively participating" in nonpartisan campaigns for city council. Bellevue #1604 took it all the way to the state supreme court, where the ordinance was overturned (*Bellevue Fire Fighters #1604 vs. the City of Bellevue*), in 1984.

More recently, many WSCFF members participated in the WSLC's Labor-Neighbor Program, which uses volunteers from member unions to doorbell other union members, in support of endorsed candidates.

Larry Vognild had served twenty-three years with Everett's Fire Department when he retired (due to disability) and was elected to the State House of Representatives. He served as representative for the next twenty years.

PHOTO BY JIM LEO

This flyer was circulated within the 38th district in 1980, when Vognild was up for his first re-election. It stated "each fireman in this state costs you $2.4 million in addition to his or her regular salary," a reference to estimates made when LEOFF 1 was targeted for reform. It went on to cite other politicians who had been defeated when "firemen from across the state converged on Tacoma," referring to the defeats of Representative Homer Humiston in 1968 and Representative Ned Shera in 1972.

WSCFF COLLECTION

In 1992, George Orr (#876) was elected District 4 representative, and was instrumental in the 1993 passage of HB 1294 (amending RCW 41.26.430). This reduced the LEOFF 2 retirement age (from 58 to 55), indexed vesting, and provided portability with other public retirement systems. In 1993, Orr worked to gain passage of HB 1541 (amending RCW 18.71.205) which created a modular EMT Testing Program.

WSCFF COLLECTION

Currently two IAFF members serve in the Washington House of Representatives:

↔ *Named the WSLC's Legislator of the Year in 1999, Mike Cooper (#1760) is president of his IAFF local and was first elected to the House of Representatives (District 21) in 1996.*

Geoff Simpson (#1747) ↔ became a member of the House of Representatives (District 47) in 2000.

WSCFF COLLECTION

profile:
Howard Vietzke

Howard Vietzke (Spokane #29) best summed up his relationship to the WSCFF as he concluded one of many interview sessions for this book, "Next to my family, it's my life." Vietzke grew up in Spokane, graduated from high school, and went to work in highway construction. At twenty-one, Vietzke was laid off for the winter. Vietzke was playing basketball at a church, and Paul Olsen, who would later become Spokane's fire chief, was there. Olsen told Vietzke he should take the fire fighter's test that would be given the next week, and offered to go over what would be on it with Vietzke. A week later Vietzke had a job through the winter.

Work as a fire fighter paid much less than construction, with a monthly salary of $285 for a seventy-two hour week. Vietzke stuck with it, in part because of the job security and a pension plan. Jack Waller was Station 3 captain, and Vietzke remembers Waller "worked on me to get me involved in the union." Nine years later, Vietzke was involved enough to be targeted by the *Spokesman Review* as one of twelve members of Spokane #29, in an October 1965 cover story that falsely alleged illegal use of union funds.

Vietzke increased his union activity, and went to the 1966 WSCFF Convention as a delegate. The following year Vietzke was promoted to lieutenant, and was elected as Spokane #29's secretary-treasurer, replacing Bob Munk who had been elected secretary-treasurer of the WSCFF in 1965.

By 1971 Vietzke remembers Munk talked about retiring as the WSCFF's secretary-treasurer and "tried to get me interested in running." But Vietzke liked working with Ken Strong, Spokane #29's president, and wasn't convinced. By the time the 1972 Convention rolled around, Vietzke had teamed up with Karl Hofmann (Everett #46), who was already on the WSCFF's executive board. Vietzke was elected secretary-treasurer of the WSCFF, and Hofmann its president. Vietzke remembers the elections were contested, but not who the opponents were.

From summer of 1972 on, Vietzke focused his union efforts on the WSCFF. He served as secretary-treasurer for the next nine years, beginning when Munk handed him two boxes of documents, the entire collection of WSCFF records. At first Vietzke operated out of his house; later he shifted to the captain's room of Station 15, where he added a mimeograph machine and a typewriter, and could enlist his coworkers to help when it came time to collate and prepare mailings. By 1974 the WSCFF had its first office, located across from the Ridpath Hotel.

Michael McGovern (#1488, WSCFF president), Howard Vietzke (#29, WSCFF legislative representative), and Ron Morehouse (#106, WSCFF s/t) fishing, circa 1984-1985.
HOWARD VIETZKE COLLECTION

⬌ *Malicious Media*
181

Signing on the purchase of the WSCFF condo in Olympia in December 1978. STANDING, L-R: *Jim Hill (#31, WSCFF vp), Walt Lambert (#29, IAFF legislative researcher), Frank Spicklemire (#468, WSCFF District 5 representative).* SEATED: *Doug McNall (#46, WSCFF president), Howard Vietzke (#29, WSCFF s/t).*
WSCFF COLLECTION

The 1990 signing of RCW 28B.15.380, which provides tuition waivers for dependents of fire fighters killed or totally disabled in the line of duty.
STANDING, L-R: **Howard Vietzke (WSCFF leg rep, #29), Michael McGovern, (WSCFF pres, #1488), Sen. Marilyn Rasmussen, Rep. Harriet Spanel, Rep. Sally Walker, Jim Cason, (WSCFF s/t, #31).**
SEATED: **Gov. Booth Gardner.**

WCSFF COLLECTION

↔ *At the End of the Day*
137

Senate Resolution 1996-8707 recognizing Howard Vietzke's "decades of service" to Washington State's fire fighters.

WSCFF COLLECTION

Vietzke became more involved in legislative lobbying during this time. The WSCFF's lobbyist, John Willis (Tacoma #31), was working out of a room in the Governor's House Hotel, and Vietzke can remember draft legislation spread on every spare surface, with little room left for Willis's residential needs. Vietzke lobbied within the WSCFF and in December 1978 income generated from the WSCFF's magazine was used to purchase a condo in Olympia which then served as the WSCFF's lobbying headquarters.

Vietzke announced his retirement as secretary-treasurer of the WSCFF in 1981. When Willis stepped down as lobbyist later that summer, President Denny Parlari (Puyallup #726) drove out to where Vietzke was fishing to offer him the job of lobbyist. Vietzke accepted. His first session in Olympia he worked under the paid tutelage of Mike Ryherd, who was also lobbying for the Teamsters, the Fred Hutchinson Cancer Research Center, and the American Federation of Teachers (AFT). Al Brisbois (of the AFT and later secretary-treasurer of the Washington State Labor Council) was also a mentor to Vietzke.

At the 1982 Convention, Michael McGovern won a three-way election to become president of the WSCFF. He immediately dismissed Ryherd, and Vietzke was on his own. Vietzke remembers the "pace picked up after Mike was in charge."

Vietzke served as the WSCFF's chief lobbyist under three governors, John Spellman, Booth Gardner, and Mike Lowry. During his first session, in 1982, Vietzke helped to gain passage of legislation that provided re-employment rights for LEOFF members returning to work following disability leave (RCW 41.26.470). Five years later he led the WSCFF's successful lobbying for RCW 51.32.185 (1987), which defines lung disease as a presumptive occupational disease for fire fighters. He also worked to pass legislation granting collective bargaining rights to port employees and paramedics (in 1984 and 1988 respectively).

Vietzke was part of a bitter 1992 battle in Olympia, and could only reduce the magnitude of cuts in retirement funding. The following year WSCFF lobbying rallied, and the LEOFF 2 retirement age (and service years) were reduced, from fifty-eight to fifty-five.

In fall 1993, Vietzke became the WSCFF's Legislative Director, with Ken Snider (Spokane #29) as assistant lobbyist. The two worked so closely that Snider now calls Vietzke's wife Mickey "Mom." After the death of Seattle fire fighters in the Pang warehouse fire, Vietzke helped gain passage of SB 5322 (RCW 41.26.048 Special death benefit—Death in the Course of Employment) which established a $150,000 payment to a fire fighter's beneficiaries or estate following death due to injuries sustained in the line of duty. Vietzke announced his retirement in 1995. Jimmy Cason (Tacoma #31) and Jim Rudd (Spokane #29) were appointed as replacements for Vietzke and Snider that September. All four lobbyists worked Olympia during the 1996 session, Vietzke's last.

Vietzke helped the WSCFF remain a critical player in Olympia for decades, and to modernize as an organization, dedicating years of service to the mission of the WSCFF: education and legislation. He became secretary-treasurer emeritus of the WSCFF in 1982 (effective June 1981), and was awarded the WSCFF's Walt Lambert Union Leadership Award in 1993.

profile:
Jim Rudd

Jim Rudd working the phones for the WSCFF as its assistant lobbyist.

Jim Rudd was twenty-four and operating a service station with his father-in-law when he tested to become a fire fighter. He was hired by the Spokane Fire Department in August 1964 and stayed with that department for thirty-two years.

At first Rudd subbed around the city, and heard a vehement range of opinions regarding Spokane #29's leadership. So for a while he kept his distance from the union. In October 1965, the *Spokesman Review* falsely accused members of Spokane #29 of illegally using union funds. Rudd decided those charged (including Jack Waller and Howard Vietzke) "were in it for the union" because there was no way they would have otherwise undergone the personal difficulties the case generated.

By 1968 Rudd was on Spokane #29's executive board. Rudd became a driver (fire equipment operator) in early 1971, and was on Spokane #29's negotiating team when Spokane became a union shop. A year later, Rudd was elected to replace Vietzke as secretary-treasurer, while Vietzke shifted his efforts to the WSCFF.

The WSCFF rallied with other state labor interests to defeat Washington's Senate Majority leader, Augie Mardesich, in 1978, and Rudd remembers riding along with busloads of fire fighters, doorbelling Mardesich's Westside district. Shortly after this, Rudd worked under Don Spangle (Spokane #29) to establish a sign shop in Spokane.

In 1988 Rudd was elected the WSCFF's District 1 representative, a position he held for the next eight years, and served twice as vice president of the WSCFF. In 1990 he defeated Dan Downs (Richland #1052). Downs then defeated Rudd in 1991. Rudd came back as vice president in 1993, winning against incumbent Ron Morehouse (Bellingham #106).

WSCFF Legislative Director Vietzke (Spokane #29) retired, and Ken Snider (Spokane #29) stepped down as legislative assistant in September 1995. Rudd was appointed as Snider's replacement, and Jimmy Cason (Tacoma #31) became the WSCFF's new legislative director. All four worked the 1996 legislative session, but Cason's appointment brought to a head the dissention within the WSCFF's executive board.

Delegates to the WSCFF's 1996 Convention elected a new president, Kelly Fox (Olympia #468), vice president, Ricky Walsh (Richland #1052, District 2 representative), and treasurer, Lonnie Hampton (Tacoma #31), ending Michael McGovern's (Lakewood #1488) fourteen-year presidency. Cason died in January 1997, which left the WSCFF scrambling for legislative representation. Rudd stayed on, and remained part of the WSCFF's legislative team until he retired in 2000.

Rudd thinks fire fighters' political success comes from a combination of fire fighters' political hustle and legwork, and the fact that there are few fire fighters, relative to the total number of public employees.

⬌ *Malicious Media* 181

⬌ *Campaigns and Candidates* 126

HANFORD I-24'S TWO STRIKES

Hanford I-24 205

In 1966 Hanford Atomic Metal Trades Council (HAMTAK) went on strike. HAMTAK is a coalition of Hanford Site's unions, including Hanford I-24. It was a bitter fight, and I-24 did not fare well, especially since "neutral gates" were allowed for security and emergency response, which were used by strikebreakers. Many of the site's trade workers went to work elsewhere, and some of their international unions allowed other, non-resident, locals to work on the site.

ITT was Hanford I-24's employer when HAMTAK staged its second strike, in 1976. Ted Ellis (Hanford I-24) remembers he was out ninety-three days, and had to wait another month for his first check. Some in I-24 say the strikes were a benefit to the corporate employers, because they allowed maintenance procedures to be performed by supervisors (including those in the fire department). Once again, union tradesmen used neutral entrances, with authorization from their non-Tri-Cities locals. Hanford's fire fighters made up less than three percent of HAMTAK's membership, and I-24 was the only local to go back to work with a pay cut.

Members of Yakima #217 gather in Station 1's "Club Room" for Chief E.G. Dawson's retirement dinner on August 9, 1919, months before their walkout.

YAKIMA FIRE DEPARTMENT COLLECTION

YAKIMA #217: A LOCAL DESTROYED

Less than a year after the IAFF was created, Yakima #217 affiliated (sometime between April 1918 and August 1919). By November 5, 1919, the local made the front page of the *Yakima Daily Record*. Yakima #217's members were so disgruntled they voted unanimously to walk out as of noon that day. When city commissioners called the potential walkout a strike and vowed to use "emergency force," local members voted again, and agreed unanimously to stay on the job for the next twenty-four hours (two shifts), to "enable city commissioners to meet the present emergency.... [and to] insure proper protection to the city." Members declared they were "not now, and never have been 'on strike' and that the emergency has been entirely created by the commissioners."

The newspaper article did not identify specific issues, although Chief Ray H. Hare offered some details in his verbal resignation shortly after his fire fighters voted to walk:

> I wish to resign as chief, because I do not care to assume the responsibility of the department with a crew of green men and broken down apparatus.

Commissioners immediately accepted Hare's resignation, declared the walkout a strike, and replaced everyone in the department. Yakima #469 reaffiliated in 1936.

Yakima #469 206

Yakima #217's walkout on November 5, 1917, made the city paper's headline. Seattle's general strike had taken place only months before, and the governor faced other possible strikes in the Olympia area.

YAKIMA FIRE DEPARTMENT COLLECTION

Pensions and Benefits

RULES and REGULATIONS

Spokane
Fire Department

BY-LAWS,
RULES and REGULATIONS

Firemen's Relief
and
Pension Fund

JUNE, 1932

Spokane #29 established a Firemen's Relief and Pension Fund prior to 1926. It was formed as a union action to take over or co-opt a "company union" style relief fund that had almost destroyed the union. The June 1932 rules and regulations of the Spokane Fire Department also included bylaws, rules and regulations for the benefits plan.

SPOKANE FIRE STATION MUSEUM
COLLECTION

PICNICS

Spokane #29's Firemen's Picnic, at Lake Wandermere in 1941.

SPOKANE FIRE STATION MUSEUM COLLECTION

At the 1949 Spokane Firemen's Picnic, one of the events was a women's rolling pin throwing competition. (Note rolling pin in mid-air, target is a dummy.) Practicing for this event may have created additional job hazards for Spokane's fire fighters.

SPOKANE FIRE STATION MUSEUM COLLECTION

Seattle #27 held many of its annual picnics at Norm's Resort (on Cottage Lake) in Woodinville. At this picnic, sometime in the 1970s, pepperonis were a dime, beers were two for a quarter, free ice cream was plentiful, and anyone with a suggestion was directed to "write it on a piece of paper, fold it, and put it in your pocket." Entertainment and events traditionally included bingo, egg tosses, leapfrog races, dancing to live music, a raffle, and softball.

RICHARD WARBROUCK COLLECTION

Benefits Enacted: *A Chronology of Pension and Benefits Legislation*

Fire fighters have been working to receive and maintain an adequate pension and benefits system for as long as they have provided fire protection in Washington State. It would be nice to think that the public they served recognized the inherent dangers and special demands of fire fighting, and then paid for such a system. In reality, the public honors fire fighters, especially in the wake of media coverage of on-duty injuries or deaths, but needs prodding to pay for their pension and benefit programs. It takes tax dollars to fund these, a "detail" that is often forgotten when public opinion swings against higher taxes.

The following chart outlines the history of Washington State's retirement and benefits for professional fire fighters from 1902 to present. The other articles in this chapter then provide a chronology of related lobbying and legislative actions, but they do not include every specific change in benefits. Although individual fire fighters, IAFF locals, and the WSCFF have always been deeply involved in these matters, specific documentation of their actions was not always available.

Year	RCW — Title — Description	Benefits: At retirement, post-retirement increases, upon disability, death benefit, medical benefits, survivors' benefits	Service Requirements and Definition of Duty
1909	RCW 41.16 — Firemen's Relief and Pension Act (Chapt 50, Laws of 1909) — pay-as-you-go pension fund administered by local governments	**Retirement pension:** 50% of salary for rank held during 12 months preceding retirement; **Disability pension:** same if disability, bed-ridden condition, or illness was incurred as a 'consequence of duty.' During first 6 months of disability, inactive fire fighters received full salary. **Death benefit:** paid 50% of salary to widow or children under 16, until either married; or to parents of fire fighters, unmarried sisters, or dependent minor brothers. Death benefit for non-duty death $1,000. **Medical benefits:** hospital bed and nursing care if sickness or disability was duty-related.	Uniformed personnel; 20 years of service, including 2 immediately before retirement; age 55
1919	RCW 41.16 — Firemen's Relief and Pension Act - Amended	**Death benefit:** extended to children under 18. Non-duty reduced 'pro-rata' for less than 1 year of service. Fire fighters with more than 15 years of service (including 10 immediately before death) had option of 25% of salary paid as pension to widow. Burial expenses of $100 paid at local pension board's option. **Medical benefits:** distinction made between illness and disability, with illness paid 50% of salary for up to 6 months; disability receiving full salary until retirement. Medical benefits given for both when bed-ridden or hospitalized. **Survivors' benefit:** initiated equal to 50% of fire fighter's pension at time of death. **Survivors' disability benefit:** applied to unmarried widows and children under 18.	Service requirement changed to include 10 years immediately preceding retirement. "Performance of duty" changed to exclude certain periods of injury (recreation, work for compensation) distinguishing non-duty-related disabilities.
1929	RCW 41.16 — Firemen's Relief and Pension Act - Amended	**Non-duty disability pension:** Contributions plus 4% refunded for 1 to 15 years of service; for more than 15 years of service pension was one-third of salary. **Death benefit:** non-duty with 15 or more years of service allows option of $1,000 or pension equal to 33% of salary. Mandatory payment of $100 for burial expenses. **Medical benefits:** distinction between sickness and disability removed. **Survivors' benefits:** increased to equal fire fighters'. Fire fighters' children added when widow absent. Benefits to child of disabled or unable to work continued "until disability removed."	Service requirement of 10 years preceding retirement eliminated.

Year	RCW — Title — Description	Benefits: At retirement, post-retirement increases, upon disability, death benefit, medical benefits, survivors' benefits	Service Requirements and Definition of Duty
1935	RCW 41.16 — Firemen's Relief and Pension Act - Amended	**Retirement pension:** set at 50% of salary, not to exceed $125 per month. Maximum duty-disability pension of $125 per month. Non-duty disability benefits granted to survivors if fire fighter served more than 15 years. **Death benefit:** set at maximum of $125 per month. For non-retired, service benefit made eligible, death benefit equal to 50% of salary (maximum $125 per month); with 4 to 15 years of service eligible for full $1,000; service of greater than 15 years had option of $1,000 payment or pension of 33% of salary. Payment of burial expenses increased to $200. **Medical benefits:** Pay for first 5 days of illness eliminated. **Survivors' benefits:** required widow to have been married to fire-fighter for 5 years prior to retirement; extension of benefits for child unable to work removed; non-duty survivors' pension of 33% of salary.	Service requirement set at 25 years of service, regardless of age.
1947	RCW 41.16 — Firemen's Relief and Pension Act of 1947 - Amended (final amendments)	**Retirement pension:** based on average salary for last 5 years worked and age at entry into system. **Death benefit:** added for service retired (greater of $1,000 or refund of contributions and interest, minus paid amounts). Widow of active fire fighters had option of 50% of salary with maximum monthly payment of $125 per month or $5,000 one-time payment. Options were the same for duty-disabled retirees, with other terms available to non-duty disabled retirees (based on years of service). **Medical benefits:** local pension boards permitted to select physician for duty-related illness or injury.	Service requirement set at 25 years' service **and** minimum age of 55. Credits given for military service of up to 5 years, if employee contribution to pension was paid. **Vesting:** fire fighters with 20 or more years of service received contributions with interest **or** a pension equal to average salary times years of service, at term or age 55 (latest of 2). Fire fighters with fewer than 20 years of service received refund of contributions.
		After 1947, no further amendments to 41.16 medical benefits	
1955	RCW 41.18 — Firemen's Relief and Pension Act — New pension system created by legislature; fire fighters had the option of retaining coverage under RCW 41.16	**Non-duty disability pension (with options):** available only to fire fighters with more than 15 years of service. Disabling events occurring on duty resulted in fire fighter's placement on "inactive" status for up to 6 months at full pay. After this 6 months received 50% of salary if less than 25 years of service or under age 55 with conversions at 55 if service requirements for retirement pension met. **Death benefit:** if no option selected, benefits ceased at death. Variable options available to service retirees (ranging from refund of contribution to 80% pension received). **Medical benefits:** coverage for duty-related disability continued for disability's duration. **Survivors' benefits:** various options	Credits given for military service of up to 5 years, no pension contribution required. **Duty vesting:** fire fighters leaving system received refund of contributions minus any payments made; **non-duty vesting:** fire fighters leaving system received refund of contribution or $1,000.
1957	RCW 41.16 — Firemen's Relief and Pension Act of 1947 - Amended	**Retirement pension:** maximum raised to $150 per month. **Post-retirement increases:** existing pensions increased by $25 per month, up to the maximum of $150. Future increases tied to the cost of living index. **Disability pension:** recipients could choose $5,000 one-time payment or pension of 50% of salary pension up to $150 per month.	
1959	RCW 41.16 — Firemen's Relief and Pension Act of 1947- Amended	**Post-retirement increases:** cost of living adjustments ruled unconstitutional and removed.	
1961	RCW 41.18 — Firemen's Relief and Pension Act of 1955 - Amended — Also called the Firemen's Pension Bill	All pensions set at 50% of "basic salary." **Post-retirement increases; Non-duty disability:** 90 days paid at full salary, then paid at 50% of salary with no escalator. **Death benefit:** duty-retired survivor received pension based on maximum of 50% of salary; non-duty survivors received pension based on 33% of salary with an additional percentage based on number of children or cash settlement. Burial expenses covered up to $500. **Medical benefits:** covered for non-duty-related disability during 90 days prior to retirement.	Retirement allowed at age 50. "Dissipation or abuse" clause added. Years of service required for vesting raised from 20 to 25.
1963	Public Pension Commission (PPC) formed (to study funding deficit)	In 1963 the Public Pension Committee (PPC) created to study and propose legislative action to address minimum of $103 million deficit between the pension systems' assets and its liabilities (projected funding vs. projected expenses).	
1967	RCW 41.16 — Firemen's Relief and Pension Act - Amended	**Post-retirement increase:** minimum pension of $150 set for fire fighters retired before January 1, 1947.	Full chiefs added to pension system.
1969	OMNIBUS PENSION BILL: RCW 41.26 — LEOFF (Law Enforcement Officers' and Fire Fighters' Retirement System) created; RCW 41.18 — Firemen's Relief and Pension Act of 1955 - Amended	Effective date: October 1, 1970. Escalator clause added 2% of salary for each year worked beyond 25 to a maximum of 60% of salary. **Post-retirement increases:** 2% non-cumulative annual COLA increase for all types of benefits. **Death benefit:** duty-retired widow and unretired same as if retired (retroactive to July 1, 1967); $5,000 option removed for fire fighters killed in line of duty and those on disability retirement; pension based on 50% of salary paid to both.	All active fire fighters transferred to LEOFF; **Military service credits:** definition of "veteran" amended. **Vesting:** required years of service dropped from 25 to 20 with option of refund of contributions **or** pension equal to 25 year pension (based on percentage multiplied by additional years of service) without escalator clause.
1970	OMNIBUS PENSION BILL: RCW 41.26 — LEOFF Amended (prior to effective date)	**Post-retirement increases:** 2% annual cost-of-living adjustment (COLA) retroactive to date of retirement. LEOFF 1 included cost-of-living increase equal to percentage increase/decrease in the Seattle area consumer price index. **Non-duty disability:** granted by local disability boards. Salary paid at 50% after 6 months at full pay (with 'offset' for outside employment including post-retirement employment). **Disability retirement:** granted by local disability boards. Salary paid at 50% after 6 months at full pay. **Death benefit:** spouse of active fire fighter received 50% of salary + additional 5% per child to maximum of 60%. **Medical benefits:** necessary hospital care and nursing expenses not payable from certain other sources. Survivors' benefits extended to a child unable to work.	5 years of service and age 50; benefits variable according to bracketed years of service. Retirement required at age 60.
1971	Pension Minimum Standards Bill RCW 41.26 — LEOFF Amended	**Death benefit:** removed pension to survivors of vested fire fighters with fewer than 20 years of service, unless death occurred after age 50. Survivors of fire fighters with less than 20 years of service received refund of contributions. **Medical benefits** to fire fighters with less than 20 years of service terminated unless they were over age 50.	
1972	RCW 41.26 — LEOFF Amended	**Disability retirement:** made option to begin disability pension immediately, in lieu of 6 months' paid leave, available.	
1973	RCW 41.16 and 41.18 — Firemen's Relief and Pension Acts of 1947 and 1955 - Amended	**Post-retirement increases:** minimum pension set at $300 per month for fire fighters covered under both RCW 41.16 and RCW 41.18. **Death benefit:** widowers (not just widows) specified as eligible beneficiaries.	

Year	RCW — Title — Description	Benefits: At retirement, post-retirement increases, upon disability, death benefit, medical benefits, survivors' benefits	Service Requirements and Definition of Duty
1974	RCW 41.26 — LEOFF Amended	Pensions set at maximum of 60% of salary. **Post-retirement increases:** minimum yearly increase of 2% per year, based on 'full compounded consumer price index increase' for 41.16 and 41.18. **Non-duty disability:** downward adjustment for other earnings removed.	
1975	RCW 41.26 — LEOFF Amended	**Post-retirement increase:** Seattle area consumer price index applied to $300 minimum pension. **Death benefit:** $300 month set as minimum for death in the line of duty or of disability retiree.	
1976	RCW 41.26 — LEOFF Amended	Local pension board decisions on increases in benefits under RCW 41.16 & 41.18 could be appealed to LEOFF Retirement Board.	
1977	RCW 41.26 — LEOFF Amended to create LEOFF 2	Effective date: October 1, 1977. Actuarial reduction. **Post-retirement increase:** increase or decrease limited to 3% and tied to cost of living; could not be decreased to less than original pension. **Death benefit:** made available as option for survivors of service retirees with a corresponding reduction of pension; active fire fighters vested with fewer than 10 years service eligible for refund of contribution only; active fire fighters with more than 10 years could opt between refund or actuarially reduced pension.	Service requirement: 5 years and age 50; 2% pension 'actuarially' reduced for age difference from 58; full pension at age 58.
1982	Job Security and Employment Rights RCW 41.26 — LEOFF Amended	(41.26.470) required LEOFF 2 members restored to work, level of duties; prohibited such salary being less than member's rank at date of disability retirement; offered statutory protection of LEOFF 2 careers from extended absence of any sort; provision for lump sum payment of retirement benefits when monthly allowance less than $50.	
1984	RCW 41.26 — LEOFF Amended	Interim legislative study of LEOFF 2 improvements; definition of disability changed.	
1985	RCW 41.26 — LEOFF Amended (HB 444: LEOFF 1 Separation of Duty and Non-Duty to Correct Tax Problems)	Disability supplement for duty-related injury (instead of sick leave, through workers' comp, goal to cover a person who doesn't have sick leave), to sunset in 1989.	
1987	RCW 51.32.185 — Occupational diseases — Presumption of occupational disease for fire fighters	Lung disease identified as presumptive occupational disease for fire fighters.	
1988	RCW 41.26 — LEOFF Amended	Retired fire fighters and law enforcement officers have right to elect and be elected as members of local disability boards.	Retirement age reduced from 63 to 58.
1989	RCW 41.26 — LEOFF Amended	Disability supplement authorized in 1985 is made permanent; terms of state service credit accrued if on paid leave and making contributions, prior to this no service credit was accrued, including disability.	
1990	RCW 41.26 — LEOFF Amended	Service credit annual notification from DRS to each member; survivor benefit from disability goes to estate if no survivors.	
1991	RCW 41.26 — LEOFF Amended	LEOFF law reorganized, right to sue provision applies to both LEOFF 1 and LEOFF 2; a housekeeping bill to simplify understanding of laws.	
1992	RCW 41.26 — LEOFF Amended	LEOFF law recodified right to sue under LEOFF 1 only. State's contribution to all retirement systems reduced by a total of $40 million, of which $32 million was from LEOFF; military service credit for both inactive and active duty if member pays all contributions within 5 years.	
1993	RCW 41.26 — LEOFF Amended	150% return of contributions plus interest on separation with less than 5 years service, indexed vesting.	Age/service years reduced to 55 (from 58) in LEOFF 2 without penalty.
1994	RCW 41.26 — LEOFF Amended	State permanent portability window created; applied to all systems but cost born by member and "very high;" elimination of "open window" periods to occasionally allow members to buy back service credit in other systems.	
1996	RCW 41.26 — LEOFF Amended	Line-of-Duty Death Benefit $150,000; PERS II fire fighters who work for universities can transfer into the LEOFF system.	
1999	RCW 41.26 — LEOFF Amended	LEOFF 1 survivor benefit clarification; LEOFF 2 cash-out provision passed to the retirement system.	
2000	RCW 41.26 — LEOFF Amended	Reduction of actuarial penalty to 3% per year from 50 to 52 years of age for earlier retirement with 20 years of service.	Retirement age reduced from 55 to 53 years of age, but with an early retirement factor: penalties for retirement (per month) before age 53.
2002	RCW 51.32.185 — Occupational diseases — Presumption of occupational disease for fire fighters - Limitations - Exception - Rules (SHB 6311)	RCW 51.32.185 (Occupational diseases - Presumption of occupational disease for fire fighters - Limitations - Exception - Rules) presumes heart problems occuring within 72 hours of exposure to smoke, fumes, or other toxins; cancer; and infectious diseases to be occupational diseases.	
2002	Initiative 790 passes	Requires all earnings of the LEOFF 2 pension fund in excess of the actuarially assumed rate of return to be used exclusively for additional benefits for members and beneficiaries. Transfers authority over LEOFF 2 to governor-appointed, 11-member board (6 members of LEOFF 2, 3 employer representatives, and 2 members of the Legislature). Board has authority to increase benefits and contribution rates for members, local government employers, and the state, to be 1) approved by the legislature (if less than 20% of members' pay) or 2) approved by the legislature by vote (if greater than 20% of members' pay).	
2003	RCW 41.26 LEOFF Amended	Legislative action on I-790 (implementation, and language changes)	

LONG JOHNS

Although this picture may have been staged, early Spokane fire fighters traditionally wore long johns so they could go from bed to work clothes in minimal time. (Note pants and boots, or "bunkers," are set up at the foot of several beds.)

NMAC COLLECTION, L93-25.149

Select but unidentified members of Spokane #29 model their long john finery in about 1951. Their clowning was part of the entertainment in the fireshows of the early 1950s, which raised money for the Firemen's Welfare Benefit Fund.

SPOKANE FIRE STATION MUSEUM

A fire fighter initiation from bygone days included wearing pink long johns for members of the Camas Department. L-R: Jim Brock, Brooks Cooper, Ken Hill.

DON FULTHORP CAMAS #2444 COLLECTION

⟷ *Fireshows* **160**, *Spokane #29* **173**

IAFF MEMORABILIA

Washington State fire fighters have been involved in the IAFF since its formation in 1918. Delegates sent to IAFF Conventions traditionally celebrated as intensely as they worked, and used the conventions as a forum for making political alliances with other IAFF locals.

Olympia #468 was a member of the IAFF prior to the formation of the WSCFF, and used the printed stationery the IAFF issued to its locals for a 1937 letter.

YAKIMA #469 COLLECTION

A certificate to attend the 1940 IAFF Convention in Des Moines, Iowa, as a delegate. This was the first IAFF convention after the formation of the WSCFF.

YAKIMA #469 COLLECTION

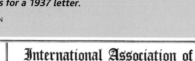

Members of the Spokane #29 delegation celebrate at the Biltmore Hotel in Los Angeles during the 1972 IAFF Convention, which was the year Vietzke was first elected secretary-treasurer of the WSCFF. L-R: Howard Vietzke (#29), unknown, Mickey Vietzke, unknown, Sherry Rudd, Ken Strong (#29), Jim Rudd (#29), Doris Strong.

HOWARD VIETZKE COLLECTION

MICHAEL MCGOVERN COLLECTION

A program from the 1974 32nd IAFF Convention in Baltimore, signed by Howard Vietzke (#29), Karl Hofmann (#46), Mickey Vietzke, Gary Brown (#29), Reanie (sic) Brown, Ken Strong (#29), Doris Strong, Doug McNall (#46), Charlene McNall, Bertine Hofmann, Ken Groth (#469), J. Groth, Walt Lambert (#29, IAFF staff), Jack Waller (#29, IAFF staff). It was at this convention John Willis (#31, WSCFF lobbyist) was narrowly defeated by incumbent Martinez (#672) in a bid for the IAFF Dist 7 vp.

HOWARD VIETZKE COLLECTION

This placard represents an interesting show of solidarity within the Washington delegation to the 1976 IAFF Convention in Denver, since signatures include many members of Seattle #27, which would re-affiliate with the WSCFF the following year. (In 1977 McNall would be elected WSCFF president.) Vietzke unsuccessfully challenged Jim Martinez (#672) for IAFF Dist 7 vice president at this convention. Signatures include those of Doug McNall (#46), Richard Warbrouck (#27), Bill Gosnell (#27), Ollie Morris (#1433), Ken Groth (#469, WSCFF pres), Howard Vietzke (#29, WSCFF vp), Dick Sparks (#27), Ralph Guelfi (#31), Bob Gough (#27), Joseph May, Dennis Brown (#27), Gary Brown (#29, WSCFF trustee), Edward Osway (sic), Don Spangle (#29), Vince Azzinnaro (#29), and Pete Todish (#469).

WSCFF COLLECTION

At the End of the Day:
The Evolution of Benefit Systems

Seattle fire fighters carry out one of their own. Fire fighter on the right is Richard Warbrouck (#27) (date unknown).

RICHARD WARBROUCK COLLECTION

1902

The State Legislature passed a law requiring fire insurance companies to pay one percent of their premiums into funding that would go to disabled fire fighters. Little information is available on whether or how this was actually carried out.

1909

Labor and a large progressive coalition supported the newly elected Republican Governor Marion Hay. The legislature passed the Employers' Liability Act, establishing employers' liability for workers' on-the-job injuries. The Firemen's Relief and Pension Act (RCW 41.16) also passed in 1909 and established a state-mandated pension plan to be administrated by the local governments on a pay-as-you-go basis, and included the first definition of a fireman:

> "Fireman" shall mean any person regularly or temporarily, or as a substitute, employed and paid as a member of a fire department, who has passed a civil examination for fireman and who is actively employed as a fireman; and shall include any "prior fireman."

Washington State's other employees would have to wait another thirty-eight years before they would be covered under a state pension plan. RCW 41.16 granted retirement after twenty years of service, at age 55, death benefits for beneficiaries, six months fully paid disability leave, and covered medical expenses related to on-duty injuries.

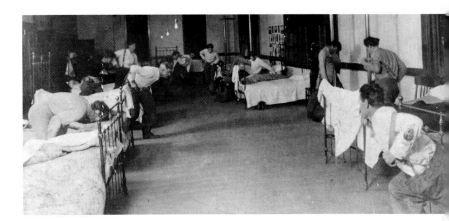

Tacoma fire fighters make a dash to respond to an alarm.

RALPH DECKER COLLECTION

1919

In 1919 the State Legislature amended RCW 41.16 to include pneumonia and tuberculosis as illnesses. This meant a fire fighter who contracted either would receive variable amounts of disability leave and/or coverage of medical expenses.

1929

RCW 41.16 was again amended, making the one hundred dollar payment for burial expenses mandatory, and medical benefits were standardized to apply equally to illness or disability. In addition fire fighters were no longer required to have served for the ten years immediately preceding their retirement.

1930s

Amendments to RCW 41.16 in 1935 allowed "firemen" to retire at any age after twenty-five years of service, but a cap of $125 per month was put on the pension received. Whether or not there was adequate municipal funding for each jurisdiction's pension was called into question. Seattle's Mayor Arthur Langlie called for a study of the city's fire fighter pension. When the study was completed it was clear there wasn't enough money in the system.

Platoons, Kelly Days and Transit Passes **57**
Yakima #469 **206**

Some accounts say this was what drove the creation of the WSCFF. During the 1930s and 1940s, IAFF locals across the state began to compare notes on pensions, benefits, wages, and working conditions. Yakima #469 in particular did an amazing amount of research, polling locals throughout Washington and Oregon on the details of their pension plans, and brought this information to the first meetings of the WSCFF.

1947

The 1947 legislature changed the way the pension was calculated with SB 226, further amending RCW 41.16. A five-year average was used to calculate a worker's salary base, instead of simply that of the last year worked. A death benefit for those who retired was also added. In the wake of the bombing of Pearl Harbor, the first military service credits were also added. Axel Drugge (Seattle #27) remembers the WSCFF supported these changes, although many in Seattle #27 opposed them, as reductions that should not be conceded.

In the 1950s, members of the Spokane Fire Department practiced with a "bangor ladder" (named after Bangor, Maine, where it was developed). To stabilize the ladder, two fire fighters hold clipping lines, and two are on outriggers, which were called "tormentors."
SPOKANE FIRE STATION MUSEUM COLLECTION

Spokane fire fighters work from a roof (unknown fire, sometime between 1948-1954).
SPOKANE FIRE STATION MUSEUM COLLECTION

1950s

A new pension system was established in 1955, also called the Firemen's Relief and Pension Act (RCW 41.18). This system set up a series of options that had variable pension and death benefits. Anyone who didn't formally choose some option was left without any benefits at death. Those covered under the earlier Firemen's Relief and Pension Act, RCW 41.16 remained under that plan.

In 1957 the legislature amended RCW 41.16, raising its $125-per-month cap on pension payments to $150 per month, and for the first time incorporated cost-of-living adjustments. Unfortunately these were ruled unconstitutional and legislatively removed in 1959.

1960s

Investigations and actuarial analyses of state-mandated pension and benefits programs continued. At the 1960 WSCF Convention, members geared up as they never had before, establishing a legislative team of Walt Lambert (Spokane #29, WSCFF treasurer), Jack Waller (Spokane #29, IAFF District 7 vice president), John Alexander (Renton #864, WSCFF president), Harold Nilsen (Seattle #27), Axel Drugge (Seattle #27 secretary-treasurer), Gordon Hovik (Everett #46, chair of this legislative committee), and John Smith (Tacoma #31 president). Members of this committee toured the state's locals, where members discussed, drafted, and redrafted legislative proposals.

Every single legislator in the state was contacted prior to the beginning of the 1961 session. Three were contacted before they left for Olympia, and agreed to sponsor the WSCFF's language. District 4 (Spokane) Representative Bill Day, a Democrat, became the bill's initial sponsor. It is fair to assume the combination of Lambert and Waller on their home turf had something to do with this. Republican Arnold Wang (District 23, Kitsap County) then signed on, pulling in significant support from other Republicans. The third sponsor to sign on was senior member Representative Captain A.E. Edwards, a Democrat who represented the 42nd District (Whatcom County). Lambert noted in a later article for Seattle #27's magazine, the *Fire Fighter*, "Captain Edwards' name on any bill is a sign of good legislation."

Hanford fire fighters "fog" an electrical fire (circa 1951-52).

HANFORD FIRE DEPARTMENT COLLECTION

State-of-the-art technology was then called into play. Another 1961 article in the *Fire Fighter,* describes the WSCFF's mail campaign:

> The response [by members] to send letters and postcards to... the Legislature in support of HB 365 was terrific and effective. I want to thank Walt Lambert, and editor Marshall Bland, who conceived the idea of identifying the addressograph plates of legislative districts; with our new addressograph machine. This gives us an alphabetical, fingertip selection of members and addresses.

But all of this effort did not move HB 365 out of committee. The WSCFF then turned to allies within the labor movement, especially the United Labor Lobby (ULL), a part of the Washington State Labor Council (WSLC). Under the direction of WSLC President Weston, union members toured the halls of the capitol letting legislators know they needed to support HB 365. Waller's post-passage commentary is pointed:

> The results were very gratifying. The concentrated effort brought about passage of this bill out of committee. This again demonstrates the importance of affiliation with the Central Labor Councils and the Washington State Labor Council.

The same process was repeated in the Senate, supported by a sea of phone calls and telegrams. Eventually, the 1961 legislature passed an amendment to RCW 41.18 (Firemen's Pension Bill). The WSCFF celebrated its victory with the same political savvy it had used to win the bill's passage. An "appreciation dinner" was held in Seattle, at the Olympic Hotel's Grand Ballroom. The July 1961 *Fire Fighter* reported:

> The ballroom was filled to capacity with firemen, senators and representatives, government officials, union officers, and their ladies.

When Governor Rosellini appeared, he was greeted with a standing ovation. Lieutenant Governor John Cherberg was also there. The *Fire Fighter* describes the events once all legislators present were introduced:

> A seemingly spontaneous roar of applause arose from the hall, and continued for three minutes. A couple of times the clapping, cheering, and whistling seemed to have reached an end, and then rose again in increasing intensity. A more evident disclosure of the fire fighters' appreciation to the state legislators and officials could not have been made.

While the Firemen's Pension Bill did amend the specific terms of RCW 41.18's programs, it also directed the Legislative Council to begin formal study of the state's pension systems. This examination documented a minimum of $103 million deficit between the pension systems' assets and its liabilities (projected funding vs. projected expenses). In 1963 the Public Pension Commission (PPC) was created to deal with this deficit, and continued to study the problem and inform the legislature of an ever-widening funding gap.

It is during this time that the lobbying efforts of the WSCFF and its members increased, setting the stage for several legislative victories. John Smith, who had lobbied Olympia as president of Tacoma #31, was elected president of the WSCFF at its 1964 Convention. Smith brought a new and blunt style of leadership with him. "I told them [the voting delegates] what I wanted to do. Some of the leadership wanted me to wait. But I ran, and I won."

In 1967 RCW 41.18 was amended to include full chiefs as the Public Pension Commission (PPC) continued its fourth year of studies. Fire fighters worked a major pension reform bill through both houses of the legislature, but Governor Daniel Evans vetoed it, although he would sign almost identical legislation three years later to create LEOFF (RCW 41.26 Law Enforcement Officers' and Fire Fighters' Retirement System).

Several other pieces of legislation affecting fire fighters were passed that same session, including RCW 41.56 (the Public Employees' Collective Bargaining Act), which granted uniformed public employees collective bargaining rights, a huge victory. In addition, the Washington State Labor Council (WSLC) and other labor organizations defeated the proposed privatization of the state workers' compensation program.

⬌ *Collectively Bargaining* **99**

1969-1970: LEOFF

In 1969 fire fighters representing both the WSCFF and individual locals swarmed Olympia, lobbying for pension reform. Seattle #27, which had disaffiliated from the WSCFF the year before, sent representatives including Secretary-Treasurer John Richmond and President Dick Sparks. Tacoma #31's president, John Willis, was also there and remembers how hard Richmond worked, and the ways in which all the IAFF locals coordinated their various lobbying efforts. John Smith (Tacoma #31), president of the WSCFF, was also there, doing something he was good at—working both sides of the aisle—Republicans and Democrats. Bob Munk (Spokane #29, WSCFF secretary) remembers, "John Smith went for the Republicans; Waller and Lambert never did."

Smith (Tacoma #31) calls his work on the draft "scalping," and recalls that the legislation that became LEOFF grew out of what was originally a bill applicable only to sheriffs:

> It was lousy. We redid it, practically from after 'therefore be it resolved,' and then we got it moving through as an amendment instead of a new bill.

Although the key fire fighter lobbyists did not agree on many things, their ways of working in Olympia complemented each other. George Roop (Spokane Valley Fire District 1 #876) helped Smith track hearings, some of which were scheduled with minimal notice when few were around the capitol. Richmond (Seattle #27) had lifetime bonds with several key legislators, including 33rd District Representative John L. O'Brien (King County), and Richmond used his renowned abilities behind the scenes to secure procedural support and votes. Smith (Tacoma #31) worked very closely with Representative Sid Morrison (15th District) who wrote the WSCFF later that spring:

⬌ *Lobbying and Lambaste* **123**

> In the opening days of the [1969] session, I began my relationship with John Smith by telling him "to go to hell...." But full credit must be given to John Smith, backed up by George Roop, for the strong position of the fire service in the final version that was signed into law.

According to both Willis and Smith (both Tacoma #31), Arnie Roundtree (Seattle #27) gave key testimony, as did Ed Garner, who spoke on behalf of the fire districts. In many ways, the real deal being negotiated was for the state to step in and assume the financial liabilities of numerous and varied municipal pension plans. Most cities just didn't have the money to cover the wave of fire fighters that had been hired after World War II, and who were fast approaching retirement. As Howard Vietzke (Spokane #29) described:

> With LEOFF, cities got off the hook. Before that, if fifty fire fighters retired, fifty guys who had been paying into their pension, the city would have had to start paying. And the cities didn't have the money.

This helped Willis and others secure the support of the Association of Washington Cities (AWC). Chester Biesen, Deputy Mayor of Spokane at the time and the AWC's lobbyist, testified in support of HB 74. Biesen's support is particularly interesting because Spokane was one of very few cities that had adequate funding to face its pension liabilities. It was in the cities' interest to find a way around what Don Meyer (Seattle #27) calls "leapfrogging." Meyer remembers fire fighters used whatever gains police pensions were awarded to lobby legislators on behalf of fire fighters, and that police would do the same, leveraging both benefits higher.

The orchestration toward pension reform continued as the bill faced another hurdle. Lieutenant Governor John Cherberg, a longtime friend of fire fighters, made the decision the "scope and object" of this bill had not changed since its original draft.

The bill continued to move forward. Meantime plenty of other fire fighters assisted: Howard Vietzke (Spokane #29), Bill Gosnell (Seattle #27), Dick Warbrouck (Seattle #27), Gordon Hovik (Everett #46), and Karl Hofmann (Everett #46, WSCFF vice president).

Governor Evans had undergone an impressive change of heart by April 25, 1969, when he signed House Bill 74 into law (RCW 41.26 Law Enforcement Officers' and Fire Fighters' Retirement System, or LEOFF). Evans referred to it as the most significant legislation of 1969, although he did apply what Wayne Williams called "a minor partial veto." Williams explained Evan's veto:

> …was to make sure certain firefighters and law enforcement officers hired after March 1, 1970 were not placed in the old systems, but could only be in the LEOFF system.

RCW 41.18 was also amended in 1969, with changes to take effect when LEOFF became effective, the following year.

RCW 41.26 consolidated a multiplicity of local law enforcement and fire fighter pensions and benefit plans into one statewide, state-administered system. LEOFF provides fire fighters, police officers, sheriffs, and deputy sheriffs with a one hundred percent state-funded pension system, transferring the responsibility for paying out pensions and benefits from the municipalities to the state:

> The purpose of this chapter [41.26] is to provide for an actuarial reserve system for the payment of death, disability, and retirement benefits to law enforcement officers and fire fighters, and to beneficiaries of such employees, thereby enabling such employees to provide for themselves and their dependents in case of disability or death, and effecting a system of retirement from active duty.

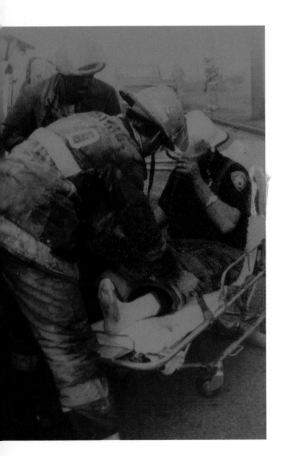

Unidentified members of Tacoma #31 treat one of their own for injuries incurred in the line of duty.

TACOMA #31 COLLECTION

In the spring of 1970 the legislature revisited LEOFF and the 1969 revisions to RCW 41.18, which were to take effect on October 10, 1970. In a way, the legislation passed in 1969 became a structural framework for major changes that were adopted during the 1970 legislative session. Smith recalled that language in the 1969 law included language stating a city would provide "medical, care." An unofficial ruling from the Attorney General's office stated that this comma "broke the thought" and would mean both medical and "care," an undefined term, would be provided. So Smith went into the 1970 legislature promising to remove the comma if fire fighters got other language included that explicitly identified areas of care, such as nursing home care, allowing widows to receive no reduction of benefits, and allowing all spouses (if a fire fighter remarried) to "buy into the medical." On March 1, 1970, what was called the Omnibus Pension Bill, which amended both RCW 41.26 and 41.18, was signed by Governor Evans. Ironically, this bill had the same number, HB 74, as the original passage of 41.26 had in 1969. The *Fire Fighter*, March 1970, summarized all the work that went into 1970's success:

> The entire legislative program was coordinated by the representatives of the four concerned groups with Charles Marsh of the Tacoma Police Department, the president of the Washington State Police Officers Association acting as chairman of the four-group organization, assisted by John W. Smith, president of the Washington State Council of Fire Fighters, George Dunn, of the Washington State Law Enforcement Association and John D. Richmond, Secretary of Seattle #27.
> ....The cooperation shown between [WSCFF] President John Smith and Vice President Karl Hofmann, Charles Marsh, and George Dunn.... was certainly conducive to the successful passage of this much needed legislation.

1970-1977: LEOFF BECOMES TWO-TIERED

LEOFF ran into difficulties faster than it could be amended. The funding deficit of all the state's pension systems became clearer when uniformed public employees pensions were unified under LEOFF. In March 1970, before LEOFF became effective but after that year's legislative amendments, LEOFF's liabilities exceeded assets by $239.6 million, even with $11.4 million in contributions from the previously existing pension systems.

Bob Munk was secretary-treasurer of the WSCFF when LEOFF was passed and enacted, and is covered under it today. "We got a good deal. All my prescriptions, whatever we need medically, everything is covered." And that, almost immediately, was part of LEOFF's problem; LEOFF was far superior to any other public employee pension system. It seemed clear other publicly-employed workers would rally to gain what uniformed personnel now had. At the same time, those who paid taxes doubted the value of providing what some called the "Cadillac of pensions" when they, as private employees, had no way of getting such coverage for themselves.

The AWC almost immediately began organizing challenges to LEOFF's un defined cost of medical coverage for fire fighters and police officers. By December of 1970, Bremerton Mayor Glenn Jarstad, chair of the AWC pension committee, was quoted in Seattle #27's *Fire Fighter*:

> Ninety-nine percent of the cities and counties did not know what was contained in the fire and police pension bill and [were] concerned over the terrific liability for off-job accidents.

Unidentified members of Tacoma #31 clipped in on the Tacoma Narrows bridge.

TACOMA #31 COLLECTION

To further compound LEOFF's funding difficulties, the legislature never appropriated to LEOFF the amount of money the state actuary projected as required. In the 1973-1975 biennium, the legislature appropriated $6.5 million for LEOFF when the actuary's projections recommended $47.8 million. In addition, an inflationary spiral pushed the Consumer Price Index (CPI) to record heights; between 1967 and 1979 the CPI rose more than 117%. This boosted the cost of post-retirement benefits as well, creating even greater expenditures, while the wages that some of the benefits were pegged to also kept climbing. Dennis Parlari (Puyallup #726) recalls that during one quarter of 1978 Puyallup may have had the highest paid fire fighters in the country because of the local's contract incorporated quarterly cost-of-living increases.

LEOFF members' use of the system's benefits didn't match actuarial projections either. While LEOFF members were claiming disabilities at a predicted level, they were filing for benefits at an earlier age than expected, driving up the total expense of the program. Part of this discrepancy came from the physical standards requirement in LEOFF. County sheriffs were suddenly required to pass the fire fighters' medical exam, and many failed, which caused them to file for disability or early retirement. In some cases, physical conditions that had not hampered an individual's performance still forced a sheriff from office.

From the beginning of LEOFF, there were many anecdotes of system abuse, and certainly there were such cases. There were also many departments that applied a liberal interpretation to what fell under LEOFF. Suddenly, all sorts of jobs were re-categorized to fit LEOFF's definition of "uniformed personnel." John Willis (Tacoma #31) remembered one example, which John Smith (Tacoma #31) confirmed:

> There was a county sheriff, and he got his secretary to wear a uniform, and then she was covered.... a lot of sheriffs—it was a time when there were a lot of appointments to office, and so you got guys who weren't ready for any kind of physical test. They were somebody's friend or relative. And then all those people were under LEOFF.

There were also examples of abuse within the fire service, and although these were rare, public sentiment had turned against the huge cost of LEOFF, and the press played up every abuse it uncovered. A Bill Mauldin political cartoon of the era depicted Joe Public pushing a wheelbarrow full of a fire fighter, a policeman, a teacher, and a street sweeper, together holding a banner that read "Public Servants on Strike." The caption read: "I'm the public, and I'm not sure I can afford servants anymore." (Pictured on page 7.)

The pendulum in Olympia continued to swing away from LEOFF, year by year. Hearings were held across the state by individual cities. Willis remembers spending more and more time tracking obscure bits of proposed legislation:

> People took revenge. Somebody would get mad and suddenly there was some bill or a rider about who was in or out of the system. I had to be everywhere watching for these things.

Bill Gosnell (Seattle #27) who was on the state pension board at the time, recalls:

> LEOFF 1 did have big problems, and few LEOFF supporters were willing to admit this, let alone address the issues. There was some basis for [Representative Helen] Sommers' opposition to LEOFF 1. There were cases of abuse, and as LEOFF 1 took effect, its financial impact was greater than had been projected...

It is worth remembering that at this point in time Washington State's fire fighters had been on an almost unbelievable legislative roll: between 1966 and 1973 they gained collective bargaining, LEOFF, and binding arbitration. Olympia didn't have the budget to give LEOFF the funding it needed, and it seems possible Olympia was not ready to give fire fighters any additional funding without a fight. It also seems that fire fighters were becoming more factionalized while LEOFF's opposition gathered steam.

⟷ *Collectively Bargaining* **99**

⟷ *Fractious Fraternity* **27**

In 1974 the legislature considered numerous changes to LEOFF, and made some changes to it, including capping its pension benefits at sixty percent of a fire fighter's final average salary. One proposal that did not pass included a two-tier system of benefits, wherein future LEOFF members would receive less, foreshadowing what LEOFF 2 would bring. During the 1974 session quite a number of IAFF locals continued to lobby privately for their own deals, and the WSCFF's lobbyist Willis (Tacoma #31) described his job that year as "full-time damage control." As the session wound down, Governor Evans made it clear he was ready for some changes to LEOFF, in comments summarized by the *Seattle Times* on April 8, 1974:

> The LEOFF system is seriously under-funded and the basic reason is the benefits simply were too rich and could not be afforded.

The next day Kent Seisher, executive secretary of the AWC, picked up where Evans left off, and was also quoted in the *Seattle Times.* "We have some pretty ridiculous examples of people getting hurt and expecting the cities to pay for them."

Thomas Bleakney, actuary for several of the state retirement systems, identified a less easily grasped and more major flaw, that legislators were delaying appropriations to the pension system. In the April 11 *Seattle Times,* he said:

> You've got this long gap between the time benefits are being earned and the time they're being paid out. The threat is not so much insolvency, but the danger that the legislature will realize too late the costs it has. In the State of Washington, there's no question that the No. 1 problem is that of financing the systems.

LEOFF was amended in both 1975 and 1976, but not in ways that addressed its funding liability. During the 1975 legislative session Willis (Tacoma #31, WSCFF lobbyist) reported back to the WSCFF that the Democratic leadership of the Senate, and Republican Governor Evans "openly threatened to hold up, kill, or veto any legislation" blocking their [legislators] pension reform." The exact fate of SB 2765 and its 107 amendments is unclear, although some amendments to 41.26 were passed.

By the 1977 legislative session it was clear there would be major pension reform, it was simply a question of how drastic it would be. Willis (Tacoma #31) continued to try to stop the tide. With Dick Sparks (Seattle #27) and Charlie Marsh (longtime president of and representative for the Washington State Council of Police), Willis met regularly with the AWC, hoping to cut a deal that would sufficiently reduce the cities' financial responsibilities without gutting LEOFF. While he lobbied, columns by feature writers in most west-side newspapers mocked fire fighters who collected disabilities. John Hinterberger's *Seattle Times* column of March 2, 1977 was a series of pointed question and answers that typified the attitudes that would drive future LEOFF legislation.

L-R: **Wayne Garden (#2175) and Baron Banks (#2175). In a mutual response situation, Banks was blown off the roof by Tacoma's hose.**

TACOMA #31 COLLECTION

Q. *How many firemen retired last year [in Seattle]?*

A. 28.

Q. *How many retired early because of disabilities?*

A. 28.

Q. *You mean that of all the firemen who retired last year, the number who retired after full service was?*

A. None....

Q. *This is a touch incomprehensible. Surely in the six years that the pension plan [LEOFF] has been in existence, SOME of the firemen must have retired because they got old and earned retirement.*

A. Absolutely. 42 firemen routinely completed their years of service.

Q. *How many became disabled?*

A. 312...

Q. *What are most of the disabilities?*

A. Back trouble. Some heart complaints, but mostly backaches....

In June 1977 the legislature passed bills revising the Public Employees Retirement System (PERS), the Teachers' Retirement System (TRS), and LEOFF, implementing a two-tier structure in each. RCW 41.26, as amended, created LEOFF 1 and LEOFF 2, which is frequently referred to as "left out." At the time, the changes were estimated to generate $1.2 million in savings over twenty-five years. In fact, legislative appropriations continued to fall short of those recommended by the State Actuary.

1978-2003

In December 1977 Willis put his notes and clippings together in a scrapbook, which he labeled *1977 Pension Reform History: The Death of LEOFF (SHB 867)*. The creation of LEOFF 2 forced leadership within Washington State's fire service to reconsider their political in-fighting. By 1979, both Seattle #27 and Tacoma #31 reaffiliated with the WSCFF. Fire fighters began to identify supportive and nonsupportive politicians and campaigned like never before. One example was fire fighter support for Larry Vognild (Everett #46), as he took on and defeated Senate Majority Leader Augie Mardesich in 1978.

But the pendulum on pension reform was still swinging toward further cuts. Bill Gosnell (Seattle #27) remembers he and Dan Downs (Richland # 1052) tried by resolution to have the WSCFF hire someone with the professional skills to assess the finances of the LEOFF system, but did not get sufficient support to make this happen. Earl J. Davis (Seattle #27) wrote in the spring 1980 *Washington Professional Fire Fighter*:

> Fire fighters in this state are under attack! October 1, 1977, became the day when the first battle was lost. We now have fire fighters in this state with substantially different pension coverage; yet, here we are almost three years later and the numbers of LEOFF 2 fire fighters increase, and still no increase in benefits for these fire fighters.... I have to give the legislators credit for winning part of the battle by establishing the LEOFF 2 System. This brings up the old ploy of "divide and conquer."

By 1982, the WSCFF and various member locals worked successfully to get minor changes to LEOFF 2. But even with these changes, the biggest issue remained funding, with that year's calculations putting LEOFF 1's liabilities at $2.2 billion with assets of only $692 million. For the 1983-85 biennium, the state actuary recommended appropriation of approximately $375 million, but the legislature appropriated only about $200 million. In 1984, the legislature approved an interim legislative study on possible ways to improve LEOFF 2. In the following year, 1985, legislative provisions were added (with a sunset clause to expire in 1989) which allowed a LEOFF 2 member to receive a supplemental disability coverage for duty-related, on-the-job injuries.

During the late 1980s and 1990s, WSCFF members lobbied together to improve their two-tiered pension plan (LEOFF 1 and 2) and to gain new benefits and coverage through other legislation. In addition, the WSCFF, led by President Mike McGovern (Lakewood #1488), established a family medical program for its members and retirees in 1986, and called it the WSCFF Health and Welfare Trust. The following year the WSCFF gained passage of presumptive occupational disease legislation (RCW 51.32.185 Occupational diseases—Presumption of Occupational Disease for Fire Fighters). Although the WSCFF worked hard to have the legislation include lung disease, heart disease, and cancer, by the time it got to Governor Booth Gardner it included only heart and lung disease. Gardner then vetoed all but coverage of lung disease, or as lobbyists explained it, "he cut the heart out of it."

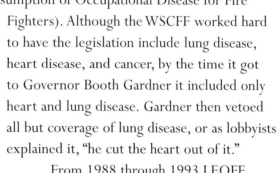

The LEOFF Health and Welfare Trust **157**

From 1988 through 1993 LEOFF (RCW 41.26) was amended in every legislative session. Improvements included reducing the age for retirement eligibility from age sixty-three to fifty-five (in two separate amendments), greater participation of LEOFF members on their local pension boards, and formal clarification and increased notification about their coverage to LEOFF members.

Howard Vietzke (#29, WSCFF leg dir) stands beside the "Last Alarm" Fallen Fire Fighters Memorial, located in the John A. Cherberg Building in Olympia. Established by an act of the 1989 legislature, it was the last indoor monument or tribute granted on the grounds of the Capitol.

WSCFF COLLECTION

While the WSCFF was working to reduce the impact of LEOFF 2 during this period, portability became more important to WSCFF members. The increase in EMS services provided by the fire service brought with it paramedics who joined fire departments, having previously been covered under PERS as non-uniformed public employees.

EMS **69**

A "portability window" which applied to all state retirement systems passed in 1994. This allowed transfer into the LEOFF system, but only if the individual was willing to assume tremendous costs: all previous contributions that would have been made by the state, the employer, and the employee, plus interest, and finally, the actuarially calculated "financial impact to system."

No matter what improvements to its members' pensions and benefits the WSCFF secured, the financial liabilities of the LEOFF system continued. With the stock market boom of the 1990s, LEOFF 2's investments generated more money than was actuarially predicted to be needed within the system in a rolling-estimate period of four years. In 1992 the state then reduced all contributions to LEOFF 2, including its own, and used its portion of these now-unappropriated funds ($32 million) to boost the general fund. This scenario actually emphasized the fiscal liability of LEOFF 2, because a downturn in investment returns has the potential to generate another deficit. Gary Locke, chair of the house appropriations committee in 1993, proposed further reductions in the pension system's contribution rates because LEOFF was well-funded according to immediate financial projections. This allowed the state to balance its budget for that year.

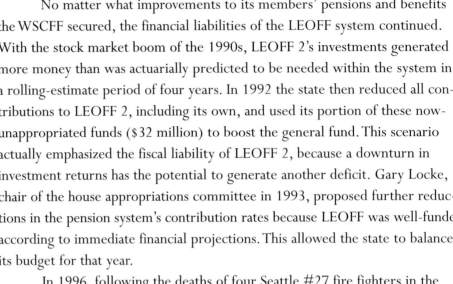

Greg Borg (#29) caught in a flashover in about 1998. He was then with Ladder Co. 4.

GREG BORG COLLECTION

In 1996, following the deaths of four Seattle #27 fire fighters in the Pang warehouse fire, WSCFF lobbyist Howard Vietzke (Spokane #29) helped gain passage of SB 5322 (RCW 41.26.048 Special Death Benefit—Death in the Course of Employment), which established a $150,000 payment to a fire fighter's beneficiaries or estate following death due to injuries sustained in the line of duty. (LEOFF members paid for this benefit.) In 2000, the WSCFF lobbied successfully to once again reduce the LEOFF 2 retirement age, this time to 53.

In response to state-dictated reductions in contributions, two resolutions passed at the 2001 WSCFF Convention. These outlined proposed legislation and a possible initiative campaign that would establish fire-fighter representation on LEOFF 2's board of trustees. Out of these emerged the Initiative 790 (I-790) campaign, which gained voter approval in November 2002.

During the 2002 legislative session, the WSCFF also successfully supported SHB 6311, which amended RCW 51.32.185 to increase coverage of medical conditions and diseases related to the occupational hazards of the fire service.

With the fall 2002 success of I-790, lobbying efforts in 2003 focused on successfully securing enabling language through HB 2197 (which implemented I-790 by amending RCW 41.26), and HB 2198 (which repealed one section of the initiative's language that would have generated possible legal challenges).

The 2003 legislative session also saw HB 1202 and SB 5089, amending RCW 41.54. This improved paramedic portability of pension benefits between PERS and LEOFF 2 systems, and is the culmination of efforts led by WSCFF lobbyists and district representatives.

Spokane #29 members Dave West and Paul Binkoski deal with a mattress as it explodes into flames. They were responding to a house fire on April 26, 1990.

DAVE WEST COLLECTION

I-790   149

I-790:
Power from the People

Initiative 790 (I-790) followed twenty-five years of work on pension reform by the WSCFF. I-790's evolution from one rank-and-file member's concerns into a successful statewide initiative also illustrates changes in the WSCFF's relationship to its membership and to its educational and political programs.

In 1977 RCW 41.26 (LEOFF—Law Enforcement Officers' and Fire Fighters' Retirement System) was amended to create a two-tier pension system, the second tier of which is called LEOFF 2. Although there were amendments passed prior to 2002 that altered aspects of LEOFF 2 provisions, two basic flaws remained. One was financial. The LEOFF 2 system allowed the return on its investments to be transferred to the state's general fund when such monies were identified as "surplus" to the actuarial needs of LEOFF 2. The second major flaw with LEOFF 2 was that those covered under its provisions were not represented in its decision-making body, the board of trustees.

Vancouver #452 member Mark Johnston was pursuing a college degree (through a cooperative program offered by Antioch College and the George Meany Labor Center) when he chose a research topic that would have significant effects for all LEOFF 2 members. As he studied and analyzed his own pension, he became familiar with the way in which LEOFF 2's funds are compared to the projected cost of its benefits, biannually. He learned that whatever amount of money in the fund is greater than its estimated expenses is labeled "surplus."

Throughout the 1990s the return on LEOFF 2 monies invested generated such so-called surpluses. The state is not allowed to directly remove funds from the pension plan, but it can and does reduce the amount of contributions, with a goal of eventually reducing all contributions to zero. Three different groups are contributors to LEOFF 2: the members covered, their employers, and the state. What the state does not consider is that those who are covered by LEOFF 2, and who also contribute to it, might

At the End of the Day
137

prefer to reinvest returns into the system to improve their benefits and/or to assure sufficient funding as the cost of services increase. Such reinvestment would also provide financial stability when investment returns do not match the cost of the LEOFF 2 system over a particular biannual actuarial period.

Ironically, the issue of what would happen if and when the LEOFF 2 system generated a "surplus" was considered when LEOFF 1 was created. John Willis (Tacoma #31), who lobbied on behalf of his local and the WSCFF from before LEOFF 1 until after passage of LEOFF 2, remembers such discussion when initial funding mechanisms were drafted for LEOFF 1. He and others were willing to include a cap on the pension fund, and didn't think such a cap would hinder the pension system in the future. Willis and others were concerned that without some limits on the pension system's funding:

> ...the fire fighters would have it too good relative to other workers. Especially when times got bad, we [fire fighters] would lose the support and sympathy that's always been our biggest political asset.

Decades later, Johnston's pension system research considered who administered LEOFF 2's investments as well as how investment returns were used. He documented that, unlike Washington, forty-six other states include police officers and fire fighters on their pension boards. Being a talkative fellow, Johnston started explaining his research to his co-workers, and began to calculate what each of them would get, given their years of service, rates of pay, the increasing cost of services, and other factors.

At this point, in spring of 2001, Vancouver #452 proposed convention Resolution 01-04, Revamp Pension System Through Initiative to the People. Vancouver #452 has a history of advocating for political change using direct means, and has sometimes challenged the WSCFF for what it considers working too much within the system, when the system is not responding. Vancouver #452 knew possible action on an initiative campaign would require full backing from the convention's delegates, so prior to the convention Johnston and others talked to locals around the state about the resolution, using individual fire fighter's pension and benefits scenarios to make their case.

⬌ Vancouver #452 **194**

Not everyone saw the fairness of letting those covered by LEOFF have input on managing their pension. This cartoon appeared in the October 31, 2002, Vancouver Columbian and helped motivate I-790 supporters using WSCFF President Kelly Fox's name in a visual pun.

DRAWING BY JEFF JOHNSON
© JOHNSON 2002

In making the issue personal, they rallied support for the content of their proposal, which was to give those covered under LEOFF 2 a voice in managing their plan. Whether or not such an initiative would receive WSCFF backing as the means of doing so was a separate consideration.

WSCFF President Kelly Fox (Olympia #468) remembers that at this point "I needed some convincing," and he was not alone. Interviews indicate that, going into the 2001 Convention, a significant number of the delegates and executive board members who eventually voted for an amended resolution had grave concerns about Vancouver #452's proposal. One was that any initiative would be seen as abandoning the legislative process, possibly alienating bipartisan support the WSCFF had worked hard to gain.

There was another factor, which was how an initiative campaign might relate to the long-term interests and participatory process of the general membership within the WSCFF. Fox also remembers considering with others how the relatively absolute demands in the proposed resolution could be shaped "into something that represented the council's membership as a whole," and he wasn't convinced that the WSCFF's membership was ready for this initiative. He knew tying the WSCFF's political actions to the will of the general membership was key.

Fox was committed to using his presidency to educate and convince the membership rather than having the elected leadership take preemptive action and then seek the support of the membership. Going into the 2001 Convention, Fox wasn't sure how the content of what Vancouver #452 was proposing fit into this approach, but he also knew it was critical that an initiative have strong grassroots support.

WSCFF Vice President Ricky Walsh (Richland #1052, WSCFF District 2 representative) was co-chair of the legislative committee. This committee and the backers of the resolution met and discussed what was seen by some as its very rigid language requesting:

> …a new, jointly trusted pension plan that includes ERISA minimum standards and a provision for collective bargaining to replace the current LEOFF Plan 2…

Those who thought the resolution, as drafted, was too absolute asked questions: "What if we go to the legislature one more time, and they give us everything but 'a new, jointly trusted pension plan?' What if they gave us LEOFF 1?"

Those meeting agreed that gaining a voice in the management of LEOFF 2 would be a huge improvement over "begging." Walsh and others could also see the potential of an initiative campaign to leverage the legislature to take action. But an initiative campaign also meant altering a style and an image the WSCFF had worked to gain, that of an organization with a commitment to working within the legislative process.

On the third day of the WSCFF Convention, Resolution 01-04 was brought to the floor by Walsh (Richland #1052), as co-chair of the WSCFF's legislative committee, with the committee's recommendation to pass it. Johnston (Vancouver #452) then moved to amend his local's resolution to gain control of the existing LEOFF 2 plan, not to create a new pension system. After discussion, the amended resolution passed unanimously. Ken Snider (Spokane #29), a member of the WSCFF's Pension Committee who had supported the original resolution going into convention, brought a new resolution from the floor (Resolution 01-25, A Bill to the Legislature):

That the WSCFF add to its 2002 legislative agenda the passage of a bill to establish a new Board of Trustees for LEOFF Plan 2... and... that the Board of Trustees be composed of plan participants.

This resolution also passed. The resolutions were put onto the agenda of the fall 2001 Educational Seminar.

Then came September 11, 2001. One of many consequences of this tragedy was postponement of the WSCFF's 2001 Educational Seminar, since all emergency response service personnel needed to stay close to home and on alert. When the seminar was finally convened in December 2001, the two resolutions on LEOFF 2 reform were on the agenda. Johnston made what would come to be the first of his road show presentations on the flaws of LEOFF 2 administration. Although his father-in-law had died unexpectedly the evening before, his wife Beth gave Johnston her blessing to stay, Johnston made his presentation, and the membership and executive board of the WSCFF left Yakima after adopting a clear agenda: get significant representation on the LEOFF 2's Board of Trustees.

From December 2001 on, the WSCFF Executive Board began to evaluate an initiative campaign, offering leadership as it worked with the other LEOFF Plan 2 organizations, the Washington Council of Police and Sheriffs (WACOPS), and the Council of Metropolitan Police and Sheriffs (COMPAS). As the campaign plan came together, Johnston (Vancouver #452) was enlisted to go on the road with his presentation. He visited local after local, talking through the details of members' actual benefits while the WSCFF sent a video of one such presentation to still other locals. Suddenly LEOFF 2 members understood that, especially if they needed to file for disability, they could receive very little under LEOFF 2, and that meanwhile the state was reducing its obligations (contributions) to LEOFF 2 to meet other state budgetary needs.

The WSCFF executive board and others within the council had no illusions the 2002 legislature would pass anything resembling the WSCFF's proposed changes to LEOFF 2. WSCFF leadership also knew that the legislature had to have this proposal in front of them as proof the WSCFF was committed to the legislative process.

By February 2002, it was clear the legislature would not grant LEOFF 2 members representation on their pension's board of trustees. HB 2931, proposing this, did make it to a hearing before the Appropriations Committee, thanks to Speaker of the House Frank Chopp. Chopp was also one of the legislators disappointed that the WSCFF was prepared to go outside of the legislative process with a possible initiative campaign. It was no surprise that Appropriations Committee Chair Helen Sommers took no further action within committee.

The WSCFF, WACOPS, and COMPAS conducted a poll evaluating support for an initiative if it were slated for November 2002. By March 2002 the coalition of police and fire fighters had approved an initiative campaign plan and the consultant to direct it, a budget of approximately one million dollars, and member groups had committed funding. In the case of the WSCFF, funding came from voluntary contributions by member locals, equivalent to $100 per member.

Union Partners 36

Representative Helen Sommers has been a major opponent of much of the pension reform supported by the WSCFF. In 1985 she did support amendments to RCW 41.26 that allowed a LEOFF 2 member to receive a supplemental disability coverage for duty-related, on-the-job injuries.

STANDING, L-R: *Michael McGovern (#1488, WSCFF president), Howard Vietzke (#29, WSCFF leg dir), Rep. Helen Sommers, Dr. Hollister (dir of retirement systems), Charlie Marsh (WSCPO).* SEATED: *Governor Booth Gardner.*

WSCFF COLLECTION

After considerable discussion, the WSCFF executive board chose this funding structure, rather than simply paying for the initiative out of the WSCFF's general coffers, to emphasize the membership was putting its money where its mouth was. Executive board members also personally "walked their talk" as they went into their districts to lay the groundwork for local speakers' bureaus and helped members prepare to explain the initiative within their communities.

At the June 2002 WSCFF Convention, I-790 campaign manager Barbara Chadwick reported WSCFF members had turned in 60,000 signatures supporting I-790. She also explained the logistics of delivering every last signature to the secretary of state in Olympia. The July WSCFF executive board's minutes, as reported in the WSCFF's August *Council Connection* newsletter reported:

> ...85,000 signatures [for I-790] have been gathered to date by fire and police union members. The paid signature gatherers are on target. Validity rate has been around 75%, better than projected. When the signatures are turned in to the Office of the Secretary of State, then the media campaign will commence. Plans include creating a speakers' bureau, purchasing of airtime, and other items. Voluntary contributions continue to come in. Approximately two thirds of the WSCFF's affiliates have contributed to the campaign.

Then came a setback. Washington's State's Office of the State Actuary and its Office of Financial Management made public their fiscal analysis of I-790, and found:

> Five-year costs could range from $1 million to $549 million for state government, from $2 million to $822 million for local governments, and from $3 million to $1.4 billion for eligible law enforcement officers and fire fighters. The higher costs are the result of increases in benefits. The lowest costs are possible only if benefits are not increased.

I-790 supporters were stunned. Just months earlier, the same changes proposed by I-790 when they appeared as HB 2931, were found to have no fiscal impact (zero dollars). Looking back at this period of the campaign, many WSCFF initiative supporters recognize the coalition erred in drafting initiative language that turned out to be vague enough to allow for interpretation. The WSCFF is relatively sure I-790 opponents sought a financial interpretation of I-790 that they could use to derail it.

The Association of Washington Cities (AWC) then weighed in heavily. The AWC objected to I-790's potential for increased required contributions by cities (as employers), but more pointedly stated on their website in October:

> ...this seriously flawed initiative [I-790] takes control of tax dollars away from elected officials, and mandates enhanced benefits for a few.

The AWC also encouraged member cities to adopt a "model resolution" opposing I-790, which it circulated and posted on its website.

Newspaper editorials generally followed the AWC's line, with few considering the discrepancy in projected fiscal impacts. At this point, weeks before the election, those advising the I-790 campaign made it clear that WSCFF members needed to stick to the campaign plan. This meant staying with the message, "we deserve a voice in our pension." I-790 campaign leadership, including WSCFF President Fox, WACOPS Executive Director Bill Hanson, and past President of the Seattle Police Officers Guild Mike Edwards coordinated responses to various unfriendly editorials. Rank-and-file WSCFF membership grumbled within the organization, but maintained discipline and put their efforts into local speakers' bureaus and city council meetings rather than editorial boards.

The campaign's TV ads were run as planned, and emphasized that those who protected the public deserved a voice in managing their own pensions. In the final weeks before the election, polls indicated the voters were going to pass I-790. The lack of last minute activity was perhaps the hardest part of the campaign for fire fighters, who generally like to make things happen rather than sit around. They did understand the importance of sticking to a plan, however, and the plan worked.

Kelly Fox (#468, WSCFF president) and Bill Hanson (WACOPS exec dir) sign I-790 before heading out to collect signatures.

KEVEN ROJECKI COLLECTION

the importance of sticking to a plan, however, and the plan worked.

The 2003 legislature passed HB 2197 (which implemented I-790), and HB 2198 (which repealed Section 6, Subsection 5), and Governor Gary Locke signed both in late April 2003.

In the meantime, the WSCFF solicited applications from active fire fighters covered under LEOFF 2, for appointment to the LEOFF 2 Pension Board of Trustees. As per I-790, three board members are to be nominated by "a recognized statewide council, affiliated with the international association representing the interests of fire fighters," for the governor's appointment. At this time, the WSCFF is the sole association fitting this description. From those who applied, the executive board nominated Johnston, Fox, and Pat Hepler (Edmonds #1828), who were confirmed in late summer of 2003.

The passage of I-790 illustrates the WSCFF's political power. More important in some ways is the process the WSCFF went through with this initiative. I-790 came from the ideas of an individual member who had literally done his homework. It focused on improvements to the LEOFF 2 pension system that the WSCFF had tried for years to get through the legislative process. Once the decision was made to use the initiative process, WSCFF membership paid for the campaign from its own pockets, gathered signatures, and campaigned locally for support, demonstrating the WSCFF is the forum for and representative of professional fire fighters within Washington State.

profile:
John Willis

John Willis put immense effort into representing the union fire fighters in Washington State, and yet is not often remembered. He served as lobbyist for the WSCFF for a total of almost nine years, during some of the WSCFF's most politically contentious and productive years, but never held any other position within the WSCFF.

Willis, who was born in 1924, remembers that during the Depression, his father, a Tacoma fire fighter, was one of only two men in his neighborhood who had steady jobs. Aldus Floyd Willis was a fire fighter for twenty-nine years, beginning in 1928, and was also an active member and officer of Tacoma #31. Willis' memories of his father's work eventually influenced his own decision to become a fire fighter.

⟷ *Service and Solidarity* 61

Three days after he graduated from high school, in 1943, John Willis joined the navy. He was "sort of shell-shocked," and chose to stick with jobs that allowed him to work outdoors. He was a union lineman for almost four years, then tested with the Tacoma Fire Department, and was hired in 1950. His first impressions of Tacoma #31 were not positive. While a lineman he had come to appreciate the formal training program and pay steps that went with becoming a trade journeyman, part of a shift he witnessed from a company union to the IBEW (International Brotherhood of Electrical Workers). In comparison, Tacoma #31 seemed to be a fraternal organization, and fairly complacent.

When Willis asked around about why fire fighters weren't focused on gaining collective bargaining rights, which he'd made use of in the IBEW, he was told to talk to the WSCFF. He remembers the WSCFF leadership at the time was not particularly interested in the issue. Then, in 1955 Willis' wife got polio, and was paralyzed for three months. Willis took the maximum sick leave at the time, twenty-five days, to stay home and take care of his wife and their two baby girls, and "went into huge debt." The fire department gave him two months pay during this time, and after this Willis felt like he "couldn't do enough for the city, and for the department."

⟷ *Collectively Bargaining* 99

Within a few years Willis was vice president of Tacoma #31, and then its president. (The exact years he was in office remain unclear, but he was local president for some eight years prior to Stanley Thaut, who was elected in about 1970.) From about 1968 to 1974 Willis also chaired the Joint Committee of Public Employees of Tacoma and Pierce County, a coalition of unions representing public employees in Pierce County and Tacoma (originally named the Public Service Employees Organization of Tacoma and Pierce County). Willis describes the Joint Committee:

> It was a novel idea. All these employees went together for "common benefits" packages. Then we used individual union negotiations to go for workplace conditions and

wages. That way we didn't let the administration back out the percentage for benefits from wage increases.

By 1970 Willis was appointed as lobbyist by the WSCFF executive board, and served for the next two years. He also directed the Tacoma Fire Department's first and second minority recruitment programs, beginning in 1971.

John Smith, also a member of Tacoma #31, was WSCFF president during Willis' first years as WSCFF's lobbyist. It is a testament to their individual commitment to the fire fighters of Washington State that Willis and Smith served together, because they did not care for each other, nor agree on many issues of the day, including the use of strikes by fire fighters.

Smith replaced Willis as lobbyist during the 1973 legislative session. It was during this session that Willis saw the legislation he had been working on for almost twenty years pass: RCW 41.56 (Mediation and Arbitration Collective Bargaining Rights Act) was amended to mandate "mediation, fact-finding, and arbitration as the means of settling contract disputes between fire fighters or police and their public employers."

Willis remembers the 1972 shift from Smith's nine-year presidency to that of Karl Hofman (Everett #46), and Howard Vietzke's (Spokane #29) election as secretary-treasurer, as "a lot of jockeying for position." A year later, Willis was reappointed lobbyist for the WSCFF.

In 1974 Willis ran for the IAFF District 7 vice presidency, encouraged to do so by Jack Waller (Spokane #29), the IAFF's national lobbyist. Willis went into the IAFF election with endorsements from Seattle #27, Walla Walla #404, and Spokane #29, among others. Jim Martinez (Boise #672) was the one-term incumbent. Some say Martinez' use of parliamentarian rule won him the election. Many wanted Willis to challenge the results but he did not, because he felt it was more important to conserve the strengths of the IAFF, which had significant financial issues as strikes occurred across the United States. It seems plausible that this election helped fuel Tacoma #31's decision to disaffiliate from the WSCFF in late 1974.

Willis remained the WSCFF's lobbyist during and after his local was disaffiliated, until 1981. He retired as a fire fighter in late 1975, after twenty-five years of service. As WSCFF lobbyist he fought hard to block the legislative tide against fire fighters' LEOFF pension system (Law Enforcement Officers' and Fire Fighters' Retirement System), but could do little to stop the 1977 passage of amendments to RCW 41.26, which created LEOFF 2. When Governor John Spellman was elected, in 1981, Willis became a lobbyist for him, working on legislation that came forward as a request from the governor. He held this position until 1985, when Booth Gardner was elected governor.

Willis' son Doug became a fire fighter, and is an active longtime member of Central Pierce County Fire Fighters #2175 (now Pierce County Professional Fire Fighters), as well as serving as District 4's representative to the WSCFF from 1996 to 2000.

The LEOFF
Health and Welfare Trust

Aberdeen made a motion at the 1984 Convention directing the WSCFF to look into the possibility of a statewide medical plan for fire fighters. The concept was to create an alternative to employer-provided insurance. It took almost three years of research and negotiation before the WSCFF Health and Welfare Trust was created in May 1987, as a 501(c)9, with Blue Cross of Washington and Alaska as its provider. Membership has always been open to active and retired LEOFF 1 and 2 fire fighters. Its purpose is to:

> provide and maintain life, accident, health and welfare benefits, including vision, drugs and pharmaceutical supplies for the employees and family members of participating unions.

Spokane #29 signed on, as did a few other locals. Rates spiked in 1988, Blue Cross changed its management, and only two more locals signed on in 1988, Snohomish and Kenmore. This brought total participation to slightly over five hundred members, plus their dependents. In the May 1988 issue of the *Washington Professional Fire Fighter*, WSCFF President Michael McGovern (Lakewood #1488) reported the trust's bylaws had been revised to allow for out-of-state IAFF locals to associate with the trust. Whether or not any out-of-state locals ever participated in the trust is not documented.

As of January 1, 1989, the trust became self-insured, but the participant pool was not large enough to beat the financial risks. That same year the WSCFF took Blue Cross of Washington and Alaska to court over previously paid premiums and possible retentions or reserves accrued in earlier years. A settlement was reached, which brought Blue Cross back as the provider.

In 1996, with the contentious election of Kelly Fox as president of the WSCFF over incumbent Michael McGovern (Lakewood #1488), the Health and Welfare trustee board became an arena for divided loyalties within the WSCFF. Spokane #29 had backed McGovern, and was the key local within the trust, both by size and historical participation. McGovern had been with the trust since its inception, whereas Fox had not. During the months after Fox was elected as WSCFF president, several changes were made within the trust.

This included shifting board makeup to six members: the president of the WSCFF (or someone he or she designates), a representative of retired fire fighters, and four trustees at large, although by tradition two come from the Eastside and two from the Westside. McGovern, although no longer president of the WSCFF, remained for a time on the board as a west-side representative. The name of the trust was changed from the WSCFF Health and Welfare Trust to the LEOFF Health and Welfare Trust. This change was made both as a marketing tool to attract non-WSCFF LEOFF participants, but also to emphasize the trust was a separate entity from the WSCFF.

McGovern resigned from the board in late 1996, and Ted Rail (Spokane #29, District 1 Representative) replaced him as chairman. Howard Vietzke (Spokane #29, former WSCFF Legislative Director), who had been the retired fire fighters' representative, also stepped down.

Since January 23, 1997, the trust has had six trustees: Kelly Fox, (Olympia #468, WSCFF president), Richard Schuerman (Spokane #29) representing retired fire fighters, Chairman Ted Rail, (Spokane #29), Bruce Tinsley (Lakewood #1488), Ken Snider (Spokane #29), and Rod Heivilin (Shoreline #1760). Dave West (Spokane #29) is the trust's program director.

Current employees participating in the plan are Seattle #27 employees residing in King County, WSCFF office employees residing in Thurston County, Lakewood Fire District, City of Spokane fire fighters, and Spokane International Airport fire fighters. Coverage is through a policy with Premera Blue Cross, a non-union member of the Washington Research Council which promotes right-to-work. The trust has approximately 484 contracts covering 1,173 members, with annual revenue of approximately $3,694,000.

EMPLOYEE BENEFIT TRUST
MEDICAL EXPENSE REIMBURSEMENT PLAN

The WSCFF's Employee Benefit Trust Medical Expense Reimbursement Plan was established in 1999 to provide post-retirement health care premiums. In particular, it was designed to provide benefits to LEOFF 2 members who receive no medical expense coverage when "separated" from employment. The trust allows members to set aside tax-free monies while still working, then withdraw the premium and interest amount without taxation.

Locals

Members of Tacoma #31 pose in 1997 while burning down a training tower.

RALPH DECKER COLLECTION

Fire departments began to stage fireshows for the public after World War II. They were generally held in large stadiums, raised money for local hospitalization and medical care programs, and were good publicity for fire fighters. Almost all of them included burning up a building that had been moved to the site.

Accounts of the 1968 Everett fireshow, in Everett Memorial Stadium, help explain why the shows are no longer performed. Fire fighters waited and watched as a house was lit on fire. When the alarm was sounded, their engine didn't start. By the time they could respond, the building had burned to the ground. Next, fire fighter Al Langton sprained his ankle as he slid down a rope that stretched from the top of the stadium to the football field. Fire fighter Gary Parks then came down the rope while on fire. When he reached the ground, expecting to be rapidly extinguished by his colleagues, no one had remembered a fire extinguisher, so instead he demonstrated the effectiveness of 'stop, drop and roll.' The final event also backfired. A magnesium fire was started in a burn pan that held traces of water and oil from previous events. A huge cloud of white smoke engulfed the grandstand. The audience fled, with nine people taken to the hospital for treatment.

FIRE SHOW GETS CROWD OF 24,000

A crowd estimated at 24,000 filled Spokane's Memorial stadium last night to witness the fire department's "Midnight Alarm" show.

According to Stadium Manager J. Fred Bohler, last night's attendance was the third largest on record for the stadium, bettered only by the 1950 Washington State-Washington football game and the 1950 Merry-Go-Round game.

Months of preparation by the more than 150 participating firemen paid off for both the department and the audience. While all receipts have not been totaled, fire officials anticipate that the show netted $5000 for their family hospitalization and medical care funds.

Mixing thrills with comedy, the firemen staged a first-rate show in a professional manner, despite the fact that very few of them had previous experience in public entertainment.

Daring stunts high on aerial ladders, 50-foot leaps into a life net, rope slides from atop a mock drill tower and other dangerous antics won rounds of applause.

Among the more spectacular displays was a colored waterfall, created by pouring tons of water from several hose leads from eight openings in the tower.

Climax of the show was the burning of a bungalow in the infield with six companies of firemen assisting to quell the blaze.

A crowd pleaser was the water fight between hose and ladder crews of No. 5 station that ended in a draw when men of both companies were thoroughly drenched.

Another highlight was the novel clown act by men of No. 4 station, who constructed a trick fire engine and attempted to extinguish an outhouse blaze.

The fire show had more clowns than a circus. Several original stunts were executed by the funnymen, while the stage was set for major acts.

Other Events Thrill

Moscow, Idaho, sent its crack drill team to perform on pompier ladders and life lines while the navy air station at Geiger field made rapid work of their realistic rescue from a burning plane.

"We want to thank the public for their exceptional response," Chief James T. Blamey said to-day. "The attendance far exceeded our expectations. We also extend gratitude to others who assisted with the show and to all who gave so much of their own time in staging it."

Suggestion that a similar program be staged by the department on a biannual basis has been made to fire officials, who said they will study the recommendation before making such a decision.

Spokane's 1952 fireshow, "The Midnight Alarm," drew a crowd of 24,000 to Memorial Stadium. "Daring stunts" were performed from aerial ladders, there were 50-foot leaps into a saftey net, and a colored waterfall "pouring tons of water from several hose leads within a tower." The show culminated when a bungalow was burned in the infield, as six companies responded.

GREG BORG COLLECTION

No. 5448

CHILD 25c

SPOKANE FIRE DEPARTMENT

FIRE SHOW

"*The Midnight Alarm*"

July 31, 1954 . . . at 8:00 P. M.

MEMORIAL STADIUM

The Spokane Fire Department pulled out all its stops to advertise its 1952 fireshow, "The Midnight Alarm."

SPOKANE FIRE STATION MUSEUM COLLECTION

AUGUST 1st

THE SPOKANE FIRE DEPARTMENT Presents

THE MIDNIGHT ALARM

Get Your Tickets Early
AVAILABLE AT ALL FIRE STATIONS OR AT THE STADIUM

Spokane Memorial Stadium

FRIDAY, AUGUST 1, 1952

7:30 p.m.

DON'T MISS
Big Water Fight
HOSEMEN vs. TRUCKMEN

Beautiful Colored Water Display
Old Horse Drawn Steamer and Apparatus that Came Around the Horn

Daring Jumps Into Life Nets

FULL 2-HOUR SHOW
With Clowns, Comedy, Thrills, Fun, Suspense and Beauty

Moscow, Idaho, Pompier Ladder and Life Rope Team

Actual House Fire and Thrilling Rescue

Spokane's 1951 Fireshow featured a grand prize of a 1951 Chevrolet Bel Aire, donated by Harms-Rofinot Dealership, valued at $1,701.98. The Spokane Fire Department put on fireshows for several years. Proceeds went to the Firemen's Pension and Trust.

SPOKANE FIRE STATION MUSEUM COLLECTION

Spokane continued fireshows into the early 1960s, each advertised as "The Midnight Alarm."

SPOKANE FIRE STATION MUSEUM COLLECTION

Spokane's 1951 fireshow was held in the Joe Albi Stadium, with proceeds to go the "Firemen's Trust."

SPOKANE FIRE STATION MUSEUM COLLECTION

FIRE SHOW
SPOKANE
MEMORIAL STADIUM

AUG. 1 8 P.M.

Adults 50¢ School Children 25¢

SEE YOUR FIRE DEPT

in 35 ACTS

THRILLING RESCUES
BURN A HOUSE
BURN A PLANE

COMEDY · ACTION

An undated poster for one of Spokane's fireshows.

SPOKANE FIRE STATION MUSEUM COLLECTION

Everett #46: *The Fire Boys*

On March 17, 1892, citizens of Everett, an unincorporated and fairly wild boomtown, elected "the Committee of Twenty-One" to "work in good harmony for certain public improvements." Although this committee had no source of funding and no authority, it was directed to improve fire protection and other community services and infrastructure. The Everett Volunteer Fire Company 1, Fire Company A, and Everett Hook and Ladder Company were formed during that same month.

A few days later these companies fought their first fire and it became clear they needed equipment. Everett's first Firemen's Ball *(sic)* was held in April 1892 and raised $150. In April 1893 Everett incorporated, electing a slate of officers nominated by the fire fighters. The new city council then approved purchase of $2,236 worth of fire fighting equipment (including eight dozen badges). Later that year the city created its own volunteer fire department to replace the three independent fire companies.

The concept of a paid department was raised at the Everett City Council meeting of April 26, 1901, when City Attorney Padget reported, "the city needs a paid fire department, but whether the taxpayers will stand for it or not is another question." The council took unanimous action authorizing a paid fire chief (seventy-five dollars per month), and six professional fire fighters (sixty dollars per month). A supporting volunteer crew received one dollar for the first hour of fire fighting, and fifty cents for each additional hour.

Working conditions were as bad as the pay. In February 1905 both paid and volunteer fire fighters threatened to walk out after receiving pay warrants that couldn't be cashed. During this same period, the city replaced rotten fire hall floors, but only after one collapsed under a horse, since a horse was considered valuable.

Engine #2 (in front of county courthouse), circa 1909.

EVERETT FIRE DEPARTMENT COLLECTION

⟷ *Platoons, Kelly Days and Transit Passes* **57**

By the end of 1916 Everett's twenty-six-member fire department gathered 4,382 signatures to put a two-platoon system on the ballot. The measure passed, but it took a superior court decision to force Everett to enact it two years later. Everett eventually enacted ten-hour day shifts and fourteen-hour night shifts, with no days off, amounting to an eighty-four-hour workweek. On February 3, 1917, Everett's fire fighters affiliated directly with the AFL. One year later, in February 1918, Everett became one of the IAFF's fifty-two charter locals, and was assigned local #46.

Everett's hand operated ladder truck, probably its 1931 American LaFrance. If so, it was kept in use until 1958, although toward the end of its life it was towed to fires.

EVERETT FIRE DEPARTMENT COLLECTION

⟷ *Fractious Fraternity*
27

There is no clear information on why Everett #46 disaffiliated from the IAFF on January 1, 1920. It reaffiliated with the IAFF as #350 in 1933, and also joined the Everett Central Labor Council and the Washington State Federation of Labor (WSFL). Everett maintained residency requirements, and it was department procedure that any fire fighter who wanted to leave the city needed to get permission, according to William E. "Earl" Brower, who had joined the Everett department in 1937. All fire fighters also had to have a phone.

At this point Everett had a complex work schedule, as described in *The Fire Boys: 100 Years of Everett Fire Fighting History*:

> Ten-hour days Sunday through Friday, then work from 0800 to 1300 on Saturday; go home for five hours and return at 1800 to begin night shifts Saturday through Friday; get off work at 0800 Saturday, go home for five hours and return to work from 1300 to 1800 hours. Then the fireman began day shifts on Sunday.

In 1939 hours shifted to twenty-four on/twenty-four off, a change the fire fighters negotiated directly with Chief Swanson. Brower remembered:

> We wanted to change our shifts....The chief agreed to try the system. The change pleased the firemen, but not the commissioner of safety who complained to the chief. Nevertheless, Chief Swanson held his ground. I think the commissioner was upset on general principles because the firemen [sic] had not supported other recommendations he had made. After all, the change did not affect the number of hours a man worked, just when he worked.

Everett #350's experience in direct negotiations must have encouraged union participation, because by 1946 Brower was both the WSCFF's director of government relations, and IAFF District 7 vice president, while Roy L. "Bob Hope" Warnock, another member of Everett #350, was president of the WSCFF. The December 1946 issue of Seattle #27's *Fire Fighter* stated Everett fire fighters were the "highest paid in the Northwest." In 1947 Everett adopted a fifty-six-hour workweek that used a three-platoon system.

Everett #350's increasing power was challenged in the 1950s. In March 1952 voters passed an initiative amending the city's charter:

> to provide for the submission of disputes arising between the firemen *(sic)* and the city as to wages, and pensions, or working conditions to a board of arbitrators.

⟷ *Collectively Bargaining* 99

The next year Everett #350 tried to collectively bargain its salaries, but could not reach agreement with the city.

The city commissioners refused to follow the arbitration procedure outlined in its new ordinance, and instead went for a court decision which found the charter amendment unconstitutional, "an unlawful delegation of legislative authority" regarding pensions and a municipal budget. Everett #350 appealed the decision to the State Supreme Court (*Everett Fire Fighters local No. 350 v. C. Arvid Johnson*, 1955) and lost. This left Everett fire fighters without binding arbitration, just like every other IAFF local in the state. By 1956 Warnock was no longer on the WSCFF's executive board, although Gordon "Denny" Hovik, another member of Everett #350, was, and would become its president in 1960.

Everett #350 regrouped. In 1964 it began an organized campaign to establish a four-platoon system under its president, Jack Scherueble. Two years later, in 1966, Everett #350 signed a binding contract with the City of Everett, establishing itself as the sole and exclusive bargaining agent for Everett's fire fighters, a first in Washington State. Everett #350 then won the forty-two-hour workweek in 1967 through a city referendum, getting its fire fighters the same hourly total as the Everett police. RCW 41.56 (Public Employees Collective Bargaining Act) passed that same year, establishing collective bargaining rights for all of Washington State's fire fighters.

The 1960s featured the Everett Fire Department Fireshows, which included such dramatic events as 1968's out-of-control magnesium fire. Everett's recruitment program during this period was "geared to the working man." Some remember most recruiting took place in a bar that attracted many of Everett's paper mill workers, with all present told they should go take the fire department tests.

Everett #350 grew along with the fire department, and bought an American Legion Hall in 1969, which became its first union hall. Karl "Hans" Hofmann, who had joined the department in 1962, was elected to the WSCFF executive board in 1969, and served as its president from 1972 to 1976. During his tenure RCW 41.56 (Public Employees' Collective Bargaining) was amended to authorize binding arbitration for uniformed personnel.

The City of Everett then showed itself to be a union adversary, and in a repeat of 1955, took Everett #350 to court. The case stemmed from 1975 negotiations between Everett #350 and the city, where the city council agreed to a ten percent pay increase but planned to reduce the number of fire fighters. Bargaining reached impasse under Everett #350's President Doug McNall.

The city refused to submit to binding arbitration, asked a superior court judge to rule 41.56's binding arbitration unconstitutional, and also to find any minimum

⬅➡ *Collectively Bargaining* **99**

⬅➡ *Fireshows* **160**

Representatives of the city, Everett #350, and the IAFF look over the local's first contract with the city, signed in 1966.

L-R: Chief Raymond Smith, Clifford Hill, Richard Rowley, Comm. of Public Works Jerry Krekow, Finance Comm. Mildred Simpson, Mayor Bud Alexander, Joseph McDonald (pres #350), Walt Lambert (IAFF Dist 7 vp, #29), Jack Scherueble.

PHOTO BY JIM LEO

Doug McNall takes a moment to joke around after a fire. Note that the only protective gear worn were helmets and jackets.

PHOTO BY JIM LEO

crew clause as outside of the realm of negotiation. Everett #350 prevailed. The City of Everett appealed, and lost before the State Supreme Court (*City of Everett v. Local 350 of the IAFF*, 1976).

While this case strengthened collective bargaining and arbitration rights statewide, fire fighters' pension and benefits programs had been taking a hit. By October, 1975 many in the state legislature were "threatening a referendum and constitutional changes on pension reform," according to a letter the WSCFF's legislative representative John Willis (Tacoma #31) sent to WSCFF President Hofmann. Willis went on to chastise Hofmann for comments Hofmann had made in Olympia that Everett #350 had been meeting with Senate majority leader Augie Mardesich. Willis suggested "…it is very important we stay away from Senate leadership and work with our friends."

In fact, Everett fire fighters were quite aware Mardesich was not their friend, although Yeldell and others remember he had been until LEOFF. After the 1977 passage of LEOFF 2, Everett #350, as part of a strong statewide labor coalition, backed former Everett fire fighter Larry "The Mole" Vognild in his successful 1978 campaign against Mardesich. In the meantime McNall had been elected vice president (1976) and then president of the WSCFF (1977). In 1980 he stepped down and was appointed chief of the Everett Fire Department, ahead of more senior personnel.

Everett #350 members had high expectations for Chief McNall. He took over a department that faced many issues of modernization. One was EMS funding. The Everett Department had provided EMS services since 1972, but there were difficulties in resolving both provider and funding mechanisms. Working with Mayor Bill Moore, McNall pulled together a paramedic plan and a six-year, five-million-dollar levy measure that passed in February 1982.

But McNall opposed the union on several issues, and a key group within #350 felt McNall had turned on them. This animosity was compounded by significant departmental problems. In response, Everett #350 sought McNall's dismissal as chief in 1987, while its contract was still in negotiation. McNall stayed on as chief until 1990, when he retired. Twenty-four-hour shifts replaced the ten-hour/fourteen-hour shifts, and went into effect on January 1, 1990, a change granted by Mayor Moore on his way out of office. Within a year and a half, in July 1991, the IAFF reassigned Everett's original local number, #46.

Members of Everett #46 take a break after the Pier 3 fire of July 10, 1979.

L-R: *Joe Johnston, Pat Lansing, Frank Anderson, Rick Brock, Larry Stubrud, Steve Turner, Steve Parker.*

PHOTO BY JIM LEO

Several members of Everett #46, who were interviewed about the reduced role their local has played in the WSCFF since McNall's era, noted a shift in the attitude of their local's membership that parallels changes in many other locals. The removal of residency requirements, changing shift structures where fire fighters no longer cross paths with all their coworkers, and a much higher standard of living have reduced the somewhat automatic camaraderie and union activism of the past.

Seattle #27:
Contentious Strength

Seattle's first organized fire protection came from the all-volunteer Seattle Engine Company 1, founded on July 6, 1876, and funded by subscription. Three years later, after almost four blocks of downtown Seattle burned, the City of Seattle passed an ordinance that eliminated wood exteriors on new buildings within a core downtown area.

Seattle took formal control of its fire department in 1884, when it created the Seattle Volunteer Fire Department. This consisted of three hose companies and three engine companies, one of which was made up of the Western Mill Company's employees and the City's handpumper, the *Sacramento*. Hose Company 4 was added in the spring of 1889, the year of the Great Seattle Fire. Fire Chief Josiah Collins was in San Francisco on June 6, when the fire began. The tide was low, which limited the volume of water steamers could draw from Elliott Bay. Seattle Mayor Robert Moran took command, and ordered buildings in the path of the fire dynamited.

Even with assistance from the Tacoma, Olympia, Snohomish, Port Townsend, Portland (Oregon), and Victoria (British Columbia) fire departments, thirty-one square blocks of Seattle were destroyed, with losses estimated at between twelve and sixteen million dollars. Insurance companies blamed the city for its inadequate water supply, and for the poor training of those in the fire department. Most of Seattle's fire fighters, including Chief Collins, resigned in response to what they felt to be unfair charges.

Seattle replaced its burned fire stations, upgraded its alarm system and alarm room, and purchased "chemical wagons" (soda-acid tanks), steam pumpers, and the fireboat *Snoqualmie*, built by Moran's shipyard (which one might guess had some connection to Mayor Moran).

Seattle tried to pre-empt future catastrophic fires with a system of new ordinances that regulated building construction. Chief Gardner Kellogg personally inspected every building and pier within Seattle. He reported to the fire commission, which had been created when the city was rechartered in 1890. In May 1891 Herman Larson was Seattle's first fire fighter to die on duty, and his death triggered the formation of the Firemen's Relief Association of Seattle. Four fire chiefs were dismissed in the next four years, and a Civil Service Commission replaced the Fire Commission in 1896.

Beginning in 1898, Seattle grew exponentially, serving as the jumping-off point for the Alaska Gold Rush. In 1901 the city hired its first fire marshal to try to keep up with building inspections and fire ordinance enforcement as the Alaska-Yukon-Pacific Exposition took over the fairgrounds (current site of the University of Washington).

Map showing the extent of Seattle's Great Fire (6-6-1889), made by George Bundy (who also served as editor of the Fire Fighter*). Everything within the dark line was destroyed.*

SEATTLE FIRE DEPARTMENT
CENTENNIAL YEARBOOK 1989

Ballard, West Seattle, South Park, Columbia City, Hillman City, and Rainier Beach were all annexed in 1907. At first Seattle could afford to provide professional fire protection only to Ballard (previously Washington's fourth largest city), which became Hose Company 18. The other new neighborhoods had to make do with individual volunteer fire departments until 1910.

Mayor Hiram Gill was elected in 1911 and had a new attitude toward vice, which he referred to as an "open city." The plan was to allow vice but to keep it within a particular neighborhood. Instead, word spread and there was enough criminal activity throughout Seattle to have it designated "off-limits" to servicemen on liberty. *The Seattle Times* led the mayoral recall campaign, and the chief of police, the fire chief, and the fire marshal were also dismissed. After months of political wrangling, Fire Chief Frank L. Stetson was hired. He purchased lighter motorized equipment to deal with Seattle's hills, remodeled stations, and had the newly created motor repair shop build "Iron Swedes," curved pipes with a nozzle, used to shoot water into basements.

⟷ *Platoons, Kelly Days and Transit Passes* **57**

In the fall of 1912 the two-platoon system was placed on the ballot in Seattle. Fire fighters and their wives successfully campaigned against Chief Stetson, the city administration, and many in the Seattle business community to win a two-platoon system utilizing an eighty-four-hour workweek that went into effect on April 2, 1913. One hundred fifty-one new fire fighters were hired, which brought the department total to 514.

Seattle fire fighter John A. Buck had worked hard on this campaign, and was a union man through and through. He organized the first News Boys Union (about 1894), then was hired as a fire fighter while on strike as a teamster. Seattle, like many cities, is rumored to have had an ordinance against municipal workers joining any union. Many fire fighters had been teamsters, however, and were not intimidated by a threatened layoff of 400. Buck personally paid the ten-dollar charter fee to the AFL (as a miscellaneous trade union) and the City Fire Fighters Union #15462 was created in 1913, and affiliated with the Seattle Central Labor Council almost immediately.

Seattle's fire department continued to modernize. In 1914 it acquired its first motorized pumping engines. Two years later the Division of Fire Protection and Inspection was created. Six inspectors were hired, and served under the fire marshal, who became a battalion chief.

In 1918 the IAFF was created and held its first convention, with Seattle #27 a charter member. Buck served as secretary of Seattle #27 until 1925, and as IAFF District 7 vice president from 1920 to 1922. Meanwhile, George M. Mentor became Seattle's chief in 1920 and ran the fire department as a business, with an outlined organizational structure, published rules and regulations, and a new program of in-school fire safety presentations. Captain Steve Snails initiated this program in response to witnessing children die in fires, and taught thousands of youngsters to "keep the bedroom door closed!" Eventually Snail's work generated the Public Education Section, under the fire marshal, and an elementary school was named after him.

Chief Mentor supervised the retirement of the department's last horses (1924), and a 1926 National Board of Underwriters' survey. This survey upgraded Seattle from Class III to Class II, which was the highest classification given to any jurisdiction. Two years later the fire department had six battalions that included thirty-two

Labels on ladder illustration (left margin): GOOSENECK, HOOK, SHIELDS, RUNGS, SPAR, BRACES, SHIELDS, STRAPS

engine companies, six hose companies, three fireboat companies, twelve ladder truck companies, and two squad companies.

The 1930s brought stiff cuts to Seattle's fire department, under Mayor John F. Dore. He began with what a 1933 IAFF article mockingly called "an innovative salary ordinance." This cut wages that had been in place since 1924 by fifteen percent. The legal authority for this action remains obscure. Seattle #27 counter-offered with a revised and reduced payroll that included voluntary acceptance of one day off in every six, without pay, but kept existing pay scales. Dore refused.

Two hundred seventy-five fire fighters were laid off, followed by the closure of the 6th Battalion, four engine companies, three hose companies, two squad companies, and a truck company. Seattle #27 organized to reinstate these fire fighters, and to reestablish the closed companies. Some sort of court action dictated placing seven companies back into service and rehiring 186 fire fighters. It also required the city to reissue payment to some fire fighters who had voluntarily signed salary waivers, thinking they might hold onto their jobs by doing so.

A total of eight companies were reinstated, but then Station 30 (which included Hose Company 30) was closed in 1935, and the Lake Union fireboat, the *Snoqualmie*, was retired. Meantime, things were so tight that no bank would cash pay warrants issued by Seattle until the city backed them for the full amount, plus five percent. According to several fire fighters, a young jeweler named Leo Weisfield cashed them without discount. (Weisfield remained a loyal supporter of Seattle's fire fighters well into the 1970s.)

During this time the fire department's motor shop took over rebuilding older equipment, since there was no money for new equipment. In 1937 Seattle did take delivery of one piece of new equipment, its first aerial truck. Mayor Art Langlie appointed Battalion Chief William Fitzgerald as chief in 1938. "Fitz" became a legend, the type of fire chief who ruled his department absolutely. Nineteen thirty-eight was also the year Seattle got its first aid car, to respond within the downtown area.

A year later the WSCFF was formed, and Chief Fitzgerald attended early meetings and supported the formation of a statewide council. Seattle #27 had two members on the WSCFF's first executive board: O.K. Coffin as secretary-treasurer, and A.D. Adams as a trustee. Max Maximilian, also a member of Seattle #27, was the IAFF's District 7 vice president at the time, and continued to serve in that position until 1944.

After years of makeshift and modified equipment, the beginning of World War II continued to keep the Seattle Fire Department from acquiring much-needed equipment. At the same time the city itself rapidly expanded, this time from war-related

EMS 69

industrial growth. Boeing created its own fire department, and required its subcontractors to meet Boeing's safety standards. As the industrial base of the city grew, Chief Fitzgerald requested and received government funds for a new station on Harbor Island, Station 31, which soon took in the fireboat *Duwamish*, and became part of a new division, the Seattle Harbor Patrol.

Like many cities during World War II, Seattle established volunteer fire department auxiliaries, assigned to specific stations, to assist professional companies. When World War II ended, Seattle #27 began a major campaign to restructure the fire fighters' work schedule. This was in part to provide jobs to returning fire fighters who had served in the military and to those new hires who had temporarily replaced them. By late 1948 Seattle #27 had won the forty-eight-hour workweek, with ten-hour day and fourteen-hour night shifts.

Technological advances followed, beginning with two-way radios in all first-line units and a central dispatch in 1950, while truck companies became ladder companies.

The 1950s saw general movement toward increased union membership, so that in September 1953, Seattle #27 had eighty-five percent of all its fire fighters as members. That October Seattle allowed Seattle #27 to collect dues through payroll deduction and began providing an annual clothing allowance of fifty dollars. Seattle #27 kept its political independence in Olympia, although it remained affiliated with the WSCFF. In addition, it had one member, Felix Arena, who served as WSCFF treasurer from the mid-1940s until 1965, in what was then one of the two most powerful offices in the WSCFF. The other position was secretary, and was held by Jack Waller (Spokane #29) and then Walt Lambert (Spokane #29). There were statewide initiative attempts at "home rule" legislation for several years, which Seattle #27 and the WSCFF lobbied against and helped to defeat.

Seattle #27's executive board, circa 1958. STANDING, L-R: *unknown, unknown, John Richmond, unknown, unknown;* SEATED, L-R: *unknown, Felix Arena, Harold Nilsen, Axel Drugge, unknown.*

AXEL DRUGGE COLLECTION

In May 1958 Ballard's Seattle Cedar Lumber Manufacturing caught fire. The fire spread along the Lake Washington Ship Canal, and became the largest fire in Seattle since 1889, injuring ten fire fighters and one harbor patrolman. A few months later the fire department added six new Ford station wagons, assigning one to each existing aid car. Using these new rigs, the department began to transport critical emergency cases rather than waiting for private ambulance service, setting the stage for the Medic One program ten years later.

The Seattle Fire Department did its part to incorporate state-of-the-art technology throughout the late 1950s and early 1960s. The possibility of atomic war and a desire to be prepared for natural disaster triggered federal and municipal plans for civil defense, and fire fighters were considered part of the response team. Seattle #27's magazine, the *Fire Fighter*, featured regular but vague articles on the need for such training to fight "A-Bomb fires." In April 1961, the world's first jet-powered fire truck went into service in Seattle. Its Boeing turbine engine was replaced later that same summer after problems that included braking. The next year Seattle hosted the "Century 21" Exposition, or World's Fair, at the new Seattle Center. The Exposition, including the 550-foot Space Needle, had its own fire protection force to support Seattle's department.

Hand-drawn map for delegates to the 1963 WSCFF Convention in Seattle, where John Smith (#31) was elected president. Note key landmarks identified: the Benjamin Franklin Hotel, department stores, Weisfield's, a bowling alley, and a liquor store.

GEORGE ROOP COLLECTION

In 1965, after more than twenty years in office, Arena stepped down as the WSCFF's treasurer, and was replaced by another member of Seattle #27, Don Meyer. John Richmond was just beginning his twelve year legacy of leadership as secretary-treasurer of Seattle #27. At the 1967 WSCFF Convention, Richmond squared off against others in the WSCFF, including Ken Strong (Spokane #29), as the WSCFF's executive board was restructured. When the convention was over, the WSCFF had combined the secretary and treasurer positions, and created seven vice presidential positions.

During this period, the WSCFF lacked solidarity. At the 1968 WSCFF Convention Seattle #27's resolution passed, barring an individual fire fighter or groups of fire fighters from introducing legislation without their local's and the WSCFF's approval. Penalties included the WSCFF's automatic opposition of the legislation and expulsion of the offending member or members from their local union. Seattle #27 disaffiliated from the WSCFF within weeks of this convention.

Richmond and Seattle #27 then joined other major IAFF locals at that fall's IAFF Convention, fighting off the enactment of a majority vote that would have required locals to affiliate with their state associations. Seattle #27 took advantage of its options and stayed out of the WSCFF until 1979, although Richard Sparks, while Seattle #27 president, made an attempt to reaffiliate in 1973. Dick Warbrouck, who would later become president of Seattle #27, remembers his local used per capitas equivalent to what would have gone to the WSCFF to buy the local its building on 1st Avenue.

While Seattle #27 focused on its political autonomy, change was coming to the fire department, and to the city of Seattle. Hiring practices needed to incorporate affirmative action, and Seattle #27 had no choice but to adapt. In January 1959 Claude Harris had been hired as the first black fire fighter in Seattle (and perhaps the state). But the city of Seattle did not begin to formally address the issue of affirmative action until 1968, when it began a minority recruitment program that applied to all of its departments. For the next eight years both the city and its fire department revamped and revisited a variety of policies and practices regarding hiring and affirmative action.

In 1976 two promotions, including Harris' to battalion chief, were legally challenged by non-minority applicants who charged they had been unfairly passed over. Seattle #27 paid for the appeal (*Maehren v. Seattle*, 1979), which was to last for another nine years. Meanwhile, minority membership in the fire department continued to rise until the mid-1980s, while Bonnie Beers became the first woman fire fighter in the Seattle Fire Department in October 1977.

During the same period hiring practices began to change, the Seattle Fire Department became a national innovator in providing on-site medical response. In 1968 Chief Vickery and Dr. Leonard Cobb, from Harborview Hospital's Cardiology Department, began trial use of the fire department's personnel and first aid cars to deliver "out-of-hospital" care to cardiac patients. Grants provided four years' funding. In 1972, as these funds expired, the City of Seattle refused to pay for the program to continue, in part because of differences with Harborview concerning funding.

Fire fighters went public, and gathered enough contributions to fund the program for several years, creating the Medic Two program. As the Seattle Fire Department led the way in integrating paramedic services into its fire department, Seattle #27 began the difficult process of integrating EMS into its contract negotiations.

Richard Warbrouck and Richard Sparks (pres #27) deliver petitions with 63,000 signatures in a campaign to recall Seattle Mayor Uhlman in 1976. Uhlman had backed a budget from the director of the city's office of management, Walter Hundley, which proposed major cuts to the fire department's arson unit. Chief Richards spoke to news media against these cuts, and was fired in December 1974. L-R: *Warbrouck, Sparks, elected official.*

RICHARD WARBROUCK COLLECTION

⟷ *Fractious Fraternity* 27

⟷ *Someone Like Me* 83

⟷ *EMS* 69

⟷ *Collectively Bargaining* 99

While branching out into broader emergency medical response, Seattle's fire department also expanded its maritime response. The 1973 tank explosion on the 560-foot tanker *Cygnus* had the US Coast Guard and the Police Harbor Patrol ferrying Seattle's fire fighters out to the burning vessel, as the fireboats *Duwamish* and *Alki* also responded. Shortly after this the US Maritime Administration provided funding to establish the Marine Division of the Seattle Fire Department, with the requirement that this division would respond anywhere in Washington State's waterways.

LEOFF 2's two-tiered retirement system (amending RCW 41.26.480) had passed in June of 1977. A period of intense negotiations between the WSCFF, Seattle #27, and Tacoma #31 (also out of the WSCFF) ensued. Final terms included formation of seven WSCFF districts, with Seattle #27 hiring its own additional lobbyist. Dick Warbrouck is credited with much of what it took to bring Seattle #27 back in.

At the 1982 Convention in Yakima, Seattle #27 asked for the WSCFF's dispensation on its per capita fees, in part because of the expense of the Maehren appeal and a drawn-out series of arbitrations and contract negotiations. Seattle's request was denied. It didn't pay its per capita and was out of the WSCFF, but not before voting in the infamous 1982 presidential election.

The Seattle Fire Department continued to modernize. By the late 1980s it had a Hazardous Materials team. Although regular units were to respond to such incidents, the department added a special van equipped with a library on hazardous materials, protective clothing, and monitoring and decontamination equipment. The van's library and microfiche was soon replaced with a computer system that tracked weather and wind conditions in addition to storing a database of product information. A second truck was added in 1988.

While this specialization and expansion was going on in the department, some workplace conditions were slower to progress. It wasn't until the mid-1980s that Seattle provided all combat fire fighters with new turnout coats, pants, boots, gloves, and other safety clothing. Before then it had paid only a clothing allowance. In 1985 Mayor Charles Royer appointed Chief Claude Harris Seattle's first minority chief, who served until the end of 1996.

Beginning in 1989, the Seattle Fire Department had a series of major fires in which fire fighters died. With each came more detailed investigations, and some changes in the department's equipment and procedures.

The first of these was the Blackstock Lumber Company fire, which resulted in the death of one fire fighter. This triggered a mandatory investigation by the Washington State Department of Labor and Industries (L&I), which found the Seattle Fire Department

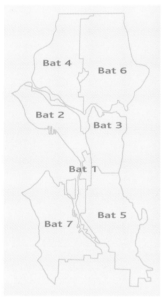

A map of Seattle's seven battalions, as of 1978.

SEATTLE FIRE DEPARTMENT YEARBOOK 1978

Unidentified Seattle #27 fire fighter "gaining entry."

SEATTLE FIRE DEPARTMENT CENTENNIAL YEARBOOK 1989

Lobbying on Olympia in 1991. L-R: *Dick Warbrouck, John D. Richmond, John O'Brien (House Speaker pro-tem), Chief Claude Harris.*

RICHARD WARBROUCK COLLECTION

negligent in two major training areas: on SCBA gear (self-contained breathing apparatus) and in tracking fire crews at large-scale operations. L&I also fined the city.

As a result, a safety officer position was created (as battalion chief). Personal Alert Safety System (PASS) devices, which sound an audible alarm when an individual stops moving for a given time, were provided to each fire fighter on the scene, and name badges for individual crews were kept with both the incident commander and crew sector officers. In addition, the fire department commissioned its own full operational study, which recommended improved fleet management, an apparatus replacement plan, and upgraded communications. In the spring of 1991 all city radios were converted to a centralized Computer Aided Dispatch (CAD) system, and new radios were added in 1994. In the midst of these upgrades, from the summer of 1992 through the winter 1993, Seattle fell victim to a serial arson spree. When Paul Keller confessed and was convicted as the arsonist, he had set more than one hundred fires.

By spring of 1992 Seattle #27 reaffiliated with the WSCFF, as District 11. Paul Harvey, president of his local since 1984, worked hard to convince members of his own local to return to the WSCFF, and negotiated so Seattle #27 was not required to pay back dues, nor to provide a second lobbyist.

Some Seattle fire fighters continued to have grave concerns about their working conditions, and filed anonymous reports to L&I in 1994. They were anonymous in part because of the fire department's negative reaction to any such concerns. The department's personnel tracking system was found to have significant problems, one of which concerned the new radios, which were "splash proof" but not waterproof.

Then came the tragic Pang Fire of January 5, 1995. What turned out to be a basement fire caused the floor to collapse; four Seattle fire fighters never made it out. All of Seattle's fire fighters have had to live with this loss.

Four independent investigations were begun by L&I, the US Fire Administration, the IAFF, and the International Association of Fire Chiefs. L&I found violations including lack of communication within the department, some safety equipment had not been provided (flame-resistant cloth hoods in particular), and that there had been interference with the safety officer and his duties. A fine was levied against the department.

Eventually Martin Pang, son of the business's owner, was arrested in Rio de Janeiro and extradited, with the understanding he could be tried only for arson. He was convicted, and sentenced to thirty-five years in 1998. All of the studies and fines

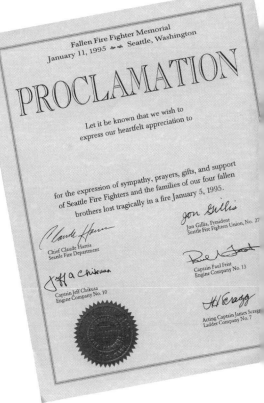

A certificate handed out by the Seattle Fire Department and Seattle #27 to supporters of the Fallen Fire Fighter Memorial, in commemoration of the four fire fighters who died in the Pang warehouse fire.

WSCFF COLLECTION

Charles Hawkins turned down an offer from Microsoft to pursue a childhood dream, to become a fire fighter. He was hired by the Seattle Fire Department in 1984, and within six years was elected Station 10's representative to Seattle #27. In 1991 the IAFF sponsored a human rights convention in Los Angeles, and Jim Fossos, secretary-treasurer of Seattle #27, worked to get Hawkins, Robin Gibson, and Melanie Anderson sent on behalf of the local.

Seattle #27 then created its own Human Relations Committee, to provide representation and direction in addressing the thorny issues of affirmative action, and as Hawkins put it "to get the change coming from within the union," with Hawkins as chairman.

Hawkins continued to be elected to this position until 1999, when he was elected president of Seattle #27. As District 11 representative, Hawkins was the first African American to serve on the WSCFF's executive board, and the only African American to have served as an IAFF president in Washington State.

did not create agreement or even acceptance within the department or within Seattle #27, as to what had gone wrong or could be improved in responding to major fires.

At the end of 1996 Claude Harris retired as chief. James Sewell was appointed Harris' successor, but not before politics within the fire department got ugly. Selection criteria had been established that virtually eliminated anyone from within the department as a finalist. The Seattle Black Fire Fighters Association (SBFFA) gave their support to Sewell; Seattle #27 gave him a vote of no confidence. Harvey, no longer president, facilitated meetings between a number of fire fighter groups in an attempt to address the divisiveness within the rank and file.

Harvey was then re-elected president of Seattle #27, in the fall of 1997, and then IAFF District 7 vice president in fall of 1998. Mike Milam was appointed to fill out Harvey's term, then lost the presidency to challenger Charles Hawkins, in 1999.

A few months later, in December 1999, the World Trade Organization (WTO) met in Seattle. Tens of thousands participated in mostly peaceful protests, including many members of AFL-CIO affiliated unions. In a crisis of ever-escalating responses by municipal and federal agencies, those in the Seattle Fire Department refused to order use of fire hoses for crowd control. Hawkins is generally credited with the decision. The refusal is in keeping with lessons learned during the race riots of the late 1960s, when those in the fire service made the decision that their work is to arrive at a situation and deliver emergency services, not law enforcement, and that it is imperative everyone involved in a situation knows this.

Seattle #27's executive board as of fall 2002. L-R: *John Hinson, Joe Coultman, Dana Caldart, Greg Scott, Paul Atwater, Theresa Purtell, Dale Watanabe, Ken Stuart, Mike Milam.*

SEATTLE #27 COLLECTION, PHOTO BY MONICA BLUM

In early 2002 Hawkins announced he was stepping down as WSCFF's District 11 representative to focus on being president of Seattle #27. Cory Bostick ran for district representative against another Seattle #27 executive board member, Kenny Stuart, and won by a vote. That fall Hawkins was defeated by current Seattle President Paul Atwater.

When Sewell was appointed chief, he had proposed hiring sixty-five new fire fighters, construction of a new training center, and the creation of an officer's training program. As of June 2002, twenty-eight fire fighters had been hired, but the training center and officers' program were still only plans. Late 2002 brought extensive budget cuts, which may close a number of stations, unless voter referendums in 2003 provide additional funding.

Spokane #29: *Longtime Leadership*

An illustration from Spokane Fire Department's "brown book," a manual on all aspects of fire fighter protocol.

GREG BORG COLLECTION

After several small grass fires during the dry summer of 1884, the Spokane Falls City Council authorized purchase of fifteen hundred feet of hose and two hose carts. In August, although this equipment had not yet arrived, twenty men joined Rescue Hose Company 1, and elected Eugene B. Hyde its president. A week later two downtown fires destroyed the Sprague House Hotel and sixteen other businesses. Within months the council had created a volunteer department by ordinance and added Spokane Hose Company 2.

For the next few years Spokane Falls' volunteer fire fighters spent much of their time on the showier aspects of their organizations. They raced hose carts in competitions throughout the Pacific Northwest, secured elaborate uniforms, hosted Firemen's Balls, and put on a performance of *The Mikado* (an operetta).

In 1889, about two months after Seattle's Great Fire, most of Spokane's Central business district burned in Spokane's Great Fire. In a legendary account of the fire, the superintendent of the city's privately owned Holly Water System, Mr. Jones, is generally held responsible for the degree of devastation. In this version Jones was off fishing at Lake Cour d'Alene when the fire started, and had with him the key to the city's waterworks. Given the tinderbox conditions and the inexperience of the volunteers, it is questionable whether Spokane's fire fighters could have further controlled the fire even with more water available.

The Great Fire pushed Spokane's City Council to pass an ordinance on December 18, 1889 which created a professional fire department of twenty-five men, with an annual budget of $33,000. By April of 1890 the city had installed an electrical alarm system and the department had six "decently trained" horses, one steam engine, a horse-drawn hook-and-ladder truck, a chemical engine, four hose carts, and two engine houses.

⬅➡ *Hose Cart Races* **59**

⬅➡ *Seattle #27* **165**

BELOW LEFT: *Undated photo of Spokane fire fighters, probably volunteers.*

SPOKANE #29 COLLECTION

BELOW RIGHT: *The entire Spokane Fire Department (all equipment, horses, and fire fighters) poses, circa 1893-94. They are in front of the Spokane Chronicle offices, located within the Auditorium Building.*

NMAC COLLECTION, L93-34.78

Once the department went professional, fire chiefs were appointed and removed from office according to the political fortunes of the mayor. Then came the 1896 appointment of Harry Meyers, a plumber and founding member of the Tiger Hook and Ladder Company. Meyers remained chief until 1912. During his term seven new wood frame fire stations were constructed. Each was built by fire fighters, in trade for Sundays off, and was designed to shelter both men and their horse-drawn equipment. The *Spokesman Review* described the fire fighters building Station 6:

⟷ *Stations* 96

> Almost without exception the members are young fellows who have been engaged in some sort of trade before joining the force. As a consequence, they include all sorts of artisans. They are good workmen, too. Time is a surplus asset among them. Indeed, the chief occupation of the men between fires is to find something to do; so it comes to pass that the carpenters and the blacksmiths and the harness makers and the wheel wrights who belong to the department spend a good many hours in fine work at their trades. It is purely a labor of love, and the things turned out in fire stations equal those produced anywhere. All the repair work of every kind is done by the firemen, and they attain all-around proficiency.

In 1912 Chief Meyers was dismissed for what one researcher called "a minor technicality" having to do with making a profit on ladders sold to the city. Almost as soon as Albert L. "Boomer" Weeks became chief, he upgraded the department's fleet. Weeks, who built his own powerboats, took a different approach than Meyers, who had purchased three "autotrucks." Weeks started by designing each new vehicle, and had a machine and paint shop built at Monroe and Sharp, behind Station 3. Then, between calls and inspections, on-duty fire fighters constructed vehicle bodies, frames, and other parts, and assembled them. Average construction time was about three weeks per vehicle. By 1916 the horses were gone.

Chief Albert L. "Boomer" Weeks supported the 1913 ballot measure that created Spokane's two-platoon system.

NMAC, COLLECTION L93-25.7

City Water Dept. Truck built by S.F.D

A City of Spokane Water Department truck, circa 1914, which was built by fire fighters, as part of their general duties.

NMAC COLLECTION, L93-25.24

⟷ *Platoons, Kelly Days and Transit Passes* 57

It was while Boomer Weeks was chief that the two-platoon system was first enacted in Spokane. In November 1913 this ballot proposition (amendment #3) was opposed by many influential parties, including the *Spokesman Review*. But Weeks supported the two-platoon system, as did Public Works Commissioner D.C. Coates, who was quoted in the *Spokesman Review*:

> Let's quit figuring on the basis of $50,000 or $70,000 and base our calculations on the average of 40 or 70 cents [per taxpayer]. Think what this amount will mean in better home life and better health for the firemen of the city.

The ballot passed and on January 2, 1914, Captain W.W. Eichelberger left work at 6 PM saying, "Good-bye boys; I guess I'll spend the evening with the wife and kids."

Cost overruns and continued opposition put the two-platoon system back on the ballot in 1914, and it was repealed as of January 2, 1915. Whether this repeal motivated Spokane's fire fighters to form a union is unclear. But on April 16, 1917, the City Firemen's Union #15,515 affiliated with the AFL (as a miscellaneous trade union) and presented its documentation to the Spokane-area central labor council.

The next day the *Spokesman Review* reported "the work of organizing the firemen has proceeded so quietly that no hint of it leaked out until mentioned in the newspaper last week." How much secrecy had cloaked the formation of a city employees' union a few weeks earlier is unclear. It is also not clear how the City of Spokane reacted to its employees going union. Fire fighter Henry C. Smith came on in 1917 or 1918 and remembers:

> We had a union that was formed before I came on, and it was against the City Ordinance for the Firemen to be organized, so some of the members decided to put out a petition and hand it to the City Fathers, and the organizers did not want their name signed on the top, so they signed their name around in a ring, but they picked the name on top and he was fired off the job. I don't remember his name. Half of the firemen only belonged to it. Most of the Captains did not belong to it as they feared it would interfere with getting a promotion.

The same week the City Firemen's Union #15,515 affiliated, H.K. Taylor, its spokesperson, told the *Spokesman Review*:

> We have long felt the need of some regular organization among the firemen. They are scattered around among fourteen stations and sometimes rarely meet one another. The purposes of the union are benevolent and are not intended to create trouble, as some would infer *[sic]*."

The *Spokesman Review* reported Chief Weeks:

> ...did not question the right of the men to join the union but saw no necessity of it in view of the rights under the civil service pension fund and sick benefits already enjoyed by the firemen.

Although the details are unclear, Spokane's local also participated when a separate international union for fire fighters, the IAFF, was created within the AFL. Later in 1917, in Buffalo, New York, AFL President Sam Gompers initiated this process. Fire fighters from around the United States and Canada convened in Washington, D.C., on February 29, 1918. Their official purpose was to write a constitution and bylaws "for the sole benefit of rank-and-file fire fighters in the United States and Canada." Spokane's representatives helped do so, and came home with a charter membership in the IAFF for Spokane #29.

From the time the City Firemen's Union #15,515 affiliated they had a single demand, a raise in pay. Members lobbied for this throughout 1917 without success. In May 1918, shortly after affiliating with the IAFF, Spokane's fire fighters went to the city council and Mayor Fassett and offered an ultimatum: either they got a raise in pay or they would resign en masse.

The council refused to authorize any raise, but made promises that there would be some increase at the beginning of 1919. Fassett went on record that all city employees deserved more pay, but made it clear nothing would be forthcoming until the next budget cycle. The council went further, informing fire fighters that if they all resigned and the civil service process couldn't keep up with the number of jobs available, the council would then shift to a more general application process. On May 29, 1918, Mayor Fassett was quoted in the *Spokesman Review*:

> We are all called upon in these times of war [World War I] to make sacrifices. I call upon you men of the fire department as patriotic and loyal citizens to join with us in running this city economically and in accordance with law by retaining your positions under your present wage until we can legally give you more. If you feel that you cannot do this and wish to resign to go elsewhere, may God be with you.

The *Spokesman Review* also reported Commissioner of Public Safety Tilsley's and Chief Weeks' acknowledgements that twenty fire fighters had quit within the last ninety days and about fifty percent of the remaining department was threatening to quit unless an increase of fifteen dollars per month was granted.

Once again, there is no clear record that might document how this stand-off was resolved. Fire fighter Smith recalls Spokane #29 was on the verge of extinction, and that the city sponsored a "relief association" to break it. Smith remembered:

> A bunch at 5's [Station 5] organized what they called a Relief Organization that paid the members one dollar a day. This broke up the union. I remember I obtained the books of the union and we had eighty-five dollars left in First National Bank. We were notified by the bank if no moneys were added, or withdrawn, in a number of years... the money would be taken over by the state. That was the state law, as it would be a defunct organization. A few of us got together to save the union. It was myself, Mr. Blunc, Al Keal, and a few other loyal members. We met at Moriarity's on East Cora Avenue, and paid our dues and revived our union. Then later, this Relief Organization merged with our union. This Relief Organization was formed for the purpose to kill our union, and the heads of it were the Chiefs, and many of the Captains and some of the members of the department [a company union].

One way or another, Spokane #29 hung on. By 1926 it was ready to work with other IAFF member locals in Washington State to sponsor a bill to enact a statewide two-platoon system. IAFF District 7 Vice President E. W. Powell (Tacoma #31) tried to pull together state locals and did gain the endorsement of the Washington State Federation of Labor (WSFL). But by December Spokane #29's secretary, A. J. Schrader, knew the bill didn't have the support of the biggest IAFF local in the state, Seattle #27. He wrote the president of the WSFL, W.M. Short:

> Seattle firemen will fight a bill of this kind. I wish you and Mr. Powell would have a talk with the President of their Local and find out for what reason they object to such a bill.

By January of 1927 Spokane #29 had taken a new tack. Schrader again wrote Short, this time asking him to withdraw the bill and outlining the plan to try for a two-platoon system within Spokane. "We are at present circulating a petition to put it before the people at the March election. May need your assistance at that time."

Once again the *Spokesman Review* led the opposition. This time it was joined by the Taxpayer's Economy League, a group formed especially to defeat this ballot measure, of which little else is known. Spokane's fire fighters were described as misrepresenting the cost of a two-platoon system, and were said to want the shift change so they could go out and work other jobs. Voters turned the proposition down.

Spokane City Firemen Strikebreakers

During the big National Railroad Shopmen's strike in the summer of 1922 the Chief of the Spokane Fire Department organized among the different fire stations in the city what was known as the professional strikebreakers on the City Fire Department.

These men were hired by the Northern Pacific Railroad, through Fire Chief Weeks, to go on their days off from duty to the railroad shops at Parkwater for strikebreaking duty, at a wage of $6.00 a day for 8 hours' work. The railroad furnished these men with a high-powered car and armed driver to drive them from their homes to the shops and from the shops to their homes.

The officers who were in personal charge of these men at the Railroad Shops were Fire Captains William Russel and Theodore Kofmehl, Fire Lieutenants Guy Hannum, Evan Johnstone, Edward Dunning and Charles Burger.

All promotions on the Police and Fire Departments are through three civil service members, who are all appointed by the five City Commissioners. These three civil service members are all outside men who do not know the least thing about either the Police or Fire Departments, which actually results in both the chiefs doing all of their own hiring, promoting and firing of their own men, which has created rank favoritism and graft and soft jobs on both the Police and Fire Departments.

Fire Chief Albert A. Weeks has four near relatives on the Fire Department besides himself, drawing a combined monthly salary of $905. These relatives are Captain George Weeks, Master Mechanic Ernie Johnstone, Lieutenant Evan Johnstone and Pipeman Cecil Weeks.

All this has been highly approved and O. K.'d by our rubber-stamp Commissioner of Public Safety, Maurice Smith.

An unsigned flyer, circa 1922, that makes undocumented accusations Chief "Boomer" Weeks arranged the hiring of Spokane fire fighters as strikebreakers (or scabs) during the 1922 Northern Railroad Shopmen's strike.

SPOKANE FIRE STATION MUSEUM COLLECTION

Platoons, Kelly Days and Transit Passes **57**

The degree of acrimony in Spokane is illustrated by a bizarre incident a few months later. Fire fighter Harry Ilse was charged with trying to blow up the *Spokesman Review* building with a bomb made of 102 sticks of dynamite. Ilse claimed he was framed by another fire fighter, a supporter of the two-platoon proposition who was angry at the *Spokesman Review's* opposition. The prosecution tried to make a case for attempted blackmail. Ilse was found not guilty, but thirteen years later, another unsuccessful bomb, also delivered to the *Spokesman Review* building, put him behind bars.

Spokane #29 kept trying for a better work schedule. In February 1928 the city did adopt a day-on/day-off shift plan which Chief Weeks was quoted as saying was "virtually... the same as the double platoon." Each fire fighter was also required to be available by phone, and also to "devote" (Week's word) two days, eight hours per day, from his off time to "carry on inspection work and drill practice."

The IAFF's magazine, the *International Fire Fighter*, reported that Spokane's city council, at the request of Public Safety Commissioner Charles A. Fleming, approved a shift to twenty-four hours on duty/twenty-four hours off. This replaced a forty-eight on/twenty-four off system, and a "working day" was reduced from sixteen to twelve hours. Fire fighters would no longer have three hours per day off for meals. Chief Weeks told the IAFF reporter:

> Under the new system with no meal hours off, sufficient men will be on duty at all times to meet any emergency. The plan will not only increase efficiencies, but will create better working conditions for the men themselves.

There is little specific information available on Spokane #29's activities between the late 1920s and the early 1940s. The WSCFF was formed in 1939, and Spokane #29 was a founding member, but it is unclear what role it played as the constitution was drafted. Jack Waller, who was to become a pillar of the WSCFF, joined the Spokane Fire Department in 1938, and considered himself the WSCFF's legislative representative as of 1941.

A 1940 American Insurance Committee report on Spokane's general safety practices noted, "relief men are now used to fill [military] vacancies as well as those caused by illnesses." This may partially explain the vehemence with which Spokane #29 went after a pay raise in 1942. Their successful campaign was covered in an April, 1944, IAFF *International Fire Fighter* article. Spokane #29's Secretary Charles McCray wrote the headline: "Spokane, Wash., Local No. 29 Wins Two Pay Raises By the Ballot Within Two Months."

First, Spokane #29 asked the city council for a twenty-dollar increase and was "turned down flat," according to McCray's article. Spokane #29 then told the city council it would take the proposal for a pay raise to the voters. The city council promised not to oppose this effort. Over 15,000 signatures were gathered, and the referendum was added to an already-slated August 1942 ballot on parking meters. "Then came the double-cross," wrote McCray. City commissioners decided such a pay raise was an administrative, not a legislative matter. This kept it off that ballot, and off the next ballot, in March 1943. McCray wrote "we [Spokane #29] decided to fight out the question in the courts regardless of the cost."

Interestingly, it was Chief W. Payne who represented the fire fighters in court. The decision upheld the commissioners' decision and dismissed the case. Chief Payne

⟷ *WW II and the Cold War* **66**

It took a state supreme court decision to allow this special election, which granted fire fighters a raise. Note the June 22, 1943, ballot is printed with a union bug.

SPOKANE FIRE STATION MUSEUM COLLECTION

immediately appealed to the state supreme court, which reversed the decision in April 1943. The commissioners appealed but were denied, and a special election was slated for June 22, 1943. The measure passed, but since the commissioners had given all city employees a ten-dollar raise during the appeal process, fire fighters could receive only ten dollars of the twenty approved.

In January 1944 fire fighters went for another ballot measure, for another twenty-dollar raise, to bring their salary to $200 per month. The commissioners ran an amendment to the city charter on the same ballot that gave the commissioners "exclusive right over the salaries of all officers and employees of the city." Spokane's 154 fire fighters, most members of Spokane #29, hit the streets while the Taxpayers' Economy League and the newspapers ran opposition. The mayor threatened to fire Chief Payne on a radio broadcast. Spokane #29 countered by having George Richardson, secretary-treasurer of the IAFF, make his own radio presentation.

Chief Payne and nine other fire fighters ran the campaign, and whatever they said needed to be done, was done. McCray's article continues:

> In our campaign we forgot about the business men and so-called money people. They were against us, so we never bothered with them. Labor, teachers, P.T.A.'s and Old-Age Groups were our source of favorable votes. Over 200 talks were made before various groups... Each member sent out a mimeographed personal letter to everybody he was acquainted with. The total of these letters numbered about 35,000.... Our total mailing ran close to 80,000 out of a population in the city of about 140,000.

Spokane #29 won their second raise and defeated the commissioners' amendment, both with a margin of three to two votes in an election where slightly over 35,000 voted.

As of January 1, 1947, Spokane gained the two-platoon system and one "Kelly Day in seven days" (making the eighth day a Kelly Day). Details of this campaign were not available.

By 1950 all of Spokane's fire fighters were also members of Spokane #29. The fact that only members of Spokane #29 could participate in what had become an excellent insurance program may have had something to do with this. Details are

AT RIGHT: *A member of Spokane #29 evacuates a female victim down a ladder, step by step, circa 1940s.*

SPOKANE FIRE STATION MUSEUM COLLECTION

FAR RIGHT: *Father Bairy (sic) stands by the recently rescued woman.*

SPOKANE FIRE STATION MUSEUM COLLECTION

sketchy, but it seems that the Relief Organization originally established in about 1917 to defeat the union evolved, and was used as the basis for an excellent and cheap insurance plan that motivated every Spokane fire fighter to join the union. To secure funding for the Spokane Firemen's Pension and Trust, the department held fireshows, beginning in the early 1950s.

⬌ *Fireshows* 160

In 1956 Spokane #29 once again tried for a pay increase by referendum and pledged two dollars per member, per month, to fund the campaign. It is not clear if this raise was approved. Nineteen fifty-six was also the year Jack Waller was elected IAFF District 7 vice president, an office he was to hold for the next eight years. Walt Lambert, also a member of Spokane #29, succeeded Waller in 1964. A year later Robert Munk added to Spokane #29's presence in the WSCFF, serving as its secretary and then secretary-treasurer from 1965 to 1972.

The next documented ballot measure put forward by Spokane #29 was scheduled for November 1965. A month before the vote the *Spokesman Review*, never a supporter of pay increases for city employees, ran a front-page article which falsely charged members of the Spokane police and fire departments with the illegal use of funds to support their campaign. Individual fire fighters and police filed lawsuits which came before the state supreme court in September 1969 (*Amsbury v. the Cowles Publishing Company* and *Tilton v. the Cowles Publishing Company*). The court majority found that those falsely accused were not technically libeled.

⬌ *Malicious Media* 181

Months earlier, Spokane #29 had hosted the WSCFF's thirtieth convention, which also celebrated the fiftieth anniversary of the formation of the IAFF. The following year Ken Strong was elected president of Spokane #29. Howard Vietzke, who had been party to the lawsuit, had served as Spokane #29's secretary-treasurer since the mid-1960s. Vietzke stepped up to follow in Munk's footsteps, serving as the WSCFF's secretary-treasurer from 1972 to 1981. When the WSCFF created districts in 1976, Spokane #29 elected Vince Azzinnaro and then Don Spangle as its WSCFF District 1 representative.

The program cover from the 1968 WSCFF Convention and IAFF Jubilee (50th Anniversary) celebration hosted by Spokane #29.

SPOKANE FIRE STATION MUSEUM COLLECTION

In 1980 Spokane #29 had a memorable set of negotiations with the city. Ted Rail (who would later become District 1 representative) was in on negotiations for the first time. He remembers that by the time the contract was settled everybody in the department got an almost seventeen percent pay increase, with almost seven percent more in benefits, including Kelly days. (Inflation during 1979-1980 was rampant.)

Then came the arson attack of July 21, 1984. Between 1:49 AM and dawn, twenty-eight Spokane fire companies and more than one hundred fire fighters fought three major fires, without a single serious injury. Three other fire departments were called in to fill Spokane's empty stations. Greg Borg (WSCFF District 1 representative) wrote an account of these events, "Out All Night, or All You Guys Do is Play Cards."

Ken Strong served as Spokane #29's president for a total of seventeen years, although he took several years off in the late 1970s and early 1980s. Using what he calls "the gift of gab," Strong was a key player in negotiating the restructuring of the WSCFF executive board in 1967, and ran for WSCFF president in 1982.

TACOMA #31 COLLECTION

Improvements within the department followed. In 1992 the city completely remodeled or rebuilt every station in town, with funding from a bond that had passed two years earlier. Spokane's fire department added a fourth platoon in 1993.

As of 1995, there were significant shifts in Spokane #29's leadership. Ted Rail had been its secretary-treasurer for almost fifteen years, and Dave West its president for almost ten. Doug Bacon defeated West, and Doug's brother, Mike Bacon, defeated Rail. Mike Bacon continues to serve as Spokane #29's secretary-treasurer. Doug served as its president until 2001, when Borg returned to that office.

The 1996 WSCFF presidential election affected Spokane's role in the WSCFF. Kelly Fox (Olympia #468) announced very late that he was challenging incumbent Michael McGovern (Lakewood #1488). Spokane was stalwartly loyal to McGovern, in part because of Vietzke's longtime work with McGovern. (Vietzke had served as the WSCFF's legislative lobbyist since months after McGovern was elected in 1982.) After Fox was elected, it took some time for Spokane #29 and Fox to work out their differences. The LEOFF Health and Welfare Trust was one forum for this lack of cooperation.

As Rail, who was elected to his current position as WSCFF District 1 representative months before that 1996 Convention, puts it, "It takes time to earn our [Spokane #29's] loyalty. We were loyal to McGovern, now we've become loyal to Fox." Spokane has fostered new leadership within its own executive board, and continues to be an active participant in the WSCFF.

➡ *Platoons, Kelly Days and Transit Passes* **57**

➡ *The LEOFF Health and Welfare Trust* **157**

SPOKANE FIRE ROYALTY

➡ *Ladies Auxiliaries* **52**

Prior to women entering the Spokane Fire Department, Spokane #29 had a ladies auxiliary, and a more informal group for the wives of its members, the Fire Belles. In addition, the Spokane Fire Department sponsored a fire queen and two princesses each year.

Spokane's Fire Department issued a special badge for its fire queen. Note that it is badge #1.

SPOKANE FIRE STATION MUSEUM COLLECTION

The Fire Royalty of Spokane (undated). L-R: *Gayle, Carol Ann, Sue (last names unknown).*

NMAC COLLECTION, L93-25.103

Malicious Media: *The Cowles Publishing Company Attacks*

Perhaps there exists a raise or workplace improvement Spokane employees sought prior to the mid-1960s that the *Spokesman Review* and the *Chronicle* supported. Records indicate these two papers led the opposition on whatever proposal municipal workers brought forward. Push came to shove over a November 1965 ballot measure. The proposal was to change the city's government from one with a city council and manager, with the mayor elected by and from council members, to a directly elected mayor and council, and no manager.

Once the proposal was on the ballot, Spokane #29 geared up its political machinery to win the election, and used the Spokane Area Public Safety Council, which was made up of all the members of Spokane #29 and of Spokane's Fraternal Order of Police Lodge #1. A new organization was also formed specifically to work on the campaign, the Committee of Interested Taxpayers and You (or CITY). The *Spokesman Review* weighed in heavily in opposition, running regular editorials against the measure. Citizens for Keeping Spokane's Family-Town Form of Government was formed to oppose the proposed charter amendment.

With the November election fast approaching, the *Spokesman Review* pulled out the stops and ran an article on the front page of its Sunday, October 24, 1965, paper. In it, the paper named members of the Spokane police and fire departments under a headline that read, "23 Named in Charges of Illegal Fund Use." Among those named were Bob Munk, Jack Waller, and Howard Vietzke, all active members of Spokane #29 and at various times, the WSCFF. *Spokesman Review* reporter Jack Roberts' article reported court summons had been issued on charges:

> ...involving alleged "unlawful" and "unauthorized" appropriation of $5,300 in Fraternal Order of Police funds for political and financial support of a City Charter change for a Strong Mayor-Council form of city government.

Vietzke remembers going in to work, where other fire fighters asked him about the charges. "I told them, sure, we did it. I hadn't seen the paper yet." By the time his mother called to ask if any of it was true, Vietzke realized how serious the allegations were. Jack Waller's sons, Harvey and Darroll, remember a meeting of "all of them [at least the fire fighters]" at the Waller home, where their father kept saying "it was going to be OK, that there was nothing to fear because they had done nothing wrong."

The article was based on Assistant Police Chief E. W. Parsons' and Police Department Secretary Wesley Natwick's pending suit to block use of the police funding

5 WAYS TO STOP

THEIR TROJAN-HORSE ATTACK ON SPOKANE'S FAMILY-TOWN FORM OF GOVERNMENT

The cover from a flyer published by the Citizens for Keeping Spokane's Family-Town Form of Government. It claimed changing to a "strong mayor" form of government would foster "Bossisms, graft, and spoils" as well as increase taxes.

SPOKANE #29 COLLECTION

in the pro-change campaign. Judge W.R. Cole of Ellensburg dismissed the six fire fighters from the action and also denied the temporary injunction because Parsons and Natwick didn't have proof.

The six fire fighters then sued the Cowles Publishing Company, owner of the *Spokesman Review*, charging malice and libel:

> The defendant published in the Sunday Edition of its *Spokesman Review* on the front page thereof, an alleged news article.... That said article... was published by the defendant, with malice, and was made for personal selfish reasons to enhance and further the objects of the defendant; and said article, as defendant well knew at the time of publication, was false and untrue.

On January 11, 1966, the week before this case, *Amsbury v. the Cowles Publishing Company* (1969), was to be heard, a second lawsuit was filed by the other seventeen police and fire fighters, *Tilton et al v. the Cowles Publishing Company* (1969). The two cases went through the judicial system together. The *Amsbury* supreme court decision describes the events that triggered the article:

> Jack Roberts, a political writer for the *Spokesman Review*, was told of the possibility that a lawsuit seeking to enjoin transfer of police union funds to CITY was to be started. His informant, a former employee in the office of the Mayor of Spokane, was then employed by an advertising agency handling publicity for the supporters of the existing city manager form of city government. Following up this tip, Mr. Roberts telephoned the Spokane police chief in an attempt to verify this story. The chief told Mr. Roberts he could release no details at the time, but agreed to give him an "exclusive" on the story. Mr. Roberts again telephoned the police chief on the evening of October 22nd, and was told that nothing definite had developed, but that something might be ready on the next day, Saturday.
>
> About noon of Saturday, October 23rd, the police chief called Mr. Roberts and told him that if he wanted the story he should be at a certain suite in a downtown office building at 1 o'clock that afternoon. Although Saturday was Mr. Roberts's day off, he went to the designated office. The office was that of one of the attorneys for the plaintiffs in the proposed suit. Mr. Roberts was there given copies of various legal papers pertaining to the proposed lawsuit.
>
> The suit was being instituted by Assistant Police Chief E. W. Parsons and Police Department Secretary W. W. Natwick for the purpose of preventing use of Fraternal Order of Police funds by the Public Safety Council to support the proposed charter change. At the time these papers were given to Mr. Roberts they had not been filed, but Mr. Roberts was told that the named defendants were being served with process at that time. (The action was filed the following Monday.)
>
> Upon leaving the attorney's office, Mr. Roberts, the police chief, and Assistant Chief Parsons went to a restaurant for lunch. Mr. Roberts then returned to his office at the *Spokesman Review* and in the course of 30 to 45 minutes wrote the story about the Parsons-Natwick lawsuit. He made no further attempt to verify the story....
>
> The mayor and chief of police of Spokane would stand to lose their jobs under a strong mayor system; the position of assistant chief of police would be removed from civil service protection; the employee of the public relations firm who gave Mr. Roberts the "tip" on the story was a former employee of the mayor; plaintiffs in the... lawsuit were high employees of the police department... and one of their attorneys was opposed to the charter change...

The jury awarded each of the plaintiffs $13,000. Cowles Publishing Company immediately appealed, requesting a new venue, which they got. The state supreme court reversed both decisions (*Amsbury* and *Tilton*) on September 18, 1969. The majority opinion determined that by virtue of being on the elected board of the

Spokane Area Public Safety Council, and by speaking in public to support the change in government, all twenty-three had become public figures, and were therefore subject to a lesser standard regarding libel. It also found that Roberts, although he made no effort to verify the charges he reported, did not do so "maliciously."

Two of the supreme court judges, J. Hale and J. Rosellini dissented vehemently:

> In a case such as this where the defendant's newspapers are virtually a monopoly and those papers have taken an editorial stand on a controversial issue of local concern, the court should be inclined to impose upon that defendant an obligation to treat those having opposing views with absolute fairness rather than to prove a protective shield for its defamatory attacks upon them, whether such attacks are disguised as a report of accusations made by third parties or published as accusations by the editors themselves. Otherwise, First Amendment rights may soon be enjoyed only by the privileged few who hold the power of the mass media and will be effectively denied to the individual, contrary, I think to the spirit of the constitution....
>
> Considering the reprehensible conduct of which the plaintiffs were accused in the publication and the fact that such charges are seldom entirely forgotten, the verdict of $13,000 for each plaintiff does not shock the conscience of this member of the court.

Cowles Publishing Company was awarded no damages. But years later, when Vietzke was ready to sell his home, he discovered Cowles had put a lien against it. Vietzke also remembers that for years these cases were used to convince new police and fire fighter recruits to stay away from the union.

During the court actions related to this case, the Spokesman Review offered front-page coverage of decisions supporting their claims.

SPOKANE #29 COLLECTION

HELMETS

Chief of Spokane Fire Department (unidentified) in full gear of the time. Note bullet hole in photo.

NMAC COLLECTION, L93-25.2BBW

This style, sometimes referred to as an "8 cone" because of its eight panels, was made by Cairns & Brothers, of New Jersey. The Spokane Department used this style of helmet from 1889 until 1942.

GREG BORG COLLECTION

This style is called the "war baby" helmet. It was designed to use less leather during WW II. The Spokane Department used them from 1942 until the late 1960's.

GREG BORG COLLECTION

This yellow plastic helmet was made by MSA (Mine Safety Association). Note plastic safety goggles. This helmet was put into use in the Spokane Department in 1972, and remained in use until 1989, when it changed to a more modern helmet. From about 1965 until 1972, the Spokane Department used black plastic helmets just like this yellow one. That year state safety standards banned black helmets because they were hard to see in the dark and smoke.

GREG BORG COLLECTION

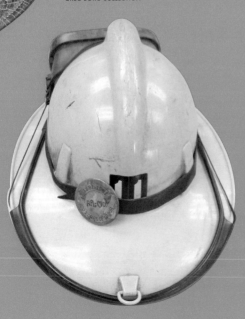

In use since the 1990s, this helmet's goggle strap holds a disposable flashlight and a door jam.

DEL SPIVEY COLLECTION

Tacoma #31:
Working-Class Power

According to *100 Years of Firefighting in the City of Destiny*, Tacoma was the "self-appointed lumber capitol of the world" in the 1880s. With so many mills, numerous and spectacular waterfront fires were guaranteed. The all-volunteer New Tacoma Hook and Ladder Company 1 was formed on May 29, 1880. Its equipment consisted of one truck. After a major fire at a downtown drugstore in October 1882, the Commencement Hook and Ladder Company 1 was created, and eventually acquired a hose cart and hose. In 1883 Tacoma adopted a "commission" form of government, including a commissioner of public safety, who oversaw the volunteer fire companies. Old Tacoma and New Tacoma were merged into one city on January 1, 1884, and as part of this, the two hook-and-ladder companies became one.

Tacoma suffered numerous large fires that year, many of which were the work of arsonists. The city's water system demonstrated itself to be woefully inadequate, so Tacoma contracted for a six-mile canal, which ran from Spanaway Lake to the city reservoir at Hood Street. The fire department was given a building to house the two hose companies and their equipment: chains and hooks (for pulling down frame buildings), one hook and ladder truck, two hose carts, and 3,200 feet of hose. Four more hose companies were created in 1885, the same year Tacoma's privately-contracted water franchise came on line, able to deliver three million gallons of water. Forty hydrants were immediately added.

The Tacoma Hook and Ladder Co. 1, in front of their station at 13th and A Street, with all of their equipment, circa 1880.

TACOMA PUBLIC LIBRARY COLLECTION

Arsonists continued to burn out many buildings and businesses throughout Tacoma. In May of 1889, after the popular Monty and Gunn's grocery store had been torched, Tacoma's Chamber of Commerce held a meeting that had the feeling of vigilantism, and created its own Committee of Safety.

A month later, on June 6, 1889, Seattle's Great Fire began. Seattle's fire department immediately sent a telegram to Tacoma Chief J.D. Rainey asking for assistance. Tacoma loaded twenty-five fire fighters and its new four-wheeled hose cart onto a railroad flatcar, which arrived in Seattle sixty-three minutes later. A second crew of eight followed on another train. Meanwhile Tacoma resident Allen C. Mason hired every Tacoma baker, and at 1 AM the next morning the first relief boat full of bread was

⬅ *Seattle #27* **165**

on its way to Seattle while a caravan of vehicles, loaded with other donated supplies, took the roads north.

Later in 1889 Tacoma established the first professional fire department in Washington State, and purchased new equipment that included four steam engines and several horses. Chief Rainey received a salary of $125 per month, while the fire fighters under him received from $70 to $90 per month. (Sometime during the next seven years these rates of pay were lowered.) Citizen support of the expanding fire department was mixed. As new fire stations were proposed, several neighborhoods fought to exclude them, objecting to their horses and clanging bells.

In 1890 the fire department submitted the first of what would be decades of unanswered requests for a fireboat. Instead, twelve fire fighters were laid off and two of the chemical engine companies were taken out of service. Both police and fire fighters were issued warrants instead of paychecks, which local merchants discounted when cashing.

On June 26, 1896, Tacoma fire fighters threatened to go out on strike as of July 1 if they did not receive eight months of back pay, which totaled between $480 and $600 per fire fighter. Insurance companies then informed the city that without its fire department all policies would be cancelled. Tacoma's merchants gathered $2,780 to cover the June salaries and food for the department's horses; the fire fighters agreed to keep working for another ninety days. During this same period Tacoma shifted its fire and police departments to a civil service system, and forty men took Tacoma's first civil service test on July 1, 1896. On December 22, the city produced the $62,000 in back pay owed to fire fighters and police.

The Tourist Hotel, which later became Tacoma's Stadium High School, had been built by the Northern Pacific Railroad and was uninsured. An arsonist used naphtha and a pile of wooden shingles to set it on fire October 11, 1898. Delayed response time and lack of full-size water mains meant there was little the Tacoma Fire Department could do to keep the inferno from spreading to adjacent property. Northern Pacific took a loss of $150,000, a hit to all of Tacoma's economy. At about this time Tacoma Tug and Barge Company agreed to have a pump and four hose connections mounted onto one of its vessels, the *Fearless*, for use by the fire department.

But even with the *Fearless*, by 1900 Tacoma was trailing other metropolitan fire departments. Most cities assigned eight fire fighters to an engine, Tacoma staffed only six. When insurance companies threatened higher premiums unless staffing improved, Chief Poyns requested and received an additional twenty fire fighters, two new engine companies, and three additional chemical engines. Fire fighters gained ten days of vacation per year, but continued to work twenty-eight days per month, twenty-one hours per day.

In 1902 a huge fire at Wheeler-Osgood Sash and Door Company forced Tacoma to make improvements. The mill had been the largest of its kind on the West Coast, and 285 jobs were lost when it burned. The city council approved purchase of a fourteen-inch water main on the tide flats, added another steam engine, a combination chemical engine, a hose wagon, and reestablished a hose company. Tacoma also began requiring fire escape inspections, forcing improvements on more than one hundred buildings.

Although the first written rule books were issued in 1907, one to a station, several sources mention scandal as a way of life in Tacoma's departmental politics in

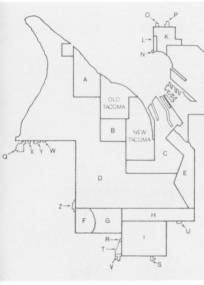

A map of the expansion of Tacoma, as of 1981. Old Tacoma was formed in 1875, and incorporated with New Tacoma in 1884. The lettered sections indicate further annexations to Tacoma, in the order they occurred.

100 YEARS OF FIREFIGHTING, TALBOT AND DECKER

1908. Mayor Wright decided to fire all the fire fighters at Station 4 and replace them with his own appointments. Then came the National Board of Fire Underwriters' inspection, which condemned the city's alarm system for faulty wiring, and found rules and regulations violated "with impunity," members dismissed without due cause, lack of discipline, inadequate engine capacity, a serious inability to respond to second alarms, no building inspections, and a "lack of aggressiveness" in fighting fires under adverse conditions. Chief McAlevy, who had himself been discharged twice for "political activity," attended the next city council meeting. Records indicate he was unrestrained in the volume and content of his comments as he informed the council they did not allocate enough money to the fire department.

In 1909 the Tacoma City Council considered abolishing its Civil Service system, but decided to keep it. Little is known about what triggered this. For the first time the council entertained the possibility of a fireboat, and asked the commissioner of public works to contract for two sets of boat plans, total cost of construction not to exceed $90,000. When the bids were presented to the council, both were immediately rejected. The following year Chief McAlevy came to the council with a budget request of $378,980, almost three times what he had received the year before. A featured and fully capitalized line item was "A $125,000 OUTLAY FOR A FIREBOAT." Voters defeated a bond issue on a fireboat that October.

McAlevy had other problems to deal with. *100 Years of Firefighting in the City of Destiny* describes an incident where two fire fighters in Engine Company 6 let a woman into their quarters after midnight. They then hosted "a disgraceful drinking party and passed out in alcoholic stupor." McAlevy used the station gong, but could not wake them. When they awoke, he accepted their resignations.

The two-platoon system first appeared on a ballot in 1912, and was defeated.

Tacoma's motorized fleet poses in front of Station 6, circa 1913. Automobiles are Stoddard-Daytons. Engine Co. 1, 3, 4, 5, and 6 had Seagrave Combination Hose and Chemical wagons.

RALPH DECKER COLLECTION

The City Firemen's Federal Union #15601 affiliated directly with the AFL in June 4, 1917. Within a week it had grown from 78 to 101 members, in a department of 105. A committee of #15601 members immediately approached the city council with a proposal for a two-platoon system. At first, the council refused to consider the proposal, then said it couldn't be done because it would require an additional $50,000, and Tacoma had a fifteen-mil levy maximum.

On August 29, 1917, every member of the fire department except the chief and assistant chief then signed a letter of resignation, effective September 10. Mayor Fawcett made his opinion clear, "Let them quit. Let the damn city burn" rather than meet their demands.

Six days later, on September 5, the city council enacted the two-platoon system with an eighty-four-hour workweek, effective September 12. Off-duty hours

⟷ *Platoons, Kelly Days and Transit Passes* **57**

Wives of Tacoma #31 members played a big part in the successful campaign for a two-platoon system in 1917.

RALPH DECKER COLLECTION

would be split between the two shifts, and after some discussion, it was agreed that off-duty fire fighters would respond when called in for a fire. The change to a two-platoon system triggered the Tacoma Fire Insurance Association to increase its premiums by fifteen percent because of the lack of coverage on all shifts, but Battalion Chief Earle Charles More, who was in the fire department from 1913 to 1959, recalled:

> You never saw such a change in the morale of the men. They felt like they had been released from prison and the old fellows, as we would refer to them, were so happy to think that by solidarity in our union, we had at last broken the backs of the politicians who labeled themselves "The Tax Payers League."

In February 1918 representatives of Tacoma #15601 went to Washington, D.C. and the local became one of the fifty-two charter members of the IAFF. Later that year Tacoma #31 tried for a salary raise. According to an article in the IAFF's September 1933 *International Fire Fighter*, the "[city] council flatly refused to act." One hundred nineteen of the one hundred twenty-two fire fighters submitted a letter of resignation unless they were given a raise. On December 31, 1918, the Tacoma City Council offered a five dollar raise, with one day off in eight. The offer was accepted, and Tacoma #31 became one of the first in the nation to have one day off out of every eight days. The department replaced all of its horses with motorized units in 1919, and sold all its horse-drawn equipment to American La France (a major fire equipment manufacturer) for twenty-five dollars a piece.

Six years later, in 1925, both police and fire fighters campaigned for a thirty-dollar-a-month raise. The city council put the matter before the voters, and after some hesitation, the fire fighters decided to support this approach. They then staged an all-

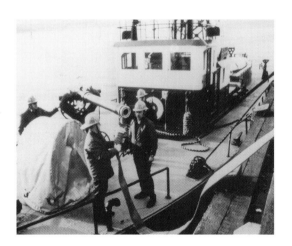

The Fireboat was built by Tacoma's Coast Lines and went into service on Oct.1, 1929. Its 10,000 gpm pumping capacity was provided by four Sterling motors (425 hp each). The deck cannon was known as Big Bertha, and could pump 5,500 gpm.

TACOMA #31 COLLECTION

out publicity campaign, including a one-reel movie of a staged fire that was shown with regular features at Tacoma's Rialto Theater. The ballot measure passed in March 1926, and the raise took effect January 1, 1927.

A bond measure passed in 1928 that funded the largest-ever expansion of the Tacoma Fire Department. In 1929 three new stations, all engine companies with new Mack pumpers, went into service. Thirty-three new fire fighters were hired, and the department finally got the fireboat it had wanted for decades, the cleverly named *Fireboat*. This vessel was put into operation on October 1, four weeks before the national fiasco of Wall Street's Black Tuesday began the Great Depression.

From then until at least the early 1940s, Tacoma cut all its employees' wages. Tacoma #31 provided many relief programs, but also took the city to court for back wages, claiming the council could not cut wages established by popular vote, and eventually prevailed. The decision was issued while fire fighters fought the infamous Tacoma Hotel fire.

World War II only increased the Tacoma Fire Department's staffing problems. Unlike Seattle and other municipalities, who used volunteer auxiliaries to supplement its workforce, Tacoma used duration men, who were exempt from hiring standards. Tacoma #31 eventually decided to allow the duration men in as members. In February 1945 a fire in the Hamilton Candy Company spread upstairs into the Maefair Apartments, and killed twenty-two of its eighty-five residents. This was the greatest loss of life from fire to date in Tacoma.

Tacoma #31 used 1946 to gear up for the 1947 legislative session. Its goal was improved pensions, and in January it requested IAFF District 7 Vice President Earl Brower put all his lobbying efforts into pension reform. That August members of Tacoma #31 assessed themselves twelve dollars each to cover lobbying expenses, which included a December dinner for all of Pierce County's state representatives and senators. The 1947 legislature amended RCW 41.16 (Firemen's Relief and Pension Act), with changes that restructured municipal pension boards, increased funding, and added vesting.

As of January 1, 1947 Tacoma instituted the three-platoon system with a sixty-three hour workweek, keeping its ten-hour day/ fourteen-hour night shifts. Throughout 1947 members of Tacoma #31 argued among themselves as to what would be the best way to reduce their workweek. Seattle #27 had successfully gained a forty-eight-hour workweek through a general ballot measure which had taken effect January 1, 1947. But Seattle #27 was still hammering out their shift scheduling, trying hard to avoid three eight-hour shifts that might remove the night shift's sleeping privileges. After Brower came to Tacoma and explained the Seattle situation, Tacoma #31 decided to try for a fifty-six hour workweek. Once again, Tacoma #31 was successful, gaining this workweek reduction in 1949.

The worst earthquake to date in Tacoma struck on April 14, 1949. Eight people died as a result, although no major fires occurred. Battalion Chief Harold Fisk won out competition for a fallen figurehead from Engine Company 6's station, and planned to use it as his headstone.

The Joint Council of Public Service Employees Organization of Tacoma and Pierce County had been formed in 1945, and Tacoma #31 had participated in it to a lesser or greater degree since its formation, depending upon how closely the two groups' interests aligned. In 1951 the Joint Council came to Tacoma #31 and explained that any cost-of-living increases to any municipal worker's salary required an emergency ordinance. This was due to the Korean War (called the Korean Incident at the time). Tacoma #31 gathered signatures for the Joint Council's petition to the city council.

When presented with the petition, one council member proposed salary increases for fire fighters, which he withdrew when another wanted to grant an emergency increase to all city employees. The council then asked the state attorney general's office for an opinion on the matter. Meanwhile Tacoma #31 proposed a limited salary increase and a clothing allowance. The attorney general issued an opinion that inadequacy of pay was not an emergency, in that it did not threaten a breakdown of city governmental functions.

By December 1951 Tacoma politics were vicious. Commissioner James T. Kerr announced the dismissal of Fire Chief Charles Eisenbacker. Kerr then postponed his action until January 1, 1952, after Mayor Anderson challenged his decision. At the last city

◄► *WW II and the Cold War* **66**

◄► *At the End of the Day* **137**

◄► *Pounding the Pavement* **63**

In 1948 the Tacoma Fire Department purchased three Pirsch aerial ladder trucks (Engine Co. 1, 2, 4 and 5) and lined them up in front of Station 2, with Truck Co. 1, 2, and 3.

RALPH DECKER COLLECTION

council meeting of 1951 the mayor announced he was ready to file impeachment charges against Kerr, in part because of Kerr's drinking, formally noted as "misconduct in office."

At the next council meeting, on January 2, the council authorized a seven percent increase in wages to all city employees. On January 9 Kerr dismissed Eisenbacker for his "belligerent, arrogant manner" and Eisenbacker's statements to the press, which Kerr characterized as "disrespectful to the commissioner of public safety." Eisenbacker retired the next day, to take a position with Civilian Defense. On January 21 Kerr resigned, and Mayor Anderson became acting safety commissioner until the following March.

The state legislature assigned a committee to investigate vice within Tacoma, and a petition was filed to have a general election to change Tacoma from a councilman form of government to that of a city manager and council. Most municipal employee unions opposed the change since it would give the city council the power to appoint the civil service board, which had been an elected body. The Civil Service Protection League was formed, and Tacoma's fire fighters assessed themselves ten dollars each to fund the league.

The November 1952 ballot measure passed, and on January 1, 1953, Tacoma gained a new form of government, which also made each council member the commissioner of one of the city's departments. This meant each union negotiated directly with its commissioner, who had broad discretionary powers over that department, limited mostly by the budget approved by the entire council.

At this point Tacoma #31 proposed a contract that required wage negotiations be settled through "boards of arbitration" should they reach impasse. The City of Tacoma refused, stating that since fire fighters were public officers, their wages and compensation could not be subject to contract. Nineteen fifty-three was also the year Tacoma initiated Rescue Company 1, nicknamed "the Breadwagon."

In 1954 the Tacoma City Council agreed the city would provide work uniforms for its fire fighters. According to Trowbridge's account, this consisted of:

> …three shirts, two pairs of pants for station wear, one pair of boots, one pair of water repellant trousers and a water repellant jacket. Officers were given three white shirts, a blue serge uniform and a white water repellant jacket.

By the late 1950s Tacoma #31 had gained significant wage and workweek improvements, and had started to work with the WSCFF as it lobbied Olympia for further improvements. Two individuals had joined the department who would play a large part in both Tacoma #31's and the WSCFF's successes.

John "Jack" Willis worked as a union lineman, then became a Tacoma fire fighter in 1950, following in the footsteps of his father, who had been a proud member of Tacoma #31 since 1928. From the beginning, Willis wanted fire fighters to have the same collective bargaining rights that privately employed union workers were allowed.

John Smith had been hired as a fire fighter in 1952, and immediately took part in union politics, making one unsuccessful bid for his local's presidency before he was elected in about 1955, after Ray Greenleaf had served one two-year term. Smith forged a relationship with Charlie Marsh, leader of the Tacoma police during this time. He also went to work to secure a building for his local.

Pat McElligott, current Tacoma #31 president and District 6 representative to the WSCFF, describes the friction between Willis and Smith as part of a tradition of

Attaching hard suction (non-collapsible hose) to Pirsch pumper, since hydrant is lower than pump.

L-R: *Armstrong, Bud Nickols, Lloyd "Bud" Card (driver), Steaves or Stevens. Card put his house up as collateral when Tacoma #31 financed its first union hall.*

RALPH DECKER COLLECTION

antagonisms. He calls it "the battle between stations," and the stations at battle have usually been Station 1, where Willis worked, and Station 13, where Smith worked. Smith and Willis also had very different styles, temperaments, and lobbying techniques.

At the 1963 WSCFF Convention, Smith was elected president, although his own local did not support him. By 1964 Willis was Tacoma #31 president. Without really working cooperatively, the two men managed to keep Tacoma #31 a key player, both within the WSCFF and in Olympia. Meanwhile, Tacoma's fire department added a second rescue unit, and had ninety EMTs trained and assigned to companies by 1973. Within three years this had expanded to 236 EMTs, at least one on every engine and truck company.

⟷ *EMS* 69

In 1963, the same year Smith stepped up as WSCFF president, there were major fires in Tacoma. The Musicbox Theater was destroyed by two separate fires later found to be the work of an arsonist. All one hundred patrons, who had been watching Hitchcock's *The Birds*, were safely evacuated. Then on July 14, approximately 150 Tacoma fire fighters responded to the Pier 7 fire. Twenty-two were injured seriously enough to require hospital care. Five other fire departments also responded: Brown's Point, Fircrest, Midland, McChord, and Buckley. The next year, a formal mutual aid policy was established between Tacoma's fire department and that of University Place (for waterfront coverage) and with Gig Harbor (for the Tacoma Industrial Airport).

Tacoma was one of several departments investigated by the US Commission on Civil Rights in 1970. In response, Tacoma #31 worked with the city to develop a recruitment program that went into effect in 1971, and the first black fire fighter was hired in Tacoma in 1972. The department continued to recruit minority fire fighters, although retention was to become a problem by the late 1970s.

⟷ *Someone Like Me* 83

Tragedy struck the department in February 1974. Fire fighter Dale Jones was killed when the Tuddí Restaurant burned, with inhalation of superheated gases cited as the cause of his death. Shortly after this, radios were issued to every on-duty fire fighter. It was during the 1970s that the marine rescue program was added as well.

Marine Rescue Unit 1, assigned to Station 15. This unit may be related to the beginning of Tacoma's Surface Effect Ships (SES). which can skim along at 30 knots and are used for security and pollution activities, on-water fire suppression, and search and rescue.

TACOMA #31 COLLECTION

Willis became the WSCFF's legislative representative in 1974, and then ran for IAFF District 7 vice president. Willis lost to Jim Martinez (Boise #672) in an election that was more than close. Many encouraged Willis to demand a recall because of procedural issues. He refused, in part because he didn't want the IAFF to shoulder the enormous expense of reconvening. Many in Tacoma #31 felt wronged, however, and Tacoma #31 joined already-disaffiliated Seattle #27 in leaving the WSCFF on September 1, 1974, in part because of the Willis-Martinez election. Willis continued to serve as WSCFF lobbyist while his local was disaffiliated.

Tacoma #31 rejoined the WSCFF in 1976, and Jim Hill was elected the first District 6 (Tacoma) representative at the 1977 WSCFF Convention. In 1978 he was elected president of his local, and vice president of the WSCFF.

By 1980 the coffers of Tacoma #31 were low, and Chuck Jenkins mounted a successful campaign for its presidency, while Jim Cason was elected Tacoma #31's secretary-treasurer. Hill then defeated incumbent IAFF District 7 Vice President Martinez (Boise #672) at that fall's IAFF Convention. Cason stepped up to replace Hill as WSCFF District 6 representative, and Willis continued as the WSCFF's lobbyist for another year, making Tacoma #31 the major player in the WSCFF.

Cason was elected WSCFF vice president in 1983, and reported in that summer's issue of the *Washington Professional Fire Fighter* that the major issue facing Tacoma #31 was a proposed re-chartering of the city, which would address municipal employees' participation in non-partisan elections. This same year the fire department

The Top of the Ocean Restaurant fire of 1977. This was not a ship, but a waterside building. The arsonist was caught hours later.

RALPH DECKER COLLECTION

Members of Tacoma #31 have done virtually all the repairs and additions to their union hall since they purchased it in the mid-1960s.

TACOMA #31 COLLECTION

returned to a 24-hour shift and reduced hours to a 46.1-hour workweek. Many of the improvements in Tacoma's fire department during the late 1980s involved its newly created Emergency Medical Divisions, rescue units each staffed with two paramedics. By 1986 all Tacoma fire fighters on engine and truck companies were also EMTs.

EMS **69**

One Vote Matters **33**

The *Morning News Tribune* named Tacoma #31 one of the ten "most influential persons or organizations in Pierce County" in 1989. That year Cason challenged Ron Morehouse to become secretary-treasurer of the WSCFF, and won by two votes. When Tacoma #31 went into caucus prior to this vote, Pat McElligott made it clear he wanted to be Cason's replacement as District 6 representative, and that unless this was part of the deal, he would not vote for Cason. Recognizing McElligott's connections with Federal Way #2024 and other locals could cost him his bid for secretary-treasurer, Cason agreed. Tacoma #31 President Al Nyman was furious, and tried to appoint

George Thornhill; Thornhill deferred to McElligott. McElligott then ran for president of Tacoma #31 in 1990, and won, defeating Nyman.

Although Tacoma #31 had been party to Tacoma's affirmative action program, many in the local still did not support it. In addition to the recruitment of minority men, women had been joining the department, beginning with Eileen Lewis in 1981. While he was Tacoma #31's president Al Nyman submitted comments to Tacoma's civil service board:

> Competitive appraisal of applicants seems racially and sexually limited to white males, while "protected classes" are offered a free ride to city employment.

Clearly, attitudes and hiring practices have since changed, given that Lewis went on to become the chief of the Tacoma Department, with the backing of Tacoma #31, in February 2000. McElligott, who worked with Lewis at Bangor Naval Base as well as in Tacoma, thinks part of the change within the local came because of the efforts of Lonnie Hampton, who served as its secretary-treasurer. Hampton demonstrated the "power of participation with new hires" showing them what others in Tacoma #31 already knew, that "the union is where you go with a problem."

By 1995 Pierce County Fire District 10 merged into Tacoma #31. Tacoma also contracted fire protection to the City of Fife and Town of Fircrest, the first time it had gone beyond its city limits to do so.

During the mid-1990s, Tacoma's role within the WSCFF shifted. In September 1995 Cason left his position as its secretary-treasurer to train as its legislative director during the 1996 legislative session, under Howard Vietzke (Spokane #29). In June 1996 WSCFF delegates elected a new president (Kelly Fox, Olympia #468), a new vice president (Ricky Walsh, Richland #1052), and a new secretary-treasurer, Lonnie Hampton.

Cason died suddenly in January 1997. His death was a shock to his friends. family, and local, and it created a hole in the WSCFF's ambitious plans for the just-beginning legislative session. At the next IAFF Convention, in fall of 1998, Hill stepped down as District 7 vice president. McElligott ran to replace him, but was defeated by Paul Harvey (Seattle #27) in an extremely close vote. McElligott continues to represent Tacoma #31 to the WSCFF, as well as serving as its president. Tacoma #31 continues its tradition of a united executive board as it moves into the future.

Tacoma #31's executive board, circa 1998.

L-R: *Trent Wohlfeil, Jolene Davis, Dan Crotty, Rodger Edington, Pat McElligott stand-in (pres), Bruce Baurichter (s/t),Christine Kaufman, Jon Lendosky (vp), Vern Heller (Ken Faulkner not pictured).*

TACOMA #31 COLLECTION

Vancouver #452

In August 1866, on the Saturday after a devastating fire that destroyed most of a city block, thirty citizens of Vancouver formed the Vancouver Engine Company 1 and contributed $265 toward the cost of a fire engine. The city then donated another $1,000 and, presumably, an engine was purchased. The city council created its fire department on April 1, 1867. Vancouver's fire fighters, along with those of Camas, affiliated with the IAFF on October 29, 1935, as Vancouver-Camas #452. At the time they worked a one-day-on, one-day-off shift schedule. Four years later, Vancouver-Camas #452 was one of the founding members of the WSCFF, with member H.L. Leach serving as the WSCFF's first vice president.

In 1957 Vancouver-Camas #452 ran a successful city ballot measure that created a three-platoon system, and reduced the workweek from seventy-two to fifty-six hours. Arnie Emter, president of Vancouver-Camas #452 during this period, was able to negotiate directly with Vancouver's mayor. Improvements included the city's assumption of the cost of uniforms, which had previously been the responsibility of individual fire fighters. It was not until the early 1980s that the majority of Vancouver #452 members worked one job, fire fighting, to support themselves and their families.

Improvements in fire service working conditions and pay also brought a dramatic increase in the number of applicants. Fewer than 15 people applied for positions within the fire department in 1968; in 1999 over 3,000 individuals applied for ten openings. During the same period the City of Vancouver bargained hard against many of the local's proposals, and yet also advertised the "generous pay and benefit package [the city] provides to our employees."

While working conditions improved, a riff developed between the Camas and Vancouver fire fighters, culminating in the creation of a separate Camas local (Camas #2444) in 1975. Union meeting minutes indicate the final disagreement which triggered the split was Camas-Vancouver #452's refusal to provide a TV for the Camas fire fighters' day room.

During the early 1990s the City of Vancouver annexed several adjacent areas, which reduced the tax base of Clark County Fire District 5. Vancouver #452 and Clark County District 5 #2491 together took the lead in merging their fire departments to protect the fire district's existing jobs. (Clark County Fire District 4 #2811 had merged with Clark County District 5 #2491 in 1988.) On April 1, 1994, the seventy members of Clark County District 5 #2491, with full seniority, joined sixty-nine member Vancouver #452. Eleven additional fire fighters were then hired. From 1994 through 1999, Vancouver #452 faced intimidation and challenges from Fire Chief Dan Fraijo, a time some members refer to as "dark days." Two former presidents of Clark County District 5 #2491 continued their union work within Vancouver #452, Jim

Platoons, Kelly Days and Transit Passes **57**

Flaherty and Mike Phillips. Phillips was elected president of his new local in 1996, and made two bids for District 5 representative of the WSCFF, in a 1997 special election to fill a vacancy created by Cody Arledge's shift to WSCFF legislative representative, and again in 1998.

During this same period, Vancouver's battalion chiefs, who had been a bargaining unit within Vancouver #452, decertified from their local and the IAFF. The decertification was led by Joe Mackey, a former president of Vancouver #452, who, in 1992, lost by one vote to Kelly Fox (Olympia #468) in the WSCFF District 5 representative election.

Meanwhile, Vancouver #452 stepped up its participation within the WSCFF. At the 1997 Convention, Vancouver #452 member Bill Garlington was elected by acclamation as a WSCFF trustee (and served until 2003). At the same convention, Vancouver #452 proposed Resolution 97-7, which sought passage of legislation providing presumptive benefits for cancer, heart, and infectious disease. Unanimous adoption of this resolution led the WSCFF to lobby for successful 2000 legislation which lowered normal retirement age from 55 to 53 (amending RCW 41.26 LEOFF). It also laid the groundwork for passage of RCW 51.32.185 (Occupational diseases—Presumption of Occupational Disease for Fire Fighters) in 2002.

↔ *At the End of the Day* 137

At the 2000 Convention, Vancouver #452 brought forward Resolution 00-06 "Subsidies for Small Locals at WSCFF Events," which passed. A year later, with Resolution 01-04 (Revamp Pension System Through Initiative to the People), Vancouver #452 sparked enormous debate and discussion. The WSCFF pulled together to gain passage of I-790, in 2002. Mark Johnston (Vancouver #452) currently serves as one of the fire-fighter representatives on the state's eleven-member LEOFF Plan 2 board of trustees.

↔ *I-790* 149

Vancouver #452 is proud of the experience and knowledge gained by the officers and members of the former locals Clark County Fire District 4 #2811 and Clark County District 5 #2491, and, as Johnston puts it, "we are stronger together."

Jeff and David Garlington join other children of Vancouver #452 members gathered to make a banner and gifts to send to the children of New York City fire fighters, in remembrance of the September 11, 2001 tragedy. The banner read "Love, Faith, Hope: from our fire fighter children to yours."

KEITH DUYUCK COLLECTION

Outside the City Limits: *Fire Districts*

Spokane Fire District 1

In about 1940, shortly after mil levies were established in Washington State, Spokane Valley Fire District 1 was formed as an all-professional department. Surrounded by this new district, Millwood, site of the Inland Paper Company paper mill, opted out. Instead, Inland Paper traded donated equipment for its own volunteer department. Spokane Valley Fire District 1 #876 was affiliated on July 29, 1946. George Roop was the district's seventeenth fire fighter hired, in 1952, and the first to take a civil service exam. Almost immediately Roop was elected president of his local.

In 1953 payroll checks were on his desk when Roop got a call from Fire Commission Secretary Ray Toole. A few days earlier, Al Parkinson, a fire fighter, had died of a heart attack after responding to a fire. Toole told Roop to pull out Parkinson's check because "we don't issue paychecks to dead men." Roop immediately got on the phone to Mrs. Parkinson, told her to get down to the station to pick up her husband's check, and to cash it as soon as she had it.

Roop knew she had done this when Toole and a fire district commissioner appeared at the station to take back the check. Roop explained that his own check came after two weeks worth of work, and that Parkinson's check was also for work previously performed. Roop also made it clear he would bear the consequences of his actions, but that Toole's order exceeded Toole's authority, since Roop had been hired by the civil service commission, not the fire district commission.

Shortly after this, Spokane Valley Fire District 1 Chief Stanley suffered from, and eventually died of, lung problems, very possibly related to his fire service duties. His widow had been told "we'll take care of you" by the fire district, with the assumption that she would receive something in accordance with the Volunteer Fire Fighters' Relief and Pensions Act (RCW 41.24). Instead, both she and Mrs. Parkinson received nothing.

Roop took what records he could find and went to Olympia, and crossed paths with Bob Grimm, newly-elected state auditor. Grimm helped Roop contact Vern Fabian, secretary of the volunteer fire fighters' association. Roop then learned that although his department had always been professional, state law categorized it within the volunteer pension system because it was a fire district rather than a first class city.

Grimm arranged to have the Spokane Valley Fire District 1 pension information (and payments) sent to its individual fire fighters. When they reviewed this information, Roop and his coworkers learned they were not on even the volunteer pension

George Roop (#876, WSCFF vp) served his local and the WSCFF in Olympia from months after he was hired (in 1952) until 1969. He still gets phone calls asking for citations on state pension law, and has his own legislative library on the subject.

system's roster; only the fire district's secretary and two fire district commissioners were listed. Roop, the Spokane county auditor, and Grimm managed to get all the district's fire fighters grandfathered into the volunteer pension system, but there was nothing anyone could do for Mrs. Stanley and Mrs. Parkinson because they were beneficiaries, not actual pension participants.

All of Roop's research made him wonder why he and his coworkers, as well as other fulltime professional fire fighters in fire districts, third-, and fourth-class cities were considered volunteers when it came to their pensions. The common response in Olympia was that they "were neither fish nor fowl." Roop toured the state, talking to fire fighters in other locals trapped in this bind. One local that was particularly interested but also extremely intimidated was Olympia #468. Olympia Fire Chief Lynch ran his fire department the way he chose, and everyone knew it. When he fired someone at will, he might also violate the terms of that fire fighter's pension and final payments. So Roop learned to call ahead, and met Olympia fire fighters in concealed locations to discuss what might be done. "This was right in Olympia" says Roop, still amazed at the inequity that occurred in the very shadow of the Capitol.

At the End of the Day 137

"It took three years to convince the legislature" to include professional fire fighters serving in fire districts, third-, and fourth-class cities under the professional fire fighters pension program. "It came down to changing one word. We got 'first class city' changed to 'municipality.' That did it."

Roop and his local then worked to gather support for a successful Spokane Valley Fire District 1 levy, which established funding to pay into the pension system. Roop didn't go out of his way to make sure fire district commissioners understood that once this levy passed, pension funding would come under operations and maintenance, making it hard to eliminate.

Roop remembers there had been other fire district levies almost annually to make up for what they couldn't get through the junior taxing district. As part of this district, Fire District 1 had to compete with other service districts such as libraries, townships, irrigation, and cemeteries. The fire district levies passed because:

> …it was cheaper. If your property didn't have any fire protection, then that made it Class 10 for insurance purposes. If you had protection, you got Class 4 or 5. And you got the other actual services, too, for free. We responded to any emergency with an aid car and a resuscitator.

Roop later used his experience and understanding of taxation to get state passage of a bill eliminating townships within Spokane Valley Fire District 1, which allowed funding from the eliminated townships to instead go directly to the fire district:

> I just went for those [within Spokane Valley vs. statewide], I didn't want to take on the whole mess. In the valley, the townships had become spit-and-whittle clubs, they didn't do a thing. People didn't realize that when townships dissolved, Spokane County automatically got all the money that would have gone to a township.

In 1965 Spokane Valley Fire District 1 #876 got its first signed contract as a result of new statewide regulation that required contracts for employees working over forty hours a week. Roop described negotiating with his employer before contracts as a process where "whoever hollered longest and the loudest" came out ahead. But Roop and Spokane Valley Fire District 1 #876 held their own even before they had a

Collectively Bargaining 99

contract, thanks in part to Roop's meticulous and clear understanding of the laws affecting his local. "I still have a box of papers. I just take a copy of the law that applies and have the person read it when there's a problem. That's usually all it takes."

King County Fire District 25

King County Fire District 25 was created in April 1945, and expanded to the north and south over the next five years. In 1971 the City of Bellevue first attempted annexation of Newport Hills. Instead, King County Fire District 25 passed a bond, improved its staffing, and held onto Newport Hills. Four years later, in April 1975, King County Fire Districts 25 and 10 contractually combined their headquarters and staffing. Within a month King County Fire District 25 #2439 affiliated with the IAFF.

In April 1993, the fire district began contracting all services from the City of Renton, and King County Fire District 25 #2439 members transferred into Renton #864. As a result of Bellevue's partial annexation of the fire district, eight members of Renton #864 voluntarily transferred to the Bellevue department in January 1995, and became members of Bellevue #1604. (Seven had originally been members of King County Fire District 25 #2439.) Another portion of the fire district then incorporated as the city of New Castle, and contracts with Bellevue for fire services. Renton is annexing other portions of the district, which at this point contracts its fire service but retains commissioners and one employee.

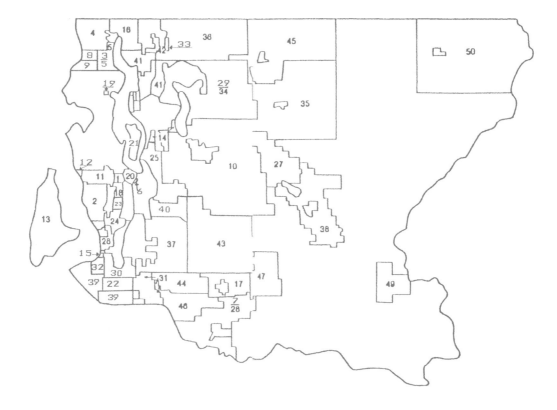

As of 1990, King County had fifty fire districts.

THE FIRE DISTRICTS OF KING COUNTY, HAROLD "JIGGS" HOYT

Rising from the Ranks: *Chiefs' Locals*

As the first fire fighter locals organized in Washington State in the early 1910s, fire chiefs' reactions ranged from strong support to firing the fledging local's leadership. Yet no matter what position each chief took on unionization, a chief's salary, work schedule, and working conditions have always been based upon what that department's fire fighters received. As John Willis (Tacoma #31) notes, "a chief's working conditions piggyback on what the fire fighters get in their contract."

Traditionally, chiefs have been selected from within the ranks of their department and are generally appointed by the mayor, council, or commissioners. Before collective bargaining rights became mandatory in 1967 (RCW 41.56 Public Employees' Collective Bargaining Act), when a fire fighter became a battalion chief, continued union membership was a matter of personal choice, and was influenced by the political climate within a department. This was in part because no fire fighter was required to be a member of his or her union.

For example, in 1941 E.C. Kuehner (Chehalis-Centralia #451) was president of the WSCFF and also chief of his department. The WSCFF's executive board determined this was acceptable since the situation wasn't covered in the WSCFF bylaws, didn't go against IAFF bylaws, and chiefs were dues-paying members of the IAFF. As late as 1958, Everett #46 (then Everett #350) member Earl Brower continued to serve as the WSCFF's legislative representative while chief of his department. Some chiefs, including former WSCFF president and Assistant Chief Michael McGovern (Lakewood #1488), continue to pay union dues after they are promoted out of their original bargaining unit, as "associate members." McGovern explains, "I'm happy to be a contributor to the on-going work of Local 1488."

Following the 1967 passage of RCW 41.56, the Department of Labor and Industries (L&I) almost immediately issued a decision regarding Seattle #27 that only "uniformed personnel below the grade of battalion chief" were part of a local's bargaining unit. Since this decision, battalion chiefs within a unionized department have been organized as separate bargaining units, as separate locals, and have chosen to stay out of the union.

Jim Rudd (Spokane #29) recalled that after the 1967 ruling, Spokane's chiefs "all but Marion Scotten, got out of the union pretty quick." When these chiefs chose to leave Spokane #29 they also lost their ability to participate in the local's insurance plan, which is sometimes credited for the rapid formation of Spokane chiefs' bargaining unit. Nineteen sixty-seven was also the year RCW 41.18 (Firemen's Relief and Pensions Act) was amended to include full chiefs.

↔ *Collectively Bargaining* **99**

↔ *Everett #46* **161**

↔ *Collectively Bargaining* **99**

↔ *Benefits Enacted* **133**

IAFF Local 1052 v. PERC (1981) was a case where Richland #1052 tried to overturn a Public Employment Relations Commission (PERC) decision that removed its battalion chiefs from the bargaining unit. In 1975, the City of Richland, represented by Cabot Dow, as he began his career as a union buster, filed a "unit clarification" petition to L&I while the fire fighters' contract was being negotiated. Dan Downs, then president of Richland #1052, remembers getting a court injunction to block it.

Richland #1052's 1975 contract was signed and included the battalion chiefs. The city quietly filed another petition as negotiations on the 1976-77 contract began. Administrative jurisdiction over bargaining units shifted from L&I to PERC when many portions of RCW 41.58 (Public Employees Collective Bargaining) were enacted on January 1, 1976. When the PERC hearings officer said he was going to conduct the Richland hearing on the merits of the case, Richland #1052 was unprepared because it thought the injunction was still in effect. The 1981 court case summarizes this event somewhat differently:

> At a [PERC] hearing in 1977, the Union [#1052] challenged the City's right to petition and requested the hearing officer not reach the merits. This request was refused. Then the Union representatives walked out and refused to participate in a hearing on the merits relying on lack of jurisdiction of PERC. The hearing officer continued to take evidence on the function of the battalion chiefs. He later decided that PERC had jurisdiction to consider the petition and found the bargaining unit should be clarified by excluding the battalion chiefs.

Richland #1052 appealed to PERC, and to superior court, and lost in both venues. When it came before the state supreme court the only issues under consideration were whether PERC should have accepted Richland's unit-clarification petition, and whether PERC's decision was "contrary to law, clearly erroneous, or arbitrary and capricious." The court ruled against the local on June 16,1981, and made it clear its decision did not make:

> ...a determination of whether the battalion chiefs are supervisory personnel or confidential employees who are ineligible for the benefits of the Public Employees' Collective Bargaining Act.

Four months later Richland #1052 filed a petition with PERC to gain representation of the battalion chief's bargaining unit. Not surprisingly, PERC ruled against the petition. Richland #1052 immediately appealed, and won a reversal in superior court. Both PERC and the City of Richland appealed the court's decision to the state supreme court and finally Richland #1052 won a precedent-setting victory in *IAFF Local No. 1052 v. PERC* (1985). The Supreme Court determined:

> Given the provisions of our act [RCW 41.56] and the fundamental difference between it and the federal act [the National Labor Relations Act (NLRA)] in the treatment of supervisors, we conclude the Commission [PERC] exceeded its statutory authority by denying the battalion chiefs the right to choose Local 1052 as its bargaining representative.

Jim Webster, labor lawyer, sees an additional reason why the decision was a win. "PERC originally ruled chiefs couldn't organize; this decision turned that around and allowed representation, and allowed representation to be in the same local." Webster believes the issue of whether chiefs choose to organize is related to the degree of solidarity and/or superiority between chiefs and fire fighters, although other factors come into play.

After passage of a wage freeze for all city employees except those covered by a collective bargaining agreement. Seattle's chiefs formed a separate bargaining unit, as did the city's police supervisors. Seattle's chiefs formed their own local, Seattle Fire Chiefs #2898, in March 1983, which has never affiliated with the WSCFF.

North Highline Chiefs #3780 affiliated in 1996. Its four members, all battalion chiefs who had come up through the ranks of North Highline #1810, petitioned PERC after fire commissioners "streamlined" several existing benefits. The chiefs served "at will," and worked under administrative contract; the district's civil service system had been eliminated in the mid-1980s. At the time, there had been ongoing negotiations between five fire districts (North Highline, Des Moines, Burien, SeaTac, and Federal Way) to consider consolidation into what would have been called Salt Water Ridge. When the non-union battalion chiefs put forward the wage scale for chiefs that were part of the consolidation discussed, the fire commissioners refused to recognize it. Interestingly, similar discussions about a consolidation that would involve all but SeaTac are currently underway, under the proposed name of Sound View Fire and Rescue. Paul Fray, current secretary-treasurer of North Highline Chiefs #3780, has hopes that should the consolidation go through, all its battalion chiefs could be members of his local.

SEATTLE'S CHIEF FITZGERALD

Seattle Chief William Fitzgerald.

SEATTLE #27 *THE FIRE FIGHTER*, AUGUST 1963

Seattle Fire Chief William "Fitz" Fitzgerald came from the ranks. Newly elected Seattle Mayor Art Langlie appointed Fitzgerald on April 26, 1938, just after the state cut "relief" payments by twenty percent. Seattle was issuing pay warrants many merchants refused to honor, the AFL and the CIO battled for political power within Seattle and the state, and there were charges of rampant corruption within the police department.

Fitzgerald ran the fire department with an iron hand, with what Bob Gough (Seattle #27) called his "intimidation factor." Yet Fitzgerald took part in some of the first meetings of 1938 that created the WSCFF, and supported its formation.

Every fire fighter who worked under Fitzgerald has a story about his appearances at middle-of-the-night fires, his requests for written explanations from every fire fighter on the scene who had not been in bunkers [turn-out gear], his personal system of merits and demerits. But at that same fire, if a neighboring business owner began to complain about a window broken by a fire fighter, Gough remembers "Fitz, all five-foot-three of him—he would have the owner saying 'yes sir, no sir, would you like a free dinner Chief, maybe our steak dinner Chief...'"

Fitzgerald retired in 1963, and with him ended an era; he had made the final decision on every hire during his term. Richard Warbrouck (Seattle #27 president) remembers Fitz studying Warbrouck's hands, to see if he did manual labor.

Bob Gough, still a rookie, recalls hauling garbage cans up a ladder, on clean up. He told the guy ahead of him on the ladder to "either move it or get the hell out of the way." The man pulled his head outside of the window and it was Fitz, who said "OK son, hand me the can."

Seattle #27 **165**

Puyallup #726

The Puyallup Fire Department in 1934. L-R: *Bill Voight, Harry Greengrass, Bill Mo, Frank Chadwick (police chief), Luke Caraway, Irving Jones, Dorman Storem, Fisher, Chet Brakefield (1st asst chief), A.J. McCarthy.*

PUYALLUP #726 COLLECTION

↔ *Platoons, Kelly Days and Transit Passes* **57**

Puyallup Ladder Truck 3 responding to a fire at the Vancouver Door company (circa 1991-1992).

PUYALLUP #726 COLLECTION

Puyallup #726 members responding to a paint store fire. The paint store, on Stewart Street, still exists.

PUYALLUP #726 COLLECTION

Three years after incorporating, in 1893, the City of Puyallup had a volunteer fire department and its first paid fire chief. Little more is known about the department until the 1930s, when it consisted of volunteers and "sleepers," (fire fighters who lived in the station in exchange for responding to fires) supervised by four paid fire fighters, all officers, including Fire Chief A.J. McCarthy. In 1936 McCarthy challenged the Puyallup City Council to boost its paid fire fighters' wages to match that of its police, who received $129 per month. Fire fighters then worked a seventy-two-hour work-week, in continuous shifts, one off and one on.

By 1942, when Puyallup #726 affiliated, the department had thirteen paid fire fighters, including officers, all of whom joined the local. Thirteen years later Puyallup #726 approached the city council with a request that their terms of employment be compared to those of tradesmen, as skilled workers vs. unskilled laborers. At the time, they worked a sixty-eight-hour workweek, and were paid $385 per month. What effect this had upon their work conditions is unclear.

RCW 49.46 (Minimum Wage Act), mandating a forty-hour workweek (with certain exceptions), was passed in 1959. Puyallup #726 took an unusual approach to its enactment. It proposed the city avoid a forty percent cut in services by granting fire fighters a forty-hour workweek, with an additional sixteen hours of volunteer work. The council accepted, and fire fighters shifted from a sixty-four to a fifty-six-hour workweek.

Puyallup #726 again demonstrated its savvy negotiating in the late 1970s, gaining bi-monthly Cost of Living Adjustments (COLAs), pegged to the Consumer Price Index. Extreme inflation resulted in a thirteen percent raise in one year, making Puyallup's fire fighters the highest paid on the West Coast. During this same period, Puyallup #726 began supporting candidates in city council elections.

In 1984 Puyallup #726 was the first Washington State IAFF local to negotiate a "Light Duty Clause," allowing fire fighters injured off the job to continue to receive full wages. This contract language was then used as a model by the state legislature when it passed RCW 41.04.520 (Disability Leave Supplement for Law Enforcement Officers and Fire Fighters) in 1985.

Given its size, Puyallup #726 has played a big part in the WSCFF. Dennis Parlari (WSCFF president 1980-1981), Dale Pierce (WSCFF trustee 1977-1994), and Dennis Lawson (WSCFF District 4 representative, 2001-current, and trustee 1994-2000) are all #726 members.

profile:
Merlin Halverson

Merlin Halverson (Lynnwood #1984) has offered leadership within the WSCFF and his local for decades. One fire fighter described him as "the backbone of integrity within the WSCFF." Halverson rarely takes credit for his efforts. He speaks softly, and delivers the proverbial big stick. In his case this is an incredible working knowledge of, and experience in, contract negotiation and arbitration.

Halverson wields his influence through hands-on support, counseling with other union fire fighters, and guiding them through innumerable contract negotiations. He has served officially as an IAFF state representative (1976-2002) and informally in thousands of conversations with negotiating team members who have questions. In the twenty-two years he represented District 3 (1978-2000), Halverson was tireless in advocating for the fire fighters he represented.

Halverson began his career as a fire fighter in March, 1972, with the Lynnwood Fire Department. Within about three months he got involved in his union. Lynnwood #1984 was entering negotiations on its second contract, and, as Halverson put it succinctly, "the department treated its fire fighters poorly." Contract terms going in included cost of living *minus* four percent. Within three years of coming into the department, in 1975, Halverson was promoted to lieutenant, and later commented, "that's as high as you can go in Lynnwood."

During the late 1970s, many in the fire service had mixed opinions as to what role fire departments should play in delivering EMS. Members of Lynnwood #1984 pressed to have all fire fighters trained as EMTs, even though the department paid only for the cost of required classes, not for their time. Halverson's personal experience with EMS made him an advocate for coordinated fire-service based EMS. His twin brother had been in a motorcycle accident and he knew well what care and treatment programs existed in his community.

As EMS was integrated into his department, Halverson saw that the only way good people would stay was if working conditions improved. Halverson continued to demonstrate his leadership and negotiating prowess. Months after his election as IAFF District 7 vice president, Jim Martinez (Boise #672) recognized this, and appointed Halverson as an IAFF state representative, certifying Halverson to negotiate contracts for other IAFF locals. This position also provided Halverson with training, and opportunities to meet other negotiation specialists.

Halverson sees his election as the first WSCFF District 3 representative in 1978 as an evolution from his work as a "service rep" to that of a spokesperson, and viewed each member of the executive board as a specialist. He identifies his own

EMS 69

specialties as the ability to provide assistance in negotiating a local's first contract, and in bringing his grassroots connections into executive board discussions and decisions.

Four years after he was elected to the executive board, Halverson ran for president against Michael McGovern (Lakewood #1488) and Ken Strong (Spokane #29), at the 1982 WSCFF Convention. All three candidates had hospitality rooms the night before the convention convened: McGovern had a well-endowed female bartender in a tight t-shirt, Strong's supporters had to scramble to deal with no liquor sales on Sunday night, and Halverson simply "provided," in keeping with his understated ways.

The next morning, in the first round of voting, Halverson led and was within a few votes of carrying a majority. McGovern came in second, and Strong trailed third. Strong's key supporters met with Halverson and McGovern separately, and listened to their pitches. Votes were again cast, and McGovern won by three.

Halverson, in keeping with his vision of the organization as bigger than any particular election, put his efforts into supporting McGovern for some years thereafter. He also continued to work extremely hard on his own circuit tour of local negotiations, whether he participated as IAFF state representative, WSCFF District 3 representative, or simply as a fire fighter who knew contract negotiations inside out.

Going into the 1991 Convention, Halverson, Dan Downs (Richland #1052, District 2 representative), and Greg Bergquist (Renton #864, District 7 representative) successfully lobbied for redistricting of the WSCFF. As part of this change, WSCFF District 3, where Merlin served, was split in two, creating District 10. Prior to this, District 3 had included almost all of Western Washington except Seattle, which meant Halverson represented more than 1,000 individual fire fighters but had only one vote on the executive board. Part of this restructuring was in preparation for Seattle #27's reaffiliation in 1992.

Halverson continued to provide continuity on the WSCFF executive board after Kelly Fox (Olympia #468) defeated McGovern as president in 1996. Two years later, Halverson had been working with WSCFF member locals in Snohomish County, and knew Snohomish Fire District 5's out-going chief was resistant to a "brand new local." One of Halverson's friends gave him an application for the chief's position as a joke. Halverson dug up a resume and turned it in. When the citizens' selection committee picked Halverson as its first choice, he considered withdrawing his application. Instead Halverson agreed to a three-month trial period. Within four months he was fulltime chief. During his "trial" period Halverson gained successful passage of a levy, after the department had run two previous levies that failed. This funding allowed Snohomish Fire District 5 to integrate paid fire fighters into a department that had been all volunteer since 1911. As usual, Halverson provided leadership to make this a smooth transition.

Appointment as chief marked a shift in Halverson's career, away from a formal role in the WSCFF, although he continues to offer guidance to union members who call him. He still works two shifts per week for the Lynnwood Fire Department, because as he says, "I like the people there. And it's good for the younger folks to have someone with more experience around, to learn their own history."

Hanford I-24

As the Hanford Site evolved, its fire and emergency response service personnel have been employed by a unique and convoluted blend of corporations and governmental departments and agencies, in conjunction with municipalities. Union fire fighters at Hanford have been members of two internationals, affiliated first as a federal and then as an industrial local. As an industrial local, I-24 members are not covered by the collective bargaining, pensions, and benefits laws affecting most other IAFF locals in Washington State.

Hanford Engineer Works was created in 1943, when the US government's Manhattan Project and the DuPont Corporation chose the site for plutonium production. Whatever fire protection was provided at the time seems to have been through the federal government. Richland #1052 first affiliated with the IAFF on December 14, 1946, and by some accounts included Hanford's fire fighters.

In 1947, the Manhattan Project ended and the Atomic Energy Commission (AEC) took over government oversight. Hanford fire fighters split off from Richland #1052 to form their own local between 1948 and 1950, but affiliated with the Building Service Employees International Union (BSEIU), supposedly because the IAFF would not allow Hanford to form a separate local. GE took over a number of operations, including the Hanford Fire Department, before 1952, and the Hanford Atomic Metal Trades Council (HAMTAK) was then created. This may have been when fire fighters switched from a federal to an industrial local. HAMTAK is a coalition of Hanford Site's unions, negotiates their contracts collectively, and at one time included Richland #1052. Guards are not in HAMTAK for security reasons, and because traditionally police are in guilds, not unions.

Officers from the various jurisdictions providing fire services for the Hanford site pose as part of a meeting, circa late 1940s. L-R: *Carl Olson (North Richland chief), Pat Quane (Richland chief) Jim Witcher (Hanford chief 1948-50), Gordon Hirst (Hanford assistant chief 1948-50, Hanford chief in 1950), Ray Hare (1st chief of Richland and Hanford 1943-1948).*

HANFORD FIRE DEPARTMENT COLLECTION

Hanford's "foam truck" delivered 13,500 cu. feet of foam per minute. It was barged to the Pasco fuel depot to check the height it could deliver to, and whether it actually put out fire.

HANFORD FIRE DEPARTMENT COLLECTION

Union Partners 36

HAMTAK went on strike in 1966. In June 1975, fire fighters successfully negotiated with BSEIU and Hanford I-24 affiliated with the IAFF. HAMTAK staged its second strike, against all of Hanford's employers, in 1976.

Hanford 1-24's Two Strikes 130

Fluor Corporation took over the fire department in 1996, as part of the Department of Ecology's increased "outsourcing." When Fluor took over, supervisory personnel were allowed union membership, something that local members had tried to negotiate in the past.

Yakima #469

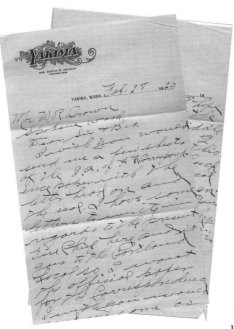

On Feb. 28, 1920, Roy Utley (Yakima #469 s/t) wrote W.R. Brown of Spokane #29, requesting "some IAFF letterhead" to use in union correspondence to the Portland, Oregon, IAFF local.

GREG BORG COLLECTION

1903 map of what was then called North Yakima.

YAKIMA #469 COLLECTION

Yakima's first fire department was a bucket brigade, in the 1880s, when Yakima City moved from what is now Union Gap. The North Yakima Volunteer Fire Department was created in 1886. Three years later the city council passed Ordinance 99, which required members of the department to pay a one-dollar initiation fee, be US citizens over eighteen, and to "converse understandable English."

Working conditions were bad enough that by March 28, 1904, everyone in the fire department voted to resign unless the city council took action. It didn't. The volunteers charged themselves $35.00 each for a sumptuous final dinner, then divided the department's funds into payments of $19.35 to each former member. A new volunteer department was created shortly thereafter, replaced in 1905 by a combination volunteer and paid department.

Yakima #217 affiliated with the IAFF between April 1918 and August 1919. On November 5 of 1919, the entire department walked out. City commissioners called it a strike and replaced everyone in the department. On May 20, 1936, Yakima's fire fighters reaffiliated. Yakima #469 then carried on frequent correspondence with other IAFF locals within the state, helping to trigger formation of the WSCFF, and became one of its charter members.

Yakima #469's Ken Weaver served on the WSCFF's executive board from at least 1949 until 1950, followed by another local member, Bus Cramer (1952 to 1955). Ken Groth (Yakima #469) served for six years as a WSCFF vice president before he was elected president (1976-1977). In 1981 Yakima hosted the WSCFF Convention, where member Tom Fieldstead was elected WSCFF's secretary-treasurer, serving until 1983, when he was promoted to deputy chief. (Yakima #469 also hosted the 1982 and 2001 Conventions.) Most recently, from 2000 to 2002, Yakima #469 member Tom Schneider served as one of the WSCFF's trustees.

⟷ *Yakima #217* 130

AT RIGHT: **Ten volunteers worked with North Yakima's first professional fire fighters, as of September 6, 1905. Paid fire fighters,** L-R: **E.G. Dawson, J.P. Bowman (asst. chief), Charles M. Hauser (chief), Marry C. Dawson, J. J. Miller.**

YAKIMA #469 COLLECTION

FAR RIGHT: **Members of the WSCFF picketed the City of Yakima while they were in town for a WSCFF event in the 1990s.**

KELLY FOX COLLECTION

The WSCFF is its membership. The following profiles of the current executive board demonstrate the personal commitment and range of skills and experience members bring to this organization. The financial resources, organizational structure, and political arena of the WSCFF have changed over the last sixty-four years. The commitment of its leadership to serve the professional fire fighters of Washington State has not.

Washington State
Council of Fire Fighters

WSCFF PRESIDENT: *Kelly Fox*

President Kelly Fox (Olympia #468).

WSCFF COLLECTION

Kelly Fox is not the first person you might notice in a room of fire fighters, but he has proven himself their leader. He did not dream as a child of becoming a fire fighter. Instead Fox worked a series of jobs: dishwasher, cook, and company service representative at a title company. During this period, a friend, Kent Ewell (Kent #1747), was a student at Bates Technical Institute. Fox observed fire fighters were well-respected, and from what Ewell told him the job itself sounded interesting, and paid more than any-thing he had been doing. He tested to get into Bates, and started classes there in April 1980. He also served as a resident in Pierce County Fire District 7 (now part of the Central Pierce County Fire District). While he was there he began to appreciate the distinction between volunteers and "the guys with the IAFF stickers [professional union fire fighters]" although he had no real idea what union membership meant.

Fox, Ewell, and another buddy, Todd Madsen (Olympia #468), all tested for the Kent and Olympia fire departments. Fox was hired by Olympia in August 1982, and Madsen was hired later that afternoon. Fox, not yet twenty-one, took his proba-tion year seriously. He knew he served "at will," and that he and Madsen had been hired to replace two other probies terminated when they failed street tests.

Fox went to Olympia #468's meetings, at first because they were opportunities to socialize with his coworkers. In 1983, he sat in a series of labor-management meet-ings. The smug attitude of the city manager, regardless of the validity of the problem being discussed, made Fox want to try to actually negotiate.

The following year he was appointed to an IAFF trial board, wherein the IAFF brought charges against an individual member of Spokane Airport #1789. This experi-ence provided Fox with the opportunity to understand how a smaller local worked, and to work with his WSCFF District 5 representative, Frank Spicklemire, also a mem-ber of Olympia #468. Fox attended his first WSCFF event as a delegate in that same year, 1984, and hasn't missed once since.

When Olympia #468 President Ron Bowen decided he would not run for re-election in 1985, Spicklemire encouraged Fox to do so. Fox knew he had little real experience, but also that he was interested in what he might accomplish within his local. He ran, and won by acclamation. Olympia #468's next negotiations began that May, and Fox led its team, assisted by a few visits with Jimmy Cason (Tacoma #31, then vice president of the WSCFF).

This round of negotiations resulted in a two-year contract. Its terms included overtime (or compensatory time) when a fire fighter worked in excess of fifty-three hours per week, in keeping with the FSLA's Garcia decision. It also granted a ten percent pay increase over the next two years. When local members challenged their negotiating team about why they hadn't gotten still more, since negotiations had gone so smoothly, Fox learned an important lesson. From then on he presented negotiated terms without emotion or personal endorsement, and let members make the call on accepting a contract.

Fox continued to attend WSCFF events as president of Olympia #468. He also worked at these events as a bartender, beginning in 1983. In 1989 Fox chaired the convention committee that hosted the WSCFF Convention. By the following spring's WSCFF Educational Seminar, Fox had decided to run for WSCFF District 5 representative, and informed his mentor, Spicklemire, of his intentions. Spicklemire then decided not to run for re-election. That June, delegates voted along north-south geographic divisions within District 5, eight for Fox and seven for Joe Mackey (then president of Vancouver #452).

Fox joined the WSCFF executive board as the organization went through a series of major changes. At its 1991 Convention, WSCFF delegates voted to add Districts 8, 9, and 10, creating the framework that would allow Seattle #27 to reaffiliate the following year, as District 11. Nineteen ninety-one was also the year that the WSCFF approved (48-44 votes) fundraising by the telemarketing company, the Gehl Group.

The next year, 1992 Convention delegates passed a resolution creating the assistant lobbyist position. Fox was one of three who applied for the position, and was disappointed when the WSCFF executive board instead appointed Ken Snider (Spokane #29) that fall. Sometime between 1991 and 1995, it became tacitly understood that Fox had the potential and support to succeed Mike McGovern (Lakewood #1488) as president of the WSCFF. What was not clear was when McGovern might choose to move on. In addition, few on the executive board understood McGovern was more interested in becoming the WSCFF's next lobbyist, than the next IAFF District 7 vice president. This matter came to a head when Howard Vietzke (Spokane #29) announced his retirement in 1995.

At this point relations between members of the WSCFF executive board and WSCFF President McGovern were not good. The board appointed Jimmy Cason (Tacoma #31) as lobbyist, and then made further appointments. Jack Andren (Pierce County Professional Fire Fighters #2175) replaced Cason (Tacoma #31) as the WSCFF's secretary-treasurer, Jim Rudd (Spokane #29) replaced Snider (Spokane #29) as its assistant lobbyist, and Ricky Walsh (Richland #1052) joined the executive

Collectively Bargaining 99

board to replace Rudd as its vice president and District 2 representative. As the 1996 Convention approached, several executive board members encouraged Fox to challenge McGovern. He decided to do so only a few weeks before the election, and then did nothing but campaign.

Once Fox won his bid for the presidency, he had his work cut out for him. The WSCFF took occupancy of its new offices in Olympia two months after the convention. Office staffing also changed, and in one case triggered litigation. In addition, rifts within the WSCFF membership between McGovern loyalists and those who had backed Fox needed to be resolved. Finally, there was all of the regular business of the WSCFF. Fox took all of this on, and slowly resolved issues, in part because he has the ability to elicit intense loyalty from those he works with. He also focused on broadening the decision-making role of the WSCFF executive board.

By 2001, Fox faced another challenge, that of an initiative campaign. He struggled with his own concerns about the WSCFF stepping away from its participation in the legislative process. However, once he was convinced the WSCFF membership backed the initiative process, he committed himself and all of the WSCFF's resources to I-790. When it passed in fall 2002, Fox immediately shifted his efforts to the legislative arena, helping the WSCFF secure enabling language for I-790 during the 2003 session.

⟷ *I-790* 149

As he completes his eighth year as president, Fox has proven himself to be a strategist, and like many in the fire service, he seeks ever larger challenges. In Fox's case he has focused on leadership within the WSCFF, the IAFF, and Washington State's labor movement. In working within these three interwoven arenas, Fox has come to appreciate the significance of labor history in shaping "who and what we are today."

WSCFF VICE PRESIDENT AND DISTRICT 2: *Ricky Walsh*

A big guy who has always had big dreams, Ricky Walsh is fiercely committed to the union movement. He came to fire fighting by way of architectural work, pitching watermelons, and the push of a friend. Part of the debt he feels toward the fire service and his union comes from the changes he sees in himself as a result of becoming a fire fighter. "It turned my life around."

Six days after he graduated from high school in eastern Oregon he was attending classes in architecture at the Phoenix (Arizona) Institute of Technology. When he received his degree there, he returned to the Hermiston area, but found that his work involved "pumping out plans" and a lot of time inside. Walsh switched to operating heavy equipment. A decline in construction meant he was laid off much of the time, so he then tested with, and was hired by, the Hermiston Fire Department in mid-1983.

While he was still on probation with the combined volunteer-professional Hermiston Department, Walsh was elected secretary-treasurer of Hermiston #2752.

Vice President and District 2 Representative Ricky Walsh (Richland #1052).

R. WALSH COLLECTION

Its seven members won exclusive use of station living quarters (rather than sharing them with volunteers) through binding arbitration. Walsh was hooked on the negotiating process. But Walsh realized he wanted to work in a "career" department rather than one that had both volunteer and professional fire fighters. He tested in Lake Oswego, Oregon, and then in 1986, with the Richland, Washington Department.

Walsh was hired by Richland in 1986. He went to Richland #1052's meetings as soon as he was hired, and immediately volunteered to work on a Muscular Dystrophy Association (MDA) function. A year later, in 1987, Walsh became a paramedic and joined Richland #1052's negotiating team. He was elected vice president of his local in 1988. Two years later, Walsh wanted greater responsibility, and ran in an uncontested race for Richland #1052's presidency, replacing Tim Sharp.

During the next four years (and four elections) Walsh served as president of his local and was promoted to lieutenant. He became close friends with Kelly Fox (Olympia # 468), whom he had met in 1988 as they participated in WSCFF activities. Walsh knew the growing intensity of his union work placed demands upon his family. He remembers asking Howard Vietzke (Spokane #29) how Vietzke's union involvement had affected Vietzke's family, "if it panned out in the end, for Howard and his kids" knowing Vietzke had served the WSCFF for decades. Vietzke assured Walsh the sacrifices his family would make to support him could be balanced by the greater fellowship and support of other WSCFF families.

In 1993 Walsh challenged Dan Downs for District 2 representative, and endured a political salvo from within his local. Downs had been the WSCFF District 2 representative since WSCFF districts were created in 1976. Although Walsh was president of Richland #1052 at the time, he was stripped of his delegate status going into the 1993 WSCFF Convention. Richland's two delegates committed their votes to Downs, as directed by a mandate of the local. Downs supporters within the local then demanded Walsh withdraw his candidacy, on the grounds he was going against the local's mandate, and therefore no longer a member in good standing.

It will surprise no one who knows him that Walsh brought in bigger guns, and received written authorization for his candidacy from the president of the IAFF, Al Whitehead. Walsh then won the 1993 election for District 2 representative, and has served in this capacity ever since. In the fall of 1995, his role in the WSCFF increased when its executive board appointed him as vice president, to replace Jim Rudd (Spokane #29), who was shifting over to serve as the WSCFF's assistant lobbyist.

Walsh was elected vice president at the next WSCFF Convention, in 1996, over Ted Rail (Spokane #29, District 1 representative). That same year, Walsh was also promoted to captain of an engine.

As Walsh continued to work as a fire fighter and paramedic, he wanted to give back to his union, because he knew that it was the union that provided the working conditions he enjoyed, and that it was the fire service that provided the discipline to allow him to focus on leadership and political activism.

In 1999 Walsh's commitment was put to a test, when he was terminated. He had spoken against possible station closures and personnel cuts, and against the recommendation of Richland at a Richland City Council meeting. Those in the fire department had been told not to make statements at council meetings. Walsh was fired one week later, on the day before Thanksgiving, and remained off the job for 317 days. Richland #1052 waived his dues, but could offer little other financial support as it faced significant arbitration expenses at the time. The WSCFF collected contributions that covered Walsh's bills during this time, an experience Walsh calls "totally humbling." Although Walsh offered to pay back these contributions, no one would accept them. Walsh's forceful support of union solidarity did not waiver. The case went to arbitration, and Walsh was reinstated, docked one day's pay, without disciplinary action with back pay.

Currently Walsh views the decrease in health care services as a sleeping giant within the fire service and EMS, since more and more of medical services are delivered on a quasi-emergency basis to people who do not have any other form of medical care. His desire for political change that addresses such issues had experience behind it. Walsh has served as part of the WSCFF's lobbying team during the 2000-2001 and 2002-2003 sessions, immersing himself in the Olympia scene.

More than a few of Walsh's fire fighter brothers and sisters tease him for his eastern-Washington ways. Walsh has trimmed his hair and mustache from his younger, wilder days, but he has kept his straightforward approach when it comes to moving toward an objective. For the last twenty years many of Walsh's goals have been political—as an individual within the WSCFF and as a representative of union fire fighters in Washington State. And although Walsh appears brash, he understands that moving ahead may mean that others receive the recognition that follows.

WSCFF SECRETARY-TREASURER: *Chris Heminger*

Secretary-Treasurer Chris Heminger (Auburn #1352).

WSCFF COLLECTION

When the volunteer fire fighter came to the door for donations in 1973, he also left an application to join King County Fire District 44. Both Chris Heminger and his father did so, although Heminger's father soon found his work as an air traffic controller made it impossible to meet scheduling demands. Heminger continued to serve as a volunteer while he attended Green River Community College ("Harvard on the hill"). He also worked at Safeway, and filled in as a "part-time" resident with King County Fire District 44.

Heminger hoped to apply to become a fire fighter for the state Department of Natural Resources (DNR). Dixie Lee Ray was governor at the time, however, and in 1977 she froze all new hires. So Heminger enlisted in the Coast Guard, and served two years of active duty. He then took another job with Safeway and tested with the Auburn Fire Department. Heminger was hired six months later, in February 1980. He chose the Auburn department because of the way its members had treated the volunteers of adjacent Fire District 44, and because he had grown up in Auburn.

Heminger was part of the first group of recruits to go through the Washington State Fire Academy, which at that time traveled around the state. He completed his EMT certification during his year of probation, and also became a member of Auburn #1352. Heminger's experience with unions up to this time had not been particularly positive.

While working at Safeway, he had been a member of Retail Clerks #1105. When he became a member of the Coast Guard Reserve, this local had not helped Heminger resolve certain issues, while the Coast Guard had. Heminger recalls that he learned "the fire service had a different attitude. They [the local and the IAFF] were there for us." After seeing both the terms his contract provided and observing that it was local members who earned these, Heminger felt it was "only fair to give something back."

He started by working on the committee that evaluated the feasibility of an apprenticeship program. He was then asked to join Auburn #1352's negotiating committee. Two years later, in 1986, Heminger was elected vice president of his local. He was elected president of Auburn #1352 in 1989, and served three consecutive two-year terms. That same year he became chair of its negotiating team, a position he held for the next six years.

At the 1991 WSCFF Convention, three new districts were created, including District 8. It took several months for the WSCFF executive board to hash out which locals would be assigned to the new districts. By about November, District 8 had been created, and included Auburn #1352. Heminger then ran for district representative, and was elected by the delegates of the locals within the district.

Heminger continued to serve as District 8 representative until 1997, when he was elected WSCFF's secretary-treasurer. He ran against incumbent Lonnie Hampton (Tacoma #31), and remembers both candidates made a point of exchanging mailings and did not attack each other. This was especially important because of the amount of change within the WSCFF executive board that had occurred in the previous two years. Once elected, Heminger worked hard to improve the financial accountability

Politics Costs Money
121

of the WSCFF, during a period that included exponential increases in income, tighter rules on public disclosure, and the continued operation and maintenance of the WSCFF's office building and condo in Olympia.

He chose not to seek re-election at the 2003 Convention. As he puts it, "it's been a hell of a ride," but he is ready for other challenges, and interested in trying a life that would include something called "free time." He hopes to remain involved in statewide pension issues and within his local, and is humbled by the privilege of having served the WSCFF membership.

DISTRICT 1: *Ted Rail*

Ted Rail is recognized as a dapper dresser; less visually obvious is his commitment to the union movement within the fire service. A lifelong Spokane resident, he completed military service and college, with a degree in marketing. The next summer he was working for an asphalt company. One housemate was a fire fighter, and from him Rail learned enough about the job to be interested. The next time the Spokane Fire Department tested, Rail applied, along with other housemates. Three of them made the grade and were hired by the Spokane Fire Department in August 1973. He was assigned to Station 5, and started to ride along on runs where the inhalator was used. In 1975 Rail became certified as an EMT, one of about ten in the department at that time.

Rail attended union meetings from the time he joined the department, and was elected to Spokane #29's executive board in 1977. In June 1980, when Gary Brown stepped down, Rail became Spokane #29's secretary-treasurer, and was part of the team that negotiated a pay raise of just over twenty-four percent. That same year he was certified as a paramedic, and six years later a paramedic lieutenant. This rank had been created within the Spokane Fire Department as a separate and parallel promotional track to that of fire lieutenant. Rail became a fire lieutenant as well in 1987. About three years later, Rail became an executive board member of what was then called the WSCFF Health and Welfare Trust. He was appointed chair of the state's EMS Licensing and Certification Committee when it was created in 1994.

⟷ *EMS* 69

District 1 Representative Ted Rail (Spokane #29).
WSCFF COLLECTION

After fifteen years as Spokane #29's secretary-treasurer, Rail lost to Mike Bacon in 1995. That September, when Jim Rudd retired, Rail replaced him as WSCFF District 1 representative. Rail also tried for appointment as the WSCFF's secretary-treasurer, a vacancy created when Jimmy Cason (Tacoma #31) shifted to WSCFF's lobbyist. The WSCFF executive board instead chose Jack Andren (Pierce County Professional Fire Fighters #2175).

Then came the WSCFF Convention of 1996. Spokane #29 supported Mike McGovern (Lakewood #1488) over Kelly Fox (Olympia #469). Soon after Fox defeated McGovern, came the election for vice president. Rail challenged Ricky Walsh (Richland #1052) who had been appointed as vice president at about the same time Rail was elected District 1 representative. Representing the largest local that had not supported Fox, and running against Walsh pretty much insured Rail would weather some political repercussions, and the WSCFF executive board meetings immediately after the 1996 Convention were not particularly cordial. Late that same summer of 1996, Rail was elected chair of the WSCFF Health and Welfare Trust, while Fox replaced McGovern on its board. The Trust then renamed itself the LEOFF Health and Welfare Trust.

⟷ *The LEOFF Health and Welfare Trust* 157

Rail is clear about his own politics and those of Spokane #29. "One of our virtues is that we're loyal. We supported Mike [McGovern], and we voted for him. It took some time after that. Kelly [Fox] earned our trust and now we're loyal to him." Rail has continued to use his EMS experience on the IAFF's EMS Committee, as well as two state committees. He chairs the Department of Health (DoH) Licensing and Certification Committee, as he has since it was formed, and also serves on the DoH Bio-Terrorism Committee.

DISTRICT 2 AND VICE PRESIDENT: RICKY WALSH

⟷ *WSCFF Vice President Ricky Walsh* 209

DISTRICT 3: *Mike Wilson*

Mike Wilson admits he had no intention of becoming a paramedic or fire fighter. He worked construction in the Lake Tahoe area, spent his free time in the woods, and liked what he did. He also saw some significant injuries on the construction site, including one where someone cut his femoral artery with a skillsaw and died almost immediately. Wilson took an EMT class so maybe the next time he could do something. Soon after, interest rates soared and construction jobs disappeared. During the EMT class, he had ridden along on calls with the Tahoe-Donner Ambulance Company, and got a job there with lots of hours, not very many calls, and working for near minimum wage.

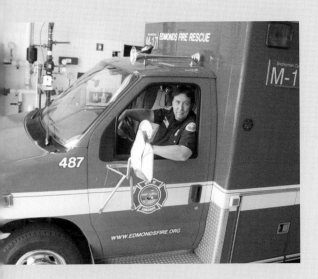

District 3 Representative Mike Wilson (Medic Seven #3524).
WSCFF COLLECTION

⟷ EMS 69

When that company was bought out by a Reno company, Wilson stayed on. The new owners came from what was then a state-of-the-art paramedic training program in Hawaii, and being around them made Wilson consider his current employment as a career. The company was sold again, this time to an ex-California State Patrol member who brought with him a management style that motivated his workers to organize. They affiliated with the Teamsters, the owner refused to bargain, and given the right-to-work provisions of Nevada, Wilson and his coworkers had few options but to strike. The shutdown service area included Lake Tahoe, Reno, Carson City, and the Truckee Donner area. The strike served as a wake-up call to the existing fire districts, who provided minimal EMS coverage, but who also realized they did not want to deal with an EMS system that could go out on strike. One of them, Carson City, sponsored Wilson in his paramedic training, although it did not pay for it.

Once he was a paramedic, he returned to the Carson City Fire Department as one of their first fire fighter/paramedics. During his eight years with the department he was an active union member, serving on the negotiations committee. Wilson was also chair of the safety and health committee as the then new NFPA 1500 standards were implemented. Only sixty percent of his coworkers were dues-paying members of the local.

During his time with the Carson City Department, Wilson kept his eye out for western Washington employment opportunities because of the area's reputation for good medical standards and practices. In the meantime he took a job in Alaska, working the unique combination of armed security and paramedic on the pipeline during the Gulf War, a position where the medical aspects of his work often conflicted with his enforcement duties.

After testing around western Washington, Wilson was hired by Lakewood. Two years later, he accepted a job offer from Medic Seven, which he took because of their reputation for excellent medicine. He didn't realize at the time that Medic Seven was neither part of the LEOFF system nor fire-service related EMS. Shortly after he was hired, Medic Seven and its local (#3524) entered years of contractual disputes and reorganization. Much of this time Wilson served as president of Medic Seven #3524.

As he and David Clark became more involved in their local, Wilson worked regularly with Merlin Halverson, who was at that time the WSCFF's District 3 representative. When Halverson stepped down after twenty-two years of service, Wilson took his place. Since then he has focused on issues that affect Washington fire fighters. He was a principal architect of the recently reformed pension plan for publicly employed paramedics. This grants portability from PERS to LEOFF 2 when their positions are absorbed by fire departments (within the state of Washington).

DISTRICT 4: *Dennis Lawson*

Dennis J. Lawson attended his first WSCFF Convention at the age of ten, in Spokane, and saw the World's Fair while he was there. His father was a member of Tacoma #31, and Lawson remembers going to his father's fire station "to shoot baskets and climb on Truck 2 [his father's rig]" with his brother Dan (Vancouver #452). By junior high he was pretty sure he wanted to be a fire fighter, too. After high school, Lawson worked a stint at Albertson's, then had the opportunity to become a resident with the Federal Way Fire Department.

As a resident, he received enough training to allow him to help when calls came in. Unlike many other residents, Lawson did not attend Bates. He still values the friendships established with the career and resident fire fighters he met while there. During his time as a resident he tested with fire departments on the Westside, "from Everett to Vancouver," and was hired in Puyallup in 1987.

Lawson completed training at the Fire Academy in North Bend. Upon finishing his probationary period, he joined Puyallup #726's negotiating team, and has been there for every contract negotiation since. He became one of his local's delegates to the WSCFF almost immediately, partly because he wanted to be involved and partly because, as he put it, "not everybody wants to go." C. Dale Pierce, also a member of Puyallup #726, stepped down as a WSCFF trustee in 1994. Lawson saw the position as a way to get more involved with the WSCFF, and was elected to replace Pierce. Lawson credits his time as a trustee with teaching him the financial aspects of the WSCFF, and with allowing him to get a better understanding of the political realities of Olympia.

Lawson served as a trustee until 2001, when he was elected District 4 representative, replacing Doug Willis (Pierce County Professional Fire Fighters #2175). Dennis considered it an honor to follow Willis and vowed to build on the foundation established by the previous 4th District representatives. Since District 4 is second only to District 11 (Seattle #27) in membership, this means Lawson has to hustle to stay in communication with all of his district.

Platoons, Kelly Days, and Transit Passes 57

District 4 Representative Dennis J. Lawson (Puyallup #726).
WSCFF COLLECTION

Through his work in Puyallup #726 and the WSCFF, Lawson has observed the small percentage of the membership who take an active part in union activities. At the 2002 Educational Seminar in Bellingham, Lawson conducted a survey and confirmed that in most small locals, union officers turn over every four or five years. From his own experience, he knows it takes about three years to get a personal understanding of how one's local functions, what it takes to negotiate a contract, and how to actively participate in the WSCFF.

Lawson has several clear goals, in addition to his duties as a district representative. He seeks to work with membership and the executive board to shape the WSCFF so more fire fighters want to have a part in the WSCFF, and so those who do participate stay involved at some level throughout their careers. He is also working to find ways for all WSCFF members to "appreciate our profession and what it provides for us and our families," while helping to make sure the membership understands "many others came before us and made many sacrifices on our behalf both in the fire service and in the labor movement."

DISTRICT 5: *Brian Hurley*

⬅ EMS 69

Brian Hurley's ties to Thurston County have helped to shape several of his professional decisions. His commitment to EMS is just as basic. As a teenager he volunteered with the Tenino/Thurston County Fire District 12, following in the footsteps of his father and brother. As soon as Hurley turned eighteen he became an EMT. Hurley fits the profile of a new generation of fire fighters, in that he received significant formal education before he came into the fire service. He got a BS in physics from the University of Puget Sound, studied applied physics at Cornell University, and, drawn back to the Pacific Northwest, completed his Ph.D. in bioengineering at the University of Washington. This desire to stay close to his roots geographically, combined with his experience of university politics, helped him decide against a career in academics. Less than a year after he received his doctorate, Hurley went to paramedic school.

After interning with Tumwater's Medic 5, his first job as a paramedic was with CARE Ambulance in Lewis County, where he learned the ropes. Hurley began to up his union involvement when he was asked to run for secretary-treasurer of Tumwater #2409. He stresses that it is a small local, with about twenty-three members. Elected in 1996, Hurley began to attend WSCFF events, drawn into more involvement by Cody Arledge, who was Hurley's shift supervisor.

District 5 Representative Brian Hurley (Tumwater #2409).

B. HURLEY COLLECTION

That same year Arledge replaced Kelly Fox as WSCFF District 5 representative. Then in 1997, Jimmy Cason (Tacoma #31) died, shortly after having been appointed WSCFF's director of government relations. Arledge was selected to replace him. Hurley then won a special election to become WSCFF's District 5 representative, and continues to serve in that position. He also serves as one of two district field service

profiles

representatives for all of the IAFF District 7 (Alaska, Washington, Idaho, and Montana). Hurley uses his experience in EMS to represent WSCFF members on three Department of Health (DoH) committees: its EMS and Trauma Steering Committee, the State EMS Education Committee, and the Bioterrorism Committee.

DISTRICT 6: *Pat McElligott*

District 6 Representative Patrick McElligott (Tacoma #31).

WSCFF COLLECTION

When Pat McElligott was growing up in Los Angeles, he went on camping trips with a friend's family. His friend's father was a fire fighter, so McElligott was included in a group of fire fighter families who did lots of things together, and credits the camaraderie of these fire fighters with his own career choice. By the time he was seventeen he had tested in Los Angeles, Ventura County, and Santa Barbara. Facing the draft, he enlisted so he could be assigned to fire protection.

When McElligott left the Air Force he tested again with the City of Los Angeles Fire Department, and was hired in 1978. Less than a year later, McElligott and his wife visited a friend who was a fire fighter at the Bangor submarine base. McElligott remembers this visit occurred during a singularly beautiful weekend, and he left thinking Bangor seemed idyllic but that there was no chance he would ever get a job there, although he had taken time to interview with the chief. At the time Bangor was run under private contract with Pan Am, and so there was no testing required. Three months later, in fall of 1979, he was offered a job at Bangor, conditional upon his beginning work immediately, which meant his wife was left to take care of their new baby and the job of moving.

One of McElligott's co-workers at Bangor was Eileen Lewis (Tacoma #31, now chief of the City of Tacoma Fire Department), who was hired in Tacoma a few years later. In March 1981 McElligott separated his shoulder while playing in a promotional softball game for Pan Am. He spent the next six months dispatching for Bangor, while his shoulder healed. During this time he tested with Federal Way, and was hired there in July 1981.

McElligott then began his EMT training, and was assigned to a two-man station as acting lieutenant before he completed EMT certification. He learned firsthand the immense responsibility of being a first responder, and he took his EMT training seriously. These classes were taught by Tacoma paramedics, and McElligott came to respect the Tacoma Department as he got to know some of its personnel. Meanwhile, Federal Way #2024 President John Rickert fostered McElligott's involvement in the local. McElligott participated in the next round of contract negotiations in 1983, where Federal Way #2024 secured a substantial raise. The city then announced fifteen fire fighters would be laid off because of this. McElligott was one of those slated to be cut. The contract was eventually renegotiated, and no one lost his job, but McElligott did not like having to wait and see if he still had a job.

He took the written test for Tacoma, then got the call to take the physical agility test shortly after he'd broken his hand in a softball game. Fairly sure he was high on the list, McElligott smashed part of his cast so he could use both hands, and passed. As soon as he was hired, in October 1984, McElligott started to attend Tacoma #31's meetings.

McElligott had gone to his first WSCFF Convention in 1983 as a delegate from Federal Way, and loved it. Two years later, Jimmy Cason, then vice president of the WSCFF and District 6 representative, along with Bill Schierman, Tacoma #31's vice president, asked McElligott to run for Tacoma's executive board. McElligott did, and was elected, in part because he was a LEOFF 2 member, unlike the rest of the board. This meant McElligott was at Tacoma #31's caucus at the 1986 WSCFF Convention in Spokane, where several delegates emerged bearing signs of a scuffle.

McElligott made a run for the vice presidency of Tacoma #31 in 1988, but his time had not yet come. A year later, at the 1989 WSCFF Convention, he demonstrated his political acumen. Cason (Tacoma #31) challenged Ron Morehouse (Bellingham #106) for WSCFF secretary-treasurer, in what promised to be a close election. McElligott knew Cason was counting on all the votes of the Tacoma delegation, and leveraged his own support and influence to secure election as District 6 representative, filling the position Cason vacated.

⬌ *At the End of the Day*
137

McElligott then ran for president of Tacoma #31 in 1990, and won, defeating incumbent Al Nyman. As one of the first wave of LEOFF 2 members, McElligott was aware of the discrepancies between his own pension benefits and those of the previous generation of fire fighters, a group which included Nyman and most of Tacoma #31's longtime leadership. McElligott focused his efforts on pension reform, and as a consequence became more involved in the WSCFF. He was appointed to the state's Department of Retirement Advisory Board during this time, and was elected to the executive board of the National Conference on Public Employee Retirement System (NCPERS) in 1995.

McElligott weathered the massive changes in WSCFF leadership that occurred from 1995 to 1996, as Cason shifted from WSCFF secretary-treasurer to join the WSCFF lobbying team, and Kelly Fox (Olympia #468) defeated Mike McGovern (Lakewood #1488) for WSCFF president. He considered running for IAFF District 7 vice president in 1996, which furthered the distance between him and Jim Hill (Tacoma #31), who had held the position since 1980, and was McGovern's mentor and close friend.

⬌ *I-790* 149

In 1997, McElligott was appointed to the Washington State Investment Board. He formally ran for IAFF District 7 vice president in 1998, losing to Paul Harvey (Seattle #27) by a few percentage points. McElligott continued to focus his efforts on pension reform through the late 1990s, and did his part to make sure the I-790 campaign gained support within the WSCFF's leadership during the 2001 Convention, and after.

McElligott has been called an Irishman's Irishman, and a kingmaker. It is true he possesses the gift of gab, and he has been a significant and influential player in the politics of the WSCFF and those of Olympia. As longtime president of Tacoma #31 and senior member of the WSCFF's executive board, McElligott has chosen to apply his influence and political savvy to represent the members of his local and the WSCFF at the municipal, state, and national level, especially on pension issues.

During his tenure as president of Tacoma #31, he has also supported the Tacoma Department's efforts to increase diversity within its ranks, and has fostered a positive working relationship between his local and management. And it was only recently, on a trip to New York City, where he visited that department's museum, that he realized he had fire fighting in his blood. His great-uncle, John McElligott, was chief engineer during LaGuardia's reign as mayor.

DISTRICT 7: *John W. Stockman*

John W. Stockman was working in plant safety at Coca-Cola when he took an industrial first aid class, then went a step further and got his EMT certification in 1975. He wanted to put the skills he was learning into use, so he joined the Redmond Fire Department as a volunteer. After about a year, Stockman realized he wanted to become a professional fire fighter.

He tested, and came in number one with Snohomish County Fire District 1. But this was in the days of LEOFF 1, and the pre-hire physical determined Stockman had minor lumbar scoliosis. He appealed to a third party doctor, but the findings were the same. So Stockman went to work for the Boeing Fire Department. In 1981 he tested in Redmond, under LEOFF 2 standards, and passed. He completed Redmond's ten-week recruitment school at a training station in Federal Way, and then his probation.

District 7 Representative John W. Stockman (Redmond #2829).

WSCFF COLLECTION

Stockman's union involvement began before he joined the fire service. He started to consider social justice and social change when he was in high school, preparing himself to file as a conscientious objector during the Vietnam War. (The draft ended before Stockman would have been drafted). He participated in the United Farm Workers (UFW) movement in the early 1970s, sponsoring educational meetings in his home. During the eight years he worked for Coca-Cola he was a member of the Teamsters, but was not at the time particularly impressed with his union's activities.

Once he was hired by the City of Redmond, he immediately became active in Redmond #2829. He was soon on its executive board, and then became its vice president in 1991, a position he held for several terms. He attended WSCFF events beginning in the mid-1980s, and was appointed to the WSCFF's standing Public Relations (PR) Committee in about 1995. In 1998, when Greg Bergquist (Renton #864) stepped down as District 7 representative, Stockman ran against Russ Caney (Bellevue #1604), and won.

Stockman has served long enough to see Redmond go from rural to "mega-suburban," which has driven an exponential increase in its need for fire protection and emergency services. He also understands from his own experience the two-tiered nature of LEOFF 1 and 2. But Stockman's biggest interest as a district representative is in increasing membership participation on all issues and improvements in medical coverage for LEOFF 2 retirees.

DISTRICT 8: *Greg Markley*

In 1983 Greg B. Markley earned a BS in accounting at Central Washington University. Immediately after graduation he was working in the construction trades. A high school buddy who was a fire fighter in Bellevue encouraged Markley to take a new hire test with the Kent Fire Department. Markley knew nothing about the fire service, and remembers putting his helmet on backwards and donning the breathing apparatus upside down. Even with these blunders he was hired in February 1984, and completed his EMT certification while on probation.

Markley became active in Kent #1747, and served on its negotiating committee team for the 1985 contract. Over the next twelve years, as Kent #1747 went from fifty to 130 members, he continued to serve on the negotiating committee. During this time he also began attending WSCFF events. He was appointed to the WSCFF's newly formed standing Public Relations Committee in 1993, by WSCFF President Michael McGovern (#1488).

In 1995 Kent #1747's longtime president, John Willits, stepped down after ten years of service. Markley ran for the office, winning a three-way race against Mike Moore and Kevin Garling. The election was cordial, and focused on establishing new leadership within the local. Markley continues to serve as president of Kent #1747.

The following year Markley served as Kelly Fox's campaign manager during Fox's very brief and successful campaign for WSCFF president in 1996. After Chris Heminger (Auburn #1352) was elected to secretary-treasurer of the WSCFF in 1997, Markley was elected District 8 representative in an uncontested race.

During Markley's nineteen years in the fire service of South King County, its fire departments and locals have grown three fold. Paramedic service in this area is provided by Medic One #2595, as a third service, funded by the Medic One levy. For the past two levy periods Markley has served as chair of the "Yes on Medic One" levy. He is also actively involved in the potential transition of paramedics into the fire departments of South King County.

In 2002 Markley ran for state representative in the 30th district (the greater Federal Way area), losing by only 634 votes of 32,000 votes cast. Major campaign issues included transportation, health care, and the state's budget deficit. Markley was motivated to run by a desire to represent the interests of the citizens of the 30th district and those of fire fighters statewide. Markley is now pursuing a more active role in the WSCFF, using his education in accounting, by running for WSCFF secretary-treasurer at the 2003 WSCFF Convention.

District 8 Representative Greg B. Markley (Kent #1747) and his daughter Maesun Boo Markley.

GREG MARKLEY COLLECTION

DISTRICT 9: *Rick Chaney*

Rick Chaney picked fire fighting as one of three possible careers while he was in high school. By the time he had finished his required coursework prior to graduation, the fire service had become his first choice, and he began taking a few classes at Bates. Chaney then tested with five fire departments, and was hired by Federal Way in July 1979. Chaney completed a one-year probationary period, but he never went to recruit school since Federal Way placed its new hires on the line immediately.

When he was hired, Chaney had little interest in his union, although he did go to its meetings. John Rickert was president of Federal Way #2024 at the time, and invited Chaney to attend what the WSCFF then called its Presidents' Meeting, which has since evolved into the Legislative Conference. Chaney realized the WSCFF and his local were fighting for issues that affected his job. He also watched management reassign his local's executive board in proportion to the degree they stood up for the fire fighters.

Then came a contract negotiation that went into arbitration, in about 1983. Federal Way #2024 was awarded a raise of more than thirteen percent, but none of its non-monetary requests. In response, the city decreed that the raise necessitated layoffs. Federal Way #2024 renegotiated. It agreed to let the pay raise take effect over two years, in exchange for receiving all of its non-monetary requests.

District 9 Representative Rick Chaney (Federal Way #2024).
WSCFF COLLECTION

Watching what his local accomplished made Chaney a believer, and an active participant in his local. He ran for and was elected Federal Way #2024's treasurer in 1986, close to the same time he made lieutenant. Chaney continued to serve on its negotiating team, and was elected vice president of his local in 1991, and then its president. He attended WSCFF events, and was encouraged by Howard Vietzke (Spokane #29), the WSCFF's legislative representative, to become more involved.

When Chaney decided to run for the position of WSCFF District 9 Representative in 1994, he was challenging the incumbent, Gerry Gores (Burien #1461). Chaney was serious enough about his campaign to secure the backing of several who were already on the executive board, as well as the WSCFF's president, Mike McGovern (Lakewood #1488). Once he was at the convention, he learned Keven Rojecki was considering running. Chaney and Rojecki decided neither wanted three candidates, and agreed Chaney would run against Gores.

Chaney won, and has been his district's representative since. Four years later, in 1998, he was again elected president of Federal Way #2024, and served one term. During this same period, the WSCFF had adopted its Strategic Plan. Chaney then stepped forward to advocate for a statewide apprenticeship program for fire fighters. He was familiar with his own local's apprenticeship program and many of the terms of which were negotiated within its contract, and could see the benefits of a more standardized program. As of spring 2003, Chaney is working to get as many locals as possible committed to the program.

⟷ *On-the-Job Training*
95

DISTRICT 10: # Don Schwab

Don Schwab was sitting in a pickup truck during a pouring rain when he realized he could get better work than foreman on a residential construction crew. He had grown up in Puyallup, where his grandfather, Adam Schwab, had been a fire fighter, so the younger Schwab knew some of what would be involved, and also knew several who still worked on the Puyallup Fire Department. He enrolled at Bates in June 1986, and received his EMT certification three months later. During the next two years Schwab became a resident fire fighter in Federal Way, tested all over the Westside, and served as a volunteer fire fighter with Pierce County Fire District 14 (Riverside).

District 10 Representative Donald Scwab (Everett #46).
WSCFF COLLECTION

He was first hired in Lakewood in September 1989. This wasn't a good match, so Schwab tested in several other departments. He was offered a position in Everett and South Tahoe (California) on the same day, chose Everett, and was placed with a company at the end of April 1990. The station he was assigned to, Station 1, put him under Captain Harold Draper. Schwab remembers Draper as an inspired and controversial individual, who was deeply involved with Everett #46. Schwab became more involved in union politics himself. He was elected to Everett #46's executive board in 1993, the same year he became a driver. In 1994 he became its secretary-treasurer, and began attending WSCFF events. Three years later he was promoted to captain, all the while continuing to pursue his interest in political action.

In 1999, Schwab ran for WSCFF's District 10 representative, and won, replacing Larry Longley, also from Everett #46, who had held the position for four years. Since he first joined the Everett Fire Department, Schwab has put a good deal of his efforts into political action, targeting Everett City Council and mayoral races. He has worked in Everett #46's sign shop since 1992, and for candidates seeking positions in the 30th State representative district and 2nd congressional district, as well as the WSCFF's success campaign on I-790.

DISTRICT 11: # Cory Bostick

Smoke from a dishwasher fire filled five-year-old Cory Bostick's house by the time a fire engine pulled up in front. When the fire was out, Cory went inside and emerged from his room wearing a child's fire helmet. Bostick remembers one of the fire fighters pointed to him and said, "There's a future fire fighter." From then on Bostick knew what he wanted to be. He joined the Santa Clara (Oregon) Fire Department as a volunteer the day after his eighteenth birthday, graduated from high school the following June, and continued to volunteer as he went to school in Salem, working toward a degree in fire science, and gaining his EMT certification.

He tested first in Salem, then continued, with his classmates, to test for other departments, including Richland, Washington, a test he took "on a whim." Bostick passed and was hired by the Richland Fire Department in August 1990. He remembers thinking at the time, "You pay some money a month, for what?" Richland #1052 Vice President Ricky Walsh had answers to this and more as the two carpooled to ski at Bluewood. Soon Bostick was involved in his local, and went to his first WSCFF event, a legislative conference. By January 1996 Bostick was secretary-treasurer of Richland #1052, and also served on the Public Relations Committee of the WSCFF.

Bostick realized by this time that he wanted to work in a bigger, more urban fire department, so he tested in Tacoma and Seattle. When he got the call from Seattle, "My wife was crushed. We loved living in Richland." They made the move, and found a place in Puyallup that had some of the rural character they liked. Since the Seattle department does not accept lateral transfers from other departments, Bostick completed recruit school and his probationary period, in January 1998.

About three months later, Charles Hawkins, then WSCFF's District 11 representative, told Bostick he wanted him on Seattle #27's PAC committee. By fall of 1999 Bostick was elected to an open seat on Seattle #27's executive board, and Hawkins was elected president of the local. In 2002 Hawkins announced he was stepping down as District 11 representative to focus on serving as Seattle #27's president. Bostick had expressed his interest in the district representative position to Hawkins earlier, making it clear he would not challenge Hawkins. But politics within Seattle #27 meant Bostick ran against another executive board member, Kenny Stuart, and won by a vote.

District 11 Representative Cory B. Bostick (Seattle #27).

B. BOSTICK COLLECTION

When asked about his goals on the WSCFF executive board, Bostick is clear. Having come from Richland #1052, he knows firsthand what the WSCFF provides to smaller locals. He also knows Seattle #27 has the reputation of a big local that throws its weight around, and that some within his local are not convinced the WSCFF provides much to Seattle #27 it couldn't get by itself. But Bostick is convinced that the WSCFF's political leverage serves all its member locals well, regardless of their size. He cites the gains the WSCFF has made for all its members on basic issues such as pensions, benefits, and portability. With the recent passage of I-790, Bostick is looking forward to working with the WSCFF to identify and move forward on other statewide issues.

LEGISLATIVE LIAISON: *Keven Rojecki*

Keven Rojecki was in high school when he drove his first fire truck. Living near Kalispell, Montana, he spent much of his time ski racing; a friend's father was a retired fire chief and got Rojecki thinking about fighting fire. So Rojecki volunteered with the Lakeside Fire Department while still in high school. After graduating from high school he moved back to Vashon Island, where he'd grown up, and volunteered there for about a year. He then became a resident with the Angle Lake Fire Department (King County Fire District 24 #2919) and earned his EMT certification.

The City of SeaTac incorporated in February 1990. Its municipal fire department was created from King County Fire District 24 only weeks before Rojecki and seventeen others were hired in February of 1991. Rojecki's group of new hires doubled the size of the department, which increased fulltime professional staffing. A volunteer station, formerly part of the Burien department, was located within the newly incorporated city, and gained professional staffing as well.

City of SeaTac #2919 members had worked hard canvassing voter support for the incorporation. Once the city was created, they shifted their efforts to creating its civil service, and to holding a line on what the fire department would and would not

Lobbyist Keven Rojecki (City of SeaTac #2919).

WSCFF COLLECTION

do as it made the shift into a municipal entity. Rojecki credits his initial union involvement to working side by side with #2919 President John Madson, during twenty-four-hour shifts. While still on probation Rojecki was elected to the City of SeaTac #2919's executive board as its first PAC director. He started to attend WSCFF events, and within four years he became a member of his local's negotiating team.

During this period, Rojecki began to stop by Tacoma #31's office, talking with Bruce Baurichter and Pat McElligott, and remembers he often brought ice cream for the inimitable Jimmy Cason. Rojecki listened and learned, and continued to work with other leaders within the WSCFF. In 1994 he considered running for WSCFF District 9 representative, but deferred to Rick Chaney (Federal Way #2024) to avoid a three-way election, since incumbent Gerry Gores was also in the running.

Rojecki was elected president of the City of SeaTac #2919 in 1996. He served for four years, until 2000, when he was appointed as the WSCFF's legislative liaison, replacing Jim Rudd (Spokane #29), who retired. Since then Rojecki has been a registered lobbyist for the WSCFF. For the past four sessions he has held the position of legislative liaison, working with WSCFF President Kelly Fox (Olympia #468) and Vice President Ricky Walsh (Richland #1052) as a lobbying team.

Rojecki utilizes the WSCFF's workplace leaders, who then talk with local members, exchanging opinions and ideas over time, as a critical pipeline for political action. Even so, the shifting and sometimes arcane details of potential legislation are difficult to communicate in a timely manner while the legislature is in session. This means the committee structure of the WSCFF also comes into play.

Good communication is only one part of political representation. Rojecki is clear that the WSCFF's success in Olympia also hinges on its finances. The success of I-790 demonstrated the WSCFF's effective use of all its resources, and Rojecki knows from experience how much work this takes within the entire organization.

Appendices

The remains of the
Everett Fire Department
Headquarters Engine Co. 2,
after a fire that began with
sparks from the courthouse,
on August 2, 1909.

EVERETT FIRE DEPARTMENT ARCHIVES

A History of Leadership: THE WSCFF EXECUTIVE BOARD SINCE 1939

Year Elected	President	Secretary Treasurer	Vice President	Legislative Team	Rep District 1 (Spokane #29 as of 1977)	Rep District 2	Rep District 3	Rep District 4	Rep District 5	Rep Distri (Tacoma as of 19.
2003	Kelly Fox (#468)	Greg Markley (#1747)	Ricky Walsh (#1052, dist 2)	Keven Rojecki (#2919), leg liaison; Fox and Walsh, registered lobbyists; (director govmt relations – OPEN)	Ted Rail	Ricky Walsh (#1052, vp)	Mike Wilson (#3524), Rick Peters (#2781) elected 10-03 when Wilson resigns	Dennis Lawson (#726)	Brian Hurley (#2409)	Pat McElli
2002	Kelly Fox (#468)	Chris Heminger (#1352)	Ricky Walsh (#1052, dist 2)	Keven Rojecki (#2919), leg liaison; Fox and Walsh, registered lobbyists; (director govmt relations – OPEN)	Ted Rail	Ricky Walsh (#1052, vp)	Mike Wilson (#3524)	Dennis Lawson (#726)	Brian Hurley (#2409)	Pat McElli
2001	Kelly Fox (#468)	Chris Heminger (#1352)	Ricky Walsh (#1052, dist 2)	Cody Arledge (#2409), director govmt relations; Keven Rojecki (#2919), leg liaison	Ted Rail	Ricky Walsh (#1052, vp)	Mike Wilson (#3524)	Dennis Lawson (#726)	Brian Hurley (#2409)	Pat McElli
2000	Kelly Fox (#468)	Chris Heminger (#1352)	Ricky Walsh (#1052, dist 2)	Jim Rudd (#29) retires 8-2000; Keven Rojecki (#2919) appt leg liaison; Cody Arledge (#2409), director govmt relations	Ted Rail	Ricky Walsh (#1052, vp)	Mike Wilson (#3524)	Doug Willis (#2175)	Brian Hurley (#2409)	Pat McElli
1999	Kelly Fox (#468)	Chris Heminger (#1352)	Ricky Walsh (#1052, dist 2)	Jim Rudd (#29), Cody Arledge (#2409) director govmt relations	Ted Rail	Ricky Walsh (#1052, vp)	Merlin Halverson (#1984)	Doug Willis (#2175)	Brian Hurley (#2409)	Pat McElli
1998	Kelly Fox (#468)	Chris Heminger (#1352)	Ricky Walsh (#1052, dist 2)	Jim Rudd (#29); Cody Arledge (#2409), director govmt relations	Ted Rail	Ricky Walsh (#1052, vp)	Merlin Halverson (#1984)	Doug Willis (#2175)	Brian Hurley (#2409)	Pat McElli
1997	Kelly Fox (#468)	Chris Heminger (#1352) [defeated Lonnie Hampton (#31)]	Ricky Walsh (#1052, dist 2)	Jim Cason (#31) dies 1-97; Cody Arledge (#2409); Pat McElligott (#31) joins Jim Rudd (#29), as assist lobbyist in leg 1997 session); Cody Arledge (#2409) appt to replace Cason as leg dir at 1997 convention	Ted Rail	Ricky Walsh (#1052, vp)	Merlin Halverson (#1984)	Doug Willis (#2175)	Brian Hurley (#2409) elected by district in 8-97 to replace Cody Arledge (#2409) who shifts to lobbyist	Pat McElli
1996	Kelly Fox (#468) [defeated Michael J. McGovern (#1488)]	Lonnie Hampton (#31) [defeated Jack Andren (#2175)]	Ricky Walsh (#1052, dist 2) [defeated Ted Rail (#29, dist 1)]	Jim Cason (#31) appt leg dir by exec bd when Howard Vietzke (#29) retires 6-96; Jim Rudd (#29) assumes asst lobbyist to replace Ken Snider (#29)	Ted Rail	Ricky Walsh (#1052, vp)	Merlin Halverson (#1984)	Doug Willis (#2175)	Cody Arledge (#2409) replaced Kelly Fox (#468) when Fox became pres	Pat McElli
1995	Michael J. McGovern (#1488)	Jack Andren (#2175) elected by exec bd 9-95, when Cason (#31) shifted to leg rep [Ted Rail (#29) and Hampton (#31) also applied]	Jim Rudd (#29, dist 1), Ricky Walsh (#1052, dist 2) elected by exec bd 9-95 as replacement	Howard Vietzke (#29), leg dir; Ken Snider (#29), asst lobbyist; Jim Cason (#31) and Jim Rudd (#29) appt as replacements 9-95; all 4 serve in 1996 leg session	Jim Rudd (vp); Ted Rail replaced Rudd in 9/95	Ricky Walsh (#1052, vp as of 9-95)	Merlin Halverson (#1984)	Michael Stead (#1488) appt 11-95 when Jack Andren (#2175) appt s/t	Kelly Fox (#468)	Pat McElli
1994	Michael J. McGovern (#1488)	Jim Cason (#31)	Jim Rudd (#29, dist 1)	Howard Vietzke (#29), leg dir; Ken Snider (#29), asst lobbyist	Jim Rudd	Ricky Walsh (#1052)	Merlin Halverson (#1984)	Jack Andren (#2175)	Kelly Fox (#468)	Pat McElli
1993	Michael J. McGovern (#1488)	Jim Cason (#31) [defeated Ronald Morehouse (#106)]	Jim Rudd (#29, dist 1) [defeated Ronald Morehouse (#106)]	Howard Vietzke (#29), leg dir; Ken Snider (#29) appt asst lobbyist fall 93	Jim Rudd	Ricky Walsh (#1052) [defeated Dan Downs (#1052)]	Merlin Halverson (#1984)	Jack Andren (#2175)	Kelly Fox (#468)	Pat McElli
1992	Michael J. McGovern (#1488)	Jim Cason (#31)	Dan Downs (#1052, dist 2)	Howard Vietzke (#29), leg dir; leg asst position created	Jim Rudd	Dan Downs (#1052)	Merlin Halverson (#1984) (dist 3 split into dist 3 & 10)	Jack Andren (#2175)	Kelly Fox (#468)	Pat McElli
1991	Michael J. McGovern (#1488)	Jim Cason (#31) [defeated Mick Crawford]	Dan Downs (#1052, dist 2) [defeated Jim Rudd (#29)]	Howard Vietzke (#29), leg rep	Jim Rudd	Dan Downs (#1052)	Merlin Halverson (#1984)	Jack Andren (#2175)	Kelly Fox (#468)	Pat McElli

The following is an incomplete compilation of information on the evolving structure of the WSCFF, and those individuals who held offices in it. Source information was piece-meal and at times anecdotal; independent confirmation of details was not always available. Note that not all positions are up for election annually. A listing of IAFF District 7 vice presidents prior to 1939 is on page 23.

Rep District 7	Rep District 8	Rep District 9	Rep District 10	Rep District 11 (Seattle #27 as of 1992)	Trustees	IAFF District 7 VP	IAFF Convention Location	Miscellaneous information about this year's members and board structure, major events	Convention Host
Stockman (#29)	Rich Merrell (#2878)	Rick Chaney (#2024)	Don Schwab (#46)	Cory Bostick	Dean Shelton (#3219), Tom Reich (#1296), John Gallup (#2919)	Paul Harvey (#27)	(no convention)	Legislature codifies I-790. WSCFF nominees appointed to state LEOFF pension board.	City of SeaTac #2919
Stockman (#29)	Greg Markley (#1747)	Rick Chaney (#2024)	Don Schwab (#46)	Cory Bostick [defeated Kenny Stewart]	Bill Garlington (#452), Tom Reich (#1296), Dean Shelton (#3219)	Paul Harvey (#27)	Las Vegas, Nevada	I-790 passes in November 2002, granting LEOFF 2 members pension board representation. Coverage of presumptive occupational diseases expanded, amending RCW 51.32.185.	Spokane Airport #1789, Spokane Co. Fire Dist. 9 #2916, Spokane Co. Fire Dist. 8 #3711
Stockman (#29)	Greg Markley (#1747)	Rick Chaney (#2024)	Don Schwab (#46)	Charles Hawkins, Jr.	Bill Garlington (#452), Tom Schneider (#469), Dean Shelton (#3219)	Paul Harvey (#27)	(no convention)	Convention resolutions direct a two-pronged effort to reform LEOFF 2: legislative action and possible initiative. The I-790 campaign begins. Power Through Participation wins 1st place in the IAFF's Media Awards.	Yakima #469
Stockman (#29)	Greg Markley (#1747)	Rick Chaney (#2024)	Don Schwab (#46)	Charles Hawkins, Jr.	Bill Garlington (#452), Tom Schneider (#469), Dennis Lawson (#726)	Paul Harvey (#27)	Chicago, Illinois	The multimedia member education program, Power Through Participation, is first presented at spring educational seminar.	Bellevue #1604, Renton #864, Kirkland #2545, Redmond #2898
Stockman (#29)	Greg Markley (#1747)	Rick Chaney (#2024)	Don Schwab (#46)	Charles Hawkins, Jr.	Bill Garlington (#452), Tom Schneider (#469), Dennis Lawson (#726)	Paul Harvey (#27)	(no convention)	Constitution is amended 8-99. Exec bd reports to membership with WSCFF Strategic Plan 2000.	Walla Walla #404
Stockman (#29) [defeated Russ ...y (#1604)]	Greg Markley (#1747)	Rick Chaney (#2024)	Larry Longley (#46)	Jon R. Gillis	Bill Anderson (#876), Dennis Lawson (#726), Bill Garlington (#452)	Paul Harvey (#27) [defeated Pat McElligott (#31)]	Lake Buena Vista, Florida (Orlando)	Constitution is amended 10-98. WSCFF Report of the Economic Summit released to membership.	Everett #46
Bergquist (#4)	Greg Markley (#1747) elected by district when Chris Heminger (#1352) elected s/t	Rick Chaney (#2024)	Larry Longley (#46)	Jon R. Gillis	Bill Anderson (#876), Dennis Lawson (#726), Bill Garlington (#452)	Jim Hill (#31)	(no convention)	Constitution is amended 7-97. McGovern awarded President Emeritus. WSCFF building named after Cason. WSCFF office workers unionize (OPEIU #23).	Spokane Valley Fire District 1 #876
Bergquist (#4)	Chris Heminger (#1352)	Rick Chaney (#2024)	Larry Longley (#46)	Jon R. Gillis (probably elected in spring)	Bill Anderson (#876), Dennis Lawson (#726), Cody Arledge (#2409)	Jim Hill (#31)	Honolulu, Hawaii	WSCFF occupies new Olympia office building in 8-96. Constitution amended 7-96. WSCFF wins passage of RCW 41.26.048 (Line of Duty Death Benefit) of $150,000. WSCFF launches website.	City of SeaTac #2919
Bergquist (#4)	Chris Heminger (#1352)	Rick Chaney (#2024)	Larry Longley (#46)	Bill Gosnell	Bill Anderson (#876), Dennis Lawson (#726), Cody Arledge (#2409)	Jim Hill (#31)	(no convention)	Focus of convention is human relations, and IAFF structure, operations, policy. Constitution is amended 7-95. WSCFF's Olympia office purchased from WEA in 12-95.	Richland #1052, Kennewick #1296, Pasco #1433, Hanford I-24
Bergquist (#4)	Chris Heminger (#1352)	Rick Chaney (#2024) [defeated Gerry Gores (#1461)]	Ron Morehouse (#106)	Bill Gosnell	C. Dale Pierce (#726), Bill Anderson (#876), Dave Neyens (#46)	Jim Hill (#31)	Detroit, Michigan	Membership authorizes exec bd to move ahead on purchasing permanent office space in Olympia.	Seattle #27
Bergquist (#4)	Chris Heminger (#1352)	Gerry Gores (#1461)	Ron Morehouse (#106)	Bill Gosnell	C. Dale Pierce (#726), Bill Anderson (#876), Dave Neyens (#46)	Jim Hill (#31)	(no convention)	LEOFF 2 is amended. Binding arbitration for dispatchers and paramedics is established, amending RCW 41.56.030. Constitution is amended 7-1993.	Spokane #29
Bergquist (#4)	Chris Heminger (#1352) (as of fall 1992)	Gerry Gores (#1461)	Ron Morehouse (#106) (dist 3 split into dist 3 and 10)	Bill Gosnell	C. Dale Pierce (#726), Bill Anderson (#876), Dave Neyens (#46)	Jim Hill (#31)	Vancouver, B.C.	Seattle #27 reaffiliates with WSCFF, creating dist 11. Leg asst position created.	Tacoma #31
Bergquist (#4)	District created	District created	District created	District created	C. Dale Pierce (#726), Bill Anderson (#876), Dave Neyens (#46)	Jim Hill (#31)	(no convention)	Resolution 91-24 establishes 3 more districts (8, 9, 10): with dist 3 split into dist 3, 9 and 10. Joe Gehl Group receives further authorization as telemarketing fundraiser.	Yakima #469

Year Elected	President	Secretary Treasurer	Vice President	Legislative Team	Rep District 1 (Spokane #29 as of 1977)	Rep District 2	Rep District 3	Rep District 4	Rep District
1990	Michael J. McGovern (#1488)	Jim Cason (#31)	Jim Rudd (#29, dist 1) [defeated Dan Downs (#1052, dist 2)]	Howard Vietzke (#29), leg rep	Jim Rudd (vp)	Dan Downs (#1052)	Merlin Halverson (#1984)	Jack Andren (#2175)	Kelly Fox (# [defeated J Mackey (#4
1989	Michael J. McGovern (#1488)	Jim Cason (#31) [defeated Ronald G. Morehouse (#106)]	Dan Downs (#1052, dist 2) [possibly defeated Jack Andren (#2175)]	Howard Vietzke (#29), leg rep	Jim Rudd	Dan Downs (#1052) (vp)	Merlin Halverson (#1984)	Jack Andren (#2175)	Frank Spicklemire (#468)
1988	Michael J. McGovern (#1488)	Ronald G. Morehouse (#106)	Jim Cason (#31, dist 6)	Howard Vietzke (#29), leg rep	Jim Rudd	Dan Downs (#1052)	Merlin Halverson (#1984)	Jack Andren (#2175)	Frank Spicklemire (#468)
1987	Michael J. McGovern (#1488)	Ronald G. Morehouse (#106)	Jim Cason (#31, dist 6)	Howard Vietzke (#29), leg rep	Gregory Borg	Dan Downs (#1052)	Merlin Halverson (#1984)	Jack Andren (#2175)	Frank Spicklemire (#468)
1986	Michael J. McGovern (#1488)	Ronald G. Morehouse (#106)	Jim Cason (#31, dist 6)	Howard Vietzke (#29), leg rep	Gregory Borg	Dan Downs (#1052)	Merlin Halverson (#1984)	Jack Andren (#2175)	Larry Churc (#2491)
1985	Michael J. McGovern (#1488)	Ronald G. Morehouse (#106)	Jim Cason (#31, dist 6)	Howard Vietzke (#29), leg rep	Gregory Borg	Dan Downs (#1052)	Merlin Halverson (#1984)	Jack Andren (#2175) [defeated Wayne Senter (#1352)]	Larry Churc (#2491)
1984	Michael J. McGovern (#1488)	Ronald G. Morehouse (#106)	Jim Cason (#31, dist 6)	Howard Vietzke (#29), leg rep	Gregory Borg	Dan Downs (#1052)	Merlin Halverson (#1984)	Greg Bergquist (#864)	Larry Churc (#2491)
1983	Michael J. McGovern (#1488)	Tom Fieldstead (#469), when Fieldstead promoted 11-83 Ron Morehouse (#106) appt [over Spicklemire (#468) and Ted Rail (#29)]	Dan Downs (#1052, dist 2)	Howard Vietzke (#29), leg rep	Gregory Borg	Dan Downs (#1052)	Merlin Halverson (#1984)	Greg Bergquist (#864)	Larry Churc (#2491)
1982	Michael J. McGovern (#1488) [defeated Halverson (#1984) and Ken Strong (#29)]	Tom Fieldstead (#469)	Dan Downs (#1052, dist 2) defeated Unknown challenger	Howard Vietzke (#29) trained by professional lobbyist Mike Ryherd	Don Spangle (#29)	Dan Downs (#1052) (vp)	Merlin Halverson (#1984)	Michael J. McGovern (#1488)	Larry Churc (#2491)
1981	Dennis Parlari (#726)	Tom Fieldstead (#469) [defeated Don Spangle (#29) and Ron Morehouse (#106)]	Dan Downs (#1052, dist 2) [defeated Ken Strong (#29, dist. 1)]	John Willis (#31), leg lobbyist; resigned before 1982 session to work at L&I	Don Spangle	Dan Downs (#1052) (vp)	Merlin Halverson (#1984)	Michael J. McGovern (#1488)	Frank Spicklemire (#468)
1980	Dennis Parlari (#726)	Howard Vietzke (#29)	Jim Hill (#31, dist 6)	John Willis (#31) leg lobbyist	Don Spangle	Dan Downs (#1052)	Merlin Halverson (#1984)	Dennis Parlari (#726), 8-80 Michael J. McGovern (#1488) appt	Frank Spicklemire (#468)
1979	Doug McNall (#46)	Howard Vietzke (#29)	Jim Hill (#31, dist. 6)	John Willis (#31) leg lobbyist	Don Spangle	Dan Downs (#1052)	Merlin Halverson (#1984)	Dennis Parlari (#726)	Frank Spicklemire (#468)
1978	Doug McNall (#46)	Howard Vietzke (#29)	Jim Hill (#31, dist 6)	John Willis (#31) leg lobbyist	Don Spangle	Dan Downs (#1052)	Merlin Halverson (#1984)	Dennis Parlari (#726)	Frank Spicklemire (#468)
1977	Doug McNall (#46)	Howard Vietzke (#29)	Jim Hill (#31, dist 6)	John Willis (#31) leg lobbyist	Vince Azzinnaro (districts created)	Dan Downs (#1052) [defeated Irwin Busby (#8760) and Galen "Ollie" Morris (#1433)] (districts created)	Merlin Halverson (#1984) (districts created)	Darrell Orndorff (districts created)	Frank Spicklemire (#468) (dis tricts create

Rep District 6 Tacoma #31 (...s of 1977)	Rep District 7 (Sea. #27 from 1978-1982)	Trustees	IAFF District 7 VP	IAFF Convention Location	Miscellaneous information about this year's members and board structure, major events	Convention Host
McElligott	Greg Bergquist (#864)	C. Dale Pierce (#726), Bill Anderson (#876), Dan Neyens (#46)	Jim Hill (#31)	St . Louis, Missouri	Compensation for district representative positions is restructured. After much discussion, Joe Gehl Group receives limited authorization as telemarketing fundraiser.	Pasco #1433, Kennewick #1296, Richland #1052
McElligott	Greg Bergquist (#864)	C. Dale Pierce (#726), Bill Anderson (#876), Dan Neyens (#46)	Jim Hill (#31)	(no convention)	Convention resolution from the floor, 89-31, passes, awarding Morehouse s/t emeritus.	Olympia #468, Tumwater #2409, Lacey #2903
Cason (vp)	Greg Bergquist (#864)	C. Dale Pierce (#726), Bill Anderson (#876), Dan Neyens (#46)	Jim Hill (#31)	Miami Beach, Florida	Vietzke reports: "more legislative issues related to the fire service (pro and con) than I have ever dealt with in one session."	Walla Walla #404
Cason (vp)	Rex Lindquist (#2545)	C. Dale Pierce (#726), Bill Anderson (#876), Ted Rail (#29)	Jim Hill (#31)	(no convention)	WSCFF participation in the NW Burn Foundation discontinued, WSCFF Burn Foundation established. Discussion of redistricting and restructuring within IAFF resolved without changes. WSCFF's *Washington Professional Fire Fighter* magazine resumes publication as a semi-annual. EMS committee reports to convention. RCW 51.32.185 passes, providing limited presumptive occupational disease legislation for fire fighters.	Tacoma #31
Cason (vp)	Rex Lindquist (#2545)	C. Dale Pierce (#726), Bill Anderson (#876), Ted Rail (#29)	Jim Hill (#31)	Las Vegas, Nevada	Exec bd representatives became "delegates at large" with voting privileges."	Spokane #29
Cason (vp)	Rex Lindquist (#2545)	C. Dale Pierce (#726), Bill Anderson (#876), Ted Rail (#29) [defeated Neyens (#46)]	Jim Hill (#31)	(no convention)	RCW 41.26 amended (LEOFF) to restructure payment for disability supplement of duty-related injury.	Bellevue #1604, Kent #1747, Kirkland #2545, Renton #864
Cason (vp)	Dist 7 created from dist 4	C. Dale Pierce (#726), Bill Anderson (#876), Gary Brown (#29)	Jim Hill (#31)	Cincinnati, Ohio	Washington State Supreme Court case (#1604 vs. *City of Bellevue*) "upholds right of all citizens to be publicly active in all elections." WSCFF constitution amended to allow WSCFF trustees to vote at convention, and establishes district representatives will be elected by district caucus (formerly exec bd appt & election). WSCFF office relocates to Bellingham. District 7 added.	Everett #46
Cason (vp)	probably Dennis Fenstermaker (#27)	C. Dale Pierce (#726), Gary Brown (#29), Bill Anderson (#876)	Jim Hill (#31)	(no convention)	Some mention of third trustee position creation. McGovern focuses on working with statewide labor coalition. NW Burn Foundation begins fundraising activities. WSCFF purchases first office computer. George Orr (#876) elected to State House of Representatives. WSCFF lobbyist becomes full-time, not contracted, position.	Spokane Valley Fire District 1 #876
Cason	Earl Davis (#27) or Dennis Fenstermaker (#27)	C. Dale Pierce (#726), Gary Brown (#29), Bill Anderson (#876)	Jim Hill (#31)	Chicago, Illinois	Parlari (#726) promoted to assistant chief in Puyallup and doesn't seek reelection. Howard Vietzke (#29) awarded newly created s/t Emeritus (effective June, 1981). WSCFF works with AWC to develop defensible minimum hiring standards. Seattle disaffiliates after convention. Special meeting to discuss Seattle #27's disaffiliation held at Alderwood.	Yakima #469 (was supposed to have been in Pasco but no union facility)
Cason	Earl Davis (#27)	C. Dale Pierce (#726), Bill Anderson (#876), Gary Brown (#29)	Jim Hill (#31)	(no convention)	Richland (#1052) and Kennewick (#1296) paramedics are included in their locals' contracts for the first time. District representatives' annual PAC report required. WSCFF's magazine reports, going into convention, "redistricting recommendation will be considered." Educational seminar held in Pasco in the spring on negotiation and arbitration.	Yakima #469
Cason appt place Jim	Earl Davis (#27)	possibly Gary Brown (#29), Dale Pierce (#726), Bill Anderson (#876)	Jim Hill (#31) [defeated Jim Martinez (#672)]	Miami Beach, Florida		Tacoma #31 sponsored (at SeaTac Thunderbird)
Hill (vp)	Earl Davis (#27)	possibly Gary Brown (#29), Dale Pierce (#726), Bill Anderson (#876)	Jim Martinez (#672)	(no convention)	WSCFF moved into Olympia condo in 1-1979. As of either 1979 or 1980, WSCFF president and s/t serve staggered 2-year terms; vp elected annually from 7 district reps, lobbyist appt by exec bd. District reps serve 2-year terms (odd districts to be elected in even years; even dist elected in odd years); trustees serve staggered 3-year terms with chair elected annually.	Spokane Valley Fire District 1 #876
Hill (vp)	Earl Davis (#27)	possibly Gary Brown (#29), Dale Pierce (#726), Bill Anderson (#876)	Jim Martinez (#672) [defeated Dick Warbrouck (#27)]	Las Vegas, Nevada	Purchase agreement for condo signed 12-78. WSCFF has 65 member locals. Parlari reports on "civilian paramedics" in King County, where CETA workers are replacing fire fighters. WSCFF and 6 other public employee unions form "United Public Employees Coalition," funded by raffles, to advocate public employees' legislative interests. Seattle #27 reaffiliates.	SeaTac #1257, Renton #864, Kent #1747, Federal Way #2024, Auburn, Tukwila #2088, Puyallup #726 (at SeaTac Motor Inn)
Hill (vp) ricts creat-	districts created, Seattle not yet affiliated	Gary Brown (#29), Bill Anderson (#876)	Jim Martinez (#672)	(no convention)	Newly drawn districts in place following negotiations for Tacoma #31's (and eventually Seattle #27's) reaffiliation. Single vp, elected from dist reps, replaces 3 vp positions. LEOFF 2 created.	Walla Walla #404

Year Elected	President	Secretary Treasurer	Vice President	Legislative Team	Executive Board and Trustee Information
1976	Ken Groth (#469)	Howard Vietzke (#29)	3 vps: 1st, Kenneth Groth (#469); 2nd, Irving Busby (#876); 3rd, John Harnett (#437)	John Willis (#31), #31 disaffiliated, position under discussion of executive board	Gary Brown (#29), Bill Anderson (#876), unkn
1975	Karl Hofmann (#46)	Howard Vietzke (#29)	3 vps: 1st, Kenneth Groth (#469); 2nd, Irving Busby (#876); 3rd, John Harnett (#437)	Willis (#31), #31 disaffiliated	Bill Anderson (#876), Don Nelson, Bill Nagy
1974	Karl Hofmann (#46)	Howard Vietzke (#29)	3 vps: Kenneth Groth (#469), Irving Busby (#876), John Harnett (#437) [appt. when DeBay retired; other 2 moved up]	John Smith (#31) retires; Ken Groth (#469), interim leg lobbyist; replaced by John Willis (#31) #31 disaffiliated	Bill Anderson (#876), Don Nelson, Bill Nagy
1973	Karl Hofmann (#46)	Howard Vietzke (#29)	3 vps: 1st, Orian DeBay; 2nd, Ken Groth (#469); 3rd, Irving Busby (#876)	John Smith (#31)	Board of trustees created. Trustees: Bill Anders chair (#876), Don Nelson, Bill Nagy
1972	Karl Hofmann (#46)	Howard Vietzke (#29)	3 vps: 1st, Orian DeBay; 2nd, Ken Groth (#469); 3rd, Irving Busby (#876)	6-72 John Smith appt. by executive board to fill "leg political dir" position	Unknown
1971	John W. Smith, Jr. (#31)	Robert E. Munk (#29)	33 vps: 1st, Karl Hofmann (#46); 2nd, Orian DeBay; 3rd, Kenneth Groth (#469)	John Willis (#31)	Unknown
1970	John W. Smith, Jr. (#31)	Robert E. Munk (#29)	3 vps: 1st, Karl Hofmann (#46); 2nd, Orian DeBay; 3rd, Kenneth Groth (#469)	John Willis (#31)	Unknown
1969	John W. Smith, Jr. (#31)	Robert E. Munk (#29)	3 vps: 1st, Edward Carroll; 2nd, Karl Hofmann (#46); 3rd, Orian DeBay	Unknown	Unknown
1968	John W. Smith, Jr. (#31)	Robert E. Munk (#29)	Unknown	Unknown	Unknown
1967	John W. Smith, Jr. (#31)	Robert E. Munk (#29), secretary; Don Meyer (#27), treasurer	1st vp, Harold Nilsen (#27); other vps John Alexander (#864), Ed Carroll (#469), George Roop (#876), Joe Roozen, Wilbur White (#462), George Wiese (#404)	George Roop (#876)	Executive board and/or trustees: Jack Scherrue (#46), Joe Roozen, Wilbur White (#462), Edwa Carroll (#469), George Wiese (#404)
1966	John W. Smith, Jr. (#31)	Robert E. Munk (#29), secretary; Don Meyer (#27), treasurer	Unknown	George Roop (#876)	Unknown
1965	John W. Smith, Jr. (#31)	Robert E. Munk (#29), secretary; Don Meyer (#27), treasurer	Unknown	George Roop (#876)	Unknown
1964	John W. Smith, Jr. (#31)	Tony Balazic (#437), secretary; Bus Cramer (#469), financial secretary; Felix Arena (#27), treasurer	Zane Mitchell (#315)	Waller (#29), educational and political director; George Roop (#876)	Trustees: Axel Drugge (#27), Dick Rowley (#46 George Weise (#404), George Roop (#876), Ro Munk (29)
1963	John W. Smith, Jr. (#31) [defeated Jack Baker (#106)]	Walt Lambert (#29), recording secretary; Bus Cramer (#469), financial secretary; Felix Arena (#27), treasurer	Tony Balazic (#437)	Waller (#29), leg rep	Trustees: Axel Drugge (#27), John Smith (#31) George Weise (#404), Zane Mitchell (#315), George Roop (#876), Dick Rowley (#46)
1962	Gordon Hovik (#46)	Walt Lambert (#29), secretary; Felix Arena (#27), treasurer	Jack Baker (#106)	Waller (#29), leg rep; Earl Brower (#46), dir govt relations	Trustees: Axel Drugge (#27), John Smith (#31) George Weise (#404), George Roop (#876), Za Mitchell (#315)
1961	Gordon Hovik (#46)	Walt Lambert (#29), secretary; Felix Arena (#27), treasurer	Jack Baker wins 3-way election [John Smith (#31) and Hal Nilsen (#27) defeated]	Waller (#29), leg rep; Earl Brower (#46), dir govt relations	Trustees: Axel Drugge (#27), John Smith (#31) George Weise (#404), George Roop (#876), Za Mitchell (#315)
1960	John Alexander (#864)	Walt Lambert (#29), secretary; Felix Arena, treasurer (#27)	Unknown	Waller (#29), leg rep; Earl Brower (#46), dir govt relations	Unknown
1959	John Alexander (#864)	Walt Lambert (#29), secretary; Felix Arena (#27), treasurer	Gordon Hovik (#46)	Waller (#29), leg rep; Earl Brower (#46), dir govt relations	Executive board: G.A. Sayan (#27), Zane Mitche (#315), Jack Baker (#106), Bus Cramer (#469) Weise
1958	John Alexander (#864)	Walt Lambert (#29), secretary; Felix Arena (#27), treasurer	Walt Barnes (#31)	Waller (#29), leg rep; Earl Brower (#46), dir govt relations	Executive board: G.A. Sayan (#27), Tony Balazic (#437), Jack Baker (#106), Bus Cramer (#469), Gordon Hovik (#46)

IAFF District 7 VP	IAFF Convention Location	Miscellaneous information about this year's members and board structure, major events	Convention Host
...artinez (#672) ...ated Howard Vietzke ...)]	Denver, Colorado	Major districting changes: Seattle #27 and Tacoma #31 (both disaffiliated) submit a joint proposal for restructure of the WSCFF and their reaffiliation. Tacoma reaffiliates. District reps elected in alternate years, but appt by exec bd.	Bellingham #106
...artinez (#672)	(no convention)	WSCFF office in Spokane relocates. Local contracts are kept on file by WSCFF for the first time. RCW 41.58 (Public Employment Labor Relations) passes, creating the Public Employee Relations Committee (PERC). WSCFf begins pubication of the *Washington Professional Fire Fighter*.	Pasco #1433
...artinez (#672) ...ated John Willis ...)]	Baltimore, Maryland	WSCFF convention overlaps Expo 1974. Tacoma #31 disaffiliates 9-74. Fire districts come under legislative consideration. Vietzke reports on possible new office locations in Spokane. First monthly newsletter mailed to membership. First WSCFF budget is submitted to trustees for study. WSCFF begins publication of the *Washington Professional Fire Fighter*.	Spokane #29
...artinez (#672)	(no convention)	WSCFF creates board of trustees. WSCFF has 1900 individual members. AWC opposes WSCFF legislative action on pension concerns. Mediation and Arbitration Collective Bargaining Rights pass, amending RCW 41.56 and includes explicit language against right to strike. WISHA passes with standards specific to fire fighters. First separate WSCFF office is established in Spokane.	Yakima #469
...artinez (#672)	Los Angeles, California	WSCFF has 38 local members. Presidents' Meeting held. Trustee board structure discussed. WSCFF returns to annual convention schedule. Smith (#31) appointed to Public Employees Collective Bargaining Committee by Governor Dan Evans.	Aberdeen-Hoquiam #3315 (in Ocean Shores)
Lambert (#29)	(no convention)	No formal WSCFF convention held in 1971, to save money. An informal "mini-convention" gathered in Yakima.	unofficial mini-convention, Yakima #469
Lambert (#29)	Miami Beach, Florida	HB 474 passes, protecting public employees' right to active participation in politics. WSCFF switches to biennial conventions. LEOFF 1 (RCW 41.26) takes effect 10-1970.	Everett #46
Lambert (#29)	(no convention)	Waller (#29) hired in newly-created position of IAFF Legislative Director by IAFF president Howie McClennan and serves in this post until 1976. RCW 41.26, LEOFF created, to take effect in 1970.	Vancouver #452
Lambert (#29)	Toronto, Ontario	"No strike" clause removed from IAFF constitution. Seattle #27 disaffiliates. IAFF celebrates 50th anniversary. Secretary and treasurer positions combined.	Spokane #29
Lambert (#29)	(no convention)	Probable year 3 vp system was adopted, with one vp to come from a fire district. Arena (#27, ret.) thanks WSCFF for securing a minimum pension of $150/mo. District reps. become elected positions (by executive board). Resolution to combine secretary and treasurer positions, with 7 vps (after lots of contentious discussion) fails to get 2/3 majority required. WSCFF passes resolutions establishing itself as sole legislative advocate for fire fighters. Following passage of RCW 41.56, Public Employees' Collective Bargaining, WSCFF outlines procedures for member locals to follow when negotiating contracts.	Bellingham #106
Lambert (#29)	Indianapolis, Indiana		Walla Walla #404
. Lambert (#29)	(no convention)	Discussion of possible initiative if legislature does not grant collective bargaining rights for fire fighters.	Vancouver #452
Lambert (#29)	San Diego, California	Al Albertoni defeats Waller (#29) for s/t of IAFF. Waller couldn't simultaneously run for District 7 vp, and was eliminated from the leadership structure of the WSCFF.	Seattle #27
Waller (#29)	(no convention)	Presidential election held to replace Hovik (#46), who had heart attack while lobbying in Olympia. Governor Albert Rosellini and Seattle Mayor Gordon Clinton attend WSCFF convention and offer their support for "mandatory collective bargaining rights for fire fighters." Public Pension Commission (PPC) formed to study pension system funding deficit.	Unknown likely Yakima #469
Waller (#29)	San Antonio, Texas	All WSCFF officers elected at-large; fire districts gain WSCFF's representation.	Unknown
Waller (#29)	(no convention)	RCW 41.18, the Firemen's Pension bill, amended to increase basic pension amount. Position of financial secretary created. Leo Weisfield and John Cherberg made honorary members of WSCFF.	Unknown
Waller (#29)	Buffalo, New York	Dick Taylor, AWC president, attends WSCFF convention.	Longview area
Waller (#29)	(no convention)		Unknown
Waller (#29)	Wichita, Kansas	WSCFF joins labor opposition to Initiative #202, which attempted to establish right-to-work laws in Washington State.	Aberdeen-Hoquiam #3315

Year Elected	President	Secretary Treasurer	Vice President	Legislative Team	Executive Board and Trustee Info
1957	John Alexander (#864)	Walt Lambert (#29), secretary; Felix Arena (#27), treasurer	Walt Barnes (#31)	Waller (#29), leg rep; Earl Brower (#46), dir govt relations	Executive board: G.A. Sayan (#27), Tony Balaz (#437), Louie Larson (#2639), Cramer (#469) Gordon Hovik (#46), George Roop (#876)
1956	John Alexander (#864)	Walt Lambert (#29), secretary; Felix Arena (#27), treasurer	George Roop (#868), 1st vp	Waller (#29), leg rep; Earl Brower (#46), dir govt relations	Executive board: G.A. Sayan (#27), Tony Balaz (#437), Louie Larson (#2639), Bob Messick (# Gordon Hovik (#46)
1955	Ray Greenleaf (#31)	Jack Waller (#29), secretary; Felix Arena (#27), treasurer	John Alexander (#864)	Waller (#29), leg rep; Earl Brower (#46), dir govt relations	Executive board: Walter Madson (#656), G.A. (#27), Charles Hall (#2369), Bus Cramer (#46 Bob Messick (#106)
1954	Ray Greenleaf (#31)	Jack Waller (#29), secretary; Felix Arena (#27), treasurer	John Alexander (#864)	Waller (#29), leg rep; Earl Brower (#46), dir govt relations	Executive board: Walter Madson (#656), G.A. (#27), Charles Hall (#2369), Bus Cramer (#46 Roy Warnock (#46), Bob Messick (#106)
1953	Bob Messick (#106)	Jack Waller (#29), secretary; Felix Arena (#27), treasurer	G.A. Sayan (#27)	Waller (#29), leg rep; Earl Brower (#46), dir govt relations	Executive board: Walter Madson (#656), Ray Greenleaf (#31), Bus Cramer (#469), C.E. Mus (#404), Roy Warnock (#46)
1952	Bob Messick (#106)	Jack Waller (#29), secretary; Felix Arena (#27), treasurer	G.A. Sayan (#27)	Waller (#29), leg rep; Earl Brower (#46), dir govt relations	Executive board: Warnock (#46), Walter Mads (#656), Ray Greenleaf (#31), Bus Cramer (#46 C.E. Musgrave (#404)
1951	Unknown	Jack Waller (#29), secretary; Felix Arena (#27), treasurer	Unknown	Waller (#29), leg rep; Earl Brower (#46), dir govt relations	Unknown
1950	Roy Warnock (#46)	Jack Waller (#29), secretary; Felix Arena (#27), treasurer	Bob Messick (#106)	Waller (#29), leg rep; Earl Brower (#46), dir govt relations	Executive board: Walter Madson (#656), Ken Weaver (#469), Doyle Graff (#27), Ray Green (#31), Carly Effnor (#437); Doyle Graff (#27), trustee
1949	Roy Warnock (#46)	Jack Waller (#29), secretary; Felix Arena (#27), treasurer	Joe Oldani (#2639)	Waller (#29), leg rep; Earl Brower (#46), dir govt relations	Executive board: Walter Madson (#656), Oska Kinerman (#31), Ken Weaver (#469), Doyle G (#27), Messick; Doyle Graff (#27), trustee
1948	Roy Warnock (#46)	Jack Waller (#29), secretary; Felix Arena (#27), treasurer	Unknown	Waller (#29), leg rep; Earl Brower (#46), dir govt relations	Trustee: Doyle Graff (#27), others unknown
1947	Roy Warnock (#46)	Jack Waller (#29), secretary; Felix Arena (#27), treasurer	Unknown	Waller (#29), leg rep; Earl Brower (#46), dir govt relations	Trustee: Doyle Graff (#27), others unknown
1946	Roy Warnock (#46)	Jack Waller (#29), secretary; treasurer unknown	Unknown	Waller (#29), leg rep; Earl Brower (#46), dir govt relations	Unknown
1945	Unknown	Jack Waller (#29), secretary; treasurer unknown	Unknown	Waller (#29), leg rep; Earl Brower (#46), dir govt relations	Unknown
1944	Unknown	Jack Waller (#29), secretary; treasurer unknown	Unknown	Waller (#29), leg rep; Earl Brower (#46), dir govt relations	Unknown
1943	Unknown	Unknown	Unknown	Waller (#29), leg rep; Earl Brower (#46), dir govt relations	Unknown
1942	Unknown	Unknown	Unknown	Waller (#29), leg rep; Earl Brower (#46), dir govt relations	Unknown
1941	Unknown	Unknown	Unknown	Waller (#29), leg rep; Earl Brower (#46), dir govt relations	Unknown
1940	Unknown	Unknown	Unknown	Unknown	Unknown
1939	E.C. "Ernie or Ed" Kuehner (#454)	O.K. Coffin (#27), secretary; F.E. Stearns (#106), treasurer	H.L. Leach (#52)		Executive board: R.L. Warnock (#46), A.D. Adam (#27), C.E. Weeks (#29), Ernest Yett (#437), E. Thompson (#31)

IAFF District 7 VP	IAFF convention location	Miscellaneous information about this year's members and board structure, major events	Convention Host
Waller (#29)	(no convention)	WSCFF focuses on collective bargaining rights and introduces its first bill on collective bargaining (HB 369, Arbitration for Firemen and Policemen).	Unknown
Waller (#29)	Montreal, Quebec		Unknown
Brower (#46)	(no convention)	Walla Walla begins hosting double-digit year conventions (1955, 1966, etc.); RCW 41.18, Firemen's Relief and Pensions, enacted as an alternate to provisions of RCW 41.16.	Walla Walla #404
Brower (#46)	Miami, Florida		Unknown
Brower (#46)	(no convention)		Unknown
Brower (#46)	Seattle, Washington	Convention held in June.	Walla Walla #404
Brower (#46)	(no convention)		Unknown
Brower (#46)	Milwaukee, Wisconsin	WSCFF convention held June 9-10, but considered itself "pre-legislative," with 13 locals participating. WSCFF authorizes no-strike pledge. Tacoma #31 also hosted the 1950 WSFL convention.	Unknown
Brower (#46)	(no convention)	Some references to executive board members as district representatives.	Unknown
Brower (#46)	Houston, Texas		Vancouver #452
Brower (#46)	(no convention)	WSCFF convention held in April. Washington State establishes retirement system for public employees; legislature amends RCW 41.16, the Firemen's Relief and Pension Act.	Everett #46 (at Monte Cristo Hotel)
Brower (#46)	Toledo, Ohio		Unknown
Brower (#46)	(no convention)		Unknown
Brower (#46)	Louisville, Kentucky		Unknown
Maximilian (#27)	(no convention)		Unknown
Maximilian (#27)	Columbus, Ohio		Unknown
Maximilian (#27)	(no convention)		Unknown
Maximilian (#27)	Des Moines, Iowa		Unknown
Maximilian (#27)	(no convention)	WSCFF drafts first constitution and receives its charter from IAFF.	Unknown

Context: A TIMELINE OF LABOR AND FIRE SERVICE EVENTS

This timeline includes events significant to the history of the fire service, the history of the WSCFF, and the history of the union movement, especially within Washington State.

Shading denotes events relating specifically to the WSCFF, including sponsorship of legislation.

1670s-1899

1678   America's first fire company forms in Boston. Early "fire societies" enroll members and protect their property indicating status in the community.

December 7, 1736   Benjamin Franklin's Union Fire Company forms—the first organization to specialize in fire suppression and rescue.

1806   In *Commonwealth of Philadelphia v. Pullis*, journeyman shoemakers in Philadelphia are convicted of conspiracy for striking to obtain higher wages.

1842   Massachusetts Supreme Court ruling, *Commonwealth v. Hunt*, establishes the fundamental legality of unions.

July 6, 1876   All-volunteer Seattle Engine Company 1 provides Seattle's first organized fire protection, funded by subscription.

May 29, 1880   New Tacoma Hook and Ladder Company 1 forms as a volunteer fire department with 1 truck.

1881   Spokane Falls City Council purchases 1,500 feet of hose and 2 hose carts; 20 men join Rescue Hose Company 1 in August.

October 1881   Spokane Falls City Council creates volunteer fire department by ordinance and adds Hose Company 2.

1882   Commencement Hook and Ladder Company 1 forms in Old Tacoma.

1884   Old Tacoma and New Tacoma merge, as do their hook and ladder companies.

1884   City of Seattle takes control of its fire department, creating the Seattle Volunteer Fire Department, with 3 hose and 3 engine companies.

1886   Skilled craft workers from 25 unions form the American Federation of Labor (AFL).

1886   Knights of Labor organizes Washington State chapters and nominates candidates for territorial legislature.

May 1, 1886   Nation-wide strike in support of the eight-hour workday begins.

May 4, 1886   Striking workers protest police brutality at Chicago's Haymarket Square. Dynamite bomb thrown by an unknown person kills a police officer immediately. (Six others die later, including some wounded by police bullets). Eight anarchists are tried and convicted.

June 6, 1889   Great Seattle Fire consumes 31 square blocks of downtown Seattle.

June 1889   Tacoma establishes first professional fire department in Washington State and purchases new steam engines and horses.

August 4, 1889   Great Fire in Spokane destroys 32 city blocks.

October 17, 1889   Seattle City Council creates the Seattle Fire Department as a full-time, paid department.

December 18, 1889   Spokane Falls establishes a professional department of 25 fire fighters.

1890   Tacoma's fire department submits first request for a fireboat.

1891   First session of the Washington State Legislature establishes Labor Day as a legal holiday.

1891   Seattle fire fighter Herman Larsen dies in the line of duty, leading to formation of the Firemen's Relief Association.

March 1892   Everett Volunteer Fire Company 1, Fire Company A, and Everett Hook and Ladder Company form.

1892   City of Everett replaces independent companies with its own volunteer fire department.

1896   Civil Service Commission replaces Fire Commission in Seattle.

1896   Tacoma shifts fire and police departments to civil service system.

1897   Labor Congress of the State of Washington forms in Olympia.

October 11, 1898   Tourist Hotel Fire highlights problems with Tacoma's water systems. Tacoma Tug & Barge Company equips a vessel for fire department use.

1900-1909

circa 1900   Average fire fighter's salary is approximately $1,000 per year. Continuous shifts with meal breaks and 1 or 2 days off per month are the norm. Hiring and promotions depend on political connections. Fire fighter fatalities are expected at major fires.

1900   Advocating "A fair day's work for a fair day's pay," the AFL gains membership of approximately 2 million workers.

1901   AFL charters first "Union of Fire Fighters" in Washington, D.C. as a directly affiliated (federal) union.

1901   Seattle hires first fire marshal to conduct building inspections and enforce fire ordinances.

1901   Everett City Council establishes a paid, professional fire department.

1902   State legislature requires fire insurance companies to pay 1 percent of premiums into fund for disabled fire fighters.

1902   Washington State Federation of Labor (WSFL) forms and affiliates with AFL, then lobbies political candidates to support labor.

May 5, 1903   Pittsburgh Firemen's Protective Association Local #1 forms, and asks AFL to organize the fire service nationally.

1903   RCW 49.08 provides state-funded mediation and arbitration services to assist labor and management in resolving disputes.

1903   Washington State's first child labor law is passed.

1904   Pittsburgh local urges AFL to organize a membership drive among paid fire fighters throughout US.

1904   Everett #46 holds the first of many Relief Balls to raise money to pay fire fighters' medical expenses and support their widows and children.

1908   Congress passes Federal Employer's Liability Act.

1908   WSFL merges with the Labor Congress of Washington, which collected statistics on elected representatives and had a nationalist agenda.

1909   Washington passes Employer's Liability Act, establishing employers' liability for on-the-job injuries.

1909   Yakima's Dart fire engine is displayed at the Alaska-Yukon-Pacific Exposition in Seattle, as the first motor-driven fire apparatus west of the Mississippi.

1909   RCW 41.16, (Firemen's Relief and Pensions), establishes state-mandated, locally-administered, pay-as-you-go pension plans and defines "uniformed personnel."

1910-1919

1911   Washington State enacts RCW 51, one of the nation's first worker's compensation laws.

1912   At national convention, AFL officers and organizers are instructed to assist fire fighters in organizing and achieving improved working conditions.

1912   Public Law 426-62 establishes the US Department of Labor. President Woodrow Wilson appoints its first secretary, William B. Wilson.

1912   Washington State adopts the initiative and referendum process.

1912   Spokane Fire Department begins fabricating its own motorized vehicles.

1913   Seattle City Fire Fighters Union #15462 affiliates with AFL, despite city threats to dismiss fire fighters who joined, and gains two-platoon system.

1914-1918   World War I.

1914   The Clayton Act establishes "the labor of a human being is not a commodity or article of commerce."

1914   Seattle acquires first motorized pumping engines.

1916   Using federal authority to regulate interstate commerce, the Keating-Owen Child Labor Act curtails use of child labor.

1916   Seventeen American and one Canadian fire fighter locals hold AFL charters. Other unions compete for jurisdiction over fire fighters.

November 5, 1916   The Everett Massacre. Sheriff and citizen deputies fire on International Workers of the World (IWW) members arriving by steamer for a labor demonstration, killing five.

1916   Spokane Fire Department replaces all horses with motorized vehicles.

April 6, 1917   US enters World War I.

1917   Congress enacts Smith-Hughes Act to provide federal funding for vocational education, set minimum standards for instructors, and create state boards of vocational education.

February 1917   Everett fire fighters affiliate directly with AFL.

April 16, 1917   Spokane fire fighters form City Firemen's Union #15515.

June 4, 1917   Tacoma City Firemen's Federal Union #15601 affiliates directly with the AFL and achieves a two-platoon system within the city.

1917   At national convention, AFL adopts resolution offered by Thomas Spellacy of Schenectady, NY, authorizing AFL President Samuel Gompers to charter International Union of Fire Fighters.

1918   US Supreme Court finds the Keatings-Owen Child Labor Act unconstitutional in *Hammer v. Dagenhart*.

1918   Average salary of top-grade fire fighter is $1,346 per year.

February 26, 1918   Twenty-four locals (including Seattle #27, Spokane #29, Tacoma #31, and Everett #46) meet at AFL headquarters to form the International Association of Fire Fighters (IAFF).

February 28, 1918   Thirty-six delegates attend IAFF charter convention in Baltimore, MD, and elect Thomas Spellacy their first president. Original constitution advises against strikes, establishes *The Fire Fighter* as IAFF's official publication, and forms legislative committee and executive board. Total individual membership is approximately 5,400.

1918   Only 34 US cities employ two shifts of fire fighters; more common is continuous duty (where fire fighters live at the fire house), or the 84-hour week. Average wage is 29 cents per hour.

1918   IAFF national convention delegates congressional representatives for two-platoon systems.

1919   Fire fighters work 84 to 168 hours per week and earn approximately $1,000 per year.

February 6-11, 1919   Seattle General Strike paralyzes local industry as 65,000 workers walk out in support of shipyard workers denied promised post-war wage increases. Strikers provided meals, supplied hospitals, and kept the peace, but were ultimately unsuccessful in their demands.

August-September 1919   IAFF convention endorses 8-hour workday, calls for universal health insurance, and reports membership of 25,000 fire fighters.

September 9, 1919   Defending their right to unionize, 1,117 Boston police officers strike, leading to violence and looting in the city. State guard restores order; all participants are fired and never rehired. Governor Calvin Coolidge states "there is no right to strike against the public safety by anybody, anywhere, any time," gains popularity nationwide.

1919   After Boston's police strike, federal law passes to prevent Washington, D.C. fire fighters from affiliating with IAFF. Other local governments follow suit. IAFF headquarters moves to Canada.

November 1919   Four Legionnaires are killed while raiding an IWW hall in the Centralia Massacre. Wobbly Wesley Everest is lynched in retaliation, and the Washington Legislature makes IWW membership illegal.

1919   RCW 49.36 establishes legality of trade unions in Washington State.

1919   Washington State Legislature amends RCW 41.16 (Firemen's Relief and Pensions Act) to include pneumonia and tuberculosis as illnesses, and categorizes them as job-related disabilities. Affected fire fighters get paid disability leave and coverage of medical expenses.

1919   Washington establishes vocational education programs with the passage of RCW 28.09.

1919   Tacoma Fire Department replaces all horses with motorized units.

1920s

1920s   The National Association of Manufacturers and other business interests sponsor the "American Plan" campaign against organized labor. It equates open shops with patriotism and union shops with Bolshevism.

1920s   No US locals affiliate with the IAFF.

January 1, 1920   Everett #46 disaffiliates from the IAFF.

1920   The 19th Amendment to the US Constitution gives women the right to vote.

1921   IAFF membership is approximately 20,000.

July 1, 1922   National rail workers walk out to protest the Railroad Labor Board's wage cut and abolition of the eight-hour day in the 1922 Shopmen's Strike.

September 1, 1922   *United States District Court: for the Northern District of Illinois, in Equity No. 2943, US v. Railway Employees' Department of the American Federation of Labor* charges AFL and affiliates with conspiracy to interrupt interstate commerce, and prohibits nearly all organized strike activity.

October 1922   National Fire Prevention Week is first observed.

1923   IAFF lobbies for the enactment of civil service laws to remove fire service from politics. IAFF membership drops further to 17,000.

1924   Last of Seattle's horses are retired from the department.

1926   IAFF membership begins to climb. IAFF convention includes first professional education (on dust explosion hazards).

December 28, 1926   Spokane #29 asks WSFL to present bill to enact statewide two-platoon system. Seattle #27 withholds support.

1928   Bond measure funds largest-ever expansion of Tacoma Fire Department.

October 29, 1929   "Black Tuesday" stock market crash marks beginning of the Great Depression.

1930s

Depression Era   IAFF "Sunshine Divisions" distribute food and clothing in their communities. Tacoma #31 sponsors a soup kitchen, firewood yards, and toy repair and distribution.

1930   IAFF formally adopts no-strike provision. Most departments operate with shifts of fire fighters, and continuous service is no longer a predominant problem.

1932   Norris-LaGuardia Act prevents federal courts from prohibiting general union activities, picketing, or actual strikes; also prohibits employers from suing employees who violate yellow dog contracts.

1932   IAFF reports 23,000 members.

1932   Tacoma #31 files suit against City of Tacoma following a 10 percent pay cut, arguing against voter-determined pay rates.

1933   Franklin D. Roosevelt is inaugurated. New Deal begins.

1933   National Industrial Recovery Act (NIRA) establishes the National Recovery Administration (NRA), which sets maximum hours and minimum wages, and grants workers the right to organize.

1933   Washington enacts "little Norris-LaGuardia Act," confirming workers' right to organize. Court-issued restraining orders or injunctions in labor disputes are limited.

1933   Everett fire fighters reaffiliate with IAFF as Everett #350, and join the Everett Central Labor Council and the WSFL.

1933   Tacoma #31 receives a second pay cut of 12 percent.

1934   1,856 work stoppages occur in US—the largest number since World War I.

May 1935   US Supreme Court overturns NIRA in Schechter *Poultry Corp. v. United States* on the grounds that price and crop controls violate states' rights.

1935   Wagner Act (National Labor Relations Act, NLRA) is enacted, establishing the National Labor Relations Board (NLRB). Provides for secret elections to determine bargaining agents and outlaws "company unions," but applies only to workers engaged in interstate commerce, not to public employees.

1935   Congress passes the Social Security Act.

1935   RCW 41.08 requires creation of civil service commissions to oversee fire departments.

1935   RCW 41.16 is amended to allow uniformed personnel to retire at any age, after 25 years of service, and caps pensions at $125 per month, increasing fiscal demands on Washington municipalities.

1935   Washington State Supreme Court awards Tacoma #31 fire fighters more than $200,000 in back pay from the City of Tacoma.

1935   Mill workers strike in Tacoma. Response includes posting National Guard troops armed with bayonets and passage of an anti-picketing ordinance. Federal mediation helps secure union recognition, wage increases, and rehire rights.

1936-1939   Spanish Civil War

1936   John Lewis leads the ten unions in the Committee for Industrial Organization (CIO) to form their own federation after expulsion from the AFL.

1936-1937   Workers at Bendix products in South Bend, IN, conduct the first sit-down strike in November 1936. Flint Sit-down Strike (December 30, 1936, to February 11, 1937) culminates in General Motors recognizing the UAW as its workers' sole bargaining representative.

1936   Newspaper Guild wins strike against William Hearst's *Seattle Post Intelligencer*.

March 1937   In *West Coast Hotel Co. v. Parrish*, the US Supreme Court upholds a Washington State law establishing a minimum wage for women.

April 1937   US Supreme Court upholds constitutionality of Wagner Act in *National Labor Relations Board v. Jones & Laughlin Steel Corporation*.

1937   US Steel signs first contract with the Steel Workers.

1937   State of Washington Employment Security Department is established to implement and provide services covered in the federal Social Security Act.

1937   Seattle takes delivery of its first aerial fire truck, with a 100' all-metal ladder.

mid-to late 1930s   Seattle Mayor Arthur Langlie initiates study of Seattle's fire fighters pension system, revealing that the system cannot pay for itself.

1938   Federal Fair Labor Standards Act (FLSA) institutes a national minimum wage of 25 cents per hour, abolishes oppressive child labor, and establishes a maximum workweek of 44 hours. Provisions apply to approximately 20 percent of US labor force.

1938   Committee for Industrial Organization changes its name to the Congress of Industrial Organizations (CIO).

1938   IAFF's *International Fire Fighter* publishes a series of articles on heart disease among fire fighters.

December 9, 1938   Delegates from 12 Washington IAFF locals discuss formation of a possible IAFF state organization and move to propose the idea to potential member locals.

1939-1945   World War II.

1939   US Congress repeals laws prohibiting the District of Columbia Fire Department from affiliating with the IAFF.

1939   IAFF's first medical advisor begins research on the physical effects of fire fighting. Heart is a particular concern.

1939   IAFF assists Pennsylvania locals in passing the Heart and Lung Act, Workers' Compensation Act, and Occupational Disease Law, the first legislation to presume the connection between these diseases and fire fighting.

January 6, 1939   Washington IAFF locals meet in Chehalis to establish the WSCFF. Its proposed goals: to advocate state legislative action, provide safer working conditions, establish fair wages, and improve benefits for members.

April 1939   Twelve Washington IAFF locals draft the WSCFF's constitution and bylaws.

July 1939   Spokane hosts first WSCFF convention.

September 1, 1939   Based upon request of the majority of Washington's IAFF locals, the IAFF issues a charter to the WSCFF.

1940s

1940s   IAFF charters first 8 federal locals. The number of state associations grows from 19 to 33.

1940   IAFF membership is approximately 45,000. The union participates in new civil defense activities in US.

March 1941   Franklin Roosevelt's Executive Order 8,716 creates National Defense Mediation Board to mediate and arbitrate labor disputes which adversely affect national defense.

April 11, 1941   Office of Price Administration and Civilian Supply is established.

December 7, 1941   US formally enters World War II after Japanese attack Pearl Harbor.

1941   RCW 49.04 creates State Apprenticeship Council.

January 1942   Executive Order 9,017 replaces the National Defense Mediation Board with the National War Labor Board, banning strikes and lockouts, and providing for "peaceful adjustment" of labor disputes.

1942   Fire departments experience wartime staffing shortages. IAFF is asked for a policy on the situation. Many departments utilize "relief," "auxiliary," or "duration" fire fighters.

February 9, 1943   FDR orders 48-hour workweek in factories.

1943   Average fire fighter earns $1908 per year and works 70 hours per week. Hourly wage is approximately 50 cents.

1943   RCW 49.12.210 requires women to be paid the same wage as similarly employed men, and provides for civil recovery of sex-based wage differential.

1944   Tacoma #31 supports substitute fire fighters who want to tests for career appointments.

December 31, 1956   National War Stabilization Board replaces National War Labor Board.

1945   RCW 39.12 establishes prevailing wages for public works .

1947 Taft-Hartley Act of 1947 (Labor-Management Relations Act) prohibits secondary boycotts and closed shops. States can enact right-to-work laws, and procedures for settling national emergency strikes are outlined.

1947 Amendment to RCW 41.16 implements use of a 5-year salary average to calculate base pension. Death benefit for retirees and military service credits are added.

1947 RCW 41.40 establishes the Washington Public Employees' Retirement System (PERS).

1947 RCW 73.04 is amended to limit veterans' preference in public employment to those subject to full, continuous military control.

1947 Workers' compensation benefits increase to 100 dollars per month for disabled workers, 75 dollars per month for widows.

1947 Seattle citizen ballot grants fire fighters a 48-hour workweek, and initiates a three-platoon system.

April-September 1948 International Association of Machinists and Aerospace Workers #751 strikes Boeing after more than a year of contract negotiations. Boeing threatens to move to Wichita, and Teamsters #451 vies for Machinists' membership.

1949 RCW 49.60.030 (Washington State Fair Employment Practices Act), prohibits discrimination in employment based on race, creed, color, or national origin.

1949 RCW 47.64 creates Marine Employees Commission, and allows striking ferry workers to retain collective bargaining rights (with terms approximating interest arbitration) upon shift from private to public employment.

1950s

June 27, 1950 US enters the Korean war, and remains involved until 1953.

1950 IAFF membership exceeds 72,000. Large metropolitan fire departments pay average annual salaries of $3,500. IAFF objectives: $5,000 annual base salary, 40-hour workweek, retirement at half pay after 20 years, a $1,200 minimum annual widow's benefit, and 75 percent pay for fire fighters disabled in line of duty.

September 7, 1950 IAFF Ladies' Auxiliary is founded at IAFF's 20th convention. Lillian Howard is its first president.

1950 WSCFF annual convention delegates pledge not to strike to advance their goals, recognizing the threat to community safety. Approximately 30 locals are affiliated with the WSCFF.

1952 Voters' initiative establishes interest (binding) arbitration to settle disputes between the City of Everett and its fire fighters.

1953 WSFL establishes Health and Welfare Services to assist affiliate unions.

1954 IAFF makes the Muscular Dystrophy Association its "charity of choice."

1954 Tacoma City Council agrees to provide work uniforms for fire fighters.

1955 The AFL and CIO merge to form AFL-CIO. IAFF remains affiliated with the new entity in the US, as well as the Canadian Labour Congress.

1955 RCW 41.16.240 grants professional fire fighters in small municipalities and fire districts inclusion in professional fire fighters' pension plan. These fire fighters are also included in RCW 41.18.

1955 RCW 41.18 (Firemen's Relief and Pensions – 1955 Act) establishes a new pension system with variable benefits to be formally selected at the risk of losing survivor benefits upon death. Continued coverage under existing plan, RCW 41.16, is an option.

1955 Fire Fighters local No. 350 v. C. Arvid Johnson overturns Everett's 1952 initiative and leaves Everett fire fighters without binding arbitration as a means of settling labor disputes.

1956 Doctors James Elam and Peter Safar develop technique of mouth-to-mouth resuscitation.

1956 IAFF represents 85 percent of all eligible professional fire fighters.

1956 Right-to-work Initiative 198 is soundly defeated through the efforts of the newly formed United Labor Advisory Committee.

1957 WSCFF establishes collective bargaining rights as primary legislative focus and introduces its first bill, Arbitration for Firemen and Policemen. Bill is defeated in March.

1957 Washington State Federation of Labor (WSFL) and the Washington State Congress of Industrial Organizations merge to form the Washington State Labor Council (WSLC).

1957 RCW 41.16 raises the pension cap from $125 per month to $150 per month, and incorporates cost-of-living adjustments (ruled unconstitutional in 1959).

1958 IAFF establishes the John P. Redmond Memorial Trust Fund for research and education about occupational hazards and diseases of fire fighters.

July 1958 WSLC holds its first convention.

1958   Fire fighters join organized labor's opposition to Washington State's right-to-work movement, and voters reject Initiative 202 (Restricting Labor Agreements).

1959-1975   Vietnam War

1959   Landrum-Griffin Labor-Management Reporting and Disclosure Act imposes controls on internal union practices, sets forth a "bill of rights" for union members, requires unions to file annual reports, and further restricts strikes, picketing, and boycotts.

1959   John's Hopkins Hospital researchers develop the first portable defibrillator and cardio-pulmonary resuscitation.

late 1950s   IAFF establishes a research department to compile statistics on fire fighter working conditions and other information useful to locals in contract negotiations.

late 1950s   IAFF opposes municipal efforts to merge police and fire departments.

1959   State legislature passes RCW 49.46 (Minimum Wage Act), setting the first statewide minimum wage at 1 dollar per hour. Unemployment benefits are extended to 30 weeks at $42 per week.

January 5, 1959   Claude Harris is hired as Seattle's first African-American fire fighter.

1960s

November 8, 1960   Washington voters approve Initiative 207, adopting state civil service law for employees of state agencies. Collective bargaining provisions are included with codification in RCW 41.06.

1960   IAFF begins providing printed materials to locals on bargaining, negotiating, public relations, and local union administration.

1961   Due to vigorous efforts of the WSCFF, HB 365 (Firemen's Pension Bill) is passed as amendment to RCW 41.18.

1962   John F. Kennedy's Executive Order 10988 grants union rights to federal workers, and by extension, other public employees.

1963   Congress passes the Equal Pay Act of 1963, requiring employers to pay all employees equally for similar work, regardless of gender.

1963   IAFF starts mailing *International Fire Fighter* to individual members.

1963   All Canadian provinces require binding arbitration of collective bargaining disputes.

1963   WSCFF passes resolution titled Arbitration, Union Recognition, and Collective Bargaining for Fire Fighters at its convention and presents it for inclusion in the Washington State Labor Council's legislative program. The resolution dies in the rules committee during the 1964 legislative session.

1963   RCW 41.52 establishes the Public Pension Committee to study the gap between pension systems' assets and their liabilities.

1963   State legislature establishes occupational and environmental research facility at the University of Washington, with funding from the state Medical Aid and Accident Funds.

August 1964   Gulf of Tonkin Resolution escalates war in Vietnam.

1964   Civil Rights Act of 1964 prohibits unequal application of voter registration requirements, bans discrimination in public accommodations, encourages school desegregation, and outlaws employment discrimination in businesses with 25 or more employees.

1965   WSCFF again supports legislation to allow for collective bargaining by public employees. Governor Dan Evans vetoes it.

October 24, 1965   *The Spokesman Review* alleges that 23 members of Spokane's police and fire departments misused union funds to support the campaign for a strong-mayor system in Spokane.

1966   Fair Labor Standards Act (FLSA) expands definition of employers subject to minimum wage and maximum hour regulations.

1966   Dr. Frank Pantridge of Belfast, Northern Ireland, develops Flying Squad to deliver pre-hospital coronary care and transport.

1966   National Academy of Sciences publishes White Paper, "Accidental Death and Disability: The Neglected Disease of Modern Society," detailing inadequacies of trauma care.

1966   National Traffic and Motor Safety Act sets national standards for ambulance design and construction, and provides for inspection of used emergency vehicles.

1966   IAFF establishes Harvard University Trade Union Program Scholarship and sponsors first IAFF participant.

1966   Fire fighters in Atlanta, Kansas City, and St. Louis go out on strike.

1966   Everett #350 is the first local to establish itself as the sole and exclusive bargaining agent for its city's fire fighters.

1966   Spokane fire fighters and police officers sue the *Spokesman Review* for 1965 libel.

1967   Dr. Peter Safar establishes Freedom House Ambulance Service in Pittsburgh.

1967   RCW 41.56 is enacted, providing collective bargaining for public employees in Washington State.

1967   WSCFF convention restructures board, including creation of a combined secretary-treasurer position. After passage of RCW 41.56, WSCFF outlines procedures for member locals to follow when negotiating contracts.

1967   State effort to replace state workers' compensation system with private insurance is defeated.

1967   RCW 41.18 (Firemen's Relief and Pensions 1955 Act) amended to include full chiefs.

1967   Seattle #27 forms Ladies' Auxiliary.

1968   Lyndon Johnson signs the Fire Research and Safety Act (PL 90-259), establishing the National Commission on Fire Prevention and Control to investigate fire problems in the US and make recommendations.

1968   Average fire fighter earns an annual salary of $6,484 and works 56 hours per week.

1968   Three votes re-elect Walt Lambert (Spokane #29) as IAFF District 7 vice president against challenger John Richmond (Seattle #27).

1968   IAFF Fiftieth Anniversary, with membership approximately 130,000. No-strike clause is removed from constitution at convention. Fire-fighter casualties resulting from civil disorder lead IAFF to form committee addressing on-duty harassment of fire fighters. Proposal for arming fire fighters is abandoned.

1968   AT&T begins to identify 9-1-1 as the universal emergency phone number.

1968   St. Vincent's Hospital in New York City establishes first pre-hospital cardiac care unit, staffed by physicians.

May 14, 1968   Department of Labor and Industries determines that only fire fighters below the grade of battalion chief are included in local bargaining units.

1968   WSCFF adopts convention resolutions restricting member fire fighters from introducing legislation without its approval.

1968   IAFF resolves to require member locals to join state associations. Opposition from large locals delays enactment.

1968   Seattle #27 disaffiliates from the WSCFF.

1968   Seattle Fire Department begins formal affirmative action with its "trainee program." Twelve black applicants are recruited by June.

1968   Tacoma Fire Department begins recruiting minority fire fighters.

1968   Funded by a research grant, the Seattle Fire Department collaborates with Harborview Hospital's cardiology department to deliver "out-of-hospital" cardiac care.

1969   Dr. Michael Criley works with Los Angeles Fire Department to establish mobile life support unit.

1969   RCW 41.56 is amended to create a panel to study optional binding arbitration (RCW 41.56.400) and to establish a commission to prevent unfair labor practices and issue remedial orders and cease-and-desist orders (RCW 41.56.160).

April 25, 1969   RCW 41.26 (Law Enforcement Officers and Fire Fighters Retirement System), known as LEOFF, consolidates local pension and benefit plans into a statewide, state-administered, and one hundred percent state-funded system.

1969   RCW 28B.16 authorizes collective bargaining between state institutions of higher education and their civil service employees.

1969   Seattle Fire Department's 14 black fire fighters represent the city's highest percentage of minority recruitment.

1970s

1970   The Occupational Safety and Health Act of 1970 establishes federal program to protect workers from job-related death, injury, and illness.

1970   Nixon names IAFF president Howie McClennan co-chair of the National Commission on Fire Prevention.

1970   IAFF charters its 2,000th local.

1970   Groundbreaking takes place for new IAFF headquarters in Washington, D.C., three blocks from White House.

March 1, 1970   Prior to being enacted, RCW 41.18 and RCW 41.26 are amended with the Omnibus Pension Bill.

1970   HB 474 passes, protecting public employees' right to active participation in politics.

March 7, 1970   Seattle Fire Department's Medic One placed into service with supervising physician on board.

| 1970 | Everett #46 (then #350) negotiates new contract under RCW 41.56, and gains first binding arbitration clause in the state, as well as pay increases and improved benefits. |

October 10, 1970   RCW 41.26 (LEOFF), as amended, takes effect.

1970   US Commission on Civil Rights investigates Tacoma Fire Department's hiring practices.

1971   IAFF conducts first Redmond Symposium on health hazards of fire service.

1971   RCW 41.26.270 removes all LEOFF members from coverage under the Industrial Insurance Act (RCW 51), and abolishes civil action for personal injury by members against employers.

1971   RCW 18.71.200 clarifies the position of EMTs.

January 1971   Physician no longer rides with Seattle Fire Department's Medic One staff, but is called by paramedics from the scene.

April 1971   Tacoma #31 and the Tacoma Fire Department develop the Minority Recruitment Program, accepting its first 2 black recruits two months later.

1972   Department of Transportation and Department of Defense initiate program to provide medical evacuation via helicopter.

1972   Television show *Emergency!* debuts on NBC. Its popularity raises the profile of paramedics.

1972   Following his final term as WSCFF president, John Smith is appointed to the Public Employees Collective Bargaining Committee by Governor Dan Evans and is named WSCFF's lobbyist.

1972-1976   Tacoma Fire Department increases number of minority fire fighters from 6 to 29.

August 1972   Seattle Mayor Wes Uhlman issues executive order establishing an affirmative action program for all city departments.

1973   Congress passes EMS Systems Act (PL 93-154) funding 300 new regional emergency medical systems.

1973   *America Burning* Report by the National Commission on Fire Prevention and Control addresses the severity of America's fire problem, and recommends establishing a United States Fire Administration and national fire training academy.

1973   Amendments to RCW 41.56 mandate mediation, fact-finding, and arbitration to settle contract disputes between fire fighters or police and their public employers, and require public employers to deduct monthly union dues from a worker's pay when so authorized. Strikes are explicitly prohibited.

1973   The Washington Industrial Safety and Health Act (RCW 49.17) is enacted to create, maintain, continue, and enhance the industrial safety and health program of the state, to equal or exceed OSHA standards.

1973   State legislature passes RCW 18.73 (Emergency Medical Care and Transportation Services).

1973   Harborview Medical Center and the Seattle Fire Department formally initiate an intensive paramedic training program.

1973   Seattle City Council extends protection in employment to lesbians and gays.

1973   Explosion aboard 560-foot tanker *Cygnus* highlights shortcomings of Seattle Fire Department's maritime response capacity. Funding from the US Maritime Administration establishes the Marine Division of the Seattle Fire Department.

1973   Tacoma Fire Department has 90 trained EMTs.

1973   WSCFF establishes its first dedicated office in Spokane.

1974   The Federal Fire Prevention and Control Act (PL 93-498) incorporates recommendations of *America Burning* report and establishes the National Fire Prevention and Control Administration and the National Fire Academy.

1974   State legislature considers numerous changes to LEOFF, including a two-tier system which foreshadows LEOFF 2. Only minor amendments pass.

February 25, 1974   On-duty death of fire fighter Dale Jones leads the Tacoma fire department to issue radios to every fire fighter.

September 1, 1974   Tacoma #31 disaffiliates from the WSCFF.

1974   WSCFF begins publishing newsletter, *Washington Professional Fire Fighter*.

January 1975   IAFF executive board adopts 9 recommendations regarding EMS systems, particularly that they should be under the jurisdiction of fire departments.

1975   RCW 41.58 (creates the Public Employment Relations Commission (PERC) to administer public employees' collective bargaining rights.

1975   Seattle #27 Ladies' Auxiliary changes its name to Seattle Fire Fighters Women's Association.

1976   WSCFF creates districts within its organizational structure.

1976   Seattle fire department conducts first paramedic training program open to those outside of its department.

1976 Six of eight female applicants enter the Seattle Fire Department's recruit class. All are terminated following drill school, and one, Lori Lakshas, files a discrimination suit against the department.

1976 *City of Spokane v. Police Guild* upholds the constitutionality of the RCW 41.56 amendment which made binding (interest) arbitration compulsory.

1976 *City of Everett v. Fire Fighters #350* establishes that compulsory binding arbitration does not violate "home rule" powers of cities.

1976 Tacoma #31 reaffiliates with the WSCFF.

September 29, 1976 President Gerald Ford signs Public Safety Officers Benefits Act (PL 94-430) which provides a $50,000 death benefit for state/local fire fighters and law enforcement officers killed in the line of duty.

June 1977 State legislature revises LEOFF, along with the Public Employees Retirement System and the Teachers' Retirement System. New two-tier structures reduce benefits for employees entering the systems. LEOFF Plan 2 members become eligible for workers' compensation under RCW 51, per RCW 41.26.480.

1977 RCW 50.04 is amended to define the state and its political subdivisions as "employing units" for the purposes of determining eligibility for unemployment insurance.

1977 RCW 18.71.205 establishes tougher certification requirements for paramedics in Washington State.

1977 Tacoma #31 agrees to the use of "the rule of three" to increase the number of minorities promoted within the Tacoma Fire Department.

1977 Seattle's trainee program is dissolved and immediately replaced with a pre-recruitment class.

October 1977 Barbara Beers becomes Seattle's first female fire fighter.

1978 Seattle #27 rejoins the WSCFF.

1978 WSCFF and six other public employee unions form "United Public Employees Coalition," funded by raffles, to advocate public employees' legislative interests.

December 1978 WSCFF purchases Olympia condominium to accommodate union members throughout legislative sessions.

1979 Circuit court upholds selective certification promotions of two minority candidates in the Seattle Fire Department in *Maehren v. Seattle*. Case is appealed using Seattle #27 funds, and the original decision is finally upheld in 1985.

1980s

1981 Federal Omnibus Budget Reconciliation Act results in the shift of funding for EMS programs to block grant funds allocated by individual states.

1981 Seventy-three percent of all fire departments in the US provide some level of EMS service.

1981 Eight thousand workers participate in labor rally to oppose HB 31, proposing the privatization of worker's compensation.

1981 WSCFF delegates resolve to establish a political action fund to collect voluntary contributions from individual members. WSCFF Voluntary Political Action Fund (WSCFF VPAF) is established by winter of the following year.

1981 Richland #1052 secures right of battalion chiefs to choose union representation in State Supreme Court ruling, *IAFF Local No. 1052 v. PERC* (1985).

1981 In *Bellevue Fire Fighters #1604 vs. the City of Bellevue* Bellevue #1604 challenges a city ordinance banning certain nonpartisan political activities by city employees.

1981 Eileen Lewis is hired as Tacoma Fire Department's first female fire fighter.

1982 The National Fire Protection Association establishes federal standards for PASS (Personal Alert Safety Systems).

1982 RCW 41.26.470 passes, protecting the rank and salary of LEOFF 2 members returning to work following disability leave.

1982 RCW 41.26.425 provides for lump sum payment of retirement benefits when monthly allowance is less than 50 dollars.

1982 WSCFF replaces contract legislative position with a full-time lobbyist.

1983 Dispute over per capita payments to WSCFF causes Seattle #27 to disaffiliate for the second time.

1982 The Tacoma YMCA offers pre-training to women interested in fire service employment, at no cost to participants.

1983 HB 884 attempts to restore LEOFF 1 benefits to LEOFF 2 members, but fails.

1983 RCW 48.48.150 requires registration of guard animals with the local fire department and posted warnings when such animals are on site.

1983	RCW 46.37 mandates that vehicles using compressed gas fuels must bear warning placards.
1983	Laws governing PERC are amended to add a six-month statute of limitations on filing grievances regarding unfair employment practices, to parallel timing specified in the National Labor Relations Act (NLRA).
1983	RCW 53.18.015 (HB 434) applies collective bargaining and binding arbitration provisions of RCW 41.56 (Public Employees' Collective Bargaining) to port district employees, including fire fighters.
1983	WSCFF restructures finances following Seattle #27's disaffiliation, raising monthly per capita assessments to $5.47 per member.
1984	Legislature approves an interim legislative study on possible improvements to LEOFF 2.
1984	HB 1257, to require that employers pay full salary for up to six months following a job-related injury, fails.
1984	Amendments to the WSCFF constitution allow locals to nominate candidates for secretary-treasurer, and to allow district caucuses, rather than the WSCFF executive board, to nominate and elect district representatives.
1984	WSCFF approves steps to make its lobbyist position a salaried position, rather than one that paid per diem on a work-replacement basis.
1984	Six women pass the Tacoma Fire Department's exams, five of them participants in the YMCA pre-training program.
1984	Seattle Fire Department employs 45 female fire fighters and paramedics.
1984	State supreme court upholds the right of public employees to engage in political activity in *Bellevue Fire Fighters #1604 vs. the City of Bellevue*.
1985	US Supreme Court decision *Garcia v. San Antonio Transit Authority* establishes overtime rights of paramedics not cross-trained as fire fighters.
1985	US Supreme Court upholds original decision allowing the use of selective certification in *Maehren v. Seattle*.
1985	RCW 41.26 (LEOFF) is amended to provide state disability supplements for duty-related injury, to sunset in 1989.
1985	Claude Harris is appointed the Seattle Fire Department's first African-American chief.
circa 1987	Port of Bellingham case addresses definitions of uniformed personnel among port employees, to determine whether workers were eligible for LEOFF and/or entitled to collective bargaining rights.
1986	Congress passes the Superfund Amendments and Reauthorization Act (SARA), which establishes worker protections against hazardous materials exposure and authorizes funding for training. First responders are encouraged to play an active role in pre-incident planning and prevention.
1986	The Public Safety Officer Benefit Act (PL 94-430) is amended to include public sector EMS personnel.
1986	The National Fire Protection Association publishes the first edition of NFPA 1500—Standard on Fire Department Occupational Safety and Health Programs.
1986	IAFF establishes its occupational medical residency program with Johns Hopkins University, supporting residents during a two-month rotation in the IAFF Department of Occupational Health and Safety.
1986	RCW 35.10.370 provides fire fighters with job security when two or more cities merge.
1986	WSCFF forms EMS Committee at its convention. It also establishes WSCFF Health and Welfare Trust.
1986	Upon becoming a paramedic, Joyce Heggen becomes first woman in the Tacoma Fire Department to achieve a rank above fire fighter.
1987	With grant funding from SARA, the IAFF establishes its HAZMAT Training Program.
1987	RCW 51.32.185 defines lung disease as a presumptive occupational disease for fire fighters.
1987	SB 5347 proposes retirement age of 54, bases pension on average salary for last 2 years worked (rather than five), and requires employer to pay costs. The bill fails.
October 15, 1988	Adjustments to benefits paid under the Public Safety Officer Benefit Act begin to reflect annual change in the Consumer Price Index.
May 1987	The WSCFF Health and Welfare Trust is created to provide an alternative to employer-based health insurance.
1987	WSCFF Burn Foundation is created.
1988	The IAFF reorganizes to expand services through the following departments: Research & Labor Issues, Governmental Affairs & Political Action, Public Relations & Communications, Education, Occupational Health & Safety, Hazardous Materials, In-House Legal Counsel, Special Events, and the Canadian Office.
1988	IAFF president Al Whitehead announces that IAFF will embrace EMS as part of the fire service.
1988	State workers' compensation benefit increases from 75 percent of average state wage to 100 percent. Maximum benefit increases from $1,300 to $1,700.

1988   Amendment to RCW 18.73.081 eliminates EMT re-certification practical exam, replacing it with continuing education requirements.

1988   Legislature amends RCW 41.56, granting binding arbitration to paramedics who are public employees, unless they work for public hospital districts.

1988   *City of Bellevue v. IAFF #1604 and PERC* considers whether it is an unfair labor practice when a city violates "good faith bargaining" in interest arbitration. City of Bellevue is ordered to provide requested information and return to bargaining.

1989   Disability supplement authorized by amendment to RCW 41.26 (LEOFF 2) in 1985 is made permanent.

1989   RCW 41.26.520 allows accrual of service credit while on paid leave and making contribution to pension plan. Previously, service credit was accrued only during actual paid employment.

1989   Establishment of "Last Alarm" Memorial in John A. Cherberg Building in Olympia.

1989   *IAFF Local #1052 v. PERC and the City of Richland* determines that employers must bargain about staffing proposals that affect safety and workload.

1989 to 1991   *City of Yakima v. IAFF Local #469, PERC, Yakima Police Patrolmen's Association; City of Yakima v. IAFF Local #469; City of Yakima v. PERC* clarify the relationship between collective bargaining rights and civil service laws. The State supreme court agrees with Yakima #469 that collective bargaining agreements take precedence over municipal civil service law.

1990-2003

November 29, 1990   The Public Safety Officer Benefit Act is amended to provide benefits to federal, state, and local fire fighters, law enforcement personnel, members of public rescue squads, and ambulance crews who suffer permanent and total disability.

1990   Congress passes the Ryan White Comprehensive AIDS Resources Emergency (CARE) Act. There are over 150,000 reported AIDS cases in the US.

1990   IAFF conducts its first regional seminar as part of a new Educational Seminar Program.

1990   RCW 28B.15.380 offers tuition waivers for dependents of fire fighters killed or totally disabled in the line of duty, upon admission to a state or regional university, or The Evergreen State College within ten years of high school graduation.

1990   HB 2673 fails, denying state portability of LEOFF 2.

1990   RCW 41.50.065 requires the Department of Retirement Services to issue annual notification of service credit to each member of Washington's public retirement programs.

1990   RCW 70.168 establishes a comprehensive statewide EMS and trauma care system, and creates the governor-appointed EMS trauma steering committee.

May 1990   *IAFF #1445 v. City of Kelso and PERC* rules that a city is not required to submit to interest arbitration on the effects of annexation.

January 16 – February 27, 1991   Persian Gulf War.

July 1991   IAFF reassigns Everett #350 its original local number, #46.

1991   SB 5044, calling for a state occupational disease study for heart disease and cancer, fails.

1991   State legislature reorganizes RCW 41.26 (LEOFF) into three sections: Plan I provisions, Plan II provisions, and provisions (including the right to sue) which apply to both. Obsolete statutes are repealed or decodified.

1991   WSCFF engages the Joe Gehl group to raise funds via telemarketing of concerts benefiting WSCFF.

circa 1991   WSCFF resumes publication of *Washington Professional Fire Fighter* magazine.

1991   Executive board is expanded to 10 districts at WSCFF convention.

1991   IAFF's first EMS conference promotes fire-based Emergency Medical Systems.

1992   OSHA adopts Bloodborne Pathogens Regulation, which prescribes safeguards to protect workers against health hazards associated with exposure to bodily fluids.

1992   SB 6286 introduces legislation to reduce the state's contribution to PERS by a total of $40 million, including $32 million from LEOFF. Following negotiation, RCW 41.45 is amended to reduce state contributions by $32 million total, with $16 million coming from LEOFF.

1992   RCW 41.26.520 provides for military service credit, if member pays all contributions within 5 years of re-employment.

1993   WSCFF adds an assistant lobbyist position to paid staff.

1992   Seattle #27 reaffiliates with the WSCFF, and is added to the executive board as District 11.

1992-1993   Serial arsonist Paul Keller sets more than 100 fires in Seattle.

1993   HB 1294, amends RCW 41.26.430, reducing LEOFF service years from 58 to 55 without penalty, and establishes portability within public retirement systems as provided by RCW 41.54.

1993   RCW 51.32.090 is amended to provide continuation of workers' compensation benefits if a state worker returns to light duty while disabled.

1993   HB 1295 fails to restore right-to-sue language to LEOFF 2.

1993   RCW 41.26.520 allows service credit for paid leave taken while acting as an elected union official.

1993   RCW 18.71.205 amended to provide option of eliminating EMT written exams in favor of modular testing.

1993   RCW 41.56.030 provides collective bargaining and binding arbitration for police and fire department dispatchers, public hospital district paramedics, and Port of Seattle airport fire fighters.

1993   HB 1295 again fails to restore right-to-sue language to LEOFF 2.

1994   Ryan White infectious disease notification for fire fighters implemented by Centers for Disease Control.

1994   State creates permanent portability which applies to all state pensions, but "very high" costs are borne by members.

January 5, 1995   Four fire fighters are killed in the Pang Warehouse Fire in Seattle.

1995   WSCFF purchases permanent office in Olympia. WSCFF moves in August 1996.

1996   Fire fighter calendars are produced to benefit the NW Burn Foundation for the first time.

1996   IAFF creates new EMS department and launches htpp://www.iaff.org.

1996   With some restrictions, an amendment to the Age Discrimination in Employment Act allows states and their political subdivisions to enforce maximum age limitations on employment as a fire fighter.

1996   WSCFF successfully lobbies for passage of RCW 41.26.048, establishing a $150,000 payment to a fire fighter's beneficiaries or estate following death due to injuries sustained in the line of duty.

1996   (SB 6154) allows PERS 2 fire fighters who work for universities to transfer into the LEOFF system.

1996   The name of the WSCFF Health and Welfare Trust is changed to the LEOFF Health and Welfare Trust.

1996   WSCFF launches website.

1997   WSCFF building named after Jimmy W. Cason (Tacoma #31).

1997   IAFF and IAFC (International Association of Fire Chiefs) sponsor Joint Labor Management Wellness/Fitness Initiative to maintain fire fighters' physical and mental capabilities. Seattle #27 is one of ten departments on its Task Force.

June 1997   *Pasco Police Officers Association v. City of Pasco* determines that management rights proposals are a mandatory subject of arbitration.

1997-1998   Fire fighters' average salary is approximately $34,400, based on a 50-hour workweek.

1998   President Clinton and Congress authorize funding for the *National Fire Fighter Fatality Investigation Project.*

November 1998   *The Police, Fire and Emergency Officers Educational Assistance Act of 1998* provides federal financial aid for higher education to the dependents of public safety officers killed or permanently and totally disabled as a result of injury sustained in the line of duty.

1998   *Seattle Local #27 v. City of Seattle* finds that a city cannot create a supplementary retirement benefit to LEOFF 2, and that such benefits are not mandatory issues in bargaining.

1998   OSHA updates Respiratory Protection Regulation applicable to Immediately Dangerous to Life and Health fire fighting. Self-contained breathing apparatus must be used, two fire fighters must remain in visual and voice contact, and two fire fighters must remain outside the structure to provide safety.

1999   IAFF issues *Emergency Medical Services: A Guide Book for Fire-Based Systems* to educate member locals in becoming EMS providers.

1999   RCW 84.52.069 allows passage of permanent levies supporting EMS, rather than only those with time limits.

1999   RCW 41.26.160 (Death Benefits—Duty Connected) and RCW 41.26.161 (Death benefits—Nonduty Connected) clarify survivor benefits for LEOFF Plan 1 members.

1999   State legislature amends RCW 41.26.470 to provide refund of contributions made in excess of payments when LEOFF Plan 2 members' disability benefits are discontinued for any reason other than disability retirement or resumption of employment.

1999   Eighty-five percent of all property and people in the United States receive fire protection from members of the IAFF, and fire fighters comprise the largest group of providers of pre-hospital emergency care in US.

November 30 – December 3, 1999   World Trade Organization (WTO) meets in Seattle. Seattle Fire Department refuses to use hoses for crowd control.

February 2000 Eileen Lewis becomes chief of Tacoma Fire Department.

2000 RCW 41.26.430 reduces the retirement age from 55 to 53 years of age for LEOFF Plan II members and reduces the actuarial penalty to 3 percent per year from 50 to 52 years of age for earlier retirement with 20 years of service.

September 11, 2001 Three hundred forty-three New York City fire fighters perish when responding to terrorist attack on the World Trade Center.

October 26, 2001 As part of the USA Patriot Act, the death benefit payable under the Public Safety Officer Benefit Act is increased to $250,000.

2001 At its convention, WSCFF resolves to lobby for passage of a bill to establish a new board of trustees for LEOFF Plan 2, comprised of plan participants.

2002 WSCFF successfully lobbies to expand coverage of presumptive occupational diseases for fire fighters (RCW 51.32.185), adding "heart problems occurring within 72 hours of exposure to smoke, fumes, or other toxins; cancer; and infectious diseases."

2002 Congress passes the Hometown Heroes Survivor Benefits Act, providing federal benefits to families of public safety officers who die of a heart attack or stroke at the scene or within 24 hours of an emergency response or training exercise.

June 2002 The Mychal Judge Police and Fire Chaplains' Safety Officers Benefit Act allows all beneficiaries designated on the fallen public safety officer's most recent life insurance policy to receive federal benefits, retroactive to September 11, 2001.

2002 WSCFF establishes the WSCFF Committee on Political Education (COPE) to prepare election endorsements.

November 2002 WSCFF, WACOPS, and COMPAS sponsor Initiative 790 to establish member representation in the management of LEOFF Plan 2. The initiative passes.

2002 In *IAFF Local #46 v. City of Everett* the state supreme court finds for Everett #46 and establishes that when wages are collected through grievance arbitration, attorney fees may also be collected unless explicitly waived.

2003 Tacoma appeals court rules that the Washington State Public Disclosure Committee cannot allow different locals of the same union to contribute to a candidate's campaign, even if parent union doesn't contribute. State Attorney General's Office appeals.

We are the WSCFF: MEMBER LOCALS

The following was compiled from a survey sent out to WSCFF member locals, IAFF and WSCFF membership records, and interviews. Independent confirmation of details was not always available.

Local #	Local Name	IAFF Affiliation/ Charter Date	WSCFF Affiliation Date	WSCFF District	Mergers, Separations, Consolidations, Disaffiliations, Misc. Details
27	Seattle	1918	1939: Charter member	11	Affiliated directly with the AFL in 1913 (unknown local number). Seattle #27 was disaffiliated from the WSCFF from 1968-1978; became WSCFF District 7 from 1978-1983; disaffiliated again from the WSCFF from 1983-1992; then became WSCFF District 11 in 1992.
29	Spokane	02-28-1918	1939: Charter member	1	Affiliated directly with the AFL (#15515) on 04-16-1917; Spokane #29 has been WSCFF District 1 since 1977.
31	Tacoma	1918	1939: Charter member	6	Affiliated directly with the AFL (#15601) on 06-14-1917. Tacoma #31 disaffiliated from the WSCFF from 1974-1976; reaffiliated and became District 6 in 1977.
46	Everett	02-03-1917 or 9-17-1917; 08-28-1933	1939: Charter member	10	Everett #46 officially affiliated with the IAFF in 1917 although the IAFF was not officially incorporated until 1918. Everett disaffiliated from the IAFF in 1920 and reaffiliated as Everett #305 in 1933. The IAFF reassigned Everett its original number in 1991.
106	Bellingham	08-09-1918	1939: Charter member	10	
315	Hoquiam	09-03-1931	1939: Charter member	5	Affiliated as Aberdeen-Hoquiam #315; Aberdeen spun off to form #2639 in 1978.
404	Walla Walla	05-29-1934	Unknown	2	Some members recall #404 had disaffiliated from the WSCFF by 1948 and that it was back in by 1953. It has since hosted every WSCFF convention in years ending in matching digits (1955, etc.) except 2000.
437	Bremerton	07-10-1935	1939: Charter member	4	There is some documentation that #437 disaffiliated at some point and then reaffiliated, but the dates and reasons are unknown.
451	Centralia	10-29-1935	1939: Charter member	5	Affiliated as Centralia-Chehalis #451; Chehalis spun off to form #2510 in 1976. In the 1930s or 1940s volunteers walked off the job and created a fully professional department.
452	Vancouver	10-29-1935	1939: Charter member	5	Affiliated as Vancouver-Camas #452; Camas spun off to form #2444 in 1975 because of a dispute over a TV. Clark County Fire District 5 #2491 merged into #452 on 04-01-1994. #452 also absorbed Clark County Fire District 4 #2811 in the 90s.
453	Wenatchee	11-21-1935 10-06-1969	1939: Charter member	3	There are also references to Wenatchee #1890, a separate local which affiliated in 1969, but was no longer affiliated with the IAFF as of 1982.
468	Olympia	05-20-1936 05-03-1945	1939: Charter member	5	There is no information on what caused this local to disaffiliate at some point and then reaffiliate. Olympia absorbed the six members of Thurston County Fire District 9/McLane #2465 when that local was dissolved on 07-01-1997.
469	Yakima	08-14-1919 05-20-1936	1939: Charter member	2	Affiliated in 1919 as Yakima #217. The City of Yakima forced union representation out in 1919; fire fighters reorganized and reaffiliated in 1936.
656	Port Angeles	03-11-1940	Unknown	3	
726	Puyallup	07-13-1942	06-16-1970	4	In 1976 the members of Puyallup #726 were the highest paid fire fighters west of the Mississippi due to contractual pay increases pegged to quarterly COLAs. Puyallup represents Edgewood/Pierce County Fire District 8 bargaining unit, as of 1999.
828	Longview	05-03-1945	Unknown	5	
864	Renton	05-08-1946	Unknown	7	Absorbed some members of King County 25 #2439 when that local dissolved in April 1993.
876	Spokane Valley	07-29-1946	Unknown	2	
1052	Richland	12-14-1946 05-03-1950	04-18-1950	2	Richland originally chartered in 1946 with Hanford I-24 as #1052.
1257	SeaTac	08-05-1955	Unknown	9	
1296	Kennewick	02-06-1958	Unknown	2	
1352	Auburn	10-05-1959	Unknown	8	
1433	Pasco	05-17-1962	Unknown	2	
1445	Kelso	08-08-1962	Unknown	5	No longer in the IAFF or the WSCFF. Merged into Cowlitz 2 #3828 in 1985.
1461	Burien	01-24-1963	Unknown	9	
1488	Lakewood Prof Fire Fighters	10-31-1963	1964	4	
1537	Anacortes Fire Fighters	06-04-1954 01-12-1965	12-1965	10	
1604	Bellevue	01-25-1966	Unknown	7	Hired some members of King County Fire District 25 #2439 when that local was dissolved in April 1993 (negotiated second start/hire date); Bellevue #1604 also absorbed some King County Fire District 14 (Eastgate area) fire fighters.

Local #	Local Name	IAFF Affiliation/ Charter Date	WSCFF Affiliation Date	WSCFF District	Mergers, Separations, Consolidations, Disaffiliations, Misc. Details
1675	Duwamish	12-07-1967	Unknown		No longer in the IAFF or the WSCFF.
1747	Kent	01-22-1968	Unknown	8	
1758	Ellensburg	05-23-1940 02-27-1968	Unknown	8	
1760	Shoreline	03-18-1968	Unknown	3	
1762	Mercer Island	03-26-1968	Unknown	7	
1789	Spokane Airport	08-06-1968	Unknown	2	
1805	Clark County 6	10-22-1968	Unknown	5	Originally included Clark County Fire Districts 3, 4, 5, and 6. Clark County Fire District 5 #2491 spun off (1975-1976) as did Clark County Fire District 4 #2811 (03-31-1981). Both were eventually absorbed by Vancouver #452. Clark County 6 #1805 bifurcated and formed Prof. Fire Fighters of Clark County 3 #4156 on 01-02-2002.
1810	North Highline	11-27-1968 or 12-27-1968	Unknown	9	
1828	Edmonds	02-24-1969	06-16-70	3	As of about 1984 #1828 incorporated an innovative fitness program with incentive pay for passing the agility test; members also tested for HAZMAT exposures.
1862	Montesano	06-30-1969	Unknown	5	
1890	Wenatchee	01-21-1935 10-06-1969	Unknown		No longer in the IAFF or the WSCFF. This local disaffiliated from the IAFF before 1982. Original Wenatchee local #453 still exists.
1892	Pullman	10-06-1969	Unknown	2	
1912	Spring Glen	11-17-1969	Unknown	8	
1919	Cheney	12-02-1969	Unknown	2	
1983	Mount Vernon	06-20-1970	Unknown	10	
1984	Lynnwood	06-23-1970	Unknown	3	
1996	Mountlake Terrace	08-12-1970	Unknown	3	
1997	Snohomish County 1	08-14-1970	Unknown	3	Silver Lake #2971 merged into #1997 in May 1995.
2024	Federal Way	12-29-1970	Unknown	9	
2032	Port Townsend	02-05-1971 reaffiliated 07-10-2003	Unknown	3	Disaffiliated between 1979-1980 from the IAFF and the WSCFF and joined city-wide affiliation with the Teamsters. Recognition required PERC decision. #2032 reaffiliated in 2003.
2052	Moses Lake	05-24-1971	Unknown	2	Some documentation of an earlier affiliation of 12-08-1956; if so, then unknown disaffiliation period; unknown original local number.
2088	Tukwila	10-28-1971	Unknown	9	
2099	Bothell	10-29-1971	Unknown	7	Spun off from King County Fire District 42 in about 1988. Currently contracts with Snohomish Fire District 10 for personnel. Bothell Fire District provides money and facilities.
2105	University Place	11-15-1971	07-16-1972	4	
2109	Ocean Shores Fire Fighters	12-27-1971	Unknown	5	
2175	Pierce County Prof. Fire Fighters	08-10-1972	Unknown	4	Spanaway/Pierce County 7 #2582 was absorbed by #2175 in 1985-1986; Pierce County Fire District 9 #2221 merged into #2175 on 01-01-1996 though the departments merged in 1994 or 1995; Graham #3125 merged into #2175 on 01-01-1999. Pierce County 17 joined #2175 as bargaining unit in fall 2003. Eatonville #3487 merged into #2175 11-2003.
2221	Pierce County 9	03-26-1973	Unknown	2	No longer in the IAFF or the WSCFF. Also known as Summit Fire & Rescue. 37 members merged into Pierce County Professional Fire Fighters #2175 on 01-01-1996 though the departments merged in 1994 or 1995.
2299	Clarkston	12-18-1973	Unknown	2	
2328	Toppenish	04-05-1974	Unknown	4	
2394	Shelton	11-07-1974	Unknown	5	
2409	Tumwater	12-27-1974	07-27-1976	5	Includes 9 paramedic positions (funded 80% by Thurston County Medic One) and 14 fire fighters.
2439	King County Fire District 25	05-22-1975	Unknown		No longer in the IAFF or the WSCFF. Known as the Kenneydale Fire District prior to King County Fire District 25; for a time remained a separate fire district contracting services from Renton. After the Bellevue annexation of a portion of the district, #2439 dissolved in April 1993 with members rehired by Bellevue #1604 and Renton #864 with 2 hire dates (start date and hire date).
2444	Camas Fire Dept.	10-29-1935 05-09-1975	1939 as part of #452	5	#452 was originally Vancouver-Camas; Camas spun off in a dispute over a TV.

Local #	Local Name	IAFF Affiliation/ Charter Date	WSCFF Affiliation Date	WSCFF District	Mergers, Separations, Consolidations, Disaffiliations, Misc. Details
2459	Northshore/ King County 16	09-03-1975	Unknown	3	
2465	Thurston County 9/ McLane	Between 09-1975 and 04-1976	Unknown	5	No longer in the IAFF or the WSCFF. #2465 was dissolved and all six members were absorbed by #468 Olympia on 07-01-1997; McLane is now a bargaining unit within West Thurston Professional Fire Fighters #3825.
2491	Clark County 5	Between 09-1975 and 04-1976	Unknown	5	No longer in the IAFF or the WSCFF. Created as a spin-off from Clark County Fire District 6 #1805. Absorbed Clark County Fire District 4 #2811 in 1988. Merged into Vancouver #452 on 04-01-1994.
2510	Chehalis	10-29-1935 04-26-1976	1939 as part of #451	5	Originally Centralia-Chehalis #451; Chehalis spun off to form #2510 in 1976.
2545	Kirkland	11-24-1976	Unknown	7	Affiliated with 7 members, currently represents 70. Received an L&I ruling in 1996 limiting volunteers as fire fighters.
2582	Spanaway/ Pierce County 7	Unknown	Unknown		Merged into Central Pierce County Fire Fighters #2175 in 1985 or 1986.
2595	King County Medics	04-05-1983	Unknown	8	Went into service on 09-02-1977 as Medic 4 and Medic 5; Medic 6 (Auburn-Federal Way) added in May or June 1979. King County took over county Fire District proprietor groups 10-01-1979. Bill Marsh elected president in 1983.
2597	Snohomish County Airport	09-12-1977	By spring 1979	10	
2639	Aberdeen	09-03-1931 05-24-1978	1939 as part of #315	5	Originally Aberdeen-Hoquiam #315; Aberdeen spun off to form #2639 in 1978.
2694	Snohomish County 4	04-17-1979	Unknown	3	
2719	Lewis County 12	07-13-1979	Unknown	5	
2776	Raymond	06-8-1980	Unknown	5	Some documentation of an earlier affiliation date of 11-07-1967; if so, then unknown disaffiliation period; unknown original local number.
2781	Snohomish County 7	06-26-1980	01-18-1982	3	
2811	Clark County #4	03-31-1981	Unknown		No longer in the IAFF or the WSCFF. Created as a spin-off from Clark County Fire District 6 #1805. Absorbed into Clark County Fire District 5 #2491 in 1988.
2819	Prof Fire Fighters of Kitsap County	03-02-1981	Unknown	4	First local in Kitsap County. Some documentation of a later affiliation date of 03-26-1982. South Kitsap #2876 separated from #2819 in about 1983. At some point multiple fire districts combined into 3 districts.
2829	Redmond	04-09-1981	Unknown	7	Began with 29 members, has grown to 125 representing both uniformed and non-uniformed employees; offering seniority and job tenure for lateral hires from mergers and consolidations. Acquired Evergreen Medic One in January 2003.
2862	No name listed	01-08-1982	Unknown		No longer in the IAFF or the WSCFF. This local is listed only by number in some WSCFF documents.
2868	Washougal Firefighters Assn	03-22-1982	Unknown	5	
2876	South Kitsap Dist 7	06-01-1982	03-26-1982	4	Separated from #2819 in 1982. There is some documentation of a later affiliation date of 07-08-1997; if so, then unknown disaffiliation/unaffiliated period.
2877	Sumner	06-1-1982 (?)	06-17-1982 (?)	4	
2878	Eastside Fire & Rescue	06-15-1982	06-17-1982	8	Original PERC unit included dispatch; North Bend #3413 merged into #2878 in 1994. Duvall Fire District 45 affiliated with #2878 in 1998 or 1999. Issaquah #3796 merged into #2878 in 1999. Fall City #4064 merged with #2878 in October 2002. See also #4028.
2898	Seattle Fire Chiefs	03-28-1983	Never in WSCFF		Never affiliated with the WSCFF.
2903	Lacey	06-6-1983	06-12-1983	5	
2916	Spokane County 9	09-22-1983	12-01-1983	2	
2919	City of SeaTac	10-24-1983	12-01-1983	9	Started as King County Fire District 24 and had 16 members as of 1983. Became City of SeaTac in 1991 and hired 18 additional fire fighters.
2933	Clallam County Fire District 3	04-2-1984	01-01-1985	3	
2950	Woodinville	09-10-1984	09-24-1984	7	
2971	Silver Lake	05-09-1985	Unknown	3	No longer in the IAFF or the WSCFF. Merged into Snohomish County 1 #1997 as of 12-01-1999.

Local #	Local Name	IAFF Affiliation/ Charter Date	WSCFF Affiliation Date	WSCFF District	Mergers, Separations, Consolidations, Disaffiliations, Misc. Details
2984	Mason County	06-07-1985	Unknown	4	
3062	Maple Valley	07-25-1986	09-1986	8	Supplements career staff with volunteers on evenings and weekends.
3125	Graham	Unknown	Unknown	4	No longer in the IAFF or the WSCFF. Merged into Central Pierce Fire Fighters #2175 on 01-01-1999.
3152	Key Peninsula	05-25-1988	Unknown	4	
3186	King County 44	11-02-1988	by 01-1990	8	Some documentation of an earlier affiliation date of 12-26-1967; if so, then unknown disaffiliation period; unknown original local number.
3219	Marysville Prof Firefighters	04-01-1989	Unknown	10	Original merge was City of Marysville and Snohomish County Fire District 12 in about 1992, which created the Marysville Fire Dept. In 1998 Snohomish County Fire District 20 merged into the Marysville Dept. and one professional fire fighter was absorbed.
3235	Snohomish County 8	06-28-1989	Unknown	10	
3266	Bellingham Airport	10-28-1989	Unknown	10	
3315	Monroe Fire Fighters	04-28-1990	1990	3	
3343	United Paramedics of Snohomish County	1990-1991	1992	5	No longer in the IAFF or the WSCFF. Unknown, may have some relation to NSCPA #3438.
3375	Longview Mid-Management	05-9-1991	1992	5	Disbanded 10-2000. One member remained and maintained membership in the WSCFF. Reinstated as a local and reaffiliated with the WSCFF 01-2003.
3390	Gig Harbor	08-15-1991	Unknown	4	
3396	Des Moines	09-16-1991	1992	9	
3413	North Bend	1992	Unknown	3	No longer in the IAFF or the WSCFF. North Bend #3413 merged into #2878 in 1994.
3427	Skagit County Paramedics	02-7-1992	by 06-1994	10	
3438	North Snohomish County Paramedics Association (NSCPA)	1992-1993	05-28-1992	3	No longer in the IAFF or the WSCFF. Merged into Arlington #3728 05-01-1999. May have had some relation to United Paramedics of Snohomish County #3343.
3482	Mukilteo	01-04-1993	1993	3	
3487	Eatonville	01-12-1993	06-02-1999	4	Merged into #2175 as South Pierce Fire and Rescue bargaining unit 11-2003.
3520	East Pierce Prof. Fire Fighters	06-17-1993	by 07-1994	4	Bonney Lake #3576 merged into East Pierce #3520 on 06-01-1999.
3524	Medic Seven	07-23-1993	by 03-96	3	No longer in the IAFF or the WSCFF. Dissolved as of 01-2003; members sent to #1828 or #1984.
3542	Sunnyside Prof. Fire Fighters	10-29-1993	12-15-1993	2	Uses professional and volunteer squad; was a professional non-union department for a long time. Although incorporated city limits are about 6 square miles, service district is 180.5 square miles.
3543	WSU Fire Fighters	10-28-1993	10-28-1993	2	Only state fire department in Washington State that is in the WSCFF, and one of 3 universities west of the Mississippi operating their own fire departments.
3576	Bonney Lake	1993-1994	1994	8	No longer in the IAFF or the WSCFF. Enumclaw #3931 was originally part of #3576 as Enumclaw unit of Bonney Lake, and spun off in about 04-1999; #3576 merged into East Pierce Prof. Fire Fighters #3520 on 06-01-1999.
3611	Evergreen Medic One	11-14-1994	11-1995	3	No longer in the IAFF or the WSCFF. Dissolved as of 01-2003; members sent to #1760 or #2829.
3628	Thurston County Fire District 2, Yelm Prof. Firefighters	Between 11-1994 and 12-1995	1996	5	No longer in the IAFF or the WSCFF. Medics transferred to West Thurston Grand Mound #3825 09-2001. Local did not file paperwork to be dissolved until 2003. Medics transferred from #3825 to #2903 in 8-03.
3674	Clark County 11	12-1-1995	01-01-1996	5	Originally Battle Ground, then Clark County 11 & 12. Clark County 12 spun off to form Local #4229 01-01-2003.
3680	Union Gap	01-18-1996	1996	2	
3689	South Beach Fire & EMS	02-29-1996	Unknown	5	

Local #	Local Name	IAFF Affiliation/ Charter Date	WSCFF Affiliation Date	WSCFF District	Mergers, Separations, Consolidations, Disaffiliations, Misc. Details
3711	Spokane County 8	07-15-1996	03-1997	2	Won national recognition from the IAFF FIREPAC for its category (less than 100 members).
3728	Arlington	11-9-1996	02-1997	10	A member of Snohomish County Fire District 20 may have been absorbed in 1996. Possible relation to NSCPA #3438.
3740	Skyway Fire Fighters Assoc.	03-03-97	03-03-1997	7	
3780	North Highline Chiefs	09-08-1997	12-01-1997	9	
3796	Issaquah	11-05-1997	03-04-1998	8	No longer in the IAFF or the WSCFF. Issaquah #3796 merged into #2878 01-01-1999.
3811	Jefferson County	12-9-1997	04-20-1998	3	
3817	South Kitsap Fire Chiefs	11-20-1997	Never in WSCFF		Never in WSCFF.
3825	West Thurston Prof. Fire Fighters	02-15-1998	03-1998	5	Medics transferred from Yelm #3628 09-2001 then transferred to Lacey #2903 08-2003. Bargaining units include: Little Rock Fire District 385, Grand Mound Thurston County Fire District 14, Rochester Fire District 1, McLane (formerly #2465).
3828	Cowlitz 2 Fire & Rescue	02-15-1998	03-16-1998	5	In 1998 merged administrative staff of fire department (not local) within Longview; Kelso #1445 merged into #3828 in 1985.
3829	Dupont	02-9-1998	06-1998	4	
3835	Chelan County 1	03-19-1998	06-1998	3	
3855	Whatcom 7	08-6-1998	02-11-1999	10	
3867	NW Whatcom Fire Fighters	08-6-1998	09-03-1998	10	
3872	Unknown	Unknown	Unknown	2	No longer in the IAFF or the WSCFF. Local cited only by number in WSCFF records, perhaps some relation to Graham #3125 which merged into Central Pierce #2175 on 01-01-1999.
3876	North Mason	10-5-1998	03-1999	4	
3889	Benton County 4	11-23-1998	02-11-1999	2	
3902	Battalion Chiefs, Spokane Airport	1999	02-22-1999	2	No longer in the IAFF or the WSCFF. Dissolved 04-2000.
3911	San Juan County Paramedics Assn.	02-1-1999	02-2000	10	No mergers, separations, consolidations, disaffiliations.
3916	Granite Falls	01-21-1999	11-10-1999	10	
3931	Enumclaw Firefighters Union	02-25-1999	05-1999	8	This local was originally part of #3576 (called the Enumclaw unit of Bonney Lake Fire Fighters), and spun off as #3576 was merging into East Pierce #3520 06-01-1999.
3999	Pacific County Fire Dist. 1	12-01-1999	01-27-2000	5	
4028	Snoqualmie Fire & Rescue	03-3-2000	08-01-2000	8	City of Snoqualmie contracted with King County Fire District 10 (staffed by #2878) until 1999, when city formed its own department.
4033	Island County District 1 Fire Fighters	04-03-2000	08-01-2000	10	
4034	Bainbridge Island	04-3-2000	06-26-2000	4	
4064	Fall City Prof. Fire Fighters	07-2000	08-16-200	8	No longer in the IAFF or the WSCFF. Merged into Eastside Fire & Rescue #2878 11-2002.
4075	Grays Harbor Paramedics	10-01-2000	Never affiliated with WSCFF		No record of ever affiliating with the WSCFF.

Local #	Local Name	IAFF Affiliation/ Charter Date	WSCFF Affiliation Date	WSCFF District	Mergers, Separations, Consolidations, Disaffiliations, Misc. Details
4086	Stanwood Fire & Rescue	02-1-2000	08-20-01	10	
4111	Burlington	06-7-2001	07-03-01	10	
4118	North County Prof. Fire Fighters	07-10-2001	11-13-01	10	No longer in the IAFF or the WSCFF. Merged with Island County District 1 #4033 on 01-01-2003.
4156	Prof. Fire Fighters of Clark County 3	01-02-2002	03-06-2002	5	Originally members of Clark County 6 #1805, which bifurcated to form Prof. Fire Fighters of Clark County 3 #4156 on 01-02-2002.
4189	Vashon Island 77	05-06-2002	07-08-2002	9	
4197	Douglas County 2 Fire Fighters	06-12-2002	08-08-2002	3	
4203	Walla Walla Airport/ College Place	07-15-2002	09-25-2002	2	
4229	Clark County 12	11-14-2002	01-07-2003	5	Spun off from Clark County 11 #3674.
4258	Grays Harbor 2	2003	05-20-2003	5	
4263	Millwood Fire Fighters	2003	05-20-2003	2	
4272	Ephrata	2003	04-23-2003	2	
4276	Pacific Prof. Fire Fighters	2003	07-07-2003	8	
I-24	Hanford	06-23-1975	Unknown	2	Hanford originally chartered in 1946; Richland #1052 also came into existence at that time.
I-66	Boeing Fire Fighters	05-2-1996	05-11-2000	9	
FD282	Puget Sound Federal Fire Fighters	07-25-1994	Federal (not affiliated)		Never in the WSCFF.
FD283	Fort Lewis	11-1-1995	Federal (not affiliated)		Never in the WSCFF; leading the effort to create an associate affiliate membership category within the WSCFF to allow federal locals to participate in the WSCFF per resolution 03-24.
FD295	Yakima Training Center Fire District	11-6-1998	Federal (not affiliated)		Never in the WSCFF.

Selected Bibliography

This listing includes sources that have been of particular assistance in writing this book. It is not a complete listing, but instead provides citations that may be of particular interest.

The following individuals were interviewed and/or provided research materials. In addition, many individual members of the WSCFF confirmed information about their locals, and shared their thoughts about the union movement and the fire service.

Bruce Ansell #1604
Doug Baier #437
Bruce Baurichter #31
Dan Baxter #3828
Bonnie Beers #27
Monica Blum
Kirby Bomgarner I-24
Greg Borg #29
Cory Bostick #27
Ric Bowman #469
Jonathan Brock
Jeanette Cason
Barbara Chadwick
Rick Chaney #2024
Dennis Cooper
Ken Dammand
Steve Davis #29
Ralph Decker
Dave DeMarko #46
Jolene Davis #31
Robert Davis #27
Bill Dopps #469
Dan Downs #1052
Axel Drugge #27
Jeff Fix #3828
Judy Fortier
Jim Fossos #27
Kelly Fox #468
Paul Fray #3780
Don Fulthorp #2444
Bill Gosnell #27
Bob Gough #27
Lance Greenwood
   #1052
Ken Groth #469
Tom Gudmestad #2596
Merlin Halverson
   #1984
Lonnie Hampton #31
Eileen Harnett
Claude Harris #27
Paul Harvey #27
Charles Hawkins, Jr.
   #27
Tom Heckler #29
Rod Heivilin #1760
Chris Heminger #1352
Jim Hill #31
David Hiltwein I-24
Lembhard Howell

American Federation of Labor and Congress of Industrial Organizations. *The Federationist*, 1894-1905, 1908-1982.

———. *The American Federationist*, 1905-1908.

———. *Why Unions?* Washington, D.C.: American Federation of Labor and Congress of Industrial Organizations, 1982.

———. American Social History Project. *Who Built America? Working People and the Nation's Economy, Politics, Culture and Society.* New York: Pantheon Books, 1992.

Ammons, D. "State Disability Plan is Crippling its Budget," *Bellingham Herald*, December 1984.

Berner, Richard C. *Seattle 1921-1940: From Boom to Bust.* Seattle: Charles Press, 1992.

———. *Seattle Transformed: World War II to Cold War.* Seattle: Charles Press, 1999.

Bollen, Peter. *Great Labor Quotations.* Los Angeles: Red Eye Press, Inc., 2000.

Bremerton Fire Department. *Bremerton Fire Department Centennial 1902-2002.* Bremerton, WA: Gene Nelson, 2002.

Brock, Jonathan. *Bargaining Beyond Impasses: Joint Resolution of Public Sector Labor Disputes.* Dover, MA: Auburn Publishing House, 1982.

Bruno, H. "Affirmative Action and the Fire Service," *Firehouse*, June 1981, 8-9.

Carruth, Gorton. *The Encyclopedia of American Facts and Dates.* 10th ed. New York: HarperCollins Publishers, 1997.

Dembo, Jonathan. *Unions and Politics in Washington State, 1885-1935.* New York: Garland Publishing, 1983.

———. *A History of the Washington State Labor Movement, 1885-1835.* Ph.D. thesis, University of Washington, 1978.

———. *An Historical Bibliography of Washington State Labor and Laboring.* Seattle, 1978.

———. *Pacific Northwest Labor During World War II: Newspaper and Periodical Index.* 1984.

Emerson, Stephen B. *The Spokane Fire Department*, research project for the Eastern Washington University Department of History, circa 1999.

Everett Fire Department Archives. Photographs, memorabilia, and equipment 1900-2003. Everett, WA.

Henderson, Charles Z. *The Fire Boys: 100 Years of Everett Firefighting History.* Virginia Beach, VA: The Donning Co. Publishers, 1992.

History of the WSFL 1902-1924, pamphlet.

Hooper, Eugene R. *Organized Labor in Transition: the Washington State Labor Council, AFL-CIO 1958-1967.* Masters thesis, University of Washington, 1969.

Howell, Lembhard. *Civil Rights in Seattle Since 1965–A Legal Perspective.* Seattle, undated.

Hoyt, Harold "Jiggs." *The Fire Districts of King County.* Seattle: Frontier Publishing, 1990.

International Association of Fire Fighters. *The IAFF: Growth, Achievement and Success.* Washington, D.C.: International Association of Fire Fighters, 1996.

———. *International Fire Fighter.* Washington, D.C., 1930s-current.

———. *An Overview of Membership Services: An Instructional Unit for State, Provincial and Local Affiliates.* Washington, D.C.: International Association of Fire Fighters, 1995.

King County Labor Council papers circa 1959-1968. University of Washington Library, Special Collections, Seattle.

Matejka, Michael G. *Fiery Struggle: Illinois Fire Fighters Build a Union, 1901-1985.* Chicago: Illinois Labor History Society, 2002.

McCann, John, Blood in the Water: *History of District Local 751 of the International Association of Machinists and Aerospace Workers.* Seattle: District Lodge 751, International Association of Machinists and Aerospace Workers, in association with the Labor Education and Research Center, The Evergreen State College, Olympia, WA, 1989.

Morris, Richard B. *A History of the American Worker.* Princeton: Princeton University Press, 1983.

Murray, R. Emmett. *The Lexicon of Labor.* New York: The New Press, 1998.

Northwestern Mutual Fire Association. *50 Years of Fighting Fires: Organization and Development of the Seattle Fire Department.* Seattle: circa 1939.

Page, James O. *The Paramedics.* Morristown, New Jersey: Backdraft Publications, 1979.

Pierce County Labor Centennial Committee. *To Live in Dignity, Pierce County Labor, 1883-1989.* Tacoma, WA: Pierce

County Labor Centennial Committee, 1989.

Phipps, Jennifer R. *The Fire Next Time: Public Response to Private Choice*. Masters thesis, The Evergreen State College, 1998.

Richardson, George J. *Symbol of Action: A History of the International Association of Fire Fighters*. Washington, D.C.: International Association of Fire Fighters, 1974.

Scott, George W. *A Majority of One: Legislative Life*. Seattle: Civitas Press, 2002.

Schneider, Richard J. *Seattle Fire Department History*. Unpublished on website of Seattle Fire Fighter Union, Local 27 (http://www.iaff27.org).

Seattle Fire Fighter Union, Local 27. *The Fire Fighter*. Seattle, 1949-1973.

——. *The Seattle Fire Fighter*. Seattle, 1946-1949, 1973-1989.

Seattle Fire Fighter Union, Local 27 (Monica Blum, ed.) *The Third Rail*. Seattle, 1992-present.

Seattle Fire Department. *Seattle Fire Department 1978*. Seattle: Seattle Fire Department, 1978.

——. *Seattle Fire Department Centennial 1889-1989*. Seattle: Seattle Fire Department, 1989.

Smith, Henry C. *Spokane Fire Department History, Report #2*. Unpublished. Spokane Fire Station Museum, Spokane.

Spokane Fire Station Museum Archives. Papers and memorabilia, 1890s-2003, Tom Heckler, archivist and president, Spokane, WA.

Stieber, Jack. *Public Employee Unionism, Structure, Growth, Policy*. Washington, D.C.: The Brookings Institution, 1973.

Tacoma #31 Archives. Papers circa 1950-2003. Tacoma, WA.

Tacoma Fire Department. *Tacoma Fire Department 1968-1978*. Tacoma, WA: Tacoma Fire Department, 1978.

——. *Tacoma Fire Department 1978-1988*. Tacoma, WA: Tacoma Fire Department, 1988.

——. *Tacoma Fire Department 1988-1998*. Tacoma, WA: Tacoma Fire Department, 1998.

Tacoma Fire Department Archives. Papers and memorabilia, 1890s-2003. Ralph Decker Collection, Tacoma, WA.

Talbot, C. and Decker, Ralph. *100 Years of Firefighting in the City of Destiny Tacoma, Washington*. Tacoma, WA: Pyro Press, 1981.

Trowbridge, Richard. *The Tacoma City Firemen's Union: A Study in Municipal Employee Unionism*. Masters thesis, University of Washington, 1956.

Washington State Council of Fire Fighters Constitution and By-Laws. April 21, 1939.

——. Convention notebooks and general archives 1939-2003, Olympia, WA.

——. *Power Through Participation*. Olympia, WA: Washington State Council of Fire Fighters, 2000.

——. *Washington Professional Fire Fighter*. Olympia, WA, 1974-current.

Washington State Federation of Labor. *The Federation Bulletin*, various issues July-November 1945.

——. *Proceedings of the Washington State Federation of Labor 1905-1957*. University of Washington Library, Special Collections, Seattle.

Washington State Federation of Labor; University of Washington Library, Special Collections, Seattle.

Washington State Labor Council. *Proceedings of the Conventions, 1957-1972*. University of Washington Library, Special Collections, Seattle.

——. *Washington State Labor News* (includes WSFL) Seattle, 1924-1968.

Washington State Labor Council. University of Washington Library, Special Collections, Seattle.

Williams, Wayne L. *Seventy Years of Washington Firefighters' Pension Systems*. Olympia, WA: Parr, Peeples & Carrier Law Firm, 1979-1980.

Yakima #469 Archives. Papers 1890s-2003. Yakima, WA.

Yakima Fire Department Archives. Papers and memorabilia, 1890s-2003. Yakima, WA.

Brain Hurley #2409
Adam Jackson #726
Ron Johnson #469
Mark Johnston #452
Roberto Jourdan #27
Sam Kinville
Ruth Lambert
Dennis Lawson #726
Dan Leahy
Jim Leo
Eileen Lewis #31
Greg Markley #1747
Jim Martinez #672
Pat McElligott #31
Don Meyer #27
Michael McGovern #1488
Rich Merrell #2878
Mike Milam #27
Don Monroe #469
Ron Morehouse #46
Bob Munk #29
George Orr #876
Dennis Parlari #726
Theresa Purtell #27
Scott Rappleye #437
Ross Rieder
Ted Rail #29
Keven Rojecki #2919
George Roop #876
Jim Rudd #29
Marvin Schurke
Don Schwab #46
Dean Shelton #3219
Alex Skalbania
John Smith, Jr. #31
Dennis Sommerville #46
Del Spivey #1604
John Stockman #29
Ken Strong #29
Howard Vietzke #29
Mickey Vietzke
Daroll Waller
Harvey Waller
Jason Walsh
Jennifer Walsh
Ricky Walsh #1052
Ryan Walsh
Dick Warbrouck #27
James Webster
Dave West #29
Ed White #452
Clarence Williams #27
Wayne Williams
Frank Wilson #2876
Mike Wilson #3524
John Willis #31
Doug Willis #2175
Jeanette Woldseth #1604

Acknowledgements

History is a slippery fish grown large as it swims the murky waters of memory. I began this project ignorant of all but the most basic outline of labor history, and with an equal dearth of knowledge concerning fire fighting and emergency services. The WSCFF provided me with a list of key individuals to contact, permission to burrow through its records, and a Masters thesis, *The Fire Next Time: Public Response to Private Choice*, by Jennifer R. Phipps. This thesis laid out certain historical events, but included only teasing references to the people who are and have been the WSCFF.

A new world opened before me as I began my research. Washington State's fire fighters are members of a fraternity (mostly male, even now) created by a desire to serve, and working conditions that demand they live together and respond on-call, as a team, to life and death situations. They took me in, told me their stories and politics, and showed me their work.

The names of many who were helpful are listed in the bibliography. In addition, Doug Baier (Bremerton #437), Bill Gosnell (Seattle #27), Michael McGovern (Lakewood #1488), and Howard Vietzke (Spokane #29) were incredibly patient and forthcoming in sharing their own sense of history, and in helping me shape a larger context for my research. WSCFF Vice President Ricky Walsh (Richland #1052) and WSCFF President Kelly Fox (Olympia #468) had the original vision for this book, and made every possible resource available to me. WSCFF Executive Assistant Helen Kramer and Legislative Secretary Debbie Guillot (both OPEIU #23 members) provided instant institutional support, friendship, and good humor in the face of my sometimes ridiculous requests. Patty Stockman relentlessly proofed and copy-edited, joined at the final hour by Mike Bacon (Spokane #29) and Layne Bladow (Tumwater #2409). Ann Miner unearthed citations and checked facts with aplomb. Karen Johnson of Level 29 Design did more, and then more again, than she thought she could.

Several librarians and archivists provided assistance and direction as I combed shelves and boxes, in particular the staff of the University of Washington's Special Collections and its Gallagher Law Library; and Archives Librarian Rayette Wilder, Northwest Museum of Arts and Culture. Dennis Cooper at the Washington State Office of Code Revision and the online resources of Municipal Research Services taught me the intricacies of RCWs and WACs, current and historical.

I would also like to thank members of the WSCFF executive board for granting me true editorial freedom to write about what matters almost the most to them. The result of my efforts and their assistance is something between journalism, oral history, and an institutional history. Doug Kilgore provided constant and steady encouragement as I disappeared into this project, and I am indebted. Finally, any errors or omissions in *Fully Involved* are my own, while whatever insights it contains come from the amazing people whose story this is.

Index

Note that the appendices are not indexed.

RCWs are listed under relevant topics.

All IAFF locals are listed by their name at the time of the reference, with the exception of Everett #350/ Everett #46, whick is listed only as Everett #46.

Page numbers in italics refer to an illustration, including its caption. When both an illustration and text refer to the same topic on the same page, only one reference is given.

Page numbers in bold refer to charts.

Top of the Ocean Restaurant fire: *192*

Trout, Carl: 205

Trout, Mickey: *205*

Tuddí Restaurant fire: 191

Tumwater #2409: *77*, 216

Tumwater's Medic 5: 216

Turner, Steve: *164*

Uhlman, Wes: 84, 91, 126, *169*

Ullrich, Ron: *98*

uniformed personnel definition: 109, 112

    fireman: 137

uniforms and personal equipment [see also self-contained breathing apparatus (SCBA)]: 81, *163*, 171, 191, *201*

    badges and buttons: 120

    helmets: 184

    long johns: *136*

    uniform allowances: 81, *120*, 168, 170, 189, 190, 194

union dues deduction: 6, 109, 168

union halls: 30, 43, 163, *191*, *192*

United Labor Lobby (ULL): 36, 140

University Place #2105: *122*

US Commission on Civil Rights (see also minorities in fire service): 87

Utley, Roy: *206*

Valley Provider Group: 78, 79, 80

Vancouver #452: 150, 194-195

Vancouver Door Company fire: *202*

Vancouver (WA) Fire Department: *81*, 194-195

Vancouver-Camas #452 (see also Camas #2444; Vancouver #452): 1, **58**, 194

VanTrojen, Karen: *52*

Vickery, Gordon F.: 71, 169

Victoria, B.C. Fire Department: 165

Vietzke, Howard: 6, 7, 8, 10, 13, 26, 30, **34**, 38, 46, 48, *74*, *98*, *107*, 108, *112*, *113*, *114*, 118, 123, 125, 127-128, 129, *136*, 142, *147*, 148, *152*, 158, 179, 181, 193, 208, 210, 221

Vietzke, Mickey: 52, 128, *136*

Vognild, Larry: 7, **34**, *108*, 111, 126, 146, 164

Voight, Bill: *202*

volunteer fire fighters: 21, 67, 78, 114, *120*, 161, 165, 166, 168, 173, 185, 196, 202, 206, 211, 219, 222, 223

    RCW 41.24: 196

Wagaman, Carroll G.: 56

wages: **58**, 65, 203, 208, 221

    ballot measures: 177-178, 179, 188

    pay warrants: 161, 167, 186

Wagner Act: See National Labor Relations Act (NIRA).

Waldrep, Royce: *87*

Walker, Sally: *128*

Walla Walla #404: 3, 27, 156

Waller, Darroll "Skip": 37, 38, 39-40, 181

Waller, Harvey: 38, 39, 53, 181

Waller, Helen: 38, 40

Waller, Jack: 3, 5, 6, 28, 33, 36, 37-40, 41, *42*, 44, *98*, *100*, *101*, 123, *124*, 127, 129, *136*, *139*, 156, 168, 177, 179, 181

Waller, Jack (grandson): 40

Waller, Lucy: 38, 40

Waller, Margaret: 37, 38, 40, *42*

Wallgren, Monrad Charles: **34**, *98*, *139*

Walsh, Jason: 54

Walsh, Jennifer: 54

Walsh, Ricky: 13, 14, 15, 17, 35, 54, 129, 151, 193, 208, 209-211, 213, 223, 224

Walsh, Ryan: 54

Walt Lambert Trade Union Leadership Award (see also emeritus positions): 42, 128

Wang, Arnold: 139

Wang, Art: *114*

Warbrouck, Richard: 7, *18*, *29*, 30, 32, 82, 85, 104, *136*, *137*, 142, *169*, 170, *171*, *201*

Ward, Howard: *85*

Warnke, Frank: *147*

Warnock, Roy L.: 2, 26, 162

Washington Council of Police and Sheriffs (WACOPS) (see also labor coalitions): 152

Washington Educational Association (WEA) (see also labor coalitions): 46, 110

Washington Federation of State Employees (WSFE) (see also labor coalitions): 46

Washington Professional Fire Fighter: 10, 12, 46, 128

Washington State Apprenticeship Training Council (WSAC) (see also apprenticeship programs): 95

Washington State Chief's Association: 1

Washington State Congress of Industrial Organizations (WSCIO) (see also CIO): 4, 36

Washington State Department of Labor and Industries (L&I) (see also binding arbitration): 6, 81, 92, 95, 103, 105, 110, 111, 170-171, 199

Washington State Federation of Labor (WSFL) (see also labor coalitions): 4, 24, 36, 37, 65, 162, 176

Washington State Fire Marshals Organization (WSFMO): 95

Washington State Fire Protection Policy Board (WSFPB): 95

Washington State Firemen's Association: 1

Washington State Labor Council (WSLC) (see also labor coalitions): 4, 5, 48, 102, *106*, 121, 126, 140, 141

Washington State Trial Lawyers Association (see also labor coalitions): 36, 46

Washougal #2868: *122*

Watanabe, Dale: *172*

Colophon

Book design by Karen Johnson
Level 29 Design, Seattle, Washington
www.level29.com

Karen Johnson is a member of the Graphic Artists Guild.
Her company, Level 29 Design, has been designing books, magazines, annual reports,
marketing materials, web sites, and identity programs since 1993.

Text composed in Perpetua Expert.
Other typography set in Bliss.

Printed and bound by Quebecor World
Kingsport, Tennessee

Text paper acid-free Productolith 80# dull coated paper

About the Author

Ellie Belew is a novelist and freelance writer who writes about the situations that push and prod us into action, the community which binds us, and the huge natural wonder of a world, as it stands witness to our all too human foibles.

Born and raised in suburban Minnesota, she migrated west and eventually northwest, moving to Washington State in 1989. Recent projects include *About Wallowa County*, a community compendium about northeastern Oregon, which she coordinated and edited. Her novel, *Run Plant Fly*, was published in 2003.

For further information please visit www.elliebelew.com.

Tacoma #31 fire fighters evacuate residents of the Tacoma Hotel during the fire of October 17, 1935. Note pompier ladder at left.

INFORMATION ON COVER ILLUSTRATIONS

Information about the illustrations appearing on the cover is given below. Note it is listed in the order the illustrations appear across the entire cover (front and back).

Several illustrations appear only on the jacket of the case bound edition, and are so labeled.

BACK FLAP
(CASE BOUND EDITION ONLY):

Everett #46 members after the Pier 3 fire (7-10-1979). L-R: *Joe Johnston, Pat Lansing, Frank Anderson, Rick Brock, Larry Stubrud, Steve Turner, Steve Parker.*

PHOTO BY JIM LEO

Spokane Fire Department's chief badge.

SPOKANE FIRE STATION MUSEUM COLLECTION

Tacoma Fire Department's fire-boat, the Defiance.

RALPH DECKER COLLECTION

Fire departments have formed formal and informal sports teams from their inception. Tacoma fire fighters line up.

TACOMA #31 COLLECTION

BACK COVER:

IN BACKGROUND: *An ad (circa 1930s-1940s) which listed all members of the Tacoma Fire Department by name, rank, and weekly rate of pay, run to defeat a ballot measure for a pay increase.*

TACOMA #31 COLLECTION

Undated photo of Spokane fire fighters, probably volunteers.

SPOKANE #29 COLLECTION

Puyallup #726 members on a practice maneuver L-R: *Carl Barker, Adam Jackson, Dale Anderson, (unnamed), Dennis Lawson (WSCFF District 4 representative).*

PHOTO BY BILL JACKSON

Industrial first aid patch.

RICHARD WARBROUCK COLLECTION

Bonnie Beers (#27) shortly after she was hired as the first woman fire fighter in Seattle.

BONNIE BEERS COLLECTION

The Camas Fire Department responding to the 1993 Crown Home Furnishings fire.

DON FULTHORP, CAMAS #2444 COLLECTION

Logo from the 1961 Puget Sound Firemen's Association directory of fire departments.

GEORGE ROOP COLLECTION

Jim Cason's (#31) pallbearers: L (BACK TO FRONT): *Pat McElligott (#31), unknown, Chuck Jenkins (#31).* R (BACK TO FRONT): *unknown, Bruce Baurichter (#31), George Orr (#876).*

TACOMA #31 COLLECTION

Spokane's Station 6.

NMAC COLLECTION, L87-1.42727-30

Dick Warbrouck and Jerry Minarich, both members of Seattle #27, during a 1963 fire.

RICHARD WARBROUCK COLLECTION

SPINE:

Greg Borg (#29) caught in a flashover in about 1998.

GREG BORG COLLECTION

FRONT COVER:

IN BACKGROUND: *The McCaan SCBA, one of the first to use an air cylinder.*

GREG BORG COLLECTION

Tacoma #31 members use their department's aerial sprayer.

TACOMA #31 COLLECTION

Seagrave 1924 pumper (1,000 gpm), restored by the Everett Fire Fighter Association.

DENNIS SOMERVILLE COLLECTION

A Cairns & Brothers "8 cone" (eight-paneled) helmet, used by the Spokane Fire Department 1889-1942.

GREG BORG COLLECTION

Members of Tacoma #31 pose in 1997 while burning down a training tower.

RALPH DECKER COLLECTION

North Yakima's first professional fire fighters, September 6, 1905. L-R: *E.G. Dawson, J.P. Bowman (asst chief), Charles M. Hauser (chief), Marry C. Dawson, J.J. Mller.*

YAKIMA #469 COLLECTION

The rear section of this rig is the same in both pictures, and was adapted by Spokane fire fighters. It originally had wooden wheels and was horse-drawn.

NMAC COLLECTION, L93-25.59

Unidentified Hanford I-24 fire fighters practice in full turnouts during the mid-1980s.

HANFORD FIRE DEPARTMENT COLLECTION

Tacoma Engine Co. 4's log book of incidents.

RALPH DECKER COLLECTION

Santa carried a bag labeled "organization benefits" while the junior fire fighter, "protecting his interests," put out the fire of "objectors to organization" in this 1938 IAFF Christmas card.

YAKIMA FIRE DEPT. COLLECTION

FRONT FLAP
(CASE BOUND EDITION ONLY):

Unidentified members of Tacoma #31 on the Tacoma Narrows bridge.

TACOMA #31 COLLECTION

This picture may have been staged. Early Spokane fire fighters respond to a call.

NMAC COLLECTION, L93-25.149

Logo from the 1958 WSCFF convention sponsored by Aberdeen-Hoquiam #315.

JERRY MCFEELY COLLECTION

The Top of the Ocean Restaurant fire (a waterside building), 1977.

RALPH DECKER COLLECTION